How To Pass

Spoken English
For
Industry and Commerce

Threshold Level

Teacher's Book

How to Pass
Spoken English for Industry and Commerce
Threshold Level

Published in 1996

ISBN 3-922514-40-5

Published by: Logophon Lehrmittel Verlag GmbH
Verlag: Alte Gärtnerei 2, 55128 Mainz
Illustrations by: Hsiang-Shan Kung-Scherer
Layout by: Lynne M Evans
Printed and bound in Slovakia.

Accompanying Material to this book:

How to Pass Spoken English for Industry and Commerce Threshold Level
Student's Book ISBN 3-922514-34-0

How to Pass Spoken English for Industry and Commerce Threshold Level
Student's Cassette ISBN 3-922514-41-3

How to Pass Spoken English for Industry and Commerce Threshold Level
Picture Book ISBN 3-922514-42-1

Acknowledgements

The authors would like to thank all those who have helped in writing this book.

Special thanks to the LCCIEB, especially Liam Swords, Dawn Postans and Rupert Jones-Parry.

Special thanks also to Jean Pierre Jouteux and Gabi Schaub at Logophon.

Many thanks especially to Lucy Davison, John Davison, Nicky Westgate and John Green.

Thanks also to Wilf Curry, Safeway, Chollerford Garage, Lloyds Bank, Humshaugh Surgery, Saxon Financial Advice, Fourstones Paper Mill, Tynedale Council, The Globe Inn, Woodlands Post Office, Hexham General Hospital, London Transport Museum, European Language Skills, Stakis Coylumbridge, The Scotsman Communications Ltd and Camelot Group plc.

Thanks also to the following: Dr John McCollum, Joy McCollum, Dick Shotton, John Davison, Mike Saxon, Hazel Saxon, Kevin Allan, Scott Swan, Joan Swan, Maggie Wardle, Pat Egglestone, Hilary Stewart, Joy Taylor and Brit, Winifried Carr, Dorothy Wilson, George Robertson, Joanne McEwan.

Introduction

This Series of books is for candidates preparing for the four levels of the Spoken English For Industry and Commerce (SEFIC) examinations. It takes the learner from beginner to advanced level in approximately 480 hours.

The Teacher's book accompanies the Student's book which prepares candidates for the second level (Threshold) SEFIC exam and is divided into 60 Units, each Unit providing approximately 2 hours of classroom teaching. At the end of each Unit there is a list of new language items divided into vocabulary and structures with room for students to paraphrase or translate. Students are encouraged to prepare each Unit by looking up the new vocabulary before the lesson. Every tenth Unit is a revision Unit which consolidates the vocabulary and structures presented in the previous nine Units.

The syllabus is a thematic content-based syllabus which emphasises the process of learning and employs task-based activities. Learners are encouraged to use the subject language to discuss their own experience and knowledge relating to the themes and to express opinions about the subject matter. Language is not treated as a subject which one can learn/acquire per se, but rather as a means of receiving and giving information about another subject, ie as a means of communication.

The themes cover **personal information** (identity, character, appearance), **house and home** (type, place, costs, furniture, rooms), **environment** (town, country, weather), **travel and transport** (public transport, private vehicles, directions), **food and drink** (mealtime, restaurant, tastes, values), **shops and shopping** (weights, measures, prices, goods), **services** (telephone, bank, post office, garage), **health and hygiene** (body, states, illness, medicine), **perception and bodily movement** (feeling, seeing, handling), **work** (place, wages, duties, boss, colleagues), **education** (school, teachers, subjects, exams, future), **foreign languages** (aims, problems, skills), **leisure** (entertainment, hobbies, sport), **human relations** (friends, clubs, contacts), and **current affairs** (news, scandal, society). The speech acts and functions learned are those required to elicit and express factual information about the themes covered and which enable students to get things done (suasion). Thus, *expressing factual information about the environment* describes such language as "It's cold", "There are 3 restaurants in this town", "This town is boring/dirty". Similarly, *getting things done in connection with food and drink* would include such language as "A packet of ..., please", "Can I have a..., please", "Can I have the bill, please?"

This level is accompanied by: a Student's book, a Picture book including full-colour photographs and a cassette containing all the listening material from the Units.

By the end of this level students should be able to cope in temporary contact with foreign language speakers in everyday situations, whether as visitors to the foreign country or with visitors to their own country.

How to Pass
Spoken English for Industry and Commerce
Threshold Level

CONTENTS

Theme	Unit	Page	Title	parts of exam practised				
				A	B	C	D	E
HOUSE AND HOME	1	1-4	Where do you live?	✓		✓		
	2	5-8	Lifestyle	✓		✓		
	3	9-12	What's he doing?	✓	✓			
	4	13-16	Would you like to live in this house?	✓		✓	✓	✓
	5	17-20	Do you have a computer?	✓			✓	
ENVIRONMENT AND WEATHER	6	21-26	Life in the country is too quiet for me.	✓	✓			✓
	7	27-30	What's the weather like?	✓		✓		
	8	31-34	How do you get from the library to the golf club?	✓		✓		✓
	9	35-38	Have you ever been sailing?	✓			✓	
	10	39-42	**REVISION**					
TRAVEL AND TRANSPORT	11	43-46	Have you ever travelled on the London Underground?	✓		✓	✓	
	12	47-52	What's the best holiday you've ever had?	✓	✓		✓	
	13	53-56	Has flight JG971 from Tokyo arrived yet?	✓		✓	✓	
	14	57-60	When's the next train to Corbridge?	✓		✓	✓	
	15	61-64	I think that cars are the safest way to travel.	✓				✓
FOOD AND DRINK	16	65-68	Going Shopping	✓		✓		
	17	69-72	Eating Out	✓		✓	✓	
	18	73-76	Eating In	✓			✓	✓
	19	77-80	A pint of beer please.	✓		✓	✓	
	20	81-84	**REVISION**					
SHOPS AND SHOPPING	21	85-88	Rubbish and Recycling	✓				✓
	22	89-92	Where can you buy a safety pin?	✓		✓		
	23	93-96	How many metres are there in a kilometre?	✓		✓	✓	
	24	97-102	At the Supermarket		✓	✓	✓	✓
	25	103-106	Which department is it in?	✓		✓	✓	✓
SERVICES	26	107-112	What's the code for Cork?	✓	✓		✓	
	27	113-118	Do you have a driving licence?	✓	✓			✓
	28	119-124	Who do you bank with?	✓	✓	✓	✓	✓
	29	125-128	Where's the nearest car park?	✓		✓	✓	
	30	129-132	**REVISION**					

How to Pass
Spoken English for Industry and Commerce
Threshold Level

CONTENTS

Theme	Unit	Page	Title	A	B	C	D	E
HEALTH AND HYGIENE	31	133-138	I've got a headache.	✓	✓	✓		
	32	139-142	Rescue at Sea	✓		✓		✓
	33	143-146	Do you live a healthy life?	✓				✓
	34	147-150	Do you have medical insurance?	✓		✓	✓	✓
WORK	35	151-156	What do you do for a living?	✓	✓			
	36	157-160	Applying for a job.	✓		✓	✓	
	37	161-164	Who do you work for?	✓		✓	✓	
	38	165-170	What happens to your waste paper?	✓	✓			
	39	171-174	At Work	✓			✓	✓
	40	175-178	**REVISION**					
EDUCATION AND LANGUAGES	41	179-182	What was your favourite subject at school?	✓		✓	✓	✓
	42	183-188	How long have you been learning English?	✓		✓	✓	✓
	43	189-192	Why are you learning English?	✓			✓	
	44	193-196	I don't have time to learn vocabulary.	✓			✓	✓
LEISURE TIME	45	197-200	What do you do in your spare time?	✓				✓
	46	201-206	Going Swimming	✓	✓		✓	
	47	207-212	What's On?	✓		✓	✓	
	48	213-216	Where did you go on holiday last year?	✓		✓	✓	
	49	217-220	What's the best book you've ever read?	✓		✓		✓
	50	221-224	**REVISION**					
CURRENT AFFAIRS	51	225-228	Which newspaper do you read and why?	✓		✓	✓	✓
	52	229-232	What would you do if you won £20 million?	✓		✓		✓
	53	233-236	What was on the news last night?	✓				
	54	237-240	Young French student requires rented accommodation.	✓		✓		✓
	55	241-244	Are you free on Tuesday afternoon?				✓	✓
	56	245-250	She's going to type a letter.	✓	✓	✓	✓	✓
EXAM PREPARATION	57	251-256	**Exam Practice 1**	✓	✓	✓	✓	✓
	58	257-262	**Exam Practice 2**	✓	✓	✓	✓	✓
	59	263-268	**Exam Practice 3**	✓	✓	✓	✓	✓
	60	269-274	**Exam Practice 4**	✓	✓	✓	✓	✓

parts of exam practised

1

UNIT 1

Where do you live?

1 a **Listen to your teacher.**

b **Ask 5 neighbours.**

c **Write 5 sentences about your neighbours.**

eg *Alison lives in Sheffield.*

1 ______________________
2 ______________________
3 ______________________
4 ______________________
5 ______________________

d **Match the pictures and the words.**

d block of flats
___ semi-detached house
___ bungalow
___ detached house
___ terraced house

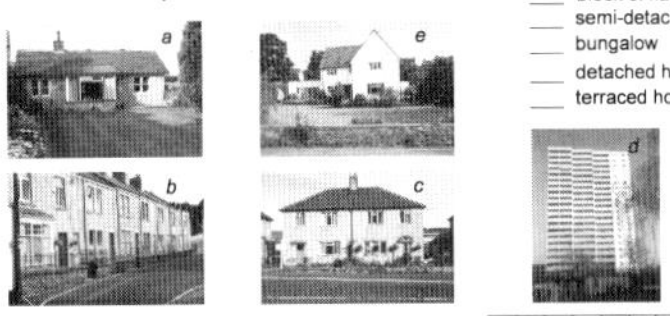

Check with your neighbour.

e **Listen to the cassette and fill in the following.**

Listen again and check.

		block of flats	semi-detached house	bungalow	detached house	terraced house	Kelso	Portsmouth	Cambridge	Sheffield	Dover
1	Alison	✓								✓	
2	Dave										
3	Sally										
4	Andy										
5	Chris										

f **Fill in the following.**

What kind of house do you live in? ______________________

g **Ask 5 neighbours.**

2

2 a **Put the words in the right space.**

bedroom bathroom hall dining room living room study kitchen

After work, I go home by bus. When I arrive home, I open my front door and go into the ____________ where I take my coat and shoes off. Then I go into the ____________ where I have a wash, and then I go into the bedroom where I change my clothes. After that I go into the ____________ and prepare something to eat for my children. They come home at 5 o'clock and we eat dinner together in the ____________. After dinner we go into the ____________ where we watch TV and relax. The children go to their bedrooms when they want to go to sleep and I normally go to my ____________ so I can do some work. When I'm tired I go into my ____________, get into bed and go to sleep.

Check with your neighbour.

b **Which rooms do you have?** ....

Fill in the column marked 'you'.

(✓= yes / x = no)

	you	your neighbour
bedroom	....	....
living room	....	....
bathroom	....	....
study	....	....
hall	....	....
kitchen	....	....
dining room	....	....

c **Ask your neighbour** ....

eg *Do you have a bedroom?*
Yes I do. / No I don't.

d **Fill in the following.**

I have ______________________ but my neighbour doesn't.

My neighbour has ______________________ but I don't.

We both have ______________________.

Neither of us have ______________________.

e **Ask your neighbour.**

1 Which room do you sleep in?
2 Which room do you eat in?
3 Which room do you watch TV in?
4 Which room do you work in?
5 Which room do you change your clothes in?

f **Can you name 3 things you both have in your rooms?**

3

3 a **Match the pictures and the words.**

8 set of scales
___ game
___ desk
___ pair of scissors
___ teddy bear
___ file
___ bottle of water
___ coat hanger
___ rubbish bin
___ coat stand

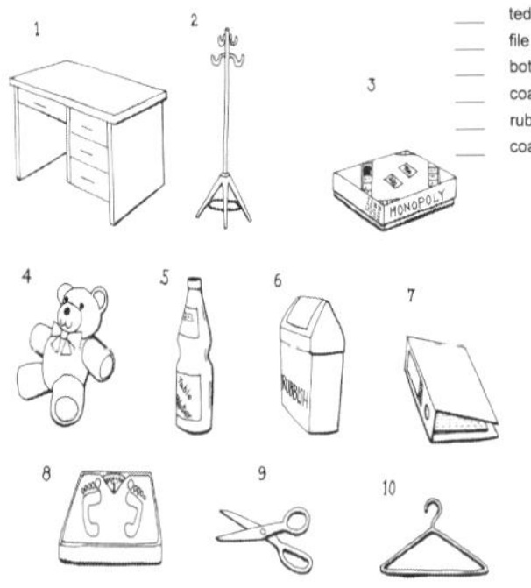

b **Ask your neighbour.**

eg *What's number 1? It's a desk.*

c **Fill in the following about yourself** ......

eg *Which room is your desk in?*
It's in my study.

	you	your neighbour
set of scales	....	....
game	....	....
desk	....	....
pair of scissors	....	....
teddy bear	....	....
file	....	....
bottle of water	....	....
coat hanger	....	....
rubbish bin	....	....
coat stand	....	....

d **Ask your neighbour and fill in the rooms** ....

4

4 a **Translate the following.**

Vocabulary

block of flats ____________
semi-detached house ____________
bungalow ____________
detached house ____________
terraced house ____________
bedroom ____________
living room ____________
bathroom ____________
study ____________
hall ____________
kitchen ____________
dining room ____________
set of scales ____________
game ____________
desk ____________
pair of scissors ____________
teddy bear ____________
file ____________
bottle of water ____________
coat hanger ____________
rubbish bin ____________
coat stand ____________

Structures

What's your name? ____________
My name's Alison. ____________
Where do you live? ____________
I live in Sheffield. ____________
Alison lives in Sheffield. ____________
What kind of house do you live in? ____________
I live in a flat. ____________
Do you have a bedroom? ____________
Yes I do. ____________
No I don't. ____________
I have a study but my neighbour doesn't. ____________
My neighbour has 3 bedrooms but I don't. ____________
We both have a kitchen and a bathroom. ____________
Neither of us have a hall. ____________
What's number 1? ____________
It's a desk. ____________
Which room is your desk in? ____________
It's in my study. ____________

Teaching Notes

Presentation and Practice

1 Introduce yourself to the class using “My name's ...” Ask each student “What's your name?” and elicit “My name's ...” Students ask two neighbours. Ask one student “Where do you live?” and elicit the answer “I live in ...”

Open the Student's book at page 1 and read the text in 1a aloud. Students read the dialogue and then ask five of their neighbours what their names are and where they live.

Two students read the text from 1a. Ask “Where does Alison live?" and elicit “She lives in Sheffield.” Ask students about their neighbours before they complete the writing exercise in 1c while you monitor and check. They then tell you where their neighbours live.

Introduce the pictures in 1d by eliciting familiar words and providing new vocabulary before students complete the matching exercise. Students check with their neighbour.

Tell students they are going to hear 5 short dialogues like the example in 1a. They are to put ticks in the columns to show where the people live and in what type of house. Play the cassette twice.

Students complete the writing task in 1f and then ask 5 more neighbours where they live. Provide feedback by asking students to tell you about their neighbours.

2 Ask students questions to elicit the rooms in 2a eg "Which room do you eat in? Which room do you work in?" Tell your students which rooms you have in your house/flat and write them on the board.

Students then complete the writing exercise in 2a and compare their work with their neighbour.

In 2b students mark which rooms they have/don't have in the column marked ‘you’. They ask their neighbour using the structure “Do you have a ...? ” and mark which rooms they have/don't have in the column marked ‘your neighbour’.

Ask one student the questions from 2b and write the rooms on the board next to your rooms. Use the information to introduce the phrases in 2d.

Students then complete the writing task in 2d while you monitor and check.

Students complete the speaking activity in 2e while you monitor and check.

In pairs students complete 2f and then tell you 3 things they both have.

3 If possible bring the objects from 3a with you to the lesson. If not introduce the words using the pictures in 3a.

Students then complete the matching task in 3a. Check by asking students questions eg “What's number 1?” “It's a desk”.

In pairs students complete the speaking activity in 3b to consolidate the new vocabulary. When they are familiar with it they complete 3c while you monitor and check.

They then complete the speaking activity in 3d by asking their neighbour. Provide feedback by asking students to tell you about their neighbour.

Revise all the structures and vocabulary before moving on to the next lesson.

At home students prepare for the next lesson by looking up the vocabulary in 4a of Unit 2.

Tapescripts

Exercise 1e

1 A What's your name?
B My name's Alison.
A Where do you live?
B I live in a block of flats in Sheffield.

2 A What's your name?
B My name's Dave.
A Where do you live?
B I live in a bungalow in Kelso.

3 A What's your name?
B My name's Sally.
A Where do you live?
B I live in a semi-detached house in Portsmouth.

4 A What's your name?
B My name's Andy.
A Where do you live?
B I live in a terraced house in Dover.

5 A What's your name?
B My name's Chris.
A Where do you live?
B I live in a detached house in Cambridge.

Answers

Exercise 1d

a bungalow
b detached house
c terraced house
d block of flats
e semi-detached house

Exercise 1e

1	Alison	block of flats	Sheffield
2	Dave	bungalow	Kelso
3	Sally	semi-detached house	Portsmouth
4	Andy	terraced house	Dover
5	Chris	detached house	Cambridge

Exercise 2a

hall
bathroom
kitchen
dining room
living room
study
bedroom

Exercise 3a

1 desk
2 coat stand
3 game
4 teddy bear
5 bottle of water
6 rubbish bin
7 file
8 set of scales
9 pair of scissors
10 coat hanger

1

UNIT 2

Lifestyle

1 a Listen to the cassette and fill in the missing information.

I have a very regular lifestyle. I work ____________ days a week from ____________ to ____________. I always get up at ____________ when my alarm clock goes off. At ____________ I have breakfast and at ____________ I leave home. It takes ____________ minutes to get to work so I normally arrive at ____________. I make a cup of coffee and then I start work at ____________. In the morning I read the post, write letters and make phone calls. I have lunch from ____________ to ____________. After lunch I have meetings and see people. I go home at ____________. In the evening I have dinner and read a newspaper. It's normally about ____________ when I go to bed.

Listen again and check.

b Tell your neighbour about Roger.

eg *He has a very regular lifestyle. He works...*

c Answer these questions about Roger.

1 How many days a week does Roger work? ____________
2 What time does he get up? ____________
3 What does he do in the office in the morning? ____________
4 What does he do in the afternoon? ____________
5 What time does he go to bed? ____________

Check with your neighbour.

d Here are some answers. Can you write the questions?

1 ____________? He has breakfast at 8.00am.
2 ____________? He leaves home at 8.15am.
3 ____________? He has meetings and sees people.
4 ____________? He finishes work at 5.00pm.
5 ____________? He has dinner and reads a newspaper.

Check with your neighbour.

2

Edward Exciting's Diary

Mon	?	Thur	?
Tues	?	Fri	?
Wed	?	Sat	?
		Sun	?

2 a Read this information about Edward.

I don't have a regular lifestyle. I start work at different times. I sometimes work at the weekend. I don't normally have lunch unless I have a business lunch. I have a company car because I travel a lot in my job. I work in different places and I often stay in hotels. I go to bed when I'm tired.

b Tell your neighbour about Edward.

eg *He doesn't have a regular lifestyle. He starts work...*

c Fill in the following.

eg *I don't have a regular lifestyle. He doesn't have a regular lifestyle.*

1 I don't have breakfast. ____________
2 ____________ He doesn't have a company car.
3 I don't travel a lot in my job. ____________
4 ____________ He doesn't often stay in hotels.
5 I don't work on Sundays. ____________

Check with your neighbour.

d Answer these questions about Edward using "Yes he does." or "No he doesn't."

eg *Does Edward have a regular lifestyle? No he doesn't.*

1 Does Edward start work at different times? ____________
2 Does he normally have lunch? ____________
3 Does he have a company car? ____________
4 Does he travel a lot in his job? ____________
5 Does he go home every night? ____________

Check with your neighbour.

3

3 a Now write about yourself using "Yes I do." or "No I don't."

eg *Do you always get up at the same time? Yes I do.*

1 Do you always have breakfast at the same time? ____________
2 Do you always start work at the same time? ____________
3 Do you always work in the same place? ____________
4 Do you always have lunch at the same time? ____________
5 Do you always go to bed at the same time? ____________

b Ask your neighbour the same questions.

c Fill in the following about yourself using the words in the box below.

always	normally	often	sometimes	rarely	never

eg *I always get up at the same time.*

1 I ____________ have breakfast at the same time.
2 I ____________ start work at the same time.
3 I ____________ work in the same place.
4 I ____________ have lunch at the same time.
5 I ____________ go to bed at the same time.

d Tell your neighbour about yourself.

e Fill in this chart about yourself. ....

		you	your neighbour
1	How many days a week do you work?	....	....
2	Do you sometimes work at weekends?	....	....
3	How long does it take to get to work?	....	....
4	How long do you have for lunch?	....	....
5	What time do you have breakfast?	....	....
6	What time do you have lunch?	....	....
7	Do you watch TV in the evenings?	....	....
8	Do you have a company car?	....	....
9	Do you travel a lot in your job?	....	....
10	What time do you go to bed?	....	....

f Ask your neighbour the questions ....

g Tell your teacher about your neighbour.

h Write 5 sentences about yourself.

eg *I never work at weekends.*

1 ____________
2 ____________
3 ____________
4 ____________
5 ____________

4

4 a Translate the following.

Vocabulary

lifestyle ____________
regular ____________
alarm clock ____________
go off ____________
take ____________
read the post ____________
write letters ____________
make phone calls ____________
have meetings ____________
see people ____________
in the morning ____________
after lunch ____________
in the afternoon ____________
in the evening ____________
at different times ____________
unless ____________
business lunch ____________
company car ____________
travel ____________
always ____________
normally ____________
often ____________
sometimes ____________
rarely ____________
never ____________

Structures

I have a very regular lifestyle. ____________
He has a very regular lifestyle. ____________
What time does he have breakfast? ____________
He has breakfast at 8.00am. ____________
I don't have a regular lifestyle. ____________
He doesn't have a regular lifestyle. ____________
Does he have a regular lifestyle? ____________
Yes he does. ____________
No he doesn't. ____________
Do you always get up at the same time? ____________
Yes I do. ____________
No I don't. ____________
I always get up at the same time. ____________
I never work at weekends. ____________

Teaching Notes

Revision

Revise all the structures and vocabulary from Unit 1 by asking students questions eg "Where do you live? Which rooms do you have in your flat? Do you have a pair of scissors in your bathroom?"

Presentation and Practice

1 Ask students questions about the picture in 1a eg "What does the man look like? What is he wearing? What is he doing?" Ask students about the diary eg "What is his name? What is in his diary for Monday?" etc.

Introduce the listening activity by telling students that Roger is going to tell them about himself and that they will hear the cassette twice. While they are listening they fill in the blanks in 1a. Play the cassette a third time for students to check.

In 1b point at the picture and tell students "This is Roger. He has a very regular lifestyle." Elicit the rest of the sentences and then students practise with their neighbour.

Students complete the writing task in 1c and compare their work with their neighbour. Provide feedback by asking one student the questions from 1c.

Write the questions from 1c on the board underlining 'does' and the verb and then students complete the writing activity in 1d. When they have compared their work with their neighbour, they close their books and ask/answer questions about Roger in pairs.

2 Introduce the picture as in 1a and then students read the information about Edward. When they have read the information they complete the speaking activity in 2b. Provide feedback by asking one student to tell you about Edward.

Write the example from 2c on the board underlining 'I don't have' and 'he doesn't have' before students complete the writing task in 2c. When they have finished they compare their work with their neighbour.

Students then answer the questions in 2d and compare their work with their neighbour. Provide feedback by asking students the questions from 2d.

3 Introduce the questions from 3a by telling students about yourself eg "I always get up at the same time. I have breakfast at different times" Using this information ask students about themselves eliciting "Yes I do" or "No I don't".

Students complete the writing task in 3a and then ask their neighbour the questions from 3a. Students then complete the writing task in 3c and tell their neighbour about themselves in 3d.

Introduce 3e by asking one student the questions from the chart. In the column marked 'you' students fill in the information about themselves and in 3f they ask their neighbour the questions, noting down the answers in the column marked 'your neighbour'. When they are finished ask students to tell you about their neighbour before they complete the writing task in 3h. Provide feedback by asking students to tell you their sentences.

Revise all the structures and vocabulary before moving on to the next lesson.

At home students prepare for the next lesson by looking up the vocabulary in 4a of Unit 3.

Tapescripts

Exercise 1a

I have a very regular lifestyle. I work 5 days a week from 9 o'clock to 5 o'clock. I always get up at half past 7 when my alarm clock goes off. At 8 o'clock I have breakfast and at quarter past 8 I leave home. It takes 30 minutes to get to work so I normally arrive at quarter to 9. I make a cup of coffee and then I start work at 9 o'clock. In the morning I read the post, write letters and make phone calls. I have lunch from 12 noon to 1 o'clock. After lunch I have meetings and see people. I go home at 5 o'clock. In the evening I have dinner and read a newspaper. It's normally about 11 o'clock when I go to bed.

Answers

Exercise 1a

5
9 o'clock
5 o'clock
7.30
8 o'clock
8.15
30
8.45
9 o'clock
12 noon
1 o'clock
5 o'clock
11 o'clock

Exercise 1c

1 He works five days a week.
2 He gets up at 7.30.
3 He reads the post, writes letters and makes phone calls.
4 He has meetings and sees people.
5 He goes to bed at 11pm.

Exercise 1d

1 What time does he have breakfast?
2 What time does he leave home?
3 What does he do in the afternoon?
4 What time does he finish work?
5 What does he do in the evening?

Exercise 2c

1 I don't have breakfast. He doesn't have breakfast.
2 I don't have a company car. He doesn't have a company car.
3 I don't travel a lot in my job. He doesn't travel a lot in his job.
4 I don't often stay in hotels. He doesn't often stay in hotels.
5 I don't work on Sundays. He doesn't work on Sundays.

Exercise 2d

1 Yes he does.
2 No he doesn't.
3 Yes he does.
4 Yes he does.
5 No he doesn't.

1

UNIT 3

What's he doing?

1 a Match the sentences and the pictures.

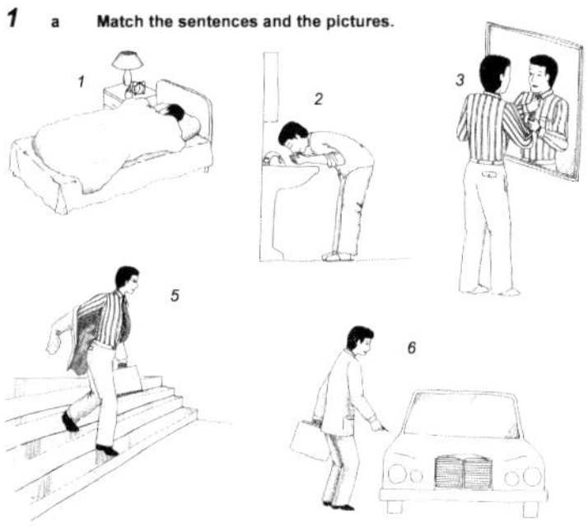

a It's 7 o'clock in the morning and Jeremy is lying in bed. [1]

b He's washing his face. [ ]

c He's looking in the mirror. [ ]

d He's eating breakfast. [ ]

e He's leaning over the wash basin. [ ]

f His alarm clock's ringing and he's trying to switch it off. [ ]

g He's getting dressed. [ ]

h He's holding a bowl in his left hand. [ ]

i He's putting his jacket on. [ ]

j He's unlocking the car. [ ]

k He's coming downstairs. [ ]

Check with your neighbour.

b Ask your neighbour about Jeremy.

eg *What's he doing in picture 1? He's lying in bed.*

c Answer the questions using "Yes he is." or "No he isn't."

eg *Is he unlocking the car in picture 1? No he isn't.*

1 Is he washing his face in picture 3? ____________________

2 Is he wearing a jacket in picture 2? ____________________

3 Is he eating breakfast in picture 4? ____________________

4 Is he coming downstairs in picture 5? ____________________

5 Is he putting his jacket on in picture 3? ____________________

Check with your neighbour.

2

2 a Describe the people in the picture to your neighbour.

eg *Tony has short dark hair and glasses.*

b Make up 5 questions about the people.

eg *What's Tony doing?*

1 ____ ?

2 ____ ?

3 ____ ?

4 ____ ?

5 ____ ?

Check with your teacher and then ask your neighbour your questions.

eg *What's Tony doing? He's drinking coffee.*

c Fill in the following using "is" or "isn't".

eg *Tony isn't typing a letter.*

1 Joe ______________ writing.

2 Roger ______________ smoking.

3 Deborah ______________ typing.

4 Sally ______________ watching TV.

5 Amanda ______________ smoking.

Check with your teacher.

d Close your book. Tell your neighbour what Tony, Deborah, Joe, Sally, Roger and Amanda are doing.

e Look around the class. Ask your neighbour what the other students are doing.

3

3 a Put the words in the right place.

sandals waistcoat shoes shirt glasses skirt dress tie suit jacket trousers shorts scarf brooch T-shirt socks necklace blouse boots bracelet earrings pullover

Tony	Deborah	Joe	Sally	Roger	Amanda

Check with your teacher.

b Write 5 questions about the people.

eg *What's Tony wearing?*

1 ____ ?

2 ____ ?

3 ____ ?

4 ____ ?

5 ____ ?

c Ask your neighbour.

eg *What's Tony wearing? He's wearing shorts, sandals, a T-shirt and glasses.*

d Look around the class. Ask your neighbour what other students are wearing.

e Answer these questions.

1 What are you wearing? ____________________

2 What is your neighbour wearing? ____________________

3 What is your teacher wearing? ____________________

f Look around your class. Describe somebody to your neighbour.

eg *She's wearing a blue dress, shoes, a brooch and earrings, and she's talking to the teacher. Who is it?*

g Look around your class. Ask your neighbour questions like these.

eg *Who's wearing a white T-shirt? What's the teacher doing?*

4

4 a Translate the following.

Vocabulary

lie ______________	sandals ______________
wash his face ______________	waistcoat ______________
mirror ______________	shoes ______________
wear ______________	shirt ______________
lean over ______________	glasses ______________
wash basin ______________	skirt ______________
ring ______________	dress ______________
try ______________	tie ______________
switch off ______________	jacket ______________
get dressed ______________	trousers ______________
hold ______________	shorts ______________
bowl ______________	scarf ______________
put on ______________	brooch ______________
unlock ______________	T-shirt ______________
come downstairs ______________	socks ______________
drink ______________	necklace ______________
smoke ______________	blouse ______________
talk ______________	boots ______________
write ______________	bracelet ______________
watch TV ______________	suit ______________
eat ______________	earrings ______________
type ______________	pullover ______________

Structures

What's he doing in picture 1? ______________

He's lying in bed. ______________

Is he unlocking the car in picture 1? ______________

Yes he is. ______________

No he isn't. ______________

Tony has short dark hair and glasses. ______________

What's Tony doing? ______________

He's drinking coffee. ______________

Tony isn't typing a letter. ______________

What's Tony wearing? ______________

He's wearing shorts, sandals, a T-shirt and glasses. ______________

What are you wearing? ______________

I'm wearing trousers, a shirt and a tie. ______________

What's she wearing? ______________

She's wearing a blue dress, shoes, a brooch and earrings. ______________

What's she doing? ______________

She's talking to the teacher. ______________

Who's wearing a white T-shirt? ______________

What's the teacher doing? ______________

Teaching Notes

Warm-up

Ask students questions from earlier Units eg "What's your name? Where do you live? How do you spell it? Which room do you sleep in? Do you have a teddy bear?"

Revision

Revise all the structures and vocabulary from the previous Unit by asking students questions eg "How many days a week do you work? Do you always have breakfast at the same time? What time do you go to bed?"

Presentation and Practice

1 Introduce the matching task in 1a by pointing at the pictures in the sequence and asking students questions eg "What's he wearing? What's he doing?"

Students complete the matching task in 1a and compare their work with their neighbour.

In 1b students look again at the picture sequence and ask each other questions eg "What's he doing in picture 1? What's he wearing in picture 2?"

Introduce 1c by asking one student "Is he unlocking the car in picture 1? and eliciting the answer "No he isn't".

Students then complete the writing task in 1c and check their work with their neighbour.

2 In 2a students describe the people in the picture to their neighbour while you monitor and check.

Introduce 2b writing "What's Tony doing?" on the board and elicit the answer "Tony's drinking coffee." Students check their work with you and then ask their neighbour the questions.

Students then complete the writing task in 2b while you monitor and check. When they are ready they ask each other their questions about the people.

Ask students "Is Tony typing a letter? " and elicit the answer "No Tony isn't typing a letter." Students then complete the writing task in 2c. Check students' work by asking one student to read out his/her sentences.

In 2d students work in pairs; one of them closes the book and answers questions about the people in the picture. In 2e they ask each other about the other people in the class, eg "What's Sarah doing? "She's speaking."

3 Point at the picture in 2a and ask one student "What's Tony wearing?" Elicit the answer and then students complete the matching task about the other people in 3a. Provide feedback by asking students what the people in the picture are wearing. Point at one of the people in the picture and elicit the question "What's ... wearing? " Students make up 5 questions in 3b and ask their neighbour their questions.

In 3d students work in pairs asking their neighbour what other students are wearing.

Students then complete the writing task in 3e. Introduce 3f by describing one of your students to the class and asking them to guess who it is. They then complete the speaking activity in 3f. Provide feedback by asking students to describe people while the rest of the class guess.

Students complete the speaking activity in 3g.

Revise all the structures and vocabulary before moving on to the next lesson.

At home students prepare for the next lesson by looking up the vocabulary in 4a of Unit 4.

Answers

Exercise 1a

a 1
b 2
c 3
d 4
e 2
f 1
g 3
h 4
I 5
j 6
k 5

Exercise 1c

1 No he isn't.
2 No he isn't.
3 Yes he is.
4 Yes he is.
5 No he isn't.

Exercise 3a

Tony	Deborah	Joe	Sally	Roger	Amanda
shorts	dress	trousers	skirt	suit	jacket
sandals	shoes	shirt	blouse	waistcoat	trousers
T-shirt	necklace	pullover	scarf	shirt	shoes
glasses		shoes	boots	tie	earrings
		socks	bracelet	shoes	brooch
					blouse

Exercise 2b

1 What's Deborah doing?
2 What's Joe doing?
3 What's Sally doing?
4 What's Roger doing?
5 What's Amanda doing?

Exercise 2c

1 Joe is writing.
2 Roger isn't smoking.
3 Deborah isn't typing.
4 Sally is watching TV.
5 Amanda isn't smoking.

Exercise 3b

1 What's Deborah wearing?
2 What's Joe wearing?
3 What's Sally wearing?
4 What's Roger wearing?
5 What's Amanda wearing?

1

UNIT 4

Would you like to live in this house?

LJ Patterson & Partners, Estate Agent, 14 Main Street, Lancaster
Tel: 01374 99476 / Fax: 01374 98345

Opening Times
Mon - Fri 9am - 5pm
Sat & Sun 10am - 4pm

For Sale
Price £95,000

17 Fairview Crescent
Lancaster

This attractive semi-detached house is pleasantly situated 2 minutes from the town centre. The house offers 2-storey accommodation including 3 bedrooms, a modernised kitchen, central heating and a patio.

Viewing by appointment only.

1 a **Ask your neighbour.**

1 What is the name of the estate agent?
2 What is the address of the house for sale?
3 What is the estate agent's telephone number?
4 What is the fax number?
5 What time do they close on Fridays?
6 Are they open on Sundays?
7 How much is the house?
8 Do I have to make an appointment to see the house?
9 Is the house in the country?
10 Does the house have central heating?

Check with your teacher.

2

2 a **Listen to the cassette and write down the names of the rooms on the house plan below.**

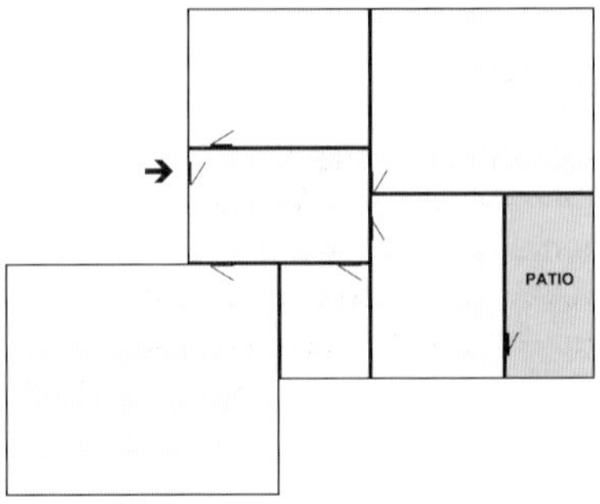

Check with your neighbour.

b **Draw a plan of your own house.**

c **Tell your neighbour what the rooms are.**

eg *This is the front door and this is the entrance hall. The first room on the left is a bedroom.*

3

3 a **Alison lives in a block of flats in Sheffield but dreams of moving to a detached house in the country one day. Read the description of Alison's ideal home.**

"My ideal home would be a detached house. It would have 9 rooms; a bathroom, a kitchen, a living room, a big dining room, a study, 3 bedrooms and an entrance hall. It would be made of stone and would be painted white. It would have views over mountains and a lake. It wouldn't have a balcony, air conditioning, a patio or satellite TV, but it would have central heating, a coal fire, a garage, a big garden, a wine cellar and a telephone. The nearest shop would be about 3 miles away, the nearest restaurant would be about 10 miles away and the nearest post office would be about 5 miles away. I would live there with my pet dog, Max."

b **Ask your neighbour.**

eg *Would you like to live in this house? Yes I would. No I wouldn't.*

c **Answer these questions about your ideal home in note form** ....

		you	your neighbour
1	What kind of house would it be?		
2	How many rooms would it have?		
3	Would it be in the town or country?		
4	What would it be made of?		
5	What colour would it be?		
6	What views would it have?		
7	Would it have a balcony?		
8	Would it have a patio?		
9	Would it have central heating?		
10	Would it have a coal fire?		
11	Would it have a garage?		
12	Would it have a garden?		
13	Would it have satellite TV?		
14	Would it have a wine cellar?		
15	Would it have a telephone?		
16	Would it have air conditioning?		
17	How far would the nearest shop be?		
18	How far would the nearest restaurant be?		
19	How far would the nearest post office be?		
20	Would you live there alone?		

d **Ask your neighbour about his/her ideal home.** ....

eg *What kind of house would your ideal home be? It would be a detached house.*

e **Tell your teacher about your ideal home.**

eg *My ideal home would be a detached house.*

4

4 a **Translate the following.**

Vocabulary

estate agent ____________
opening times ____________
for sale ____________
price ____________
attractive ____________
pleasantly situated ____________
offer ____________
2-storey ____________
accommodation ____________
modernised ____________
central heating ____________
patio ____________
appointment ____________
front door ____________
entrance hall ____________
approximately ____________
on the left ____________
opposite ____________
next to ____________
shower ____________
outside ____________
south facing ____________
wonderful views ____________
master bedroom ____________
garage ____________
mountains ____________
lake ____________
balcony ____________
air conditioning ____________
satellite TV ____________
coal fire ____________
garden ____________
wine cellar ____________
telephone ____________
10 minutes away ____________

Structures

It would be a detached house. ____________
It would be made of stone. ____________
It would be painted white. ____________
It would have central heating. ____________
It wouldn't have air conditioning. ____________
I would live there alone. ____________
This is the front door. ____________
This is the entrance hall. ____________
The first room on the left is a bedroom. ____________
Would you like to live in this house? ____________
Yes I would. ____________
No I wouldn't. ____________
What kind of house would it be? ____________
It would be a detached house. ____________
Would it have a balcony? ____________
My ideal home would be a detached house. ____________

Teaching Notes

Warm-up

Ask students questions from earlier Units eg "What's your name? Do you live in a semi-detached house? What time do you have breakfast? Do you always have breakfast at the same time?" etc.

Revision

Revise all the structures and vocabulary from the previous Unit by asking students questions eg "What is Tony doing? What are you wearing? Is Tony wearing a white T-shirt?" etc.

Presentation and Practice

1 Introduce the activity in 1a by asking students if it is normal to rent or buy property in their country. Ask them where they look if they want to rent or buy a flat. Explain that this is the type of advertisement you would see in an estate agents.

In pairs students ask and answer the questions in 1a about the advertisement while you monitor and help. Provide feedback by one pair asking and answering the questions.

2 Introduce 2a by telling students that they are going to hear a recording of an estate agent showing someone around a house which is for sale. Students should listen to the cassette and write down the names of the rooms. Play the cassette twice. The first time students should listen and not write anything. The second time they should write the information on the plan and then compare their work with their neighbour. Provide feedback by asking one student to explain what the rooms are.

Students then draw a rough outline of one floor of their house/flat in 2b. When they are finished they explain to their neighbour what the rooms are.

3 Students read through the information in 3a and complete the speaking activity in 3b. Ask the class how many people would like to live in this house and how many would not. Elicit one or two reasons for this from different students. Ask one student who wouldn't like to live here what their ideal home would be like.

Students then read through the questions in 3c and make notes in the column marked 'you'. When they are finished students ask their neighbour the questions making notes in the column marked 'your neighbour'. Provide feedback by asking students to tell you about their ideal home.

Revise all the structures and vocabulary before moving on to the next lesson.

At home students prepare for the next lesson by looking up the vocabulary in 4a of Unit 5.

Tapescripts

Exercise 2a

Here we are at the front door. I'll just find my key and open the door.

This is the entrance hall which is very light as you can see.

The first room on the left is a bedroom which is approximately 3m x 3m.

Opposite this room is the living room which is 6m x 5m and has a real coal fire in it.

Next to the living room is the bathroom with a shower and bath and next to that is the kitchen which was fully modernised last year.

The kitchen door leads outside to the patio which is south facing and has wonderful views.

The last room is the master bedroom which is 5m x 4m.

The bungalow is warm in winter and cool in summer. It has a garage and full central heating and I think it would be ideal for you.

Answers

Exercise 2a

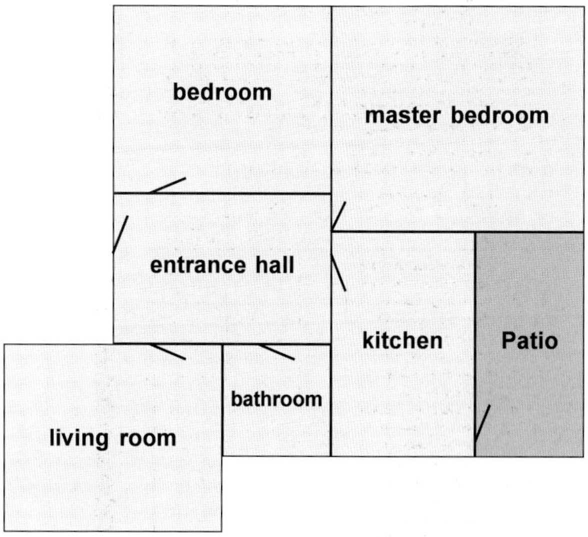

1

UNIT 5

Do you have a computer?

1 a Match the sentences and the pictures.

1 The TV remote control has buttons. [b]
2 The cassette recorder has buttons. [ ]
3 The oven has dials. [ ]
4 The iron has a dial. [ ]
5 The hairdryer has a switch. [ ]
6 The computer keyboard has keys. [ ]

b Now complete the sentences below using the words in the box.

press - turn

eg To operate the computer, you press the keys.

1 To operate the TV, you ______________________.
2 To operate the cassette recorder, you ______________________.
3 To operate the iron, you ______________________.
4 To operate the hairdryer, you ______________________.
5 To operate the oven, you ______________________.

Check with your teacher.

c Ask your neighbour.

eg Do you have a computer? Yes I do. How do you operate it? I press the keys.

d Fill in the following about your class.

1 How many people in your class have a computer? ______________________
2 How many people in your class have a TV with remote control? ______________________
3 How many people in your class have an oven? ______________________
4 How many people in your class have an iron? ______________________
5 How many people in your class have a hairdryer? ______________________

2

2 a Here is a picture of an electric kettle. See if you can match the numbers and the words.

[7] stand
[ ] cable
[ ] spout
[ ] lid
[ ] plug
[ ] max. fill level
[ ] socket
[ ] min. fill level
[ ] handle
[ ] on/off switch

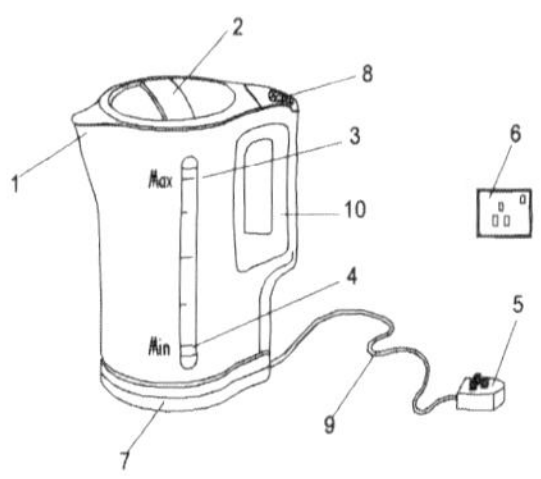

b Ask your neighbour these questions.

1 Have you ever used a kettle?
2 When was the last time you used it?
3 What did you use it for?

c Read the instructions.

Kettle Instructions

1 Take the kettle off the stand.
2 Remove the lid.
3 Check how much water is in it.
4 Fill the kettle to the required level.
5 Put the kettle back on the stand.
6 Put the plug in the socket and switch it on.
7 Put the on/off switch to the 'on' position.
8 Leave for a few minutes.
9 The kettle will automatically switch off when the water boils.
10 Take the kettle off the stand before pouring the water.

Guaranteed for 5 years.

d Ask your neighbour.

1 What do you have to do first?
2 What do you have to check?
3 What do you have to do with the plug?
4 Do you have to switch the kettle off?
5 What do you have to do before pouring the water?

3

3 a Match the pictures and the words.

[i] kettle
[ ] coffee machine
[ ] toaster
[ ] sewing machine
[ ] mixer
[ ] electric shaver
[ ] telephone
[ ] CD player
[ ] vacuum cleaner

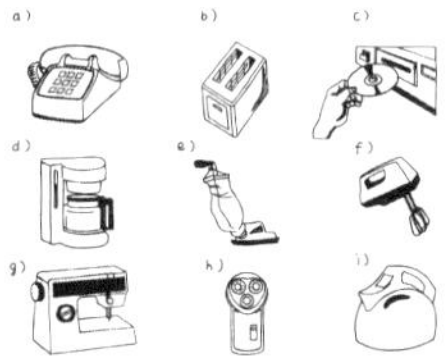

b Ask your neighbour.

eg How do you operate a telephone? You press the buttons.

c Fill in the following chart about yourself ....

(✓= yes / x = no)

	you	your neighbour
Have you got a telephone?		
Have you got a sewing machine?		
Have you got a mixer?		
Have you got an electric shaver?		
Have you got a vacuum cleaner?		

d Ask your neighbour and fill in this column..................................

e Fill in the following.

eg What do you use an iron for? You use it for ironing clothes.

1 What do you use a ______________ for? You use it for making and mending clothes.
2 What do you use a ______________ for? You use it for making toast.
3 ______________________________? You use it for cleaning your room.
4 What do you use a CD player for? ______________________
5 What do you use a mixer for? ______________________

f Ask your neighbour about the other objects in 3a.

g How to make toast. Put these instructions in the correct order.

_1_ Take a slice of bread.
___ Put the bread in the toaster.
___ Eat the toast.
___ Wait for the toaster to switch off automatically.
___ Take out the toast.
___ Switch the toaster on.
___ Put the plug in the socket.
___ Put some butter on the toast.

h Ask your neighbour.

1 How do you make a cup of coffee?
2 How do you make a cake?
3 How do you make a telephone call?

4

4 a Translate the following.

Vocabulary

computer ______	max. fill level ______
keyboard ______	socket ______
iron ______	min. fill level ______
oven ______	handle ______
hairdryer ______	on/off switch ______
remote control ______	coffee machine ______
key ______	toaster ______
dial ______	vacuum cleaner ______
button ______	CD player ______
switch ______	electric shaver ______
press ______	sewing machine ______
turn ______	mixer ______
operate ______	mend ______
electric kettle ______	toast ______
stand ______	clean ______
cable ______	slice of bread ______
spout ______	switch on/off ______
lid ______	butter ______
plug ______	

Structures

The TV remote control has buttons. ______________________
To operate the computer you press the keys. ______________________
Do you have a computer? ______________________
Yes I do. ______________________
How do you operate it? ______________________
I press the keys. ______________________
Have you ever used a kettle? ______________________
Yes I have. ______________________
When was the last time you used it? ______________________
This morning. ______________________
What did you use it for? ______________________
To make a cup of tea. ______________________
What do you have to do first? ______________________
You have to take it off the stand first. ______________________
How do you operate a telephone? ______________________
You press the buttons. ______________________
What do you use an iron for? ______________________
You use it for ironing clothes. ______________________

Teaching Notes

Warm-up

Ask students questions from earlier Units eg "What is your neighbour wearing? What are you doing? What do you do in the evenings? Do you have a set of scales in your house?"

Revision

Revise all the structures and vocabulary from the previous Unit by asking students questions eg "Would your ideal home have a coal fire? Would it have central heating?"

Presentation and Practice

1 Introduce the objects in 1a by pointing at them and asking questions eg "Is this a cassette recorder?" When students are familiar with the words they complete the matching task in 1a. Check their work by asking students eg "What has buttons?" Ask students how they would operate the remote control and introduce 'press' and 'turn' by miming. Ask about the other objects and then students complete the writing task in 1b. Provide feedback by asking one student to read out the completed sentences.

In pairs students complete the speaking activity in 1c and then bring one student to the front to ask how many of the class have the objects from 1a.

2 Students complete the activity in 2a by matching the numbers and the words. Provide feedback by asking students what number 1 is, etc.

Introduce the speaking activity in 2b by asking one student the questions from 2b. When students have completed the speaking activity ask them how they use a kettle, eg "What do you do first, what do you do after that?" etc If they don't have kettles ask them how they boil water eg, "What do you do first?" etc.

In pairs students read the kettle instructions and then complete the speaking activity in 2d. Provide feedback by asking one pair to ask and answer the questions in front of the whole class.

3 Introduce the vocabulary in 3a by asking students what electrical items they have in their home. Elicit as much vocabulary as possible, but only write the words from 3a on the board. When you have them all students can complete the matching task in 3a.

Introduce the speaking activity in 3b by writing the question "How do you operate a telephone?" on the board and eliciting the answer. In pairs students ask and answer about the other objects.

Students fill in the column marked 'you' about themselves and then fill in the column marked 'your neighbour' by asking their neighbour questions eg "Have you got a telephone? " Ask one or two students to tell you about their neighbour.

Introduce 3e by asking who has an iron and what they use it for. Students then fill in the missing information in 3e and compare with their neighbours before completing the speaking activity in 3f. Find out who has a toaster and ask them how they make toast.

In pairs students read through the instructions in 3g and try to put them in the correct order. Bring two students to the front. One gives the instructions for making toast while the other one mimes the actions. The rest of the class may help with the instructions.

In pairs students work out the instructions for 3h. Bring pairs out to the front to demonstrate how to make a cup of coffee etc.

Revise all the structures and vocabulary before moving on to the next lesson.

At home students prepare for the next lesson by looking up the vocabulary in 4a of Unit 6.

Answers

Exercise 1a

1 B
2 F
3 C
4 D
5 E
6 A

Exercise 1b

1 .... press the buttons.
2 .... press the buttons.
3 .... turn the dial.
4 .... press the switch.
5 .... turn the dials.

Exercise 2a

1 spout
2 lid
3 max. fill level
4 min. fill level
5 plug
6 socket
7 stand
8 on/off switch
9 cable
10 handle

Exercise 3a

a telephone
b toaster
c CD player
d coffee machine
e vacuum cleaner
f mixer
g sewing machine
h electric shaver
I kettle

Exercise 3e

1 sewing machine
2 toaster
3 What do you use a vacuum cleaner for?
4 You use it for playing music.
5 You use it for making cakes.

Exercise 3g

1 Take a slice of bread.
2 Put the bread in the toaster.
3 Put the plug in the socket.
4 Switch the toaster on.
5 Wait for the toaster to switch off automatically.
6 Take out the toast.
7 Put some butter on the toast.
8 Eat the toast.

1

UNIT 6

Life in the country is too quiet for me.

1 a Ask your neighbour and point at the pictures.

eg Can you see a litter bin? Yes it's here.

gate
birds
fence
queue
hedges
litter bin
bus stop
fruit trees
traffic lights
pedestrian crossing
parking meter
pavement
mini bus
hay bale
car park
stream
tractor
sheep
shops
forest

b Fill in the following about yourself.

	you	your neighbour
1 Do you live in a city?		
2 Do you live in a town?		
3 Do you live in a village?		
4 How many people live there?		
5 How far is the nearest shop?		
6 How far is the nearest bus stop?		
7 How far is the nearest restaurant?		
8 How long have you lived there?		
9 Would you like to move house?		
10 Can you see a bus stop from your living room?		

c Ask your neighbour the questions.

2

2 a Ask your neighbour questions using the words in the box.

eg Do you think life is quieter in the town or the country?

quiet	noisy	busy	hectic	exciting	boring	smelly

b Read the following and mark in the box if you agree (✓), or disagree (x).

1 Life in the country is too quiet for me. ☐
2 Life in the town is too busy for me. ☐
3 Life in the country is too boring for me. ☐
4 Life in the town is too hectic for me. ☐
5 Life in the country is too noisy for me. ☐
6 Life in the town is too noisy for me. ☐
7 Life in the country is too smelly for me. ☐
8 Life in the town is too smelly for me. ☐
9 Life in the country is too exciting for me. ☐
10 Life in the town is too quiet for me. ☐

c Tell your neighbour what you think.

eg I agree with sentence 1. I think that life in the country is too quiet.
I disagree with sentence 2. I don't think that life in the town is too busy.

d Write down 3 advantages and 3 disadvantages of living in a town.

eg near to shops.

Advantages	Disadvantages
1 ______	1 ______
2 ______	2 ______
3 ______	3 ______

e Tell your neighbour.

eg One advantage is that you are near to shops.

f Write down 3 advantages and 3 disadvantages of living in the country.

Advantages	Disadvantages
1 ______	1 ______
2 ______	2 ______
3 ______	3 ______

g Ask your neighbour.

eg What are the advantages of living in the country?

h Do you think there are more advantages of living in a town or in the country?

3

3 a Look at photograph sequence 1 'A Walk in the Country' on the next pages and see if you can find the following items.

trees clouds cows a castle a bridge a gate

b Ask your neighbour the following questions.

eg What can you see in photograph 1?
I can see some houses, a car, some trees, a woman and a dog. The woman and her dog are walking along the pavement.

1 What can you see in photograph 2?
2 What can you see in photograph 3?
3 What can you see in photograph 4?
4 What can you see in photograph 5?
5 What can you see in photograph 6?

c Now ask your neighbour these questions about the woman.

eg What's she doing in photograph 1?
She's walking towards the houses.

1 What's she doing in photograph 2?
2 What's she doing in photograph 3?
3 What's she doing in photograph 4?
4 What's she doing in photograph 5?
5 What's she doing in photograph 6?

d Read these sentences and then match them with the correct photographs.

Yesterday morning Mrs Taylor took her dog, Brit, for a walk.

The sun was shining and it was a lovely day.

3 She stopped at a gate and enjoyed the view of the castle.

___ She walked through the village towards the terraced houses.

___ She crossed a bridge over a little stream.

___ She walked through some fields.

___ She walked down a narrow lane.

Her house was at the end of the lane. When she arrived home she made a cup of tea and gave Brit some water.

Check with your teacher.

e Tell your neighbour the story using:

'first', 'then', 'next', 'after that', 'finally'.

f Now ask your neighbour these questions.

1 What time of year do you think it is in the photographs? Why?
2 What time of day do you think it is in the photographs? Why?
3 What is the lady wearing?
4 When was the last time you went for a walk in the country? Where? Why?
5 Do you have any pets? Why (not)?

4

4 a Translate the following.

Vocabulary

litter bin ______	town ______
gate ______	country ______
hedges ______	quiet ______
pedestrian crossing ______	noisy ______
birds ______	hectic ______
traffic lights ______	boring ______
fence ______	busy ______
queue ______	smelly ______
bus stop ______	exciting ______
fruit trees ______	castle ______
hay bale ______	village ______
tractor ______	bridge ______
sheep ______	narrow ______
stream ______	lane ______
shops ______	field ______
parking meter ______	first ______
forest ______	then ______
mini bus ______	next ______
pavement ______	after that ______
car park ______	finally ______

Structures

Can you see a litter bin? Yes it's here. ______
Do you think life is quieter in the town or in the country? ______
Life in the country is too quiet for me. ______
I agree with sentence 1. ______
I think that life in the country is too quiet. ______
I disagree with sentence 2. ______
I don't think that life in the town is too busy. ______
One advantage is that you are near the shops. ______
What are the advantages of living in the country? ______
What can you see in photograph 1? ______
I can see some houses, a car, some trees, a woman and a dog. ______
The woman and her dog are walking along the pavement. ______
What's she doing in photograph 1? ______
She's walking towards the houses. ______

Teaching Notes

Warm-up

Ask students questions from earlier Units eg "Does your home have double glazing? Do you have a pair of scissors in your flat? What kind of house do you live in?"

Revision

Revise all the structures and vocabulary from the previous Unit by asking students questions eg "How do you operate a computer? How do you make a slice of toast? What do you use a sewing machine for?"

Presentation and Practice

1 Ask students whether they live in the town or the country. Ask two or three students what they can see from their living room window. Students then complete the speaking activity in 1a while you monitor and check.

Students then read the questions in 1b and fill in the information about themselves in note form in the column marked 'you'. They ask their neighbour the questions about where they live and fill in the information in the column marked 'your neighbour'. Provide feedback by asking students to tell you about their neighbour.

2 Students complete the speaking activity in 2a and then read the sentences in 2b noting whether they agree or disagree.

They then complete the speaking activity in 2c expressing their opinions. Provide feedback by asking students about the statements.

Draw two columns on the board with the headings 'advantages' and 'disadvantages' and elicit advantages and disadvantages of living in a town/city. Clean the board. Students note down three advantages and three disadvantages of living in a town/city and then complete the speaking activity in 2e with their neighbour while you monitor and check.

Students note down three advantages and three disadvantages of living in the country and tell their neighbour in 2g. Elicit as many different advantages and disadvantages as possible from students. In 2h find out how many people think there are more advantages of living in a town and how many think there are more advantages of living in the country.

3 Students look at the sequence of photos and find the items in 3a, while you monitor and help. Students then complete the speaking activity in 3b. Provide feedback by asking students the questions.

Demonstrate the speaking activity in 3c and then students ask and answer the questions. Provide feedback by asking students the questions.

Students then complete the matching task in 3d while you monitor and check.

Students then tell their neighbour the story using 'first', 'then' etc. Check by asking students questions eg "What did Mrs Taylor do first?"

Students complete the speaking activity in 3f. Provide feedback by asking students the questions and checking their answers.

Revise all the structures and vocabulary before moving on to the next lesson.

At home students prepare for the next lesson by looking up the vocabulary in 4a of Unit 7.

Answers

Exercise 3d

1 She walked through the village towards the terraced houses.
2 She walked through some fields.
3 She stopped at a gate and enjoyed the view of the castle.
4 She crossed a bridge over a little stream.
5 She walked down a narrow lane.

1

UNIT 7

What's the weather like?

1 a Here are some pictures of the weather. Match the descriptions and the pictures.

[5] It's windy.	[ ] It's snowing.	[ ] It's cold and foggy.
[ ] It's hot and dry.	[ ] It's cold and dry.	[ ] It's raining.

b Ask your neighbour.

1 What's the weather like now?
2 What was the weather like yesterday?

c Complete the questions below and then answer what you like doing.

eg What do you like doing in hot, dry weather? I like lying on the beach.

1 ______________________________ in cold, dry weather?
____

2 ______________________________ in foggy weather?
____

3 ______________________________ when it's raining?
____

4 ______________________________ when it's snowing?
____

5 ______________________________ in cold, wet weather?
____

d Ask your neighbour.

2

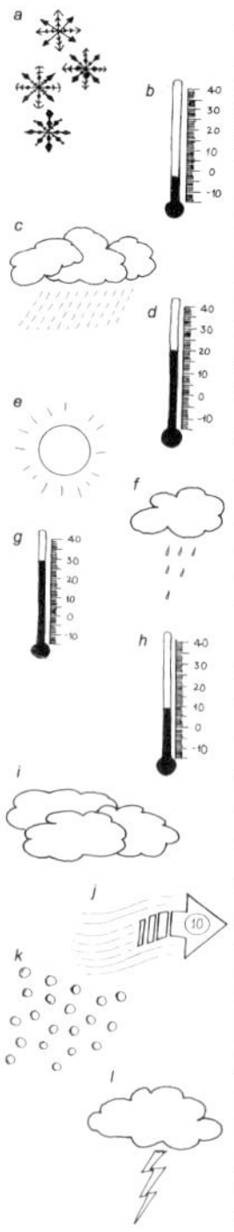

2 a Put the phrases in the correct place. It is now Wednesday morning!

1 tomorrow morning
2 last night
3 yesterday afternoon
4 the day after tomorrow
5 tonight
6 this afternoon
7 tomorrow night
8 yesterday morning
9 the day before yesterday
10 tomorrow afternoon

Monday	Tuesday	Wednesday	Thursday	Friday
		this morning		

b Ask your neighbour.

eg What's the day after tomorrow? The day after tomorrow is Friday.

c Match the sentences and the weather symbols.

_b_ It'll freeze with temperatures reaching -3 degrees.
___ There'll be hail.
___ There'll be snow.
___ There'll be showers.
___ It'll be hot with temperatures reaching 28 degrees.
___ There'll be strong winds.
___ It'll be warm.
___ There'll be heavy rain.
___ There'll be thunder and lightning.
___ It'll be sunny.
___ There'll be a lot of cloud.
___ It'll be cool.

d Write your own forecast using the sentences above.

This morning will start off bright and warm with temperatures reaching about 14°.
This afternoon ______________________________.
and tonight ______________________________.
Tomorrow morning ______________________________.
Tomorrow afternoon ______________________________,
and by tomorrow night ______________________________.

e Listen to your neighbour's forecast and make notes.

this afternoon	tonight	tomorrow morning	tomorrow afternoon	tomorrow evening

f Next to each of these sentences, write D for definite, or P for possible.

eg There'll be snow. D / There may be snow. P

1 There'll be heavy rain. ___
2 There may be heavy rain. ___
3 Temperatures will reach 28°. ___
4 Temperatures may reach 28° ___
5 There may be showers later. ___
6 There'll be thunder and lightning tonight. ___
7 It'll be a wonderful day tomorrow. ___
8 It may rain tomorrow. ___

3

3 a Listen to the cassette and fill in the missing information.

And now for the weather. In Scotland there will be ______________ coming in from the west this morning, but by lunchtime it will be calm and ______________ with temperatures rising to 16 degrees. In the north there will be ______________ and ______________ which will clear by lunchtime, but it will remain ______________. Temperatures may reach ______________ degrees. The Midlands will have a ______________ with ______________ and ______________. In the south, however, there will be ______________ all day with temperatures averaging ______________ degrees. Wales will have ______________ and ______________ in the morning, and may have some ______________ and ______________ later on. In the south west there may be some ______________ but this will have cleared up by lunchtime and in the afternoon there'll be ______________ and temperatures reaching ______________ degrees. In Northern Ireland there'll be ______________ and ______________ in the morning but this will ______________ by lunchtime.

Listen again and check.

b Now complete the weather map for <u>this morning</u>. Use the weather symbols from 2c.

4

4 a Translate the following.

Vocabulary

windy ______	tomorrow afternoon ______
snowing ______	this morning ______
cold ______	freeze ______
foggy ______	temperatures ______
hot ______	degrees ______
dry ______	hail ______
raining ______	snow ______
tomorrow morning ______	showers ______
last night ______	strong winds ______
yesterday afternoon ______	warm ______
the day after tomorrow ______	rain ______
tonight ______	thunder ______
this afternoon ______	lightning ______
tomorrow night ______	sunny ______
yesterday morning ______	cloud ______
the day before yesterday ______	cool ______

Structures

It's windy. ______________________________
It's snowing. ______________________________
What do you like doing in hot weather? ______________________________
I like lying on the beach. ______________________________
What's the day after tomorrow? ______________________________
The day after tomorrow is Friday. ______________________________
It'll freeze. ______________________________
There'll be hail. ______________________________
It'll be hot. ______________________________
There'll be snow. ______________________________
There'll be heavy rain. ______________________________
There may be heavy rain. ______________________________
There may be snow. ______________________________
It may be cold. ______________________________

Teaching Notes

Warm-up

Ask students questions from earlier Units eg "Where do you live? How do you spell it? What is an estate agent? How do you make a cup of coffee?"

Revision

Revise all the structures and vocabulary from the previous Unit by asking students questions eg "Would you prefer to live in the town or in the country? Why? How far is the nearest restaurant from your home?"

Presentation and Practice

1 Students look at the pictures and complete the matching task in 1a while you monitor and check. Ask one student the questions from 1b and then in pairs students ask each other the questions from 1b.

Write the question 'What do you like doing in hot, dry weather? ' on the board and elicit answers from several students. Students then complete the writing task in 1c by writing the questions 1 - 5 while you monitor and check. When they are finished, elicit answers from different students before they write their own answers to the questions.

In pairs students ask their neighbour the questions. Provide feedback by asking students to tell you about themselves.

2 In 2a draw a similar diagram on the board with the day and time of your lesson on it. Ask students to come to the front and put the other phrases in the correct place as you say them.

Students complete the activity in 2a and in pairs ask each other questions as in 2b. Ask students if they watch weather forecasts on TV and ask them what kind of symbols are used to show this. Encourage students to draw the symbols on the board and explain what they mean to the rest of the class. When students are familiar with the symbols they complete the matching task in 2c. Explain that these are phrases used by weather forecasters and make up a weather forecast using the phrases from 2a and 2c eg "This morning it'll be very hot with temperatures reaching 28 degrees. This afternoon there'll be some strong winds and tonight it'll freeze."

Students then make up their own weather forecasts in 2d and in 2e they tell their neighbour their forecast while their neighbour listens and makes notes.

Provide feedback by asking students to tell you their neighbour's forecast.

Introduce 2f by writing the two examples on the board underlining 'there'll' and 'there may be' and explaining that 'there'll' is definite whereas 'there may be' is possible.

Students then complete the activity in 2f while you monitor and check.

3 Tell students that they are going to listen to a recording of a weather forecast and that they are to fill in the missing information. Tell them that they will hear the recording three times; the first time they should listen; the second time they should fill in the missing information and the third time they should check their answers. Play the cassette three times and then let students compare their work with their neighbour.

Using the symbols from 2c students draw the weather forecast for this morning on the map in 3b.

Revise all the structures and vocabulary before moving on to the next lesson.

At home students prepare for the next lesson by looking up the vocabulary in 4a of Unit 8.

Tapescripts

Exercise 3a

And now for the weather. In Scotland there will be <u>strong winds</u> coming in from the west this morning, but by lunchtime it will be calm and <u>warm</u> with temperatures rising to 16 degrees. In the north there will be <u>rain</u> and <u>cloud</u> which will clear by lunchtime but it will remain <u>cool</u>. Temperatures may reach <u>10</u> degrees. The Midlands will have a <u>lovely day</u> with <u>sunshine</u> and <u>clear skies</u>. In the south, however, there will be <u>showers</u> all day with temperatures averaging <u>14</u> degrees. Wales will have <u>strong winds</u> and <u>hail</u> in the morning and may have some <u>thunder and lightning</u> later on. In the south west there may be some <u>hail</u> but this will have cleared up by lunchtime and in the afternoon there'll be <u>sunshine</u> and temperatures reaching <u>20</u> degrees. In Northern Ireland there'll be <u>cloud</u> and <u>rain</u> in the morning but this will <u>clear up</u> by lunchtime.

Answers

Exercise 1a

1 It's cold and foggy.
2 It's hot and dry.
3 It's raining.
4 It's snowing.
5 It's windy.
6 It's cold and dry.

Exercise 2f

1 D	5 P
2 P	6 D
3 D	7 D
4 P	8 P

Exercise 3a

See tapescript 3a

Exercise 2a

Monday	Tuesday	Wednesday	Thursday	Friday
the day before yesterday	yesterday morning	this morning	tomorrow morning	the day after tomorrow
	yesterday afternoon	this afternoon	tomorrow afternoon	
	last night	tonight	tomorrow night	

Exercise 2c

b It'll freeze, with temperatures reaching -3 degrees.
k There'll be hail.
a There'll be snow.
f There'll be showers.
g It'll be hot with temperatures reaching 28 degrees.
j There'll be strong winds.
d It'll be warm.
c There'll be heavy rain.
l There'll be thunder and lightning.
e It'll be sunny.
i There'll be a lot of cloud.
h It'll be cool.

1

UNIT 8

How do you get from the library to the golf club?

1 a **Ask your neighbour.**

eg *What's number 1? It's a hospital.*

1 hospital
2 leisure centre
3 swimming pool
4 hotel
5 tourist information centre
6 railway station
7 bowling green
8 tennis court
9 car park
10 post office
11 golf club
12 library
13 bus station
14 museum
15 cinema

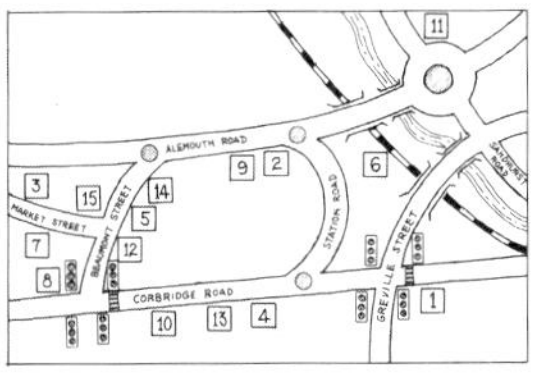

b **Ask your neighbour questions like these.**

eg *Where's the hotel? It's in Corbridge Road next to the bus station.*

c **Ask your neighbour these questions.**

1 How many roundabouts can you see on the street plan?
2 How many bridges can you see on the street plan?
3 How many crossroads can you see on the street plan?
4 How many pedestrian crossings can you see on the street plan?
5 How many traffic lights can you see on the street plan?

d **Where are you? Read the directions and write down where you are.**

1 Go along Market Street and turn right into Beaumont Street. Turn left into Corbridge Road at the traffic lights. It's the first building on your right just after the pedestrian crossing.
Where are you? ______

2 Go along Beaumont Street. Go past the library, the tourist information centre and the museum. Turn right into Alemouth Road at the roundabout and it's on your right next to the car park.
Where are you? ______

3 Go along Station Road and turn right into Corbridge Road at the roundabout. Go past the hotel and it's on your left just before the post office.
Where are you? ______

e **Fill in the following.**

eg *To get from the hospital (1) to the swimming pool (3), you go along Corbridge Road. You go past the hotel, the bus station and the post office. Then you turn right at the traffic lights into Beaumont Street. Take the first left, go straight on for about 100 metres and the swimming pool is on your right just after the cinema.*

1 To get from the swimming pool (3) to the railway station (6), you go along ______ Street. Turn left into ______ Street and then right at the roundabout. You go along ______ Road and at the next roundabout you turn right into ______ Road. Go straight on for 50 metres and the railway station is on your left.

2

2 To get from the railway station (6) to the post office (10), you ______ Station Road. You ______ into Corbridge Road. You ______ the hotel and the bus station, and the post office is ______.

f **Now ask your neighbour for directions.**

eg *How do you get from the library (12) to the golf club (11)?*

2 a **Fill in the following about your home town .....**

	you	your neighbour
1 How many hospitals are there in your town?	....	....
2 How many leisure centres are there in your town?	....	....
3 How many hotels are there in your town?	....	....
4 How many car parks are there in your town?	....	....
5 How many cinemas are there in your town?	....	....
6 How many libraries are there in your town?	....	....
7 How many swimming pools are there in your town?	....	....
8 How many railway stations are there in your town?	....	....
9 How many golf clubs are there in your town?	....	....
10 How many post offices are there in your town?	....	....

b **Ask your neighbour the questions ....**

c **Tell your teacher about your town.**

d **Here is some information about the library, swimming pool and leisure centre. Listen to the cassette and fill in the missing information.**

Library	Swimming Pool	Leisure Centre
Beaumont Street	______	Wentworth Park
Tel: 01434 ______	Tel: 01434 604903	Tel: 01434 ______
Opening Hours	***Opening Hours***	***Opening Hours***
Mon - Fri 9am - 8pm	Weekdays:	Daily ______
Sat 9am - 12 noon	12 noon - ______	
Closed all day ______	Weekends:	
	______ - 8pm	
Admission	***Admission***	***Admission***
______	Adults £1.80	Adults £______
	Juniors £______	Juniors £1.50
		Students £______

Listen again and check.

e **Ask your neighbour.**

1 Where is the library located?
2 What is the telephone number of the swimming pool?
3 How much is admission to the swimming pool for an adult?
4 How much is admission to the leisure centre for a junior?
5 Is the leisure centre open every day?

f **Ask your neighbour 5 more questions.**

3

3 a **Match the pictures and the words.**

[5] crossroads [ ] no entry [ ] give way [ ] roundabout [ ] traffic lights
[ ] stop [ ] dead end [ ] roadworks [ ] junction [ ] one-way street

b **Ask your neighbour.**

1 How many roundabouts are there between your house and your school?
2 How many crossroads are there between your house and your school?
3 How many one-way streets are there between your house and your school?
4 How many sets of traffic lights are there between your house and your school?
5 How many roadworks are there between your house and your school?

c **In Britain people drive on the left. Which side of the road do people drive on in your country?**

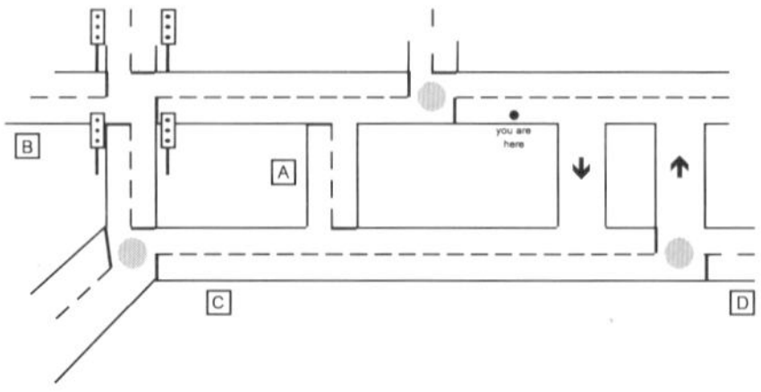

d **This diagram shows the traffic system in Britain. Show your neighbour how you would drive to A, B, C and D. Make sure you are on the correct side of the road.**

e **Ask your neighbour these questions.**

1 Do you think it would be difficult to drive on the left? Why (not)?
2 Do you think it would be easy to drive on the left? Why (not)?

4

4 a **Translate the following.**

Vocabulary

hospital ______	opening hours ______
leisure centre ______	closed ______
swimming pool ______	admission ______
hotel ______	adults ______
tourist information centre ______	juniors ______
railway station ______	daily ______
bowling green ______	weekdays ______
tennis court ______	weekends ______
post office ______	students ______
golf club ______	no entry ______
library ______	give way ______
bus station ______	stop ______
museum ______	one-way street ______
cinema ______	roadworks ______
roundabout ______	junction ______
crossroads ______	dead end ______

Structures

Where's the hotel? ______
It's on Corbridge Road next to the bus station. ______
How do you get to the golf club? ______
You go along Market Street. ______
You go past the post office. ______
You turn right into Beaumont Street. ______
You turn left into Beaumont Street. ______
Turn left at the traffic lights. ______
Turn right at the crossroads. ______
It's just before the post office. ______
It's just after the pedestrian crossing. ______
Take the first left. ______
Take the second left. ______
Take the first right. ______
Take the second right. ______
Go straight on. ______
Go straight on for about 100 metres. ______
The station is on your left. ______
The station is on your right. ______

Teaching Notes

Warm-up

Ask students questions from earlier Units eg "What do you do in the evenings? Have you ever used a kettle? What do you use to make clothes?"

Revision

Revise all the structures and vocabulary from the previous Unit by asking students questions eg "What's the weather like? What was the weather like yesterday? What's the forecast for tomorrow?"

Presentation and Practice

1 Students look at the town plan and ask each other questions from 1a and 1b eg "What is number 1? It's a hospital" to familiarise themselves with the plan.

Students complete the speaking activity in 1c. Provide feedback by asking students the questions.

Introduce phrases for giving directions by explaining how to get to different places and pointing at the map. Students then complete the activity in 1d and compare their work with their neighbour.

Write the example from 1e on the board underlining the phrases used for giving directions and demonstrating the directions on the plan. Students fill in the missing information in 1 and 2 while you monitor and check before asking each other for directions in 1f.

2 Students read the questions in 2a and fill in the information about their home town in the column marked 'you'. They ask their neighbour the questions and note down the information in the column marked 'your neighbour'. Provide feedback by asking students to tell you about their home town.

Introduce the listening activity by telling students that they are going to hear a recording which will give them information about the library, swimming pool and leisure centre. They will hear it twice; once to fill in the missing information and once to check. Students listen to the cassette twice and then compare their work with their neighbour.

In pairs they complete the speaking activity in 2e and then ask their neighbour 5 more questions about the information which they make up themselves.

3 Students complete the matching task in 3a while you monitor and check and then complete the speaking activity in 3b. Provide feedback by asking students to tell you about their neighbour.

The diagram in 3d shows the traffic system in Britain. Draw the diagram on the board and mark how you would get from the starting point to A. Make sure you stay on the left side of the road and go around roundabouts the correct way.

Students then complete the activities in 3d. Provide feedback by bringing students to the front and asking them to draw on the diagram how they would get from one place to another while driving on the left. Ask if anyone has driven on the left and ask them where and if they found it difficult.

Students then complete the speaking activity in 3e.

Revise all the structures and vocabulary before moving on to the next lesson.

At home students prepare for the next lesson by looking up the vocabulary in 4a of Unit 9.

Tapescripts

Exercise 2d

The library is located in Beaumont Street, and the number is 01434 607272. It is open Monday - Friday 9am to 8pm and Saturday 9am to 12 noon. It is closed all day Thursday. Admission is free.

The swimming pool is located in Market Street and is open from 12 noon - 9pm on weekdays. At the weekend it is open from 9am - 8pm. Admission for adults is £1.80 and for juniors, that means children under age 14, it is £1.00. If you need any further information, ring 01434 604903.

The leisure centre is located in Wentworth Park. The telephone number is 01434 607080. It is open daily from 9am - 10pm. Admission is £3.00 for adults, £1.50 for juniors and £2.00 for students.

Answers

Exercise 1d

1 You are at the post office.
2 You are at the leisure centre.
3 You are at the bus station.

Exercise 3a

1	roundabout	6	no entry
2	give way	7	one-way street
3	traffic lights	8	roadworks
4	stop	9	junction
5	crossroads	10	dead end

Exercise 2d

Library
Beaumont Street
Tel: 01434 607272
Opening Hours
Mon - Fri 9am - 8pm
Sat 9am - 12 noon
Closed all day Thursday
Admission
Free

Swimming Pool
Market Street
Tel: 01434 604903
Opening Hours
Weekdays:
12 noon - 9pm
Weekends:
9am - 8pm
Admission
Adults £1.80
Juniors £ 1.00

Leisure Centre
Wentworth Park
Tel: 01434 607080
Opening Hours
Daily 9am - 10pm
Admission
Adults £ 3.00
Juniors £1.50
Students £ 2.00

Exercise 1e

1 To get from the swimming pool (3) to the railway station (6), you go along Market Street. Turn left into Beaumont Street and then turn right at the roundabout. You go along Alemouth Road and at the next roundabout you turn right into Station Road. Go straight on for 50 metres and the railway station is on your left.

2 To get from the railway station (6) to the post office (10), you go along Station Road. You turn right into Corbridge Road. You go past the hotel and the bus station, and the post office is on your left.

1

UNIT 9

Have you ever been sailing?

1 a **Match the pictures and the activity.**

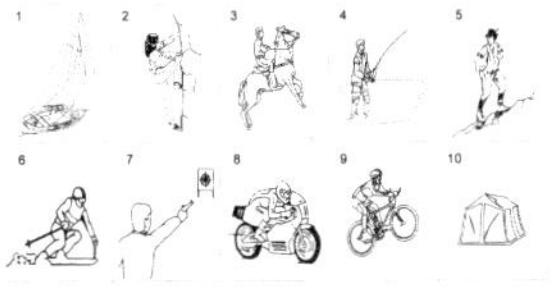

1 sailing
__ pony trekking
__ camping
__ skiing
__ walking
__ shooting
__ mountain biking
__ motorcycling
__ fishing
__ climbing

Check with your neighbour.

b **Ask your neighbour these questions.**

eg *Which activity do you need a rope for? You need a rope for climbing.*

1 Which activity/activities do you need boots for?
2 Which activity/activities do you need a gun for?
3 Which activity/activities do you need a rod and bait for?
4 Which activity/activities do you need a lifejacket for?
5 Which activity/activities do you need a helmet for?

Check with your teacher.

c **Answer these questions about yourself in note form.**

eg *Have you ever been sailing? Yes. When? Last summer. Where? Mediterranean.*

1 Have you ever been sailing? ________ When? ________ Where? ________
2 Have you ever been climbing? ________ When? ________ Where? ________
3 Have you ever been pony trekking? ________ When? ________ Where? ________
4 Have you ever been skiing? ________ When? ________ Where? ________
5 Have you ever been shooting? ________ When? ________ Where? ________
6 Have you ever been fishing? ________ When? ________ Where? ________
7 Have you ever been mountain biking? ________ When? ________ Where? ________
8 Have you ever been walking? ________ When? ________ Where? ________
9 Have you ever been motorcycling? ________ When? ________ Where? ________
10 Have you ever been camping? ________ When? ________ Where? ________

d **Ask your neighbour questions like these.**

eg *Have you ever been sailing? Yes I have. When was the last time you went sailing? It was last summer. Where did you go sailing? In the Mediterranean.*

e **Tell your teacher about yourself.**

eg *I've never been sailing. I've been climbing 4 times. Once in 1989 in the Dolomites, once in 1990 in the Alps and twice in Scotland. I can't remember when. I've been pony trekking once in Scotland. Never again!*

2

Glenhead Arms Hotel

Bed & Breakfast

Single Room £52
Twin/Double Room £92
Rates per room, per night.

Glenisla
Blairgowrie
Scotland
Tel 01575 582273
Fax 01575 582274

Summer Breaks

(2 nights or more)
Dinner, bed and breakfast
April - October £45
Rates per person, per day.
All rates inclusive of VAT at 17.5%.

Fishing Breaks

7-day stay £700 (Sat - Sat)
Includes dinner, B&B (bed and breakfast), picnic lunch, single room with private facilities and 6 days fishing.

Horse Riding Breaks

7-day stay £600 (Sat - Sat)
Includes dinner, B&B, picnic lunch, sharing twin/double room with private facilities and 6 days horse riding.
Please bring own hat.

Golf Breaks

7-day stay £800 (Sat - Sat)
Includes dinner, B&B, lunch in clubhouse every day, sharing twin/double room with private facilities.
Green fees extra.

All prices inclusive of VAT (Value Added Tax) at 17.5%.

2 a **Here is an advertising leaflet from the Glenhead Arms Hotel in Scotland. Look at the information and answer these questions.**

1 What is VAT? ________
2 How much is VAT? ________
3 How much is a single room for one night? ________
4 How much is a double room for one night? ________
5 What is B&B? ________

Check with your neighbour.

b **Answer the following.**

1 If I want a fishing break, is the picnic lunch included in the price? ________
2 If I want a golf break, is everything included in the price? ________
3 If I want to book a room, what number should I call? ________
4 If I want a summer break, is it £45 per person, or per room? ________
5 If I have a riding break, do I have to bring anything extra with me? ________

Check with your neighbour.

c **Ask your neighbour.**

1 Can I have a summer break in November?
2 Can I arrive for a golf break on a Tuesday?
3 How much does it cost for 3 nights in a single room in January?
4 How much does it cost for 3 nights in a single room in May?
5 How much does it cost for 2 nights in a double room in December?

3

3 a **You have decided to take a short holiday. Choose one of the breaks available and fill in the booking form below.**

Booking Form

Name ....
Address ....
....
Telephone ....
Fax ....

Please reserve the following accommodation:
single room ☐
twin room ☐
double room ☐

Date of Arrival ....
Date of Departure ....

fishing break ☐ golf break ☐
horse riding break ☐ summer break ☐

I/we enclose £ .... as full payment.

cheque ☐ amex ☐ visa ☐ mastercard ☐

Please enter card number:

☐☐☐☐ ☐☐☐☐
☐☐☐☐ ☐☐☐☐

Expiry Date ....
I understand and accept the conditions of booking.
Signed ....
Dated ....

b **You are the receptionist at the Glenhead Arms Hotel. Your neighbour is going to telephone you and make a reservation. Fill in the booking form below during the telephone call.**

Booking Form

Name ....
Address ....
....
Telephone ....
Fax ....

Please reserve the following accommodation:
single room ☐
twin room ☐
double room ☐

Date of Arrival ....
Date of Departure ....

fishing break ☐ golf break ☐
horse riding break ☐ summer break ☐

I/we enclose £ .... as full payment.

cheque ☐ amex ☐ visa ☐ mastercard ☐

Please enter card number:

☐☐☐☐ ☐☐☐☐
☐☐☐☐ ☐☐☐☐

Expiry Date ....
Booking made by ....
Signed ....
Dated ....

4

4 a Translate the following.

Vocabulary

sailing ________	double ________
climbing ________	break ________
pony trekking ________	VAT (Value Added Tax) ________
camping ________	picnic lunch ________
skiing ________	private facilities ________
walking ________	golf ________
shooting ________	clubhouse ________
mountain biking ________	green fees ________
motorcycling ________	date of arrival ________
fishing ________	date of departure ________
rope ________	enclose ________
gun ________	full payment ________
rod ________	cheque ________
bait ________	amex ________
lifejacket ________	visa ________
helmet ________	mastercard ________
Mediterranean ________	expiry date ________
B&B (Bed & Breakfast) ________	signed ________
single ________	dated ________
twin ________	reservation ________

Structures

Which activity do you need a rope for? ________
You need a rope for climbing. ________
Have you ever been sailing? ________
Yes I have. ________
When was the last time you went sailing? ________
It was last summer. ________
Where did you go sailing? ________
In the Mediterranean. ________
I've never been sailing. ________
I've been climbing 4 times. ________
Once in 1989 in the Dolomites. ________
Once in 1989, once in 1990 and twice in Scotland. ________
I can't remember when. ________
I've been pony trekking once in Scotland. ________
Never again! ________

Teaching Notes

Warm-up

Ask students questions from earlier Units eg "What do you do after work? Do you live in a block of flats?"

Revision

Revise all the structures and vocabulary from the previous Unit by asking students questions eg "How many roundabouts are there between your house and school? Why do you go to a leisure centre? How do you get from here to the station?"

Presentation and Practice

1 Students complete the matching task in 1a and then compare their work with their neighbour.

In pairs students ask and answer the questions in 1b. When they are finished ask one pair to demonstrate their activity to the rest of the class.

One student asks you the questions in the example. Answer the questions demonstrating the note form students are to use during this activity before they answer the questions about themselves.

In pairs students then use this information to complete the speaking activity in 1d. Provide feedback by asking students to tell you about themselves as in 1e.

2 Look at the information and ask students questions about it eg "What's the name of the hotel? What's the fax number? What's the address?"

Students answer the questions in 2a and then compare their work with their neighbour. Students read through the information in 2b and then answer the questions. When they have compared their work with their neighbour they complete the speaking activity in 2c.

3 Introduce the activity in 3a by telling students that they are going to have a short holiday at the Glenhead Arms Hotel and they should choose which break they would like to take. When they have chosen their break they fill in the booking form while you monitor and check.

Introduce the next activity by asking one student questions to elicit the information on his/her booking form eg "What's your name? Which break would you like to take?" etc. Bring one student to the front and demonstrate the telephoning roleplay. Explain that you are the hotel receptionist and the student is telephoning to book a short holiday. Sit back to back and start the roleplay by answering the phone with "Glenhead Arms Hotel. This is ... speaking. How can I help you?" Students then carry out the roleplay in pairs. When they have finished, they compare their booking forms to check.

Revise all the structures and vocabulary before moving on to the next lesson.

At home students revise all the vocabulary and structures from Unit 1 to Unit 9.

Answers

Exercise 1a

1 sailing
2 climbing
3 motorcycling
4 fishing
5 walking
6 skiing
7 shooting
8 pony trekking
9 mountain biking
10 camping

Exercise 2a

1 Value Added Tax
2 17.5%
3 £52
4 £92
5 Bed and Breakfast

Exercise 2b

1 Yes it is.
2 No it isn't.
3 01575 582273
4 Per person.
5 Yes you do.

UNIT 10

Revision

1 a Ask your neighbour the following questions.

1 What's your name?
2 How do you spell it?
3 Where do you live?
4 What kind of house do you live in?
5 How many rooms does your house/flat have?
6 Which room do you eat in?
7 Which room do you work in?
8 Do you have a coat stand in your house/flat? Where?
9 Do you have a set of scales in your house/flat? Where? Why?
10 Can you name 3 objects in every room of your house/flat?

2 a Look at the information below and tell your neighbour about Roger and Edward.

eg Roger has a regular lifestyle. Edward doesn't have a regular lifestyle.

	Roger	Edward
have a regular lifestyle	✓	x
start work at the same time every day	✓	x
have a company car	x	✓
travel a lot in his job	x	✓
go home every night	✓	x
go to bed at different times every night	x	✓

b Complete the sentences below about yourself using: always, normally, often, sometimes, rarely, never.

1 I ________________ have breakfast at the same time.
2 I ________________ start work at the same time.
3 I ________________ work in the same place.
4 I ________________ have lunch at the same time.
5 I ________________ go to bed at the same time.

c Ask your neighbour the following questions.

1 How many days a week do you work?
2 Do you sometimes work at weekends?
3 How long does it take to get to work?
4 How long do you have for lunch?
5 What time do you have breakfast?
6 What time do you have lunch?
7 What do you do in the evenings?
8 Do you have a company car?
9 Do you travel a lot in your job?
10 What time do you go to bed?

3 a Describe the people in the picture to your neighbour. They have to guess who you are describing. You may describe their clothes, their appearance, and what they are doing.

b Look at the other people in your class and ask your neighbour these questions.

1 Can you see anyone who is wearing a skirt? Who is it?
2 Can you see anyone who is wearing a tie? Who is it?
3 Can you see anyone who is wearing a brooch? Who is it?
4 Can you see anyone who is wearing a suit? Who is it?
5 Can you see anyone who is wearing a scarf? Who is it?

4 a Ask your neighbour these questions about their ideal home.

1 How many rooms would it have?
2 Which rooms would it have?
3 What views would it have?
4 Would it have central heating?
5 Would it have air conditioning?
6 What would it be made of?
7 What colour would it be?
8 How far would the nearest shop be?
9 What kind of house would it be?
10 Would you live there alone?

5 a How many objects can you name in your house which have: a) keys b) dials c) buttons d) switches?

b What is it? See if you can guess and then compare with your neighbour.

1 You use it for making clothes.
2 You use it for cleaning your room.
3 You use it for listening to music.
4 You use it for making cakes.
5 You use it for making toast.

c How do you make a slice of toast? What do you do first? What do you do after that? Tell your neighbour.

6 a Look at the words and then put a 'C' next to it if you would find it in the country, and a 'T' next to it if you would find it in the town. You may put a 'C' and a 'T' if you would find them in both.

1 queues ___
2 traffic lights ___
3 sheep ___
4 hedges ___
5 fences ___
6 shops ___
7 bus stops ___
8 litter bins ___
9 pedestrian crossings ___
10 forests ___

b Now try and explain the words to your neighbour.

eg You often find queues outside shops when people are waiting to buy something.

c Ask your neighbour these questions.

1 Do you live in a town, a city, or a village?
2 How far is the nearest bus stop from your house/flat?
3 How long have you lived there?
4 What can you see from your bedroom window?
5 Would you like to move house/flat? Why (not)?

d Discuss with your neighbour the advantages and disadvantages of living in the country, or living in the town.

7 a Today is Wednesday 10 January. Answer these question and then check with your neighbour.

1 What was the day before yesterday? ________________
2 What is the day after tomorrow? ________________
3 When was Tuesday 9 January? ________________
4 When is Friday 12 January? ________________
5 What is tomorrow? ________________

8

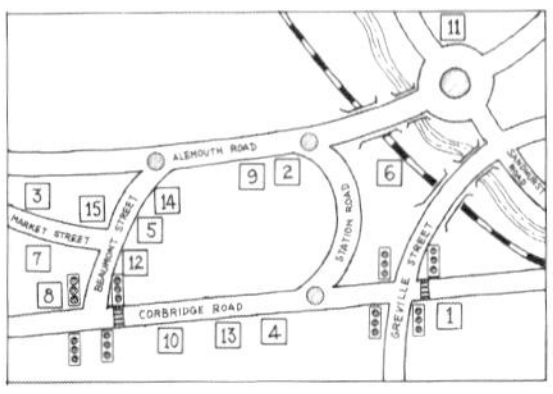

8 a Ask your neighbour these questions using the street plan.

1 How do you get from the hospital (1), to the railway station (6)?
2 How do you get from the swimming pool (3), to the post office (10)?
3 How do you get from the railway station (6), to the library (12)?
4 How do you get from the golf club (11), to the swimming pool (3)?
5 How do you get from the library (12), to the hospital (1)?

b Now ask your neighbour about their own home town.

1 How many hospitals are there in your town?
2 How many leisure centres are there in your town?
3 How many libraries are there in your town?
4 How many car parks are there in your town?
5 How many post offices are there in your town?

c Ask your neighbour these questions.

1 Why would you go to a library?
2 Why would you go to a railway station?
3 Why would you go to a swimming pool?
4 Why would you go to a hotel?
5 Why would you go to a tourist information centre?

9 a Which activity is it? Look at the equipment and then write next to it which activity/activities it is. When you have finished, check with your neighbour.

eg a rod and bait - fishing.

1 a rope ________________
2 a lifejacket ________________
3 a helmet ________________
4 a pair of boots ________________
5 a tent ________________

b Ask your neighbours these questions.

1 Have you ever been sailing? When? Where?
2 Have you ever been climbing? When? Where?
3 Have you ever been fishing? When? Where?
4 Have you ever been mountain biking? When? Where?
5 Have you ever been camping? When? Where?

10 a You are now going to tell your neighbour about yourself. Try and keep talking for at least 3 minutes. Here are some things you can talk about.

- your name, age, address
- your daily routine
- your house/flat
- the town where you live
- your ideal home
- disadvantages and advantages of living where you do.

Teaching Notes

Warm-up

Ask students questions from earlier Units eg "Have you ever been sailing? What kind of house do you live in? What do you like doing in hot weather?"

1 In pairs students complete the speaking activity in 1a while you monitor and check.

2 Students read through the information about Roger and Edward and then complete the speaking activity in 2a. Provide feedback by asking students to tell you about Roger and Edward. In 2b students complete the questions about themselves. When they have finished ask two or three students to tell you about themselves. In pairs students then complete the speaking activity in 2c while you monitor and check. Provide feedback by asking one pair to demonstrate their activity.

3 In 3a one student describes the people in the picture to his/her neighbour who then has to guess who it is.

In 3b students ask each other about other members of the class while you monitor and check.

4 In pairs students ask and answer questions about their ideal home while you monitor and check.

5 In pairs students complete the activity in 5a and then compare their answers to see who has the most objects with keys etc. Students read the descriptions 1 - 5 and guess what the object is. They compare their answers with their neighbours. In 5c one student tells his/her neighbour how to make a slice of toast, while the neighbour makes sure that nothing is left out or forgotten. Provide feedback by asking one student to describe the process to the rest of the class.

6 Students complete the activity in 6a and then compare their work with their neighbour. In pairs they then try to explain the words while you help and correct. Provide feedback by asking students to explain the words while the rest of the class guess what it is. Students complete the speaking activities in 6c and then 6d while you monitor and check.

7 Students complete the task in 7a and compare their work with their neighbour. Provide feedback by one pair asking and answering the questions for the rest of the class.

8 In pairs students revise directions in 8a based on the plan. They then complete the speaking activity in 8b about their own home towns while you monitor and check. Students then complete the speaking activity in 8c.

9 Students complete the task in 9a and compare their work with their neighbour. In pairs they complete the speaking activity in 9b. Provide feedback by asking students to tell you about their neighbour.

10 Students are given 3 minutes each to practise talking about themselves. They may make a few notes if they wish, but they should follow the points given and talk about themselves for at least 3 minutes.

At home students prepare for the next lesson by looking up the vocabulary in 4a of Unit 11.

Answers

Exercise 6a

1 T
2 T
3 C
4 C/T
5 T
6 T
7 T
8 T
9 T
10 C

Exercise 7a

1 Monday 8 January.
2 Friday 12 January.
3 Yesterday.
4 The day after tomorrow.
5 Thursday 11 January.

Exercise 9a

1 climbing, sailing
2 sailing
3 climbing, pony trekking, mountain biking, motorcycling
4 climbing, pony trekking, fishing, mountain biking, walking, skiing, motorcycling
5 camping

1

UNIT 11

Have you ever travelled on the London Underground?

1 a Match the words and the pictures.

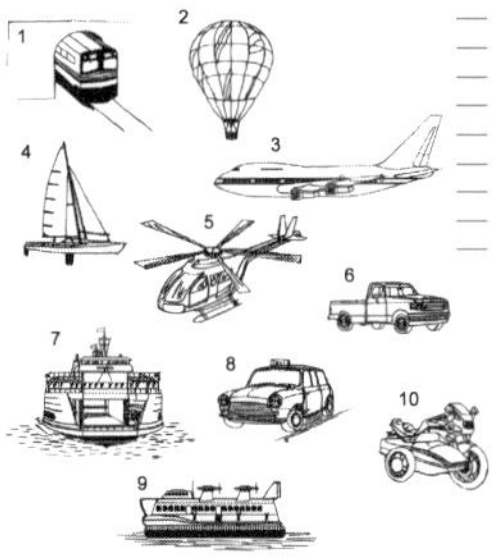

3	jumbo jet
___	taxi
___	pick-up truck
___	sailing boat
___	underground
___	helicopter
___	hovercraft
___	hot-air balloon
___	ferry
___	motorbike and sidecar

b Now point at the pictures and ask your neighbour.

eg *What's this? It's a jumbo jet.*

c Ask your neighbour questions like these.

eg *Have you ever travelled by jumbo jet?*
Yes, when I went to America. I went by jumbo jet because it's the fastest way to get there.

d Now ask your neighbour these questions.

eg *How would you go to America? I would go by jumbo jet because it's the fastest.*

1 How would you go to work or college every day? Why?
2 How would you visit friends in another town? Why?
3 How would you go on holiday to Britain? Why?
4 How would you go shopping? Why?
5 How would you go to your English lesson? Why?

e Tell your teacher about your neighbour.

f Ask your neighbour about different means of transport.

eg *Do you like travelling by bus? No I don't like travelling by bus because it's always full. I have to walk to the bus stop and wait for a bus to come. I prefer travelling by car.*

1 Do you like travelling by train? Why (not)?
2 Do you like travelling by motorbike? Why (not)?
3 Do you like travelling by plane? Why (not)?
4 Do you like travelling by bicycle? Why (not)?
5 Do you like travelling by ship? Why (not)?

2

2

Key to Lines

Bakerloo
Central
Circle
District
Hammersmith & City
Jubilee
Metropolitan
Northern
Piccadilly
Victoria

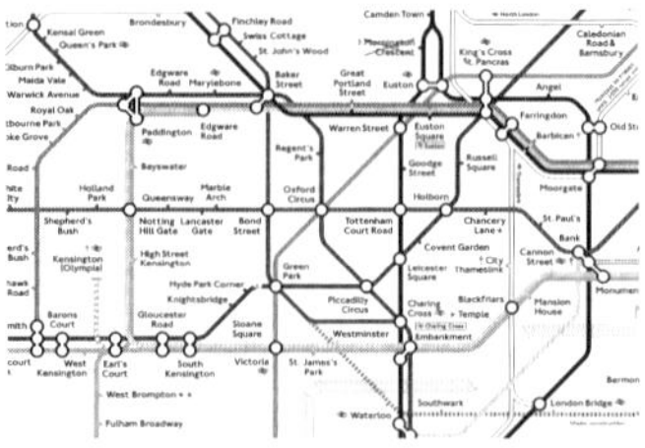

a Ask your neighbour the following questions.

eg *Which line is Bond Street on? It's on the Jubilee line and the Central line.*

1 Which line is Goodge Street on?
2 Which line is Marble Arch on?
3 Which line is Regent's Park on?
4 Which line is St Paul's on?
5 Which line is Knightsbridge on?

b Look at the example.

eg *How do you get from Victoria to Covent Garden?*
The best way is to take the Victoria line to Green Park. You can change there to the Piccadilly line and the third stop is Covent Garden.

Now you try. How do you get from Paddington to Marble Arch? ______________________________

____

Check with your neighbour.

c Ask your neighbour 3 more questions.

eg *How do you get from Baker Street to the Embankment?*
The best way is to take the Bakerloo line. It's only 5 stops and you don't have to change.

d You are going to hear some information about opening and closing times for the stations below. Listen to the cassette and make notes.

	Monday - Friday	Saturday	Sunday
Aldwych Station Barbican Station City Thameslink Station Mornington Crescent			
Further Information			

3

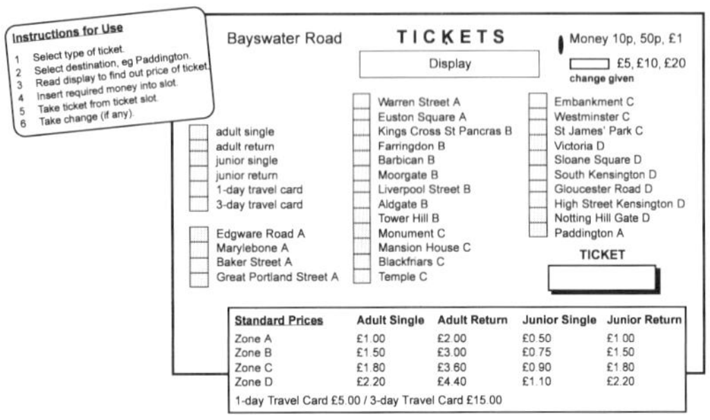

Standard Prices	Adult Single	Adult Return	Junior Single	Junior Return
Zone A	£1.00	£2.00	£0.50	£1.00
Zone B	£1.50	£3.00	£0.75	£1.50
Zone C	£1.80	£3.60	£0.90	£1.80
Zone D	£2.20	£4.40	£1.10	£2.20
1-day Travel Card £5.00 / 3-day Travel Card £15.00				

3 a Fill in the following.

eg *How much is an adult single to Baker Street? £1.*

1 How much is an adult return to Paddington? ____________.
2 How much is a junior single to Gloucester Road? ____________.
3 How much is a junior return to the Embankment? ____________.
4 How much is an adult single to Tower Hill? ____________.
5 How much is a 3-day travel card? ____________.

b Ask your neighbour 5 more questions.

eg *How much is an adult single to Blackfriars? £1.80.*

c Now answer these questions.

eg *Which button do I press first? You press the type of ticket you want first.*

1 Which button do I press next? ______________________________.
2 How do I know how much the ticket costs? ______________________________.
3 Does the machine accept 5p pieces? ______________________________.
4 Does the machine give change? ______________________________.
5 Where do I get my ticket from? ______________________________.

d Ask your neighbour.

1 How do I buy a return ticket to Notting Hill Gate?
2 How does my 8 year old daughter buy a single ticket to Marylebone?
3 If I want to buy a ticket for several journeys on one day, what kind of ticket should I buy?
4 Have you ever travelled on the London Underground? When? Why?
5 Where else would you find a machine like this?

4

4 a Translate the following.

Vocabulary

jumbo jet ____________	rebuilding ____________
taxi ____________	pay your fare ____________
pick-up truck ____________	fine ____________
sailing boat ____________	adult single ____________
underground ____________	adult return ____________
helicopter ____________	junior single ____________
hovercraft ____________	junior return ____________
hot-air balloon ____________	1-day travel card ____________
ferry ____________	3-day travel card ____________
motorbike and sidecar ____________	select ____________
to prefer ____________	destination ____________
peak hours ____________	display ____________
open ____________	insert ____________
repair work ____________	slot ____________

Structures

Have you ever travelled on the London Underground? ____________
Have you ever travelled by jumbo jet? ____________
I went to America by jumbo jet. ____________
It was the fastest way to get there. ____________
How would you go to America? ____________
I would go by jumbo jet because it's the fastest. ____________
Do you like travelling by bus? ____________
I don't like travelling by bus. ____________
It's always full. ____________
I have to walk to the bus stop. ____________
I have to wait for a bus to come. ____________
I prefer travelling by car. ____________
Which line is Bond Street on? ____________
It's on the Jubilee and Central line. ____________
How do you get from Victoria to Covent Garden? ____________
The best way is to take the Victoria line to Green Park. ____________
You can change there to the Piccadilly line. ____________
The third stop is Covent Garden. ____________
It's only 5 stops and you don't have to change. ____________
How much is an adult single to Baker Street? ____________
Which button do I press first? ____________
You press the type of ticket you want first. ____________

Teaching Notes

Warm-up

Ask students questions from earlier Units eg "What do you do after work? What's your neighbour wearing?"

Presentation and Practice

1 Introduce the subject of travel and transport by asking students to think of as many means of transport as possible. Write them on the board.

Students then complete the matching task in 1a while you monitor and check. In pairs they practise the new words by pointing at the pictures and asking each other questions eg "What's this?"

Introduce the speaking activity in 1c by finding out who has travelled by jumbo jet. Students then complete the speaking activity in 1c. Provide feedback by asking students to tell you about their neighbours.

Introduce 1d by asking one student how they would go to America. Ask why they would use this means of transport eg "Because it's the fastest, it's the most convenient".

In pairs students complete the speaking activity in 1d. Provide feedback by asking students to tell you about their neighbour.

Students then complete the speaking activity in 1f. Ask various students for their opinions to check.

2 Introduce 2a by asking if anyone has travelled on the London Underground and whether they found it easy to use. Point at the section of the underground map in the book and explain that there are 10 different lines which are named as shown. Give one or two examples eg "Bond Street is on the Jubilee Line and the Central Line."

In pairs students complete the speaking activity in 2a.

Introduce the activity in 2b using the given example before students complete the writing task in 2b. Students compare their work with their neighbour while you monitor and check.

In pairs students then complete the speaking activity in 2c.

Introduce the listening task in 2d by telling students that they are going to hear an announcement giving them information about some stations. They will hear the cassette twice and are to make notes about the stations listed. Students compare their work with their neighbour and may hear the cassette a third time if they wish.

3 Find out which students use public transport to come to the lesson and ask them where they buy their tickets. Find one student who buys the ticket from a machine to explain how to use the ticket machine. Provide any missing vocabulary (eg slot). Students look at the drawing of an underground ticket machine and before they complete the writing task in 3a ask them about the information given, eg "What different types of ticket are there? Where is the display? How many different zones are there?"

Students then complete the speaking activity in 3b while you monitor and check. Provide feedback by students asking their questions to the rest of the class.

Students then complete the writing task in 3c and compare their work with their neighbour.

In pairs students ask and answer the questions in 3d. Check by asking students the questions.

Revise all the structures and vocabulary before moving on to the next lesson.

At home students prepare for the next lesson by looking up the vocabulary in 4a of Unit 12.

Tapescripts

Exercise 2d

Please note that Aldwych Station is open Monday to Friday during peak hours, but is closed on Saturdays and Sundays.

Barbican Station is open all day Monday to Friday, on Saturday from 7.15am to 11.45pm and on Sunday from 8am until 11.45pm. This station will be closed on Sundays during the month of July for essential repair work.

The City Thameslink Station is open from 6am until 8.45pm, Monday to Friday. On Saturdays and Sundays it is closed all day.

Mornington Crescent is closed for rebuilding. If you would like any further information, call Travel Information on 0171 222 1234, and when travelling in London, don't forget to pay your fare and avoid a £10 fine.

Answers

Exercise 1a

1 underground
2 hot-air balloon
3 jumbo jet
4 sailing boat
5 helicopter
6 pick-up truck
7 ferry
8 taxi
9 hovercraft
10 motorbike and sidecar

Exercise 2b

The best way is to take the Circle or District line to Notting Hill Gate. You can change there to the Central line and the third stop is Marble Arch.

Exercise 2d

OPENING TIMES			
	Mon - Fri	**Sat**	**Sun**
Aldwych Station	peak hours	closed	closed
Barbican Station	all day	7.15am - 11.45pm	8am - 11.45pm (closed in July)
City Thameslink Station	6am - 8.45pm	closed	closed
Mornington Crescent	closed for rebuilding		
Further Information: 0171 222 1234			

Exercise 3a

1 £2
2 £1.10
3 £1.80
4 £1.50
5 £15

Exercise 3c

1 You press the destination you want to go to next.
2 You read the display.
3 No.
4 Yes.
5 From the ticket slot.

1

UNIT 12

What's the best holiday you've ever had?

1 a Put the words in the column you think is correct before reading the stories.

Los Angeles   Yosemite Park   Scone Palace   greyhound bus   Boston   California   golf   wet
air-conditioning   drive-ins   foggy   whisky distillery   motels   New York   Grand Canyon   salmon
Death Valley   convertible car   Glencoe   waterproof trousers   hamburgers   mosquito repellant

UNITED STATES OF AMERICA	SCOTLAND

b Read the paragraphs below and mark in the box if they are Story A (Clive's holiday to the USA) or Story B (Nick's holiday to Scotland).

1 He returned the hired car to Las Vegas and took a plane back to New York where he caught his connecting flight back to London. A friend picked him up in London and gave him a lift back to Manchester and that was the end of the holiday. story [A]

2 Last summer Clive went on holiday to the USA for 3 weeks. He started off from Manchester where a friend gave him a lift to the motorway junction. From there he hitched down to London and took the tube and then a taxi to Gatwick Airport. story [ ]

3 There were roadworks on the M1 motorway so it took longer than usual but at about 11.30pm he arrived at the hotel in Glencoe. story [B]

4 In the last few days he went fishing in the River Tay, one of the best salmon fishing rivers in Scotland. On the last day he visited Scone Palace, then he got back in the car and drove south, and that was the end of his holiday. story [ ]

5 He visited Dalwhinnie Distillery where they produce malt whisky. He saw how they made the whisky and at the end of the tour he was invited to taste the whisky. It tasted very good. The weather was still foggy and wet when he came out. story [ ]

6 It was his first time to the USA and he decided the best way to see it would be to travel to California by train, which he did. The train took 72 hours to get there. Unfortunately the journey wasn't as interesting as he had hoped, but he definitely saw a lot of the USA. story [ ]

7 He travelled across the Atlantic in a jumbo jet and after 8 hours he arrived in New York. He had friends, Peggy and Phil, in Boston so he took a greyhound bus up there. He rang Phil from Boston bus station which was very busy and dirty. Phil came and collected him on his motorbike. story [ ]

8 The weather in Boston was lovely and warm and he spent the next few days walking around Boston. After he had seen all the sights, he decided to head west. story [ ]

9 Last summer Nick went on holiday to Scotland for 3 weeks. He lives in Brighton but loves the mountains and countryside. He packed his rucksack with waterproof trousers and jackets and took some mosquito repellent and one Friday morning he got in his car and drove north. story [ ]

10 The weather cleared up the next day so he played a round of golf in the morning at Dalmunzie, the highest 9-hole course in Britain. The wind was very strong so he did not play very well, but he thoroughly enjoyed the game. story [ ]

11 He went to the Grand Canyon and took a helicopter ride over it. He also visited Yosemite Park and Death Valley, and soon the 3 weeks were gone. story [ ]

12 The first few days he climbed mountains near the hotel. He was lucky with the weather and it didn't rain at all. He met a lot of people and in the evenings he ate and drank in the hotel before going to bed. story [ ]

13 Then the weather turned bad; it was foggy and wet so he decided to leave Glencoe and visit some other places. story [ ]

14 He arrived in Los Angeles at 3pm and hired a convertible car. However, the next day he changed it for a car with air conditioning as the weather was too hot. He travelled around and saw a lot. He ate hamburgers which he bought from drive-ins and stayed in motels. story [ ]

c Put the paragraphs in the correct order.

Story A (Clive / USA) ______________________

Story B (Nick / Scotland) ______________________

Check with your teacher.

2

2 a Answer the following questions about the best holiday you have ever had in note form using one or two words. Do not write full sentences.

eg Where did you go? Ireland.

1 Where did you go? ______
2 How long were you there? ______
3 Did you stay in one place or travel around? ______
4 What was the accommodation like? ______
5 Who did you go with? ______
6 What did you see? ______
7 How did you get there? ______
8 What was the weather like? ______
9 Why was it the best holiday ever? ______
10 Would you go back again? ______

b Ask your neighbour about their best holiday.

eg Where did you go? I went to Ireland.

c Now tell your class about yourself.

eg The best holiday I've ever had was in 1993 when I went to Ireland.

d Ask your neighbour.

1 What is this an advertisement for?
2 What is the address of the company?
3 What number do I dial to fax a reservation?
4 How much is it for 2 people on a motoring holiday?
5 What is another name for Finland, Sweden and Denmark?

Check with your neighbour.

Finland, Sweden and Denmark

Finest lake and seaside Chalets
Hotel Touring City Breaks
Our specialist programme of motoring holidays
£210 per person.

Scandinavia awaits your visit!

Skandika Holidays, 8 Rhos Way, Wrexham
Tel 01978 843241 / Fax 01978 9120719

LONDON

Best rates in London!

single from £20
double from £15 per person
families 3/4/5 from £13 p.p.

Windsor Cottage Hotel
12 Persevny Road
London W1 2LT
Tel 0171 374 9087
Fax 0171 385 2147

5 minutes from Piccadilly tube station.

Call, fax or write now!
Welcome to London

e Ask your neighbour.

1 What is this an advertisement for?
2 What is the name of the hotel?
3 What is the address of the hotel?
4 How much is a double room for 2 people?
5 How much is a room for a family of 3?
6 What is the post code of the hotel?
7 What is the fax number?
8 Which is the nearest underground station?
9 How can I reserve a room?
10 Is this hotel cheaper than other hotels in London?

f Ask your neighbour.

Would you prefer to go to London or Scandinavia? Why?

3

3 a Look at photograph sequence 2 'Going on Holiday' on the next pages. John and his wife, Lucy, are going on holiday. His mother, Freda, is going to look after their house while they're away. Describe the people to your neighbour.

b Match the sentences below and the photographs.

1 She's putting the cat out. [3]
2 She's packing a suitcase. [ ]
3 He's saying goodbye to his mother. [ ]
4 He's putting the suitcases in the car. [ ]
5 She's putting the milk bottles out. [ ]

c Now ask your neighbour these questions.

1 What's she doing in photograph 1?
2 What's she doing in photograph 2?
3 What's she doing in photograph 3?
4 What's he doing in photograph 4?
5 What's he doing in photograph 5?

d Look at the photographs and complete these sentences using 'before' or 'after'.

eg She put the milk bottles out before she put the cat out.

1 She packed the case ______ she put the milk bottles out.
2 She put the cat out ______ she put the milk bottles out.
3 She gave the suitcase to her husband ______ she put the cat out.
4 He put the suitcases in the car ______ they drove away.
5 They said goodbye to his mother ______ they packed the car.

e Read this text and then answer the questions below.

Last Saturday Lucy and John got up early. John went to the bathroom and washed himself. He got dressed, went to the kitchen and made breakfast. Lucy washed and dressed herself and then they had breakfast together. After breakfast Lucy went back to the bedroom and opened her wardrobe. She took out her suitcase and started to pack. She packed a pair of sandals, a dress, 2 skirts, 3 blouses, a pair of shorts, a pair of earrings, a bracelet, a necklace, a jacket and a scarf. Then she took the suitcase downstairs and gave it to John. She went back to the bedroom and found John's suitcase under the bed. She opened it and packed 3 pairs of socks, 2 pairs of trousers, 2 shirts, a T-shirt, a tie, a jacket and 2 pairs of shoes. She took the suitcase downstairs and gave it to John. Then she went into the kitchen, washed the milk bottles and put them out. She went inside to look for the cat but she couldn't find it. After half an hour she found the cat asleep on her bed. She picked it up, carried it downstairs and put it out. John put the cases in the car and Lucy gave the house keys to his mother. They got into the car, said goodbye to his mother and drove away.

1 Who made breakfast? ______
2 How many skirts did Lucy pack? ______
3 Where was John's suitcase? ______
4 Where did Lucy find the cat? ______
5 Who did they give the house keys to? ______

f Work with your neighbour. You are going to continue the story. Use these questions to help you.

1 Where did they go on holiday?
2 How long did they stay?
3 Where did they stay?
4 What did they do in the mornings, afternoons and evenings?
5 What was the weather like?

g Now tell your class about John and Lucy's holiday.

4

4 a Translate the following.

Vocabulary

salmon ______
waterproof trousers ______
motels ______
mosquito repellent ______
drive-ins ______
lucky ______
to pack ______
the weather turned bad ______
produce ______
to invite ______
to taste ______
thoroughly ______
to collect ______
to see the sights ______
to head west ______
unfortunately ______
advertisement ______
seaside ______
chalets ______
motoring holiday ______
per person ______
wife ______
mother ______
husband ______
to put out ______
suitcase ______
cat ______
milk bottles ______
before ______
after ______
to drive away ______
to look after ______
to wash ______
to find ______
asleep ______
to carry ______
house keys ______

Structures

What's the best holiday you've ever had? ______
Where did you go? ______
I went to Ireland. ______
The best holiday I've ever had was in 1993. ______
She's putting the cat out. ______
She put the milk bottles out before she put the cat out. ______

Teaching Notes

Warm-up

Ask students questions from earlier Units eg "How do you make a piece of toast? What are you doing? Where would you find a pedestrian crossing?"

Revision

Revise all the structures and vocabulary from the previous Unit by asking students questions eg "Have you ever travelled on the London Underground? Which line is Green Park on? How do you buy a ticket for the London Underground?"

Presentation and Practice

1 Ask if anyone has been to the USA and ask them where they went and what they saw. Then ask if anyone has been to Scotland and ask them the same questions. Ask students what they think of when you mention Scotland and elicit a few words. Do the same for the USA before students complete the task in 1a. Ask students to tell you the words/names they put in each column.

Introduce the reading activity in 1b by telling students that the paragraphs belong to two stories: one about Clive's holiday to the USA and the other about Nick's holiday to Scotland. They are to read the paragraphs and mark in the box whether they belong to Story A (Clive) or Story B (Nick). One paragraph for each story is already marked. Students compare with their neighbours and then work together to put the paragraphs in the correct order. Provide feedback by listing the correct order on the board.

2 Revise note forms by one student asking you the questions from 2a. Write your answers in note form on the board. Students then complete the note-taking task in 2a. Introduce 2b by using your notes on the board to answer the questions in full sentences. In pairs students complete the speaking activity in 2b. Students then tell the rest of the class about their best holiday as in 2c. Introduce 2d by asking students how they choose their holidays (eg brochures, adverts, recommendations) and ask them what information such an advert normally contains. Students then complete the writing task in 2d and compare their work with their neighbour. In 2e students ask their neighbour the questions about the 'London' advert.

In pairs students complete the speaking activity in 2f.

3 Introduce photograph sequence 2 and tell students that the photographs show John and Lucy who are going on holiday. Students describe the people to their neighbour while you monitor and check. Students then read the sentences in 3b and write which photograph they refer to. Check their work. Students complete the speaking activity in 3c while you monitor and check. Introduce 3d by asking students what Lucy did first, what she did after that etc. Students complete the sentences in 3d by looking at the order of events in the photographs. Students read the text in 3e and answer the questions. Provide feedback by asking students the questions. In pairs students make up more details and continue the story while you monitor and check. Pairs then tell the rest of the class their version of John and Lucy's holiday.

Revise all the structures and vocabulary before moving on to the next lesson.

At home students prepare for the next lesson by looking up the vocabulary in 4a of Unit 13.

Answers

Exercise 1a

The United States of America	**Scotland**
Los Angeles	Scone Palace
Yosemite Park	golf
greyhound bus	wet
Boston	foggy
California	whisky distillery
air-conditioning	salmon
drive-ins	Glencoe
motels	waterproof trousers
New York	mosquito repellent
Grand Canyon	
Death Valley	
convertible car	
hamburgers	

Exercise 1b

Story A (Clive / USA)	1, 2, 6, 7, 8, 11, 14
Story B (Nick / Scotland)	3, 4, 5, 9, 10, 12, 13

Exercise 1c

Story A (Clive)	2, 7, 8, 6, 14, 11, 1
Story B (Nick)	9, 3, 12, 13, 5, 10, 4

Exercise 3b

1 Photograph 3
2 Photograph 1
3 Photograph 5
4 Photograph 4
5 Photograph 2

Exercise 3d

1 She packed the case <u>before</u> she put the milk bottles out.
2 She put the cat out <u>after</u> she put the milk bottles out.
3 She gave the suitcase to her husband <u>after</u> she put the cat out.
4 He put the suitcases in the car <u>before</u> they drove away.
5 They said goodbye to his mother <u>after</u> they packed the car.

Exercise 3e

1 John made breakfast.
2 Lucy packed 2 skirts.
3 John's suitcase was under the bed.
4 Lucy found the cat asleep on her bed.
5 They gave the house keys to John's mother.

1

UNIT 13

Has flight JG971 from Tokyo arrived yet?

1 a Listen to the cassette and fill in the missing information.

DEPARTURES			
Flight Number	Destination	Gate	Comments
BA 739	Copenhagen	7	Boarding
________	Brussels	___	Final Call
BM 805	________	___	Boarding
________	________	3	Proceed to Gate 3
SA 191	Madrid	11	________
________	________	14	Delayed
Passenger Information			
Passenger ________ to go to the airport information desk.			

Listen again and check.

Compare with your neighbour.

b Ask your neighbour.

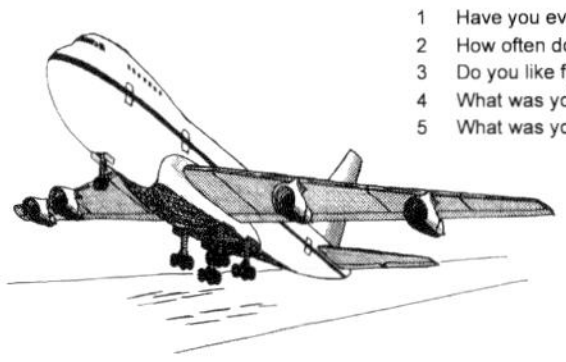

1 Have you ever travelled by plane?
2 How often do you travel by plane?
3 Do you like flying? Why (not)?
4 What was your best flight? Why?
5 What was your worst flight? Why?

c What is most important for you when you're flying?

✓✓ = very important ✓ = important x = not important

- [ ] good, calm weather
- [ ] smooth landing
- [ ] good food
- [ ] free drinks
- [ ] friendly cabin crew
- [ ] punctual departure and arrival
- [ ] duty free goods
- [ ] safety
- [ ] travelling with somebody
- [ ] getting your luggage back

d Ask your neighbour.

eg *Is good, calm weather important for you when you're flying? Yes it is.*

e Tell your teacher about yourself.

eg *For me the most important thing is good, calm weather.*
I hate flying in bad weather.

2

2 a Look at the information below and ask your neighbour.

eg *Has the plane from Tokyo arrived yet? No it hasn't.*

1 Has the plane from Berlin arrived yet?
2 Has the plane from Bucharest arrived yet?
3 Has the plane from Beijing arrived yet?
4 Has the plane from Dubai arrived yet?
5 Has the plane from Paris arrived yet?

ARRIVALS					Time Now 11:20
Flight Number	Scheduled Arrival Time	Estimated Arrival Time	Landed Time	Arriving From	Flight Information
JG 971	11:00	11:44		TOKYO	Delayed
EA 391	11:05		11:07	BERLIN	Baggage in Hall
HX 472	11:10		11:10	BUCHAREST	Landed
WV 714	11:15			BEIJING	Cancelled
YI 362	11:20	11:30		DUBAI	Delayed
QZ 580	11:25			PARIS	On Time

b Match up the flight numbers, where they are from and the flight information.

1 JG 971 Tokyo
2 QZ 580 ________
3 WV 714 ________
4 EA 391 ________
5 HX 472 ________
6 YI 362 ________

It's on time. [ ]
It's been delayed. [ ]
It's already landed. [ ]
It's been delayed. [1]
The baggage is in the hall. [ ]
It's been cancelled. [ ]

Check with your teacher.

c Ask your neighbour 5 questions.

eg *Has flight JG 971 from Tokyo arrived yet? No it hasn't. It's been delayed.*

d Ask your neighbour.

1 Has flight YI 362 been delayed?
2 Has flight HX 472 been cancelled?
3 Has flight JG 971 arrived?

e Write 5 more questions.

eg *Has flight YI 362 been delayed?*

1 ________________________________?
2 ________________________________?
3 ________________________________?
4 ________________________________?
5 ________________________________?

Check with your teacher.

f Ask your neighbour your questions.

3

LONDON - MUNICH

Depart: Heathrow Airport
BA flights Terminal 1 (min check in time at gate - 20 mins)
Other flights Terminal 2 (min check in time at gate - 30 mins)

Arrive: Munich Airport

Frequency 1234567	**Aircraft** Dep	Arr	Via	Flight
12345..	0700	0830	non-stop	LH 971
1234567	0820	1145	Düsseldorf	BA 709
12345..	1005	1135	non-stop	LH 391
1.3.5..	1200	1330	non-stop	BA 743
1.34.6.	1445	1800	Frankfurt	LH 242
1234567	1745	2105	Hanover	LH 372
.2.4.6.	1905	2035	non-stop	BA 552
12.456.	2025	2205	non-stop	LH 721

(1 = Monday / 7 = Sunday)

Flight Enquiries

Flight Reservations	0171-322-9476
Flight Information	0171-391-4672
Cargo Sales Office	0171-242-9733

24-hour service

3 a Look at the information and ask your neighbour.

eg *Does the 0820 plane fly on Sundays? Yes it does.*

1 Does the 1445 plane fly on Tuesdays?
2 Does the 2025 plane fly on Saturdays?
3 Does the 1200 plane fly on Tuesdays?
4 Which days does the 1905 plane fly on?
5 Which days doesn't the 1200 plane fly on?

b Answer the following questions.

eg *What time does the 0820 arrive? It arrives at 1145.*

1 What time does the 1745 arrive? ________
2 What time does flight BA 709 depart? ________
3 Is flight BA 552 non-stop? ________
4 Which flight goes via Düsseldorf? ________
5 Which terminal does flight BA 709 leave from? ________

Check with your neighbour.

c Ask your neighbour 5 more questions.

eg *Which flight goes via Hanover? Flight LH 372.*

d Ask your neighbour the following questions.

1 Which number do I ring if I want to find out departure times?
2 What is the latest check in time for flight LH 391?
3 Can I reserve a ticket at 3am?
4 If I have to be in Munich for 1430, which flight should I take?
5 If I have to be in Munich at 1300, which flight should I take?

Check with your teacher.

4

4 a Translate the following.

Vocabulary

departures ________
flight number ________
comments ________
boarding ________
final call ________
check in ________
smooth ________
cabin crew ________
punctual ________
arrival ________
duty free goods ________
safety ________
luggage ________
arrivals ________
scheduled arrival time ________
estimated arrival time ________
landed time ________
flight information ________
yet ________
on time ________
delayed ________
already ________
landed ________
baggage in hall ________
cancelled ________
frequency ________
aircraft ________
via ________
enquiries ________
reservations ________
cargo sales ________
24 hour service ________

Structures

Has flight JG 971 from Tokyo arrived yet? ________
Is good calm weather important for you when you're flying? ________
For me the most important thing is good, calm weather. ________
I hate flying in bad weather. ________
Has the plane from Tokyo arrived yet? ________
No it hasn't. ________
Yes it has. ________
It's been delayed. ________
It's already landed. ________
Has flight YI 362 been delayed? ________
Does the 0820 plane fly on Sundays? ________
Yes it does. ________
What time does the 0820 arrive? ________
It arrives at 1145. ________
Which flight goes via Hanover? ________
Flight LH 372. ________

Teaching Notes

Warm-up

Ask students questions from earlier Units eg "What's your name? How do you spell it? Where do you work?"

Revision

Revise all the structures and vocabulary from the previous Unit by asking students questions eg "What's the best holiday you've ever had? What can you remember about Clive's holiday to the USA?"

Presentation and Practice

1 Find out who has travelled in an aeroplane. Ask them when, where to, which airline they used and why.

Introduce the activity in 1a by telling students that they will hear an announcement giving them information about departing flights. While they listen they fill in the missing information. Play the cassette a second time for them to check, before they compare their work with their neighbour.

Students then complete the speaking activity in 1b. Provide feedback by asking students to tell you about their neighbour. Make sure that students understand the vocabulary in 1c before they mark what is important for them.

Students then complete the speaking activity in 1d. Provide feedback by asking students to tell you about themselves in 1e.

2 Introduce the information in 2a by asking students the example question in 2a before they complete the speaking activity. Check by asking students the questions before they complete the matching task in 2b.

Students then complete the speaking activity in 2c and go on to 2d while you monitor and check.

Students complete the writing task in 2e and then they ask their neighbour their questions. Provide feedback by asking pairs to demonstrate their activity.

3 Ask students what they think this timetable is for, who would use it and why. Explain that 'frequency' refers to the days of the week (1 = Monday, 2 = Tuesday, etc) and then students complete the speaking activity in 3a. Provide feedback by asking pairs to demonstrate their activity.

Students then complete the writing task in 3b and compare their work with their neighbour. Students make up 5 more questions and ask their neighbour while you monitor and check.

Students then complete the speaking activity in 3d. Provide feedback by eliciting the answers to the questions.

Revise all the structures and vocabulary before moving on to the next lesson.

At home students prepare for the next lesson by looking up the vocabulary in 4a of Unit 14.

Tapescripts

Exercise 1a

British Airways announce the departure of flight BA739 to Copenhagen. Boarding now at Gate 7.

This is the final call for Air UK flight UK504 to Brussels. Would passengers please go immediately to Gate 23.

British Midland announce the departure of flight BM805 to Glasgow. Boarding now at Gate 19.

This is the final call for KLM flight KL433 to Amsterdam. Would passengers please proceed to Gate 3.

Would passengers for Air Spain flight SA191 to Madrid please go to the check in desk.

This is an urgent call for passenger Kevin Allan. Would Kevin Allan please go to the airport information desk.

Lufthansa regret to announce that flight LH731 to Berlin has been delayed.

Answers

Exercise 1a

DEPARTURES			
Flight Number	Destination	Gate	Comments
BA 739	Copenhagen	7	Boarding
UK 504	Brussels	23	Final Call
BM 805	Glasgow	19	Boarding
KL 433	Amsterdam	3	Proceed to Gate 3
SA 191	Madrid	11	Go to check in desk
LH 731	Berlin	14	Delayed
Passenger Kevin Allan to go to the airport information desk.			

Exercise 2b

1 JG 971 Tokyo
2 QZ 580 Paris
3 WV 714 Beijing
4 EA 391 Berlin
5 HX 472 Bucharest
6 YI 362 Dubai

It's on time.	2	It's been delayed.	1
It's been delayed.	6	The baggage is in the hall.	4
It's already landed.	5	It' been cancelled.	3

Exercise 3b

1 It arrives at 2105.
2 It departs at 0820.
3 Yes it is.
4 BA 709.
5 Terminal 1.

1

UNIT 14

When's the next train to Corbridge?

1 a **Match the pictures and the words.**

3 handbag
___ sports bag
___ holdall
___ suitcase
___ briefcase
___ rucksack
___ box
___ garment bag
___ vanity case
___ hat box

Check with your neighbour.

b **Ask your neighbour.**

eg *What's number 1? It's a rucksack.*

c **Look at the instructions for the left luggage locker below and then answer these questions.**

eg *When should I key in the number? When I want to retrieve my luggage.*

1 What colour is the light when I take my ticket? ______________________

2 What number do I key in to retrieve my luggage? ______________________

3 Does the machine give change? ______________________

4 When do I insert the money? ______________________

5 How do I know how much it costs? ______________________

d **You want to leave a suitcase in the left luggage locker. Discuss with your neighbour what you have to do.**

e **Tell your teacher how to use the left luggage locker.**

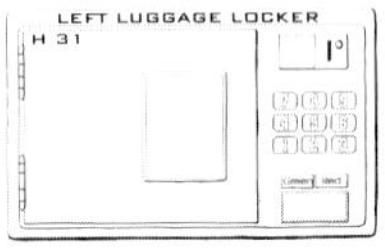

Instructions for Use
1 Place luggage in locker.
2 Close locker and wait for green light.
3 Insert required amount as shown on display (no change is given).
4 Wait for red light.
5 Take ticket.

To Retrieve Luggage
1 Key in the number on your ticket.
2 Wait for door to open.
3 Take your luggage.

2

2 a **Listen to the cassette and fill in the missing information.**

TRAIN TIMETABLE				
Platform	**Departure Time**	**Destination**	**Via**	**Comments**
7	12:06	York	Durham Darlington	on time
5	______	______	Manchester Preston	on time
4	______	Glasgow		delayed
______	12:24	______	Darlington York	on time
3	______	Cardiff		cancelled
______	12:30	______		on time

Listen again and check then compare with your neighbour.

b **Look at the following information and answer the questions below.**

eg *When is New Year's Day? Monday January 1.*

Bank and Public Holidays

New Year's Day	Mon	Jan 1
Good Friday	Fri	Apr 5
Easter Monday	Mon	Apr 8
May Day Holiday	Mon	May 6
Spring Bank Holiday	Mon	May 27
Summer Bank Holiday	Mon	Aug 26
Christmas Day	Wed	Dec 25
Boxing Day	Thur	Dec 26

1 When is Spring Bank Holiday? ______________________

2 When is Summer Bank Holiday? ______________________

3 When is May Day Holiday? ______________________

4 When is Boxing Day? ______________________

5 When is Easter Monday? ______________________

c **Ask your neighbour 5 questions.**

eg *What is August 26? It's Summer Bank Holiday.*

d **How many bank and public holidays do you have in your country?**

3

3 a **It's Thursday and you're in Newcastle. Look at the train timetable below.**

1 It's 0715. When's the next train to Corbridge? ______________________

2 It's 0935. When's the next train to Corbridge? ______________________

3 It's 1700. When's the next train to Corbridge? ______________________

Train Timetable Newcastle - Hexham

	x	+	o	+	*	o	*	+	*	*	+
Newcastle	0700	0725	0800	0815	..07	1610	1645	1705	1845	1905	2300
Dunstable	0705	0730	0805	|	..12	1615	1650	|	1850	1910	2305
Metro Centre	0710	0735	0810	|	..17	1620	1655	|	1855	1915	2310
Blaydon	0715	0740	0815	|	..22	1625	1700	|	1900	1920	2315
Wylam	0720	0745	0820	|	..27	1630	1705	|	1905	1925	2320
Prudhoe	0725	0750	0825	|	..32	1635	1710	|	1910	1930	2325
Stocksfield	0730	0755	0830	|	..37	1640	1715	|	1915	1935	2330
Corbridge	0735	0800	0835	|	..42	1645	1720	|	1920	1940	2335
Hexham	0740	0805	0840	0835	..47	1650	1725	1725	1925	1945	2340

Bank and Public Holidays

x every day, except Sunday + only weekdays o every day, including bank holidays * every day, except bank holidays

b **Now ask your neighbour these questions.**

eg *What time does the 0800 train arrive in Prudhoe? It arrives at twenty five past eight.*

1 What time does the 0800 train arrive in Stocksfield?
2 What time does the 0725 train arrive in Hexham?
3 What time does the 1407 train arrive in Wylam?
4 What time does the 1645 train arrive in the Metro Centre?
5 What time does the 2300 train arrive in Blaydon?

c **Ask your neighbour 5 more questions.**

eg *What time does the 1705 train arrive in Hexham? It arrives at twenty five past five.*

d **Answer the following questions.**

eg *I have to be in Stocksfield for 0845. Which train should I take? You should take the 0800.*

1 I have to be in Prudhoe for 1150. Which train should I take? ______________________

2 I have to be in Corbridge for 0900. Which train should I take? ______________________

3 I have to be in the Metro Centre for 0945. Which train should I take? ______________________

4 I have to be in Hexham for 1200. Which train should I take? ______________________

5 I have to be in Stocksfield for 1430. Which train should I take? ______________________

e **Ask your neighbour 5 more questions.**

eg *I have to be in Hexham for 1730. Which train should I take? You should take the 1705 express.*

f **Answer the following questions**

eg *Does the 1705 run on Sundays? No, it only runs on weekdays.*

1 Does the 0800 run on Good Friday? ______________________

2 Does the 1307 run on Sundays? ______________________

3 Does the 0725 run on Wednesdays? ______________________

4 Does the 1845 run on Boxing Day? ______________________

5 What is the last train to run on Saturday night? ______________________

4

4 a **Translate the following.**

Vocabulary

handbag ______________________
sports bag ______________________
holdall ______________________
briefcase ______________________
rucksack ______________________
box ______________________
garment bag ______________________
vanity case ______________________
hat box ______________________
left luggage locker ______________________
place ______________________
to retrieve ______________________
to key in ______________________
no change is given ______________________
delay ______________________
apology ______________________
due to ______________________
derailment ______________________
New Year's Day ______________________
Good Friday ______________________
Easter Monday ______________________
May Day Holiday ______________________
Spring Bank Holiday ______________________
Summer Bank Holiday ______________________
Christmas Day ______________________
Boxing Day ______________________
express ______________________

Structures

When's the next train to Corbridge? ______________________
When should I key in the number? ______________________
When I want to retrieve my luggage. ______________________
When is New Year's Day? ______________________
Monday January 1. ______________________
What is August 26? ______________________
It's Summer Bank Holiday. ______________________
What time does the 0800 train arrive in Prudhoe? ______________________
It arrives at twenty five past eight. ______________________
What time does the 1705 arrive in Hexham? ______________________
It arrives at twenty five past five. ______________________
I have to be in Stocksfield for 0845. ______________________
Which train should I take? ______________________
You should take the 8 o'clock. ______________________
Does the 1705 run on Sundays? ______________________
No, it only runs on weekdays. ______________________

Teaching Notes

Warm-up

Ask students questions from earlier Units eg "What do you dry your hair with? Can you name 5 electrical items which have dials? Have you ever been to the USA?"

Revision

Revise all the structures and vocabulary from the previous Unit by asking students questions eg "Have you ever flown? What is important for you when you are flying?"

Presentation and Practice

1 Introduce the activity in 1a by asking students to put their bags on their desks. Ask students what kind of bag it is and elicit the answers providing vocabulary where necessary (eg plastic bag, briefcase). Students complete the matching task in 1a and compare their work with their neighbour. To reinforce the words they complete the speaking activity in 1b.

Introduce 1c by asking students what the diagram is, where they would find it and why they would use a locker. Find out who has used a luggage locker and ask them to explain how it works.

In pairs students answer the questions in 1c while you monitor and check.

Students then complete the speaking activity in 1d. Provide feedback in 1e by asking one student how to use a luggage locker.

2 Introduce 2a by asking who regularly takes the train. Ask them where they find out information about train times. Ask students questions about the timetable in 2a eg "What time does the train to York leave? Which platform does the train to Cardiff leave from?" When they are familiar with the timetable, explain that they are going to listen to an announcement which they would hear in a railway station. While they are listening they are to fill in the missing information. Play the cassette a second time for them to check their work.

Ask two students how many public holidays they have per year in their country and find out what and when they are. Explain that the list shows public & bank holidays in the UK.

Students answer the questions in 2b and then make up 5 more questions about the information. Provide feedback by students asking the rest of the class their questions.

In 2d find out how many bank and public holidays students have in their country.

3 Explain to students that they are going to use the train timetable given for these exercises. Point out the footnotes explaining where necessary.

Students answer the questions in 3a. Students complete the speaking activity in 3b and then make up 5 more questions in 3c. When students have finished they complete the writing task in 3d.

In pairs they then complete the speaking activity in 3e. Next students complete the writing task in 3f. Provide feedback by one pair asking and answering the questions.

Revise all the structures and vocabulary before moving on to the next lesson.

At home students prepare for the next lesson by looking up the vocabulary in 4a of Unit 15.

Tapescripts

Exercise 2a

The train now standing at platform 7 is the 12:06 to York, calling at Durham and Darlington.

The next train to arrive at platform 5 will be the 12:15 to Birmingham calling at Manchester and Preston.

The 12:17 Inter-City train to Glasgow has been delayed. This train is now running 10 minutes late and will now depart at 12:27. We apologise to passengers for the delay.

The train now arriving at platform 2 is the 12:24 to London calling at Darlington and York.

We are sorry to announce that the 12:25 train to Cardiff has been cancelled due to derailment. We apologise to passengers for the inconvenience.

The inter-city train to Newcastle will depart from platform 6 at 12:30.

Thank you for your attention.

Answers

Exercise 1a

1 rucksack
2 hatbox
3 handbag
4 suitcase
5 box
6 sports bag
7 vanity case
8 briefcase
9 holdall
10 garmant bag

Exercise 1c

1 Red.
2 The number on my ticket.
3 No.
4 When I see the green light.
5 The required amount is shown on the display.

Exercise 2a

TRAIN TIMETABLE				
Platform	Departure Time	Destination	Via	Comments
7	12:06	York	Durham/Darlington	on time
5	12:15	Birmingham	Manchester/Preston	on time
4	12:27	Glasgow		delayed
2	12:24	London	Darlington/York	on time
3	12:25	Cardiff		cancelled
6	12:30	Newcastle		on time

Exercise 2b

1 It's Monday May 27.
2 It's Monday August 26.
3 It's Monday May 6.
4 It's Thursday December 26.
5 It's Monday April 8.

Exercise 3a

1 0725
2 1007
3 1845

Exercise 3d

1 1107
2 0800
3 0907
4 1107
5 1307

Exercise 3f

1 Yes
2 Yes.
3 Yes.
4 No.
5 1905.

1

UNIT 15

I think that cars are the safest way to travel.

1 a Fill in the following using a tick (✓) for yes or a cross (x) for no and a question mark (?) for don't know.

	comfortable	safe	expensive	slow	crowded	enjoyable	healthy	convenient	environmentally friendly
cars									
buses									
trains									
motorbikes									
bicycles									

b Fill in the following.

I think that ________________ are the most comfortable way to travel.

I think that ________________ are the safest way to travel.

I think that ________________ are the most enjoyable way to travel.

I think that ________________ are the most convenient way to travel.

I think that ________________ are the most environmentally friendly way to travel.

c Ask your neighbour what he/she thinks.

eg *I think that cars are the most comfortable way to travel. What do you think? I think they're very comfortable but the disadvantages are that they're expensive and not very environmentally friendly.*

d Fill in the following in note form.

eg *What are the advantages of cars? Comfortable, safe and convenient. Take you door to door. You can leave when you want.*

1 What are the disadvantages of buses? ________________

2 What are the advantages of trains? ________________

3 What are the disadvantages of cars? ________________

4 What are the advantages of buses? ________________

5 What are the disadvantages of trains? ________________

e Ask your neighbour the questions above.

2

2 a Read the following information.

"...and now for the traffic news. The M1 motorway northbound is blocked between junctions 3 and 4 due to an overturned lorry. Tailbacks are already 2 miles long. Drivers are requested to leave the motorway at junction 3 and follow police diversion signs. Meanwhile, roadworks due to worn-out surface on the M25 are causing congestion between junctions 24 and 25. Drivers are advised to avoid this section."

15 injured in motorway pile-up

A pile-up on the M4 last night was caused by careless driving according to the police.

11 cars were involved in the pile-up which happened at about 6.30pm last night and 15 people were taken to hospital.

A police spokesman said "Motorists were driving at speeds over 70mph despite the thick fog and visibility of around 100 yards. We were lucky that no one was seriously injured."

One of the drivers who was in hospital last night suffering from whiplash said "I was driving at around 40mph because of the bad conditions. Suddenly I saw brake lights ahead. I braked hard but could not avoid the cars in front."

Sheila Jameson who was travelling in the inside lane said "They were all travelling like maniacs - far too fast and far too close. I'm surprised nobody was killed. People who drive like that shouldn't be allowed on the roads."

Police have reminded motorists to drive with extra care when conditions are bad.

"Yesterday afternoon traffic congestion caused smog levels in central London to rise to a dangerous level. Motorists were requested to turn off their engines at traffic lights and when standing in traffic jams. People living in the area were advised to close all windows and keep children inside. It is feared that levels will rise again today."

b Ask your neighbour. What do you think these words mean?

1 tailback 3 seriously injured 5 whiplash 7 brake lights 9 motorist
2 pile-up 4 traffic jam 6 bad conditions 8 smog 10 overturned

Check with your teacher.

c Fill in the following in note form. Use the information from the text, as well as your own examples.

Problem	Cause
accidents	eg *driving too fast/drivers falling asleep*
roadworks	
diversions	
congestion	
smog	

d Discuss these in your group.

eg *What causes accidents? I think that people drive too fast or they drive when they are tired. They're both very dangerous.*

3

3 a Read the following statements and decide if you agree, disagree, or if you don't know. Put a tick (✓) in the box.

		agree	disagree	don't know
1	Motorways should have more lanes.	❑	❑	❑
2	Public transport is not efficient.	❑	❑	❑
3	The driving test is too easy.	❑	❑	❑
4	I can't remember the last time I went by train.	❑	❑	❑
5	I don't know how much it costs to come to my English lesson by bus.	❑	❑	❑
6	Cars should be made which don't go faster than 120km.	❑	❑	❑
7	I want to open my windows when I want, not when it's safe.	❑	❑	❑
8	Motorways should be privatised.	❑	❑	❑
9	I take public transport more than once a week.	❑	❑	❑
10	Bad drivers should be banned.	❑	❑	❑

b Discuss your answers with 2 neighbours.

eg *I think that motorways should have more lanes. What do you think? I agree - there are too many cars on the road and if there were more lanes there wouldn't be as many accidents.*

c Read the following text.

Whether you listen to the radio, watch TV, or read newspapers, you will always hear some traffic news. Occasionally you will hear some good news (eg repairs to the road are now finished) but normally you will hear bad news - traffic jams, road repairs, accidents. Of course, when this happens people do not decide to put their car in the garage and take public transport. No they stay in their cars and find other roads, side roads and B-roads in order to continue their journey. Statistics show that more and more new cars are being sold. By 2010 the number of cars will have doubled. This is not just Britain, this is true of most cities in the world and many towns in more developed countries. The problems created are not just traffic problems. More traffic means more pollution, more exhaust fumes going into the air which are breathed in by pedestrians and children as well as motorists. More traffic means more accidents. But whose responsibility is it to take action? Who should be doing something about it now? Some people say it is the government's responsibility - they should build better roads which need fewer repairs, wider roads with more lanes, and more roads. Others say it is the individual's responsibility. We should all use public transport wherever possible and when we have to travel by car, try to find somebody else going to the same place and travel together in one car. If you look at cars on any road today, 90% only have one person in them. So it's clear that some solution has to be found. The question is, what is the best solution?

d Read the sentences and based on the text write T for true, or F for false.

eg *Traffic news is normally bad news. T*

1 Fewer cars are being sold. ________

2 This problem is world-wide. ________

3 There will be twice as many cars in 2010. ________

4 More traffic means fewer accidents. ________

5 10% of cars on the road have more than 1 person in them. ________

Check with your teacher.

4

4 a Translate the following.

Vocabulary

comfortable ________	to brake hard ________
safe ________	inside lane ________
expensive ________	maniacs ________
slow ________	far too close ________
crowded ________	killed ________
enjoyable ________	to remind ________
healthy ________	extra care ________
convenient ________	whether ________
environmentally friendly ________	occasionally ________
disadvantage ________	good news ________
advantage ________	repairs ________
traffic news ________	bad news ________
northbound ________	traffic jams ________
blocked ________	road repairs ________
overturned ________	accidents ________
tailbacks ________	side roads ________
drivers ________	B-roads ________
to leave ________	to continue ________
diversion signs ________	journey ________
meanwhile ________	true ________
congestion ________	developed countries ________
to avoid ________	pollution ________
injured ________	exhaust fumes ________
pile-up ________	to breathe in ________
spokeswoman ________	pedestrians ________
speed ________	responsibility ________
despite ________	to build ________
visibility ________	fewer ________
seriously injured ________	wider ________
to suffer from ________	individual ________
whiplash ________	public transport ________
bad conditions ________	solution ________
suddenly ________	privatised ________
brake lights ________	banned ________

Structures

I think that cars are the most comfortable way to travel. ________

I think that buses are the safest way to travel. ________

What do you think? ________

I think they're very comfortable. ________

The disadvantages are that they're expensive. ________

What causes accidents? ________

I think people drive too fast or they drive when they are tired. ________

I think that motorways should have more lanes. ________

I agree. ________

Teaching Notes

Warm-up

Ask students questions from earlier Units eg "What's the best holiday you've ever had? What do you use a sewing machine for?"

Revision

Revise all the structures and vocabulary from the previous Unit by asking students questions eg "What is December 25th? When is Easter Monday? When's the next train to Stocksfield?"

Presentation and Practice

1 Introduce the activity in 1a by asking students how they come to their English lesson and why they use that means of transport. Elicit reasons why they don't use other means of transport and list the vocabulary from 1a on the board. Students complete the activity in 1a and compare their work with their neighbour. Students then complete the writing task in 1b and in 1c they ask their neighbour what he/she thinks. Before students complete the writing activity in 1d revise note forms by giving your own examples. Students then ask their neighbour the questions from 1d while you monitor and check.

2 Find out which students listen to the traffic news. Elicit words which often appear on the traffic news eg roadworks, traffic jam etc. Students then read the news and try to explain the meanings of the words in 2b while you monitor and check. Find out if anybody has been involved in an accident and elicit reasons as to why accidents happen. Students think of as many reasons for accidents as possible which you note on the board and then students complete the task in 2c. Students discuss their reasons in groups of 4 while you monitor and check.

3 Students read through the questionnaire in 3a and put a tick in the appropriate box. They then discuss their opinions with 2 neighbours in 3b while you monitor and check. When students have finished they read the text in 3c and complete the task in 3d. Check their work and then ask students what they think the best solution is.

Revise all the structures and vocabulary before moving on to the next lesson.

At home students prepare for the next lesson by looking up the vocabulary in 4a of Unit 16.

Answers

Exercise 1d

1 crowded and slow / not many buses in the country
2 comfortable and safe / you can work on a train
3 expensive / not environmentally friendly / traffic jams
4 environmentally friendly / cheap / safe
5 expensive / can be delayed

Exercise 3d

1 Fewer cars are being sold - False
2 This problem is world-wide - True
3 There will be twice as many cars in 2010 - True
4 More traffic means fewer accidents - False
5 10% of cars on the road have more than 1 person in them - True

Exercise 2c

Problem	Cause
accidents	driving too fast / falling asleep / ice
roadworks	worn-out surface / too many lorries
diversions	accidents / roadworks
congestion	too many cars / not enough roads / roads closed
smog	exhaust fumes / too many cars / industry

1

UNIT 16

Going Shopping

1

a **See if you can find these items in the shopping basket.**
Bread, milk, eggs, potatoes, onions, tinned peas, cooking oil, apples, mince and pork chops.

b **Write down 8 items which you normally buy when you go shopping.**

1 ______ 5 ______
2 ______ 6 ______
3 ______ 7 ______
4 ______ 8 ______

c **Ask 3 neighbours what they buy and then tell your teacher which items all of you buy.**

d **Answer the following questions using .... 'always', 'usually', 'sometimes', 'seldom', 'never'**

	you	your neighbour
1 How often do you eat at home?	....	....
2 How often do you go shopping?	....	....
3 How often do you cook for yourself?	....	....
4 How often do you cook for other people?	....	....
5 How often does someone else cook for you?	....	....
6 How often do you wash up?	....	....
7 How often do you eat the same thing?	....	....
8 How often do you eat frozen food?	....	....
9 How often do you eat from tins or packets?	....	....
10 How often do you eat too much?	....	....

e **Ask your neighbour and note down the answers ....**

f **Tell your teacher about your neighbour.**

eg *My neighbour normally eats at home. He seldom cooks for himself and never cooks for other people. His wife usually cooks for him...*

2

2 a **Look at the words and put them in one of the columns below.**

deodorant cat food soap grapes milk leeks barbecue sauce
curry sauce cheese dog food carrots cherries mayonnaise
oranges bananas toothpaste potatoes salad dressing shampoo
cabbage butter apples shower gel onions tomato sauce yoghurt

I know what it is	I think I know what it is	I don't know what it is

b **Compare with 2 neighbours.**
Ask your teacher the words you don't know.

c **Where would you find these in a supermarket? Work with your neighbour and put the above words in one of the categories.**

Dairy Products	______	Fruit	______
Toiletries	______	Pet Food	______
Sauces	______	Vegetables	______

Check with your teacher.

3

3 a **Here is a plan of a supermarket. The following items are missing: sauces, ordinary fruit, tinned fruit, biscuits, tea and coffee, mixers, spirits, rice, sugar and fresh meat.**
Listen to the cassette and put the items in the correct place. You may listen to it twice.

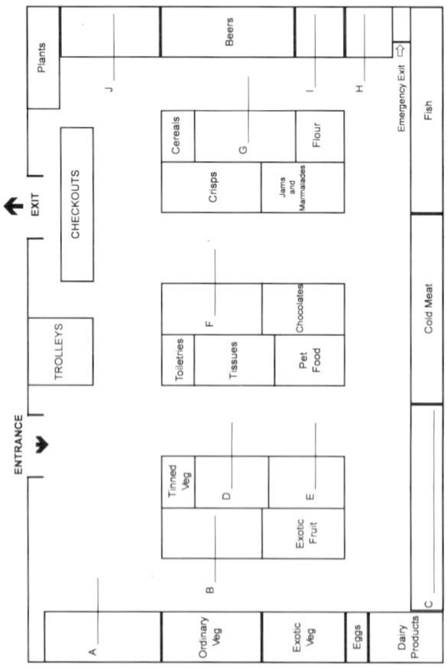

b **Ask your neighbour.**

eg *Where are the crisps? They're next to the jams and marmalades.*

1 Where are the trolleys?
2 Where is the cold meat?
3 Where is the emergency exit?
4 Where are the tissues?
5 Where is the pet food?
6 Where are the cereals?

c **Ask your neighbour 5 more questions.**

eg *Where are the tinned vegetables? They're opposite the toiletries.*

4

4 a **Translate the following.**

Vocabulary

shopping basket ______	pet food ______
to contain ______	sauces ______
tinned peas ______	trolleys ______
mince ______	checkouts ______
pork chops ______	entrance ______
deodorant ______	exit ______
curry sauce ______	ordinary ______
bananas ______	exotic ______
cabbage ______	tinned vegetables ______
cat food ______	tinned fruit ______
dog food ______	fresh meat ______
grapes ______	cold meat ______
salad dressing ______	jams ______
shower gel ______	marmalades ______
cherries ______	crisps ______
leeks ______	cereals ______
tomato sauce ______	flour ______
barbecue sauce ______	emergency exit ______
mayonnaise ______	biscuits ______
yoghurt ______	rice ______
dairy products ______	spirits ______
toiletries ______	mixers ______

Structures

My neighbour normally eats at home. ______
He seldom cooks for himself. ______
He never cooks for other people. ______
His wife usually cooks for him. ______
Do you know what deodorant is? ______
I know what it is. ______
I think I know what it is. ______
I don't know what it is. ______
Where are the crisps? ______
They're next to the jams and marmalades. ______
The tissues are between the toiletries and the pet food. ______
The trolleys are on the left when you walk in. ______
Where are the tinned vegetables? ______
They're opposite the toiletries. ______

Teaching Notes

Warm-up

Ask students questions from earlier Units eg "Have you ever travelled by plane? What is important for you when you are travelling by plane? How do you use a ticket machine?"

Revision

Revise all the structures and vocabulary from the previous Unit by asking students questions eg "Do you agree that the driving test in your country is too easy? What are the advantages of travelling by train?"

Presentation and Practice

1 Ask students if they can find the items listed in the picture in 1a of the shopping basket. Find out how often students go shopping, where they go shopping and why.

Students complete the task in 1b and then in 1c ask 3 neighbours what they normally buy. Ask each group which items they all buy.

Students complete the questionnaire about themselves in 1d and then ask their neighbour noting down the answers in the column marked 'your neighbour'. Provide feedback by asking students to tell you about their neighbour.

2 Students put the words in the appropriate column and then compare their work with their neighbour while you provide missing vocabulary and check. Find out who does their shopping in a supermarket and which sections supermarkets have. Elicit the words from 2c and then students put the words from 2a in the correct category. Provide feedback by asking students to tell you which items they have put in each category.

3 Introduce the listening activity In 3a by asking students if they know where things are in their local supermarket, eg "Which items are near the entrance? Which items are near the checkout?" etc. Before introducing the cassette ask students about the diagram, eg "Where are the toiletries? Where are the eggs?" etc to help familiarise themselves with the diagram. Explain that students are going to hear some information about the layout of a supermarket and they are to fill in the missing items on the supermarket plan. Play the cassette twice and then students compare their work with their neighbour.

Students then complete the speaking activity in 3b while you monitor and check. Provide feedback by asking students about the items in the supermarket, eg "What is between the dairy products and the cold meat?"

Students then complete the speaking activity in 3c.

Revise all the structures and vocabulary before moving on to the next lesson.

At home students prepare for the next lesson by looking up the vocabulary in 4a of Unit 17.

Tapescripts

Exercise 3a

The sauces are on the right as you walk into the store.

The ordinary fruit is next to the exotic fruit.

The tinned fruit is opposite the tissues.

The biscuits are next to the chocolates and opposite the crisps.

The tea and coffee is next to the tinned fruit and opposite the pet food.

The mixers are opposite the flour.

The spirits are next to the emergency exit.

The rice is next to the plants.

The sugar is between the flour and the cereals.

The fresh meat is between the dairy products and the cold meat.

Answers

Exercise 2c

Dairy Products
milk
cheese
butter
yoghurt

Fruit
grapes
cherries
oranges
bananas
apples

Toiletries
deodorant
soap
toothpaste
shampoo
shower gel

Pet Food
cat food
dog food

Sauces
barbecue sauce
curry sauce
mayonnaise
salad dressing
tomato sauce

Vegetables
leeks
carrots
potatoes
cabbage
onions

Exercise 3a

A sauces
B ordinary fruit
C fresh meat
D tinned fruit
E tea and coffee
F biscuits
G sugar
H spirits
I mixers
J rice

1

UNIT 17

Eating Out

1 a Look at the information and answer the questions below.

eg What kind of food does the Jasmin Garden serve?
It serves Chinese food.

Jasmin Garden Chinese Restaurant
66 Victoria Road, Wrexham
Tel 01978 443322
Mandarin Chinese Specialities
Party Bookings Welcome
Licensed Bar
Opening Hours:
Mon - Thu 10am - 11.15pm
Fri & Sat 10am - 11.45 pm
Sun 1pm - 11.15pm

Royal Country Restaurant
24 Markington Place
Stratford-upon-Avon
Tel 01789 516437
Traditional English Dishes
Sunday Lunches
Roast Beef and Yorkshire Pudding £5.25
Opening Times
Mon - Sat 12pm - 2pm / 6.30pm - 10pm
Sun 12pm - 2pm / 7pm - 9pm

Fortini's Restaurant
78-80 King George Street
Blackpool
Tel 01253 462613
Real Italian Cuisine
Licensed Bar
Open 7 days a week
11am - 2.30pm
6pm - 11pm

Shalimar Indian Restaurant
19 Trent Street, Derby
Tel 01332 242464
Specialist Tandoori Dishes
Opening Hours
Daily 11am - 2.30pm / 6pm - 12am
Licensed Bar

1 When is the Royal Country Restaurant open on Sunday? ______.
2 Which restaurant is in Blackpool? ______.
3 What is the telephone number of the Indian restaurant? ______.
4 01978 is the area code for which town? ______.
5 Which restaurant closes daily at midnight? ______.

b Ask your neighbour the following questions.

eg What is the address of the Indian restaurant? It's 19 Trent Street, Derby.

1 Can I drink wine in the Italian restaurant?
2 What is the telephone number of the Italian restaurant?
3 In which restaurant can I order a Sunday lunch?
4 Which restaurant opens at 7pm on Sunday evenings?
5 What time does the Chinese restaurant close on Saturdays?

c Match the menu below and the restaurant from 1a.

1 ______	2 ______	3 ______	4 ______
chicken soup roast lamb and mint sauce potatoes, carrots and peas apple pie	garlic bread spaghetti carbonara ice cream	bird's nest soup sweet 'n' sour pork boiled rice lychees	poppadoms basmati rice, naan bread tandoori chicken assam tea

Check with your teacher.

d Ask your neighbour the following questions.

1 When was the last time you were in a restaurant?
2 Who were you with?
3 What kind of food did it serve?
4 What did you eat?
5 Would you recommend the restaurant?

e Tell your teacher about your neighbour.

2

2 a Look at the information and ask your neighbour the following questions.

eg What shape is table 3? It's round.

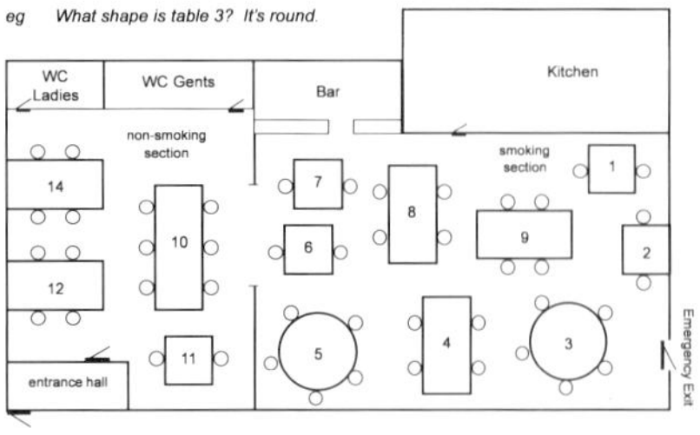

1 What shape is table 8?
2 How many tables are there altogether?
3 Which table number is missing? Do you know why?
4 How many square tables are there?
5 Which tables are non smoking tables?

b Here is the reservations diary for the Royal Country Restaurant. Listen to the cassette and fill in the missing information. You will hear the cassette twice.

Royal Country Restaurant - Reservations - Saturday November 5						
6.00	Mr Nixon	(4 people)	Table 14	8.30	(people)	Table
6.30	Walkers	(4 people)	Table	9.00	(people)	Table
	Johnsons	(people)	Table 1	9.30	(people)	Table
7.00		(4 people)	Table	10.00	(people)	Table
7.30	Mr Armstrong	(people)	Table			
		(people)	Table 10			
8.00		(people)	Table			

c Ask your neighbour the following questions.

eg Who will have table 14? Mr Nixon.

1 Who will have table 5?
2 Will the Johnsons have table 1?
3 Is table 3 a smoking table?
4 How many people are in Miss Brown's party?
5 What time are the Benfords coming?

d Answer the following questions (you may listen to the cassette again).

eg What time is the first reservation? It's at 6.00pm

1 Are the Taylors regular visitors?
2 How old is Mr Armstrong's daughter?
3 What is Miss Brown celebrating?
4 Do the Benfords smoke?
5 Is Saturday night normally busy?

Check with your teacher.

3

Menu

Soup of the Day	£2.15
Prawn Cocktail	£2.30
Paté with Toast	£2.20
Roast Beef and Yorkshire Pudding	£6.75
Roast Lamb and Mint Sauce	£6.75
Roast Pork and Apple Sauce	£7.35
Roast Turkey and Cranberry Jelly	£6.95
All served with boiled potatoes and vegetables	
Ice Cream (strawberry, vanilla)	£1.90
Apple Crumble	£2.50
Cheese and Biscuits	£2.20
Coffee and Mints	£1.30

Wine List

White	Glass	Bottle
German		
Liebfraumilch	80p	£5.95
Piesporter	85p	£6.15
Italian		
Lambrusco	75p	£5.25
Frascati	85p	£6.25
Australian		
Jacobs Creek	85p	£6.10
Red		
Italian		
D'Abruzzo Montepulciano	90p	£7.95
Californian		
Paul Masson	85p	£7.10
French		
St Emilion	£1.10	£8.95

3 a Fill in the following.

eg soup - paté
The soup is cheaper than the paté.
The paté is more expensive than the soup.

beef - lamb
The beef is the same price as the lamb.

1 prawn cocktail - paté ______
______
2 ice cream - apple crumble ______
______
3 lamb - beef ______
______
4 lamb - turkey ______
______
5 Liebfraumilch - Lambrusco ______
______

Check with your teacher.

b Look at the menus again. Decide what you would like to eat and fill in the following.

1 What would you like as a starter? ______
2 What would you like as a main course? ______
3 What would you like for dessert? ______
4 Would you like coffee and mints? ______
5 What would you like to drink with your meal? ______

c Roleplay in a restaurant. A customer (C) is ordering a meal from the waiter/waitress (W). Read the dialogue through then practise ordering a meal for yourself.

W Good evening. Can I help you?
C Yes please, I'd like a table for two.
W Come this way please. Here's the menu.
W Are you ready to order?
C Yes please. What's the soup of the day?
W It's cream of tomato.
C Okay, we'll have 2 soups and then one roast beef and one roast pork.
W One beef, one pork, fine. Would you like anything to drink with the meal?
C Yes please, a bottle of D'Abbruzo Montepulcciano
W Okay, fine.
(later)
W Was everything all right?
C Yes thanks. Can we have the bill please?
W Yes of course. Here's your bill.
C Okay here you are, keep the change.
W Thank you.

4

4 a Translate the following.

Vocabulary

Indian ______
Chinese ______
specialities ______
specialist ______
party bookings ______
licensed bar ______
cuisine ______
traditional ______
roast beef ______
yorkshire pudding ______
to serve ______
to recommend ______
round ______
square ______
rectangular ______
soup of the day ______
paté ______
prawn cocktail ______
roast lamb with mint sauce ______
roast pork with apple sauce ______
roast turkey with cranberry jelly ______
boiled potatoes ______
ice cream ______
strawberry ______
vanilla ______
apple crumble ______
cheese and biscuits ______
mints ______
wine list ______
French ______
German ______
Australian ______
Californian ______

Structures

What kind of food does the Jasmin Garden serve? ______
It serves Chinese food. ______
What is the address of the Indian restaurant? ______
It's 19 Trent Street, Derby. ______
What shape is table 3? ______
It's round. ______
Who will have table 14? ______
Mr Nixon. ______
What time is the first reservation? ______
It's at 6.00 pm. ______
The soup is cheaper than the paté. ______
The paté is more expensive than the soup. ______
The beef is the same price as the lamb. ______
Come this way please. ______
Are you ready to order? ______
Was everything all right? ______
Keep the change. ______

Teaching Notes

Warm-up

Ask students questions from earlier Units eg "What can you remember about Nick's holiday to Scotland? Have you ever used the London Underground? Can you name 10 items in your kitchen?"

Revision

Revise all the structures and vocabulary from the previous Unit by asking students questions eg "What do you normally buy when you go shopping? How often do you eat from tins? What are grapes?"

Presentation and Practice

1 Ask one student about the last time they ate in a restaurant, eg "When was the last time you ate in a restaurant? Where was it? What kind of restaurant was it? Why did you go there? Would you recommend it?"

In pairs students ask their neighbour about the last time they ate in a restaurant and report back to you. List the different kinds of restaurants on the board and elicit types of food/dishes you might find in these restaurants.

Students then look at the adverts for restaurants in 1a and answer the questions as quickly as possible. Check these answers before students complete the speaking activity in 1b.

In pairs students complete 1c while you monitor and check.

Students then complete 1d with another neighbour. Provide feedback by asking students to tell you about their neighbour.

2 Explain to students that the diagram shows the plan of the Royal Country Restaurant.

In pairs they complete the speaking activity in 2a. Explain to students that 2b shows the reservations diary for the restaurant and they are going to listen to the restaurant manager and head waiter checking the reservations and planning where their customers will sit. Students then listen to the cassette and fill in the missing information. When they have listened a second time to check they complete the speaking activity in 2c. Students then answer the questions in 2d.

3 Introduce the menus in 3a by asking students questions about the items, eg "How much is the soup of the day? How much is a bottle of Paul Masson wine?" Write the two examples from 3a on the board before students complete the exercise. Check by asking students to tell you what they have written. Tell students what you would order if you were in this restaurant and then students complete the activity in 3b.

Demonstrate the roleplay in 3c with one student and then put students in pairs to practise the roleplay. Provide feedback by asking pairs to demonstrate their roleplays.

Revise all the structures and vocabulary before moving on to the next lesson.

At home students prepare for the next lesson by looking up the vocabulary in 4a of Unit 18.

Tapescripts

Exercise 2b

Mr Nixon is coming with his wife and 2 children at 6pm. We'll put them in the non-smoking area at table 14. The next reservations are at 6.30pm. The Walkers have reserved a table for 4 and the Johnsons have reserved a table for 2. The Walkers are regulars and they can have their usual table, number 8. I don't know the Johnsons. They didn't ask for non-smoking so we'll put them at table 1. The next reservation is the Taylors at 7pm. They can have table 4. They're regulars too. We have 2 reservations for 7.30pm, a Mr Armstrong, who's celebrating his daughter's 21st birthday and has reserved a table for 5, so they can have table 5, and a Miss Brown who has booked a table for 6. She passed her driving test yesterday and is celebrating. She asked for a non-smoking table, so we'll give her table 10. At 8pm there is a reservation for 2 under the name Bell. I don't know them, so when they come in, ask if they would like smoking or non-smoking and give them either table 2 or table 11. The only other booking is the Benfords at 9.30pm for 2 people. They're smokers so they can have table 7. I hope we have some more customers between 8pm and 9.30pm, but Saturday night is normally busy, so I'm sure we will.

Answers

Exercise 1a

1 12pm - 2pm / 7pm - 9pm
2 Fortini's Restaurant
3 01332 242464
4 Wrexham
5 The Shalimar Indian Restaurant

Exercise 1c

1 Royal Country Restaurant
2 Fortini's Restaurant
3 Jasmin Garden Chinese Restaurant
4 Shalimar Indian Restaurant

Exercise 2b

6.00	Mr Nixon	(4 people)	Table 14
6.30	Walkers	(4 people)	Table 8
	Johnsons	(2 people)	Table 1
7.00	Taylors	(4 people)	Table 4
7.30	Mr Armstrong	(5 people)	Table 5
	Miss Brown	(6 people)	Table 10
8.00	Bell	(2 people)	Table 2 or 11
8.30	-		
9.00	-		
9.30	Benfords	(2 people)	Table 7

Exercise 2c

1 Mr Armstrong
2 Yes
3 Yes
4 6
5 9.30pm

Exercise 3a

1 The prawn cocktail is more expensive than the pate.
The pate is cheaper than the prawn cocktail.
2 The ice cream is cheaper than the apple crumble.
The apple crumble is more expensive than the ice cream.
3 The lamb is the same price as the beef.
4 The lamb is cheaper than the turkey.
The turkey is more expensive than the lamb.
5 The Liebfraumilch is more expensive than the Lambrusco.
The Lambrusco is cheaper than the Liebfraumilch.

1

UNIT 18

Eating In

1 a **Match the words and the pictures.**

3 casserole dish
___ frying pan
___ kettle
___ pot
___ saucepan
___ roasting tray

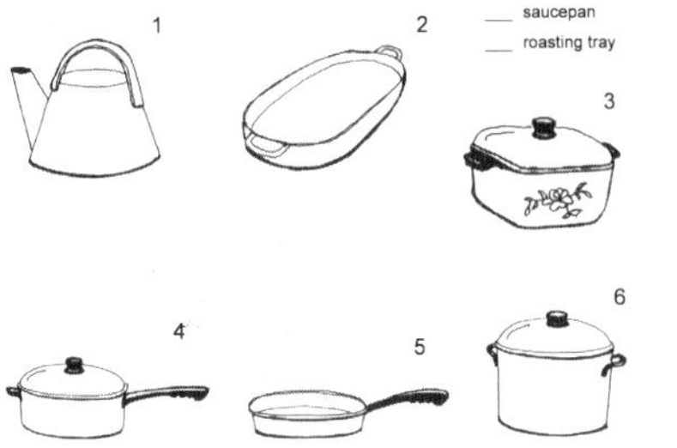

Check with your teacher.

b **Answer the following questions using the words from 1a.**

eg *Which would you use to roast a chicken? A roasting tray.*

1 Which would you use to fry potatoes? ____________
2 Which would you use to boil water? ____________
3 Which would you use to make a cheese sauce? ____________
4 Which would you use to boil potatoes? ____________
5 Which would you use to make a chicken casserole? ____________

Check with your neighbour.

c **Ask your neighbour these questions.**

1 Have you ever visited people in another country?
2 Did they prepare a typical meal for you?
3 How many courses did it have?
4 What did they make?
5 Did you enjoy it?

d **Discuss with your neighbour.**

1 What is a typical meal for your country?
2 How many courses does a typical meal have?
3 How would you make it?
4 What do you normally drink with it?
5 Which pots/pans would you use?

2

2 a **Match the abbreviations and the words.**

lb g tblsp tsp ml fl oz $^1/_2$ $^1/_3$

1 tablespoon *tblsp* 2 pound ___ 3 millilitre ___ 4 fluid ounces ___
5 teaspoon ___ 6 gram ___ 7 a half ___ 8 a third ___

b **Look at the recipe for tomato and basil soup.**

- Tomato and Basil Soup -

Ingredients

1½ lb (700g) tomatoes (chopped in quarters)
1 medium onion (chopped small)
1 medium potato (chopped small)
1½ tblsp olive oil
10 fl oz (275ml) stock
1 clove garlic (crushed)
1 tsp dried basil
salt and pepper

Instructions

1 Heat the oil in a saucepan.
2 Add the onion and potato and soften them slowly. This takes 10 - 15 minutes.
3 Add the tomatoes, stir well and let them cook for one minute. Pour in the stock and stir. Add the basil, salt and pepper and crushed garlic. Cover and leave to simmer for 25 minutes. Taste to check before serving.

c **Answer the following questions.**

eg *How much basil do you need? 1 teaspoon.*

1 What do you have to do first? ____________
2 How much oil do you need? ____________
3 Do the tomatoes have to be crushed? ____________
4 Do you add the tomatoes before the stock? ____________
5 How many millilitres is 10 fluid ounces? ____________

d **Look at the instructions below and answer these questions.**

eg *What is this? It's an instant soup.*

1 What do you do first? ____________
2 Do you need a pan? ____________
3 How much water do you add? ____________
4 Do you need a spoon? ____________
5 What flavour is it? ____________

Cream of Tomato Soup
Instant Cup Soup
Instructions for Use
1 Empty packet into cup or mug.
2 Pour on $^1/_3$ pint (190ml) of boiling water.
3 Stir well.

e **Ask your neighbour**

eg *Do you prefer home-made soup or instant soup? Why?*

f **Tell your teacher about yourself.**

eg *I prefer home-made soup because it tastes better.*

3

3 a **Look at the information and ask your teacher about food you don't know.**

Good Luck Food Palace
12 Marine Parade, Leeds, LS1 7JH
(0113) 2573157
Takeaway
We are open during Chinese New Year
Home Deliveries available
Telephone orders welcome

Duck Dishes	
Roast Duck with Mushrooms	£4.25
Roast Duck with Pineapple	£4.25
Chicken Dishes	
Fried Chicken with Pineapple	£3.25
Fried Chicken with Lemon Sauce	£3.65
Beef Dishes	
Fried Beef with Onion	£3.25
Fried Beef with Mushrooms	£3.25
Pork Dishes	
Fried Pork with Pineapple	£3.25
Fried Pork Chinese Style	£3.45
Set Meal for 2 Persons	£16.00

Joe's Fish 'n' Chip Shop
17 Ashford Road, Kendal
Tel 01539 243941
Open
Mon - Sat 11.30am - 1.30pm
Mon - Sat 4.30pm - 9.30pm
Closed on Sundays
Telephone your orders and they'll be ready for collection.

Cod & Chips	£2.25
Scampi & Chips	£2.25
Fishcake & Chips	£2.10
Steak 'n' Kidney Pie	£1.60
Chicken 'n' Mushroom Pie	£1.50
Sausage	£1.20
Portion of Chips	60p
Extra Portions	
Curry Sauce	50p
Mushy Peas	50p

Francesca's Italian Takeaway
Open 7 days a week
143 South Street, Perth
Tel 01738 667829
Delivery Service Available
no extra charge

Pizzas	10"	12"	Pastas	
Margherita	£2.80	£4.00	*Spaghetti Marinara*	£4.30
Cheese & Tomato			Tomato Sauce & Seafood	
Romana	£3.20	£4.70	*Lasagne*	£3.30
Cheese, Tomato & Ham			Freshly Made	
Funghi	£3.00	£4.70	*Tagliatelle al Tonno*	£4.20
Cheese, Tomato & Mushroom			Tomato Sauce & Tuna	

Diwan-E-Kash
4/5 County Mills, Edinburgh
Tel 0131 606575
Takeaway Menu
15% Discount
Open daily
12 noon to 1.45pm / 6pm to 11.15pm
Sunday 6.30pm to 10.30pm

Poppadom	35p
Bhuna Beef Served with a special blend of spices - medium hot	£4.90
Balti Gosth Tender diced lamb - very spicy	£5.70
Chicken Vindaloo Very hot	£4.30
Lamb Korma Cooked with fresh cream and coconut - very mild	£4.90

b **Answer the following questions.**

eg *How much is curry sauce? It's 50p.*

1 How much is cod & chips? ____________
2 Is roast duck with mushrooms cheaper than fried beef with mushrooms? ____________
3 What is the area code for Leeds? ____________
4 How much is steak 'n' kidney pie and a portion of chips? ____________
5 What is on a pizza fungi? ____________

c **Ask your neighbour 5 more questions.**

eg *What's the name of the Chinese restaurant? The Good Luck Food Palace.*

d **Practise ordering a takeaway meal with your neighbour.**

eg *Hello, I'd like to order a pizza Romana, 12 inch please.*
Will you collect it or would you like it delivered?
I'll collect it in half an hour.
Okay, what's the name?
Simon Rogers.
Fine, see you soon.
Bye.

4

4 a **Translate the following.**

Vocabulary

casserole dish ____	salt ____
frying pan ____	pepper ____
pot ____	chopped ____
saucepan ____	crushed ____
roasting tray ____	dried ____
tablespoon ____	to heat ____
pound ____	to add ____
millilitre ____	to soften ____
fluid ounce ____	slowly ____
teaspoon ____	to stir ____
gram ____	to simmer ____
to roast ____	delivery service ____
to fry ____	takeaway ____
courses ____	available ____
recipe ____	no extra charge ____
tomatoes ____	closed on Sundays ____
onion ____	discount ____
potato ____	spice ____
olive oil ____	mild ____
stock ____	medium ____
garlic ____	cream ____
basil ____	coconut ____

- Structures

Which would you use to roast a chicken? ____________
A roasting tray. ____________
How much basil do you need? ____________
1 teaspoon. ____________
What is this? ____________
It's an instant soup. ____________
Do you prefer home-made soup or packet soup? ____________
I prefer home-made soup because it tastes better. ____________
How much is curry sauce? It's 50p. ____________
What's the name of the Chinese restaurant? ____________
I'd like to order a pizza. ____________
I'll collect it in half an hour. ____________
What's the name? ____________

Teaching Notes

Warm-up

Ask students questions from earlier Units eg "What can you remember about Roger Regular?" Tell me about your normal day. What does your neighbour normally do in the evenings?"

Revision

Revise all the structures and vocabulary from the previous Unit by asking students questions eg "When was the last time you were in a restaurant? What did you eat? Would you recommend the restaurant?"

Presentation and Practice

1 Introduce 1a by asking students what they use to cook.

Students then complete the matching task in 1a. Elicit what you do with the different kinds of cooking utensils and then students complete 1b.

Students compare their work with their neighbour. Students ask their neighbour the questions in 1c while you monitor and help. Provide feedback by students telling you about their neighbour.

Students work in pairs and complete the speaking activity in 1d. Provide feedback by pairs telling you what they would make and how they would make it.

2 Students try and complete the matching task in 2a while you monitor and check.

Ask if anyone knows how to make tomato soup. Ask them which ingredients they use and how they make it.

Students then read the page from a recipe book and answer the questions in 2c. Students look at the instructions for making an instant tomato soup and answer the questions.

In pairs students complete the speaking activity in 2e. In 2f students tell you about themselves.

3 Students read through the information in 3a before answering the questions in 3b. Check students work by asking one pair to ask and answer the questions from 3b.

In pairs students then complete the speaking activity in 3c.

Demonstrate the roleplay in 3d with one student and then in pairs students practise the dialogue. Provide feedback by asking pairs to demonstrate their activity.

Revise all the structures and vocabulary before moving on to the next lesson.

At home students prepare for the next lesson by looking up the vocabulary in 4a of Unit 19.

Answers

Exercise 1a

1 kettle
2 roasting tray
3 casserole dish
4 saucepan
5 frying pan
6 pot

Exercise 1b

1 A frying pan.
2 A kettle.
3 A saucepan.
4 A pot.
5 A casserole dish.

Exercise 2a

1 tblsp
2 lb
3 ml
4 fl oz
5 tsp
6 g
7 $^1/_2$
8 $^1/_3$

Exercise 2c

1 Heat the oil in a saucepan.
2 $1^1/_2$ tablespoons oil.
3 No, chopped.
4 Yes.
5 275 millilitres.

Exercise 2d

1 Empty packet into a cup or mug.
2 No.
3 $^1/_3$ pint / 190 millilitres.
4 Yes, to stir.
5 Tomato.

Exercise 3b

1 £2.25
2 No.
3 0113
4 £2.20
5 Cheese, tomato and mushroom

1

UNIT 19

A pint of beer please.

1 a **Read the following text.**

In England and Wales pubs can only open between 11am (opening time) and 11pm (closing time). If you go to a pub you will hear the owner (landlord) shouting "last orders please" at 10.50pm. When you hear this you have 10 minutes to order your last drink of the evening. At 11pm the landlord will shout "time please". When you hear this you may not order any more drinks, however, you do have 20 minutes to enjoy your last drink. This time is called "drinking up time". The pubs in England and Wales are normally empty by 11.30pm. In Scotland pubs can open for 12 hours maximum, but there is no legal closing, or opening time. Most pubs all over Britain serve food as well (bar snacks) and normally offer hot meals as well as sandwiches. In fact many pubs in Britain serve excellent food.

b **Ask your neighbour.**

eg *What is "opening time"? It's when pubs open.*

1 Who is the landlord?
2 How long is "drinking up time"?
3 What are the differences between pubs in England and Scotland?
4 When does the landlord shout "time please"?
5 Do most pubs serve food as well?

c **Ask your neighbour.**

eg *What would you like to drink?*
I'd like a gin and tonic please.
Ice and lemon?
Yes please.
Anything else?
A glass of coke please.
Ice and lemon?
No thanks. How much is that?
That's £2.60.
Here you are.
Thanks and here's your change.

d **Practise the dialogue with your neighbour.**

The Globe Inn
24 Stamford Road, Oakleigh

Price List

Lager	pint	£1.60	Vodka	£1.30
	half	£0.80	Gin	£1.30
Bitter	pint	£1.60	Whisky	£1.20
	half	£0.80	Coke half	£0.80
Cider	pint	£1.50	Fruit Juice	£0.85
	half	£0.75	Glass of Wine	£0.90
Peanuts		£0.40	Mixers	£0.50
Crisps		£0.40	*(tonic, lemonade, etc)*	

All prices include VAT @ 17.5%

2

2 a **Match the definition and the phrases and then check with your teacher.**

eg *What is happy hour?*
Happy hour is an hour (or more) when drinks are cheaper than normal.

Happy hour is... ____
Quiz night is... ____
Karaoke is... ____
Darts is... ____
A double is... ____

1 An idea from Japan. People can sing their favourite songs to background music. The best singers can win prizes.
2 A game where people throw darts at a board on the wall.
3 An evening when groups of people answer questions on different topics. There are often prizes.
4 An hour (or more) when drinks are cheaper than normal.
5 Two normal measures of spirits (eg whisky, gin, vodka)

b **Look at the notices and answer the questions below.**

eg *When is karaoke night? It's on Saturday 14.*

Darts Competition
Tuesday 17
Entry Free

Karaoke night
Saturday 14
8pm onwards
All welcome
Prizes to be Won

Quiz Night
every Friday night
8pm
£3 per team entry
Prizes up to £10

Bar Snacks
Open Daily
Lunchtime 12pm - 2.30pm
Evenings 5pm - 8.30pm
Kiddies Menu available

Happy Hour
5.30pm - 6.30pm
Thursday - Sunday
All Pints 95p
Doubles for the price of singles

1 What time does happy hour start? ____
2 What time do they stop serving bar snacks in the evening? ____
3 How much can a team win on quiz night? ____
4 Can I get a bar snack at Sunday lunchtime? ____
5 How much is a pint during happy hour? ____

Check with your teacher.

c **Ask your neighbour.**

eg *What's happening on Tuesday 17? It's darts night.*

1 How often is the quiz night?
2 What time does the karaoke night start?
3 Is a double the same price as a single during happy hour?
4 Are there any prizes on the karaoke evening?
5 Do I have to pay to enter the darts competition?

Check with your teacher.

d **Ask your neighbour.**

1 Do you have happy hour in your country?
2 Have you every played darts?
3 What pub games do people play in your country?

e **Tell your teacher.**

3

3 a **You are going to take part in a pub quiz. Work in groups of 3. Make up a name for your team.**

Listen to the questions on the cassette and write down the answers. You may discuss these in your group and you may listen to the question 3 times. Your teacher will check your answers at the end of each section (answers must be in English).

QUIZ CARD

Name of Team ____

House and Home	Transport and Travel	Food and Drink
1 ____	1 ____	1 ____
2 ____	2 ____	2 ____
3 ____	3 ____	3 ____
4 ____	4 ____	4 ____
5 ____	5 ____	5 ____
Total Correct ____	Total Correct ____	Total Correct ____

Environment and Weather	Languages	Sport and Hobbies
1 ____	1 ____	1 ____
2 ____	2 ____	2 ____
3 ____	3 ____	3 ____
4 ____	4 ____	4 ____
5 ____	5 ____	5 ____
Total Correct ____	Total Correct ____	Total Correct ____

Now add up your score to find your final total.

Final Total ____

Which group has the most correct answers?

b **Work in groups of 3. Each group makes up 5 questions. When you are ready ask the other groups your questions.**

4

4 a **Translate the following.**

Vocabulary

opening time ____
closing time ____
landlord ____
owner ____
last orders ____
time please ____
drinking up time ____
empty ____
legal ____
bar snacks ____
happy hour ____
quiz night ____
karaoke ____
darts ____
competition ____

Structures

What is "opening time"? ____
It's when pubs open. ____
What would you like to drink? ____
I'd like a gin and tonic please. ____
Ice and lemon? ____
Yes please. ____
Anything else? ____
A glass of coke please. ____
How much is that? ____
That's £2.60. ____
What is happy hour? ____
Happy hour is an hour (or more) when drinks are cheaper than normal. ____
When is karaoke night? ____
It's on Saturday 14. ____
What's happening on Tuesday 17? ____
It's darts night. ____

Teaching Notes

Warm-up

Ask students questions from earlier Units eg "What do you do at work in the morning? What is your neighbour wearing?"

Revision

Revise all the structures and vocabulary from the previous Unit by asking students questions eg "How do you make tomato soup?"

Presentation and Practice

1 Find out who has visited Britain and if they went to a pub while they were there. Ask them what they know about pubs, eg opening times, eating possibilities. Students then read the text in 1a and complete the speaking activity in 1b. Demonstrate the roleplay in 1c and then students practise with their neighbour.

2 Students complete the matching activity in 2a while you monitor and check. Students use the information from the adverts to complete the writing activity in 2b as quickly as possible. Provide feedback by asking students to answer the questions. In pairs students then complete the speaking activity in 2c while you monitor and check. Students then discuss the questions in 2d and tell you about themselves in 2e.

3 Explain to students that they are going to do a pub quiz. Put them in groups of 3 and tell them that they will hear the questions on the cassette. They may discuss the answers but have to write the final answer in their books. Play the questions for the first category. Students may hear them 3 times. Check the answers and note down the scores before going on to the next category. When students are finished all the categories add up the points and see which is the winning team. Students then complete the activity in 3b.

Revise all the structures and vocabulary before moving on to the next lesson.

At home students prepare for the next lesson by revising the structures and vocabulary from Units 11 - 19.

Tapescripts

Exercise 3a

House and Home
1 Does a computer have keys or dials?
2 Do you find blocks of flats in the town or in the country?
3 Which room do you sleep in?
4 Would a man or a woman wear a skirt?
5 What do you use to mend clothes?

Transport and Travel
1 Name 1 way of travelling by air.
2 Do trains leave from gates or platforms?
3 Name 1 way of travelling by land.
4 Are departures leaving or arriving?
5 Name 1 way of travelling by water.

Food and Drink
1 What would you use to fry potatoes?
2 What kind of restaurant would you go to if you liked pizza?
3 If a restaurant has a licensed bar, can I get a pint of beer?
4 Name 1 type of vegetable.
5 Name 1 type of fruit.

Environment and Weather
1 Name 1 kind of animal.
2 Where do you go if you want to borrow books?
3 Do you find pedestrian crossings in the town or in the country?
4 Does it normally snow in summer or winter?
5 Is 3° warmer than 10° ?

Languages
1 What language do people speak in Italy?
2 How many letters are there in the alphabet?
3 How do you spell the word scissors?
4 In which European country do people speak French?
5 What language do they speak in Spain?

Sport and hobbies
1 Name 1 sport which you need boots for.
2 Where do you go if you want to learn to swim?
3 Which hobby do you need a lifejacket for?
4 What do you need if you want to go camping?
5 Which sport do you need a rod and bait for?

Answers

Exercise 2a

Happy hour is	4
Quiz night is	3
Karaoke is	1
Darts is	2
A double is	5

Exercise 3a

House and Home
1 keys
2 In the town.
3 A bedroom.
4 A woman.
5 A sewing machine.

Transport and Travel
1 Aeroplane, jumbo jet, helicopter, hot-air balloon. (Any form of travelling by air accepted)
2 Platforms
3 Car, train, bus, pick-up truck, bicycle. (Any form of travelling by land accepted)
4 Leaving
5 Boat, sailing ship, hovercraft, ferry. (Any form of travelling by water accepted)

Exercise 2b

1 5.30pm
2 8.30pm
3 up to £10
4 Yes
5 95p

Food and Drink
1 A frying pan.
2 An Italian Restaurant.
3 Yes.
4 (Any vegetable accepted)
5 (Any fruit accepted)

Environment and weather
1 (Any animal accepted)
2 A Library.
3 In the town.
4 In winter.
5 No.

Languages
1 Italian
2 26
3 scissors
4 France (or Belgium)
5 Spanish

Sport
1 (Any sport needing boots accepted)
2 Swimming pool.
3 Sailing.
4 A tent.
5 Fishing.

1

UNIT 20

Revision

1 a **Ask your neighbour these questions.**

1 What means of transport would you use to go on holiday to Britain? Why?
2 What means of transport would you use to go shopping? Why?
3 What means of transport would you use to go on holiday to America? Why?
4 What means of transport would you use to move house? Why?
5 What means of transport do you use to go to your English lesson? Why?
6 Do you like travelling by train? Why (not)?
7 Do you like travelling by motorbike? Why (not)?
8 Do you like travelling by plane? Why (not)?
9 Do you like travelling by bicycle? Why (not)?
10 Do you like travelling by ship? Why (not)?

2 a **Now tell your neighbour about the best holiday you've ever had. Use the following questions as a guide.**

1 Where did you go?
2 How long were you there?
3 Did you stay in one place or travel around?
4 What was the accommodation like?
5 Who did you go with?
6 What did you see?
7 How did you get there?
8 What was the weather like?
9 Why was it the best holiday you've ever had?
10 Would you go back again?

3 a **Ask your neighbour these questions.**

1 Have you ever travelled by air?
2 How often do you travel by air?
3 Do you like flying?
4 What was your best flight?
5 What was your worst flight?

b **Look at the information and ask your neighbour about the flights.**

eg *Has the plane from Athens arrived yet? Yes it has.*

ARRIVALS					Time Now 08:10
Flight Number	Scheduled Arrival Time	Estimated Arrival Time	Landed Time	Arriving From	Flight Information
GA 247	08:00	07:55	07:55	ATHENS	Baggage in Hall
SA 495	08:05	08:05	08:05	MADRID	Landed
IA 297	08:10	08:45	______	DUBLIN	Delayed
DA 373	08:15	08:15	______	FRANKFURT	On Time
IT 444	08:20	08:30	______	ROME	Delayed

c **Now ask your neighbour questions like this.**

eg *Has flight number DA373 been delayed? No it hasn't. It's on time.*

d **Tell your neighbour the status of each flight.**

eg *Flight GA247 has already landed and the baggage is in the baggage hall.*

2

4 a **Ask your neighbour 10 questions about the bank and public holidays below.**

eg *When is Spring Bank Holiday?*
What is August 26?

Bank and Public Holidays		
New Year's Day	Mon	Jan 1
Good Friday	Fri	Apr 5
Easter Monday	Mon	Apr 8
May Day Holiday	Mon	May 6
Spring Bank Holiday	Mon	May 27
Summer Bank Holiday	Mon	Aug 26
Christmas Day	Wed	Dec 25
Boxing Day	Thu	Dec 26

b **Look at the timetable below and ask your neighbour 5 questions.**

eg *What time does the 0800 train arrive in Corbridge?*
Does the 0907 train run on bank holidays?

Newcastle - Hexham

	x	+	o	+	*	o	*	+	*	*	+
Newcastle	0700	0725	0800	0815	..07	1610	1645	1705	1845	1905	2300
Dunstable	0705	0730	0805	|	..12	1615	1650	|	1850	1910	2305
Metro Centre	0710	0735	0810	|	..17	1620	1655	|	1855	1915	2310
Blaydon	0715	0740	0815	|	..22	1625	1700	|	1900	1920	2315
Wylam	0720	0745	0820	|	..27	1630	1705	|	1905	1925	2320
Prudhoe	0725	0750	0825	|	..32	1635	1710	|	1910	1930	2325
Stocksfield	0730	0755	0830	|	..37	1640	1715	|	1915	1935	2330
Corbridge	0735	0800	0835	|	..42	1645	1720	|	1920	1940	2335
Hexham	0740	0805	0840	0835	..47	1650	1725	1725	1925	1945	2340

Bank and Public Holidays

x every day, except Sunday + only weekdays o every day, including bank holidays * every day, except bank holidays

5 a **Ask your neighbour these questions.**

1 Which means of transport do you think is the most comfortable? Why?
2 Which means of transport do you think is the safest? Why?
3 Which means of transport do you think is the most convenient? Why?
4 Which means of transport do you think is the most enjoyable? Why?
5 Which means of transport do you think is the most environmentally friendly? Why?

b **Note down one advantage and one disadvantage of each of these means of transport and then compare with your neighbour. See if you agree or disagree.**

	advantages	disadvantages
cars		
buses		
trains		
motorbikes		
ships		

3

5 c **Read these statements and discuss with your neighbour whether you agree or disagree.**

1 The driving test in my country is too easy.
2 Public transport is too expensive.
3 There are too many cars on the road.
4 People would not use cars if petrol was more expensive.
5 I always take public transport if I can.

6 a **Read these questions and say how often you do these things using always, usually, sometimes, seldom, never.**

1 How often do you do eat at home? ______________
2 How often do you go shopping? ______________
3 How often do you cook for yourself? ______________
4 How often do you eat frozen food? ______________
5 How often do you eat from tins or packets? ______________
6 How often do you eat the same thing? ______________

Tell your neighbour about yourself.

b **Here are 5 items which you can buy in a supermarket. Tell your neighbour why you would buy them and what you would do with them.**

eg *I would buy milk to make a sauce or to put on my cornflakes or to drink.*

1 butter 2 apples 3 toothpaste 4 tomatoes 5 shampoo

7 a **Here is an advertisement for the Royal Country Restaurant.**

Ask your neighbour 5 questions about it.

eg *What is the area code?*

Royal Country Restaurant

24 Markington Place
Stratford-upon-Avon
Tel 01789 516437

Traditional English Dishes
Sunday Lunches
Roast Beef and Yorkshire Pudding £5.25

Opening Times:
Mon - Sat 12pm - 2pm / 6.30pm - 10pm
Sun 12pm - 2pm / 7pm - 9pm

b **Now ask your neighbour these questions.**

1 When was the last time you were in a restaurant?
2 Who were you with?
3 Where did you go?
4 What did you eat?
5 Would you recommend the restaurant?

4

8 a **Answer these questions and then compare with your neighbour.**

1 What would you use a frying pan for? ______________
2 What would you use a kettle for? ______________
3 What would you use a saucepan for? ______________
4 What would you use a roasting tray for? ______________
5 What would you use a casserole dish for? ______________

b **Look at the advertisement below and ask your neighbour 5 questions about the information.**

eg *Is the restaurant open on Sunday?*

Francesca's Italian Takeaway

Open 7 days a week
11.30am - 11.00pm

143 South Street, Perth, PH1 8TW
Tel 01738 667829
Fax 01738 167888

Delivery Service Available
no extra charge

9 a **Here are some words and phrases to do with pubs. Try and explain them to your neighbour.**

1 opening times
2 landlord
3 closing time
4 last orders
5 bar snacks

10 a **You are going to tell your neighbour about yourself now. Try and keep talking for at least 4 minutes. Here are some ideas to help you.**

- the best holiday you have ever had
- advantages and disadvantages of public transport in your town
- what you normally buy in the supermarket and why
- what you normally eat
- the last time you were in a restaurant
- your best and worst flight

Teaching Notes

Warm-up

Ask students questions from earlier Units eg "How do you make a cup of coffee? What are the disadvantages of travelling by bicycle?"

Presentation and Practice

1 In pairs students complete the speaking activity in 1a while you monitor and check. Provide feedback by asking students to tell you about their neighbour.

2 Students tell their neighbour about the best holiday they have ever had based on the questions in 2a. Provide feedback by asking students to tell you about their neighbour.

3 In pairs students complete the speaking activity in 3a while you monitor and check.

In 3b and 3c students ask their neighbour questions about the flight information.

In 3d students tell their neighbour the status of each flight.

4 In 4a students ask and answer questions about the bank and public holidays shown. Provide feedback by asking pairs to demonstrate their activity.

Students then complete the speaking activity in 4b based on the timetable given while you monitor and check.

5 Students complete the speaking activity in 5a and go on to the activity in 5b while you monitor and check.

In pairs students read the statements in 5c and discuss their opinion with their neighbour. Provide feedback by asking students for their opinion.

6 Students answer the questions in 6a before discussing their answers with their neighbour while you monitor and check.

In 6b students tell their neighbour why they would buy these items and what they would do with them. Provide feedback by asking students to tell you what they would use the ingredients for.

7 In 7a students ask their neighbour questions based on the advert shown. They then complete the speaking activity in 7b while you monitor and check.

8 In 8a students answer the questions before comparing their work with their neighbour.

In 8b students ask and answer questions about the advert shown. Provide feedback by asking pairs to demonstrate their activity.

9 In pairs students try and explain the words and phrases given in 9a. Provide feedback by asking students to explain the phrases to the rest of the class.

10 Students practise fluency in this exercise. Students tell their neighbour about themselves based on the ideas in 10a. Tell students when 4 minutes is up so that every student speaks for 4 minutes. Provide feedback by asking students to tell the rest of the class about themselves.

At home students prepare for the next lesson by looking up the vocabulary in 4a of Unit 21.

Answers

Exercise 8a

1 To fry potatoes.
2 To boil water.
3 To make a cheese sauce.
4 To roast a chicken.
5 To make a chicken casserole.

1

UNIT 21

Rubbish and Recycling

1 a **Match the objects and the words.**

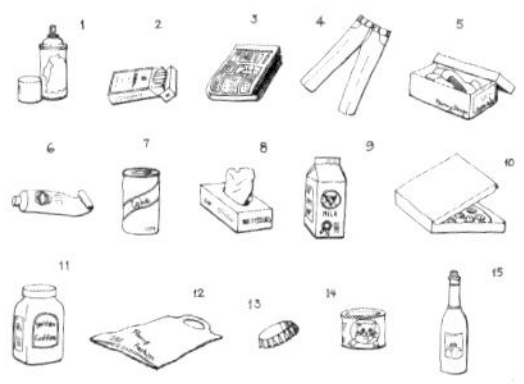

2 cigarette packet
___ tissues
___ jar
___ trousers
___ bottle
___ can
___ bottle top
___ tin
___ aerosol can
___ shoe box
___ plastic bag
___ newspaper
___ carton
___ tube of toothpaste
___ pizza box

Check with your neighbour.

b **Which of these can you recycle? Put the objects in the correct places.**

Non-recyclable items: ____________

c **What do you do with your empty cans? Put a tick (✓) in the correct box.**

I throw them away ☐ I take them to a recycling bank ☐ I use them again ☐

d **Ask your neighbour.**

1 What do you do with your empty bottles?
2 What do you do with your old newspapers?
3 What do you do with your old clothes?
4 What do you do with your empty tins?
5 What do you do with your plastic bags?

e **Fill in the following.**

1 Is your household rubbish collected? ____________
2 How often is it collected? ____________
3 Who collects it? ____________
4 Where is it collected from? ____________
5 Where does it go to? ____________

f **Ask your neighbour.**

2

2 a **Did you know...?**

1 The average European family throws away 50 kilograms of paper per year.
2 The average European family throws away 60 kilograms of metal per year.
3 The average European family throws away 45 kilograms of plastic per year.

Do you think your family throws away more or less? ____________

b **What did you throw away last week?** ....

Fill in the following about yourself.
eg *2 cans, 3 tins, 2 jars.*

	you	your neighbour
drink cans	....	....
food tins	....	....
jars	....	....
bottles	....	....
newspapers	....	....
cartons	....	....
tissues	....	....
cigarette packets	....	....
plastic bags	....	....
pizza boxes	....	....

c **Ask your neighbour and fill in the information** ....

d **If you multiply these numbers by 52 you will find out how many of each object your neighbour throws away per year (approximately!).**

1 How many cans does your neighbour throw away per year? ____________
2 How many tins does your neighbour throw away per year? ____________
3 How many jars does your neighbour throw away per year? ____________
4 How many bottles does your neighbour throw away per year? ____________
5 How many newspapers does your neighbour throw away per year? ____________
6 How many cartons does your neighbour throw away per year? ____________
7 How many tissues does your neighbour throw away per year? ____________
8 How many cigarette packets does your neighbour throw away per year? ____________
9 How many plastic bags does your neighbour throw away per year? ____________
10 How many pizza boxes does your neighbour throw away per year? ____________

Find out who throws the most away and who throws the least away.

3

3 a **Match the descriptions and the words.**

1 I put rubbish in these.
2 I need this to tie parcels up.
3 I need this when I go to the toilet.
4 I use this to kill flies.
5 I take these when I have a headache.
6 I use this to keep my furniture clean.
7 I need these when I cut myself.
8 I need this to make my hair stay in the same place.
9 I use this to decorate my flat.
10 I use this to wash my clothes.

5 headache tablets
___ bin bags
___ plasters
___ wallpaper
___ toilet paper
___ furniture polish
___ washing powder
___ string
___ hairspray
___ fly spray

b **Ask your neighbour.**

eg *What do you need headache tablets for? You need them when you have a headache.*

c **Put the words in 3a in the correct category. What do you buy them in?**

Packet *eg headache tablets* **Roll** ____________ **Can** ____________

d **You are in a shop. Look at the price list and ask your neighbour.**

eg *Can I have a packet of washing powder please?*
Yes of course. Here you are. Anything else?
No thank you.
That's £1.92 please.

Price List

tablets	£1.30
bin bags	£1.99
plasters	72p
washing powder	£1.92
hairspray	99p
wallpaper	£2.85
toilet paper	32p
furniture polish	99p
string	£1.08
fly spray	£1.29

e **You buy chocolates in a box, orange juice in a carton and shampoo in a bottle. What else do you buy in boxes, cartons and bottles?**

List 2 things.

boxes ____________ ____________
cartons ____________ ____________
bottles ____________ ____________

f **Read through the questionnaire. Make sure you understand the questions, then fill in your answers.**

Questionnaire

		yes	*it depends*	*no*
1	When you go shopping, do you take a bag with you?	☐	☐	☐
2	Do you think supermarkets should give plastic bags free of charge?	☐	☐	☐
3	Do you buy products in refillable containers?	☐	☐	☐
4	Do you buy brand products?	☐	☐	☐
5	Do you think packaging is a waste of money?	☐	☐	☐

g **Ask your neighbour the questions, then ask why or why not.**

eg *When you go shopping do you take a bag with you?*
Yes, because it's easier to carry my shopping home.

4

4 a **Translate the following.**

Vocabulary

cigarette packet ____________
tissues ____________
jar ____________
bottle ____________
can ____________
bottle top ____________
tin ____________
aerosol can ____________
shoe box ____________
plastic bag ____________
carton ____________
tube ____________
to recycle ____________
bottle bank ____________
save-a-can bank ____________
textile bank ____________
paper bank ____________
non-recyclable items ____________
to throw away ____________
household rubbish ____________
average ____________
to tie up ____________
parcels ____________
flies ____________
to decorate ____________
headache tablets ____________
bin bags ____________
plasters ____________
wallpaper ____________
toilet paper ____________
furniture polish ____________
washing powder ____________
string ____________
hairspray ____________
fly spray ____________
packet ____________
roll ____________
it depends ____________
free of charge ____________
refillable ____________
containers ____________
brand products ____________
packaging ____________
waste of money ____________

Structures

I throw my empty bottles away. ____________
I take my empty bottles to a recycling bank. ____________
I use my empty bottles again. ____________
What do you need headache tablets for? ____________
You need them when you have a headache. ____________
Can I have a packet of washing powder please? ____________
Yes of course. ____________
Here you are. ____________
Anything else? ____________
No thank you. ____________
That's £1.92 please. ____________
Can I have a roll of bin bags please? ____________
Can I have a can of hairspray please? ____________
When you go shopping do you take a bag with you? ____________
Yes, because it's easier to carry my shopping home. ____________

Teaching Notes

Warm-up
Ask students questions from earlier Units eg "How do you get to work everyday? What do you think is the most environmentally-friendly means of transport?"

Presentation and Practice
1 Ask your students what rubbish they throw out at work every day and what rubbish they throw out at home every day, helping with vocabulary where necessary.

Students complete the matching task in 1a and compare their work with their neighbour.

Students then work in pairs to decide which of the items are recyclable and write the name of the item in the appropriate 'bank' in 1b. Provide feedback by asking one student to tell you where he/she has put the items. Students then tick the appropriate box in 1c. In pairs students complete the speaking activity in 1d while you monitor and check. Students answer the questions in 1e before asking their neighbour in 1f.

2 Students read the 3 questions in 2a and answer whether they think their family throws away more or less rubbish per year. Students then fill in the chart about themselves before asking their neighbour and noting down his/her answers in the column marked 'your neighbour'.

Students then complete the activity in 2d and tell you who throws away the most and who throws away the least rubbish per year.

3 If possible bring the items from 3a with you to the lesson. Introduce the objects by asking students if they know what they are and what you do with them. Elicit as much information as you can about the objects.

Students then complete the matching exercise in 3a while you monitor and check. In pairs students then complete the speaking activity in 3b.

Introduce the words packet, roll and can and then students put the words from 3a in the category they think is correct. Before students complete the speaking activity in 3d ask students questions about the price list eg "How much is the hairspray?"

Demonstrate the speaking activity from 3d with one student and then students continue with their neighbour. When students have completed the task in 3e provide feedback by asking students to tell you what they have written.

Introduce the activity in 3f by telling students about yourself. They then complete the questionnaire about themselves.

Students then complete the speaking activity in 3g. Provide feedback by pairs demonstrating their speaking activity to the rest of the class.

Revise all the structures and vocabulary before moving on to the next lesson.

At home students prepare for the next lesson by looking up the vocabulary in 4a of Unit 22.

Answers

Exercise 1a

1 aerosol can
2 cigarette packet
3 newspaper
4 trousers
5 shoe box
6 tube of toothpaste
7 can
8 tissues
9 carton
10 pizza box
11 jar
12 plastic bag
13 bottle top
14 tin
15 bottle

Exercise 1b

Bottle Bank
bottle
jar

Save-a-Can Bank
can
bottle top
tin

Textile Bank
trousers

Paper Bank
cigarette packet
tissues
shoe box
newspaper
pizza box
carton

Non recyclable items
aerosol can
plastic bag
tube of toothpaste

Exercise 3a

1 bin bags
2 string
3 toilet paper
4 fly spray
5 headache tablets
6 furniture polish
7 plasters
8 hairspray
9 wallpaper
10 washing powder

Exercise 3c

Packet	Roll	Can
headache tablets	bin bags	furniture polish
plasters	wallpaper	hairspray
washing powder	toilet paper	fly spray
	string	

1

UNIT 22

Where can you buy a safety pin?

1 a Match the objects and the words.

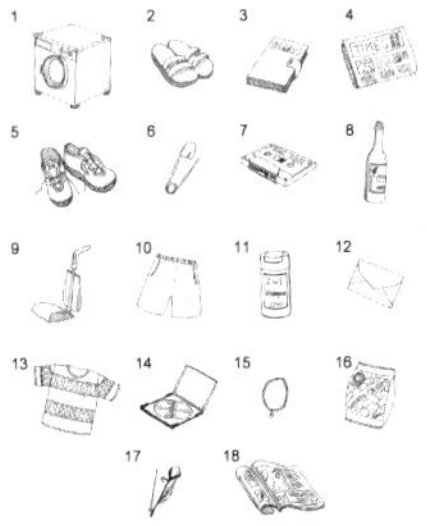

_6_ safety pin
___ brooch
___ washing machine
___ T-shirt
___ cassette
___ envelope
___ CD
___ newspaper
___ bottle of wine
___ necklace
___ vacuum cleaner
___ magazine
___ trainers
___ shorts
___ sandals
___ shampoo
___ crisps
___ diary

Check with your neighbour.

b Put the objects where you would buy them.

Electrical Shop	Jeweller's	Music Shop
eg washing machine		
Chemist's	**Shoe Shop**	**Stationer's**
Clothes Shop	**Off-Licence**	**Newsagent's**

c Ask your neighbour.

eg *Where can you buy a safety pin? You can buy a safety pin at a chemist's.*

Think of one other item which you can buy in each of these shops.

d Ask your neighbour about these items.

eg *Where can you buy a pair of boots? In a shoe shop.*

2

2 a Put the words in one of these categories.

flowers
petrol
socks
jewellery
magazine
birthday card
sticky tape
whisky
handbag
chocolate
shoes
coat
CD
hairdryer
newspaper
maps
plants
diary
iron
perfume
belt
wrapping paper
cassette
envelopes
beer
books

I know what these words mean.

I think I know what these words mean.

I don't know what these words mean.

b Compare your list with your neighbour's and look up the words you don't know.

c Fill in the following. Tick (✓) the boxes to show what you can buy in each shop (you may tick more than 1 box).

	flowers	socks	jewellery	magazine	birthday card	sticky tape	whisky	handbag	shoes	coat	chocolate	hairdryer	CD	plants	maps	newspaper	iron	diary	perfume	belt	wrapping paper	cassette	envelopes	beer	books	petrol
newsagent's																										
garage																										
off-licence																										
stationer's																										
chemist's																										
book shop																										
music shop																										
electrical shop																										
shoe shop																										
clothes shop																										
florist's																										
jeweller's																										

d Ask your neighbour.

eg *Where can you buy flowers? You can buy them in a garage or a florist's.*

e Tell your neighbour about the last time you bought any of these items.

eg *I rarely buy flowers. The last time was for my Mother's birthday. I bought them from a garage because I had forgotten it was her birthday.*

3

3 a You've just arrived at your holiday apartment and the receptionist is telling you about local shopping facilities. Listen to the cassette and note down the names of shops A and F and the opening times. You will hear the cassette twice.

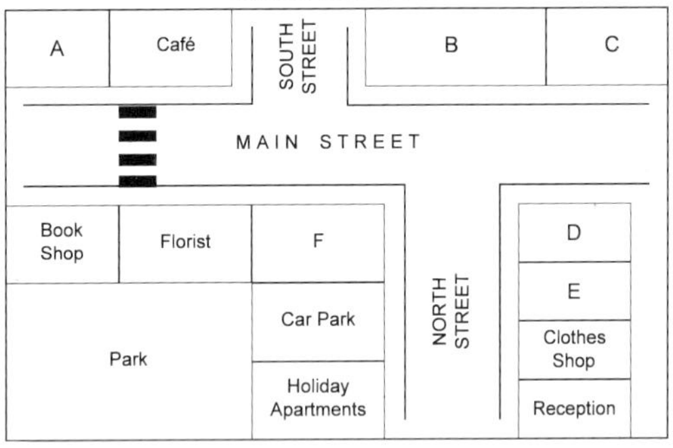

b Now ask your neighbour questions.

eg *What time does the baker's close?*

c Answer the following questions.

1 Which shop has got a red door? ___
2 Is the supermarket cheap? ___
3 Where can you buy postcards? ___
4 Which shop opens at 7.30am? ___
5 Which days does the receptionist work? ___

d Ask your neighbour the following questions.

1 How do I get to the chemist's?
2 Where is the newsagent's?
3 What time does the post office close on Wednesdays?
4 How do I get to the post office?
5 What time does the chemist's close?

e Ask your neighbour 5 more questions.

eg *How do I get to the newsagent's?*
You go down North Street. Turn left at the end. It's on the other side of the road, just after the pedestrian crossing.

f Make a list of 3 things you need from each of the shops. You are the customer and your neighbour is the shop assistant. Your neighbour starts the roleplay.

eg *Hello. Can I help you?*

4

4 a Translate the following.

Vocabulary

safety pin ___	birthday card ___
washing machine ___	sticky tape ___
cassette ___	maps ___
envelope ___	plants ___
CD ___	diary ___
wine ___	perfume ___
magazine ___	belt ___
trainers ___	wrapping paper ___
shampoo ___	beer ___
electrical shop ___	bookshop ___
jeweller's ___	florist's ___
music shop ___	supermarket ___
chemist's ___	baker's ___
shoe shop ___	holiday apartment ___
off-licence ___	receptionist ___
newsagent's ___	shopping facilities ___
stationer's ___	reception ___
clothes shop ___	greengrocer's ___
flowers ___	half-day closing ___
petrol ___	foreign newspapers ___
jewellery ___	

Structures

Where can you buy a safety pin? ___
You can buy a safety pin at a chemist's. ___
Where can you buy a pair of boots? ___
In a shoe shop. ___
Where can you buy flowers? ___
You can buy them in a garage or a florist. ___
I rarely buy flowers. ___
The last time was for my Mother's birthday. ___
I bought them from a garage because I had forgotten it was her birthday. ___

How do I get to the newsagent's? ___
You go down North Street. ___
Turn left at the end. ___
It's on the other side of the road, just after the pedestrian crossing. ___

Teaching Notes

Warm-up

Ask students questions from earlier Units eg "Where do you live? What do use a coat hanger for? Do you have a set of scales? What do you use them for?"

Revision

Revise all the structures and vocabulary from the previous Unit by asking students questions eg "What did you throw away yesterday? What do you use string for? Do you normally buy brand products? What do you do with your old clothes?"

Presentation and Practice

1 Students try and match the pictures and the words. (Some words should be familiar). They then check their work with their neighbour. Provide feedback by asking students eg "What is number 1? Which one is the necklace?" When students are familiar with the words they complete the activity in 1b while you monitor and check.

In 1c students ask their neighbour where they can buy the items. Provide feedback by asking pairs to demonstrate their activity. Students think of one other item and repeat the activity using the new items. Students then ask the rest of the class about their new items.

2 Students read the words in 2a through and put them in the appropriate category. In pairs they compare their work and look up any unknown words. In 2c they put a tick in the box/es to show where you can buy the items while you monitor and check. Students then complete the speaking activity in 2d. Provide feedback by asking pairs to demonstrate their activity.

Introduce 2e by telling students about the last time you bought 5 of these items as in the example. Provide feedback by asking students to tell you about their neighbour.

3 Introduce the activity in 3a by explaining that students have just arrived at a holiday apartment and they are going to hear the receptionist giving them information about local facilities. Before they listen to the cassette ask students about the diagram, eg "Where is B? How do you get from the holiday apartment to A?". Tell students that they will hear the cassette twice so if they do not hear all the information the first time they can listen for it the second time. Students then listen to the cassette twice and complete the task.

Students complete the speaking activity based on their notes while you monitor and check. Provide feedback by students asking the rest of the class their questions. Students then answer the questions in 3c and 3d. Check by asking students the questions.

Demonstrate 3e by asking one student for directions to the newsagent's and then pairs ask each other for directions to the shops while you monitor and check.

Set up the roleplay by asking students to write a list of 3 things they need from the shops. Explain the situation and then students act out the roleplay. Provide feedback by pairs demonstrating their activity to the rest of the class.

Revise all the structures and vocabulary before moving on to the next lesson.

At home students prepare for the next lesson by looking up the vocabulary in 4a of Unit 23.

Tapescripts

Exercise 3a

This is your holiday apartment and here are your keys. If you have any problems, the reception is just across the road, directly opposite the entrance to the flats. I work there on Mondays, Wednesdays and Fridays, but there is somebody there every day between 8.30am and 6pm.

Now, you asked about shopping. Well, you can get everything you need within 5 minutes of the flats. There's a very good baker's on North Street. You go out of the apartments, turn left and it's on the other side of the road on the corner of Main Street and North Street. It's open from 7.30am - 5pm every day, except Sunday. Just before the baker's is a greengrocer's on the same side of the road, which opens at 9am and closes at 5pm. If you walk to the end of the street, you'll see a supermarket opposite you. You can get everything there but it's not cheap. They are open 6 days a week from 9am to 6pm. There's also a chemist's which is in North Street, opposite the baker's. The opening times are the same as the greengrocer's, 9am to 5pm, Monday to Friday. There's a post office which you'll find if you walk down North Street, turn right at the end, and cross the road. It's next to the supermarket, but you can't miss it - it's got a red door and a letter box outside. It opens at 9.30am and closes at 5pm Monday, Tuesday, Thursday, Friday and Saturday, but closes at 12 o'clock on Wednesday, it's half day closing! Finally, if you want a newspaper or magazine, there's a newsagent's on Main Street. Go down North Street, turn left at the end and it's on the other side of the road, just after the pedestrian crossing. They have some foreign newspapers there and a nice selection of postcards. The newsagent's is open every day including Sunday from 7am to 7pm. I think that's everything. Hope you enjoy your stay.

Answers

Exercise 1a

1	washing machine	10	shorts
2	sandals	11	shampoo
3	diary	12	envelope
4	newspaper	13	T-shirt
5	trainers	14	CD
6	safety pin	15	necklace
7	cassette	16	crisps
8	bottle of wine	17	brooch
9	vacuum cleaner	18	magazine

Exercise 1b

Electrical Shop
washing machine
vacuum cleaner

Jeweller's
brooch
necklace

Music Shop
CD
cassette

Chemist's
safety pin
shampoo

Shoe Shop
trainers
sandals

Stationer's
envelope
diary

Clothes Shop
T-shirt
shorts

Off-Licence
bottle of wine

Newsagent's
newspaper
magazine
crisps

Exercise 3a

A	Newsagent's	Open every day including Sun 7am - 7pm
B	Supermarket	Open 6 days a week from 9am to 6pm
C	Post Office	Open Mon, Tue, Thur, Fri, Sat 9.30am - 5pm Wed 9.30am - 12 noon
D	Baker's	Open 7.30am - 5pm every day, except Sunday
E	Greengrocer's	Open 9am - 5pm Mon - Fri
F	Chemist's	Open 9am - 5pm Mon - Fri

Exercise 3c

1 The Post Office
2 No it isn't
3 At the newsagent's
4 The baker's
5 Mondays, Wednesdays and Fridays

1

UNIT 23

How many metres are there in a kilometre?

1 a Look at the following information.

Measurements (approximations)

Area

1 square foot = 0.09 square metres (m^2)
1 square yard = 0.84 square metres (m^2)
1 acre = 4046 square metres (m^2)

Weight

1 ounce (oz) = 28 grams
1 pound (lb) = 0.45 grams
1 stone = 6.4 kilograms

Fluids

1 pint = 0.57 litres
1 gallon = 4.5 litres

Length

1 inch = 2.5 centimetres (cm)
1 foot = 30 centimetres
1 yard = 90 centimetres
1 mile = 1.6 kilometres (km)

Temperature

°C	°F
-30	-22
-20	-4
-10	14
0	32
5	41
10	50
15	59
20	68
25	77
30	86
35	95
40	104
45	113
50	122

b Ask your neighbour the following questions.

eg How many centimetres are there in an inch? There are 2.5 centimetres in an inch.

1 How many grams are there in an ounce?
2 How many litres are there in a gallon?
3 How many kilometres are there in a mile?
4 How many square metres are there in an acre?
5 How many kilograms are there in a stone?

c Say whether the following are true (✓) or false (x).

eg 20ºF is colder than 20ºC. ☑

1 A kilometre is shorter than a mile. ☐
2 A square foot is smaller than a square metre. ☐
3 A pound is heavier than a kilogram. ☐
4 14ºF is colder than 14ºC. ☐
5 A pint is more than a litre. ☐

d Fill in the following.

eg There are 28 grams in an ounce.

1 There are __________ litres in a pint.
2 There are __________ grams in a pound.
3 There are __________ centimetres in an inch.
4 There are __________ centimetres in a foot.
5 There are __________ inches in a foot.

2

2 a Match the phrase and the definition.

1 bargain ☐ When all items are sold at discount but no new items are bought.
2 closing down sale ☐ When old items are sold at discount and new items are bought.
3 end of season sale ☐ An item which is cheaper than normal.

- Special Offer -
Heineken Lager
89p can (50ml cans)
2 cans for the price of 1
While Stocks Last

CLOSING DOWN SALE
Everything has to go
All Items
½ Price

Bargain Counter
Every item
99p

This Week Only
Tomatoes
Save 16p per lb
~~75p~~ **59p**

Buy one get one
FREE
Buy any CD from this stand and get another from this stand FREE

End of Season
Sale
everything reduced by 30%

b Answer the following questions.

eg How much is one item from the bargain counter? 99p.

1 If I buy 2 cans of Heineken lager, is it more expensive than if I buy 1 can? __________
2 If I buy 3 items from the bargain counter, how much will it cost? __________
3 If I buy 2lbs of tomatoes this week, how much will it cost? __________
4 If I buy 1 CD from this stand, can I get a second one from another stand free? __________
5 In the end of season sale, how much is everything reduced by? __________

c Ask your neighbour.

eg How much are 2 cans of Heineken lager? 89p.

1 How much do tomatoes usually cost per pound?
2 Is everything in the closing down sale reduced by 50%?
3 How much lager is in each can?
4 How much do I save per pound of tomatoes I buy?
5 How long does the special offer on Heineken lager last?

d Ask your neighbour.

1 When was the last time you bought an item in a sale or special offer?
2 What was it?
3 Why did you buy it?
4 Do you look for special offers? Why (not)?
5 Do you usually go to sales? Why (not)?

e Tell your teacher about your neighbour.

3

3 a You are with a tour group who are visiting a shopping centre. The tour guide is about to give you some information. Look at the following and put a question mark (?) against the information you think you will hear.

	?	✓		?	✓
where you are now	___	___	what time the shops close	___	___
the time now	___	___	how to get to the nearest railway station	___	___
where you will meet	___	___	where the bus is parked	___	___
what time you will meet	___	___	which restaurant is the cheapest	___	___
the names of all the shops	___	___	where you can get money from	___	___

b Listen to the cassette and tick (✓) the information you hear. Did you hear what you expected?

Notes

c Look at the following diagram and listen to the cassette again. Make notes as you listen to the information and then compare with your neighbour.

KING'S HALL SHOPPING CENTRE - FIRST FLOOR LAYOUT PLAN

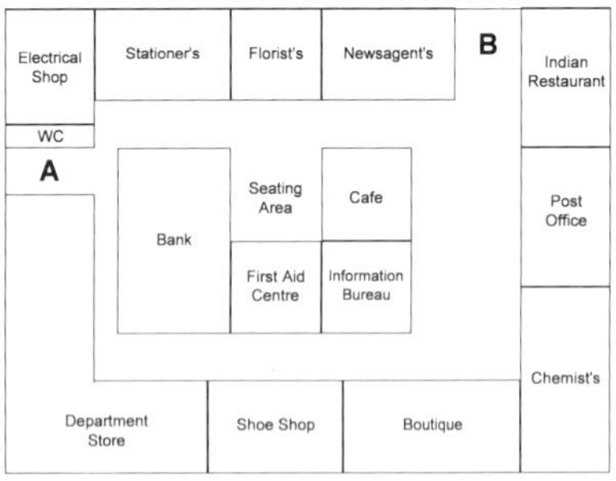

d Answer the following questions.

1 What closes at 3 o'clock? __________
2 What is closed for redecoration? __________
3 What will happen at 4.45pm on the dot? __________
4 When does the first aid centre close? __________
5 Where is the end of season sale? __________

e Ask your neighbour these questions.

1 Can I get money after 3 o'clock?
2 Where is the shoe shop?
3 What time is the local band playing?
4 How can I pay in shops?
5 Where is the bus parked?

4

4 a Translate the following.

Vocabulary

measurements __________
approximations __________
area __________
square metre __________
fluids __________
weight __________
length __________
temperature __________
bargain __________
closing down sale __________
end of season sale __________
special offer __________
item __________
to save __________
reduced __________
meeting point __________
on the dot __________
cash machine __________
redecoration __________
department store __________
first aid centre __________

Structures

How many metres are there in a kilometre? __________
How many centimetres are there in an inch? __________
There are 2.5 centimetres in an inch. __________
20° F is colder than 20° C. __________
There are 28 grams in an ounce. __________
How much is one item from the bargain counter? __________
How much are two cans of Heineken lager? __________

Teaching Notes

Warm-up

Ask students questions from earlier Units eg "How many rooms do you have in your house? What do you in the mornings?"

Revision

Revise all the structures and vocabulary from the previous Unit by asking students questions eg "Where can you buy a magazine? When was the last time you used a safety pin? Where would you buy a brooch?"

Presentation and Practice

1 Introduce measurements by asking students questions eg "How tall are you? What was the temperature today? How big is your flat?"

Students look at the information in 1a and then try and answer the questions in 1b. Provide feedback by asking students the questions and checking their answers.

Students then read the sentences in 1c and say whether they are true or false. Provide feedback by students telling you what they have written. They then complete 1d while you monitor and check.

2 Introduce this activity by asking students if and when shops have sales in their country. Find out when they are eg "January sales" and find out which students go to them. Students match the phrase and the definition before reading through the notices and answering the questions in 2b. Check the answers from 2b by asking students the questions.

Students then complete the speaking activity in 2c while you monitor and check. They then complete the speaking activity in 2d. Provide feedback by asking students to tell you about their neighbour.

3 Introduce the listening activity by setting the scene in 3a. Before students hear the cassette they put a question mark next to the information they think they will hear. They then listen to the cassette and put a tick next to the information they hear. Check this and then play it again so that students can make notes using the plan in 3c.

Students then answer the questions in 3d while you monitor and check.

Students then complete the speaking activity in 3e. Provide feedback by asking students to tell you about their neighbour.

Revise all the structures and vocabulary before moving on to the next lesson.

At home students prepare for the next lesson by looking up the vocabulary in 4a of Unit 24.

Tapescripts

Exercise 3b & c

Welcome to the King's Hall Shopping Centre. The time is now half past two. We will meet at half past four at the meeting point which is next to the seating area in the middle of the shopping centre. You have 2 hours to look around and do your shopping. We are now at Entrance A, and in case you are late, the bus is in the car park outside Entrance B. It will leave at quarter to five on the dot.

In the middle of the shopping Centre you will find an information bureau.

There is one bank in the centre, which you will find opposite Entrance A. It closes at three o'clock, but there is a cash machine outside it if you need money after 3 o'clock. Most shops accept cash and cheques and they usually display stickers on the shop window to show which credit cards they accept.

The Indian restaurant, which is on the right of Entrance B is closed this week for redecoration, but all the other shops are open until 5pm.

There is a local band playing folk music between 12 o'clock and 1 o'clock next to the information bureau.

Today is also the first day of the "End of Season Sale" in the department store, which is on the right. There will be a lot of bargains there.

Finally, there is a first aid centre between the bank and the information bureau. This closes at 3.30pm. In case of emergency after this, go to the information bureau.

So have fun, and we'll meet at 4.30pm.

Answers

Exercise 1c

1 True
2 True
3 False
4 True
5 False

Exercise 1d

1 0.57
2 0.45
3 2.5
4 30
5 12

Exercise 2a

1 An item which is cheaper than normal.
2 When all items are sold at discount but no new items are bought.
3 When old items are sold at discount and new items are bought.

Exercise 2b

1 No - same price
2 £2.97
3 £1.18
4 No - only from this stand
5 30%

Exercise 3d

1 The bank.
2 The Indian restaurant.
3 The bus will leave.
4 3.30pm
5 In the department store.

1

UNIT 24

At the Supermarket

1 a **Look at photograph sequence 3 'At the Supermarket' on the next pages and put the photographs in the correct order.**

1 *eg B* ____ 3 ____ 5 ____ 7 ____
2 ____ 4 ____ 6 ____

b **Tell your neighbour and explain why you chose that order.**

eg *I think that B is the first photograph because the trolley is empty.*

c **What has Mrs Mills just done? Read the sentences below and write which photograph each sentence refers to.**

eg *She has just picked up a bag of potatoes.* [F]

1 She has just put some bananas on the scales. [ ]
2 She has just given the assistant some money. [ ]
3 She has just picked up a carton of orange juice. [ ]
4 She has just left the supermarket. [ ]
5 She has just taken the celery out of the trolley. [ ]
6 She has just taken a shopping trolley from the trolley park. [ ]

d **Ask your neighbour these questions.**

eg *What has she just done in photograph A? She's just taken the celery out of the trolley.*

1 What has she just done in photograph B?
2 What has she just done in photograph C?
3 What has she just done in photograph D?
4 What has she just done in photograph E?
5 What has she just done in photograph F?
6 What has she just done in photograph G?

e **Now ask your neighbour these questions about the photographs.**

eg *What do your think she's holding in her left hand in photograph G?*
I think she's holding a shopping list in her left hand.

1 What do you think she's saying to the assistant in photograph D?
2 What do you think she's holding in her left hand in photograph C?
3 What is she wearing?
4 How much are beef tomatoes?
5 What time of year do you think it is? Why?

f **Ask your neighbour these questions.**

1 When was the last time you went to a supermarket?
2 Where was the supermarket?
3 What did you buy?
4 Do you often go to that supermarket?
5 How do you get there?

2

2 a **Listen to the cassette. Jamie and Gillian are writing a list of the shopping they need and deciding who is going to get what. You will hear the dialogue twice. Write down who is going to buy what.**

Jamie's Shopping List	Gillian's Shopping List

b **Listen again and answer the following in note form.**

1 Where do they want to park the car? ____
2 Where do they want to buy the toilet rolls from? Why? ____
3 Where do they want to buy the eggs from? Why? ____
4 What does Jamie want to buy from the off-licence? ____
5 What does Jamie want to buy from the newsagent's? ____

c **Ask your neighbour about 5 items on the shopping lists.**

eg *Where do you buy washing up liquid? In the supermarket.*
Why do you buy it there? Because it's cheap and convenient.

d **You are going shopping with your neighbour. Make a list of 9 items which you and your neighbour want to buy.**

1 ____	4 ____	7 ____
2 ____	5 ____	8 ____
3 ____	6 ____	9 ____

e **Decide who will get what.**

eg *I'll get the washing up liquid. Can you get the toilet rolls?*

f **Tell your teacher what you've decided.**

eg *I'm going to get the washing up liquid from the supermarket.*
My neighbour's going to get the toilet rolls from the chemist's.

3

3 a **Look at the advertisement below and answer the questions.**

eg *What is this an advertisement for? It's an advertisement for a TV and video recorder.*

1 What is the name of the shop? ____
2 What is the telephone number? ____
3 When are they open? ____
4 What do they sell? ____
5 What is the address? ____

END OF SEASON SALE

- Everything Reduced -

Save money when you buy yourself and your family a new TV and/or video recorder from Walker's Electrical Shop.

Grundy C211343 21" colour TV
Comes complete with trolley stand.
Normal Price £399.99

Sale Price £369.99

Walker's Electrical Shop
42-44 Sands Way
Oldham
OD21 5TU
Tel: (0161) 793211
Mon - Sat: 9am - 5.30pm

Grundy VTM 112 Video Recorder
Includes remote control
Normal Price £339.99

Sale Price £299.99

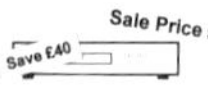

b **Ask your neighbour these questions about the advertisement.**

eg *What type of video recorder is it? It's a Grundy VTM 112.*

1 How much does the video recorder normally cost?
2 How big is the TV?
3 How much does the TV cost in the sale?
4 If I buy the TV and the video recorder in the sale, how much will it cost?
5 How much do I save if I buy the TV in the sale?

c **Now ask your neighbour these questions.**

1 Would you buy this TV? Why? Why not?
2 Do you prefer to pay for something monthly?
3 Do you prefer to pay in a lump sum? Why (not)?
4 If you have a TV, how did you pay for that?
5 What monthly instalments do you pay?

d **You have seen this advertisement in the newspaper and have decided to buy the Grundy C211343 21" colour TV. Telephone the shop and ask if they still have one. Check the price and tell them how you are going to pay. Arrange when you will collect it. You are the customer and your neighbour is the assistant. Start the roleplay.**

eg *Walker's Electrical Shop. Susan speaking. How can I help you?*

4

4 a **Translate the following.**

Vocabulary

trolley ____	frozen chicken ____
to pick up ____	butcher's ____
to put ____	sausages ____
to take ____	piece of beef ____
shopping list ____	tinned food ____
cooking oil ____	peas ____
washing up liquid ____	milk ____
toothpaste ____	eggs ____
soap ____	free-range ____
bread ____	silver foil ____
large white loaf ____	advert ____
small brown loaf ____	TV ____
vegetables ____	video recorder ____
fruit ____	normal price ____
peppers ____	sale price ____
mushrooms ____	to include ____
lettuce ____	to buy ____
cauliflower ____	to pay for ____
apples ____	lump sum ____
meat ____	monthly instalments ____

Structures

I think that B is the first photograph because the trolley is empty. ____
She has just picked up a bag of potatoes. ____
What has she just done in photograph A? ____
She's just taken the celery out of the trolley. ____
What do you think she's holding in her left hand in photograph G? ____
I think she's holding a shopping list in her left hand. ____
Where do you buy washing up liquid? ____
In the supermarket. ____
Why do you buy it there? ____
Because it's cheap and convenient. ____
I'll get the washing up liquid. ____
Can you get the toilet rolls? ____
I'm going to get the washing up liquid from the supermarket. ____
My neighbour's going to get the toilet rolls from the chemist's. ____
What's this an advertisement for? ____
It's an advertisement for a TV and video recorder. ____
What type of video recorder is it? ____
It's a Grundy VTM 112. ____
Susan speaking. ____
How can I help you? ____

Teaching Notes

Warm-up

Ask students questions from earlier Units eg "Does your house have double-glazing? How do you make a cup of coffee?"

Revision

Revise all the structures and vocabulary from the previous Unit by asking students questions eg "How many centimetres are there in a metre? Is 100 mph faster than 100 km/h? Have you ever bought anything in a sale?"

Presentation and Practice

1 Find out who goes shopping in a supermarket and ask them to explain what they do from leaving their car to returning to it. Other students may help.

Students then look at the photograph sequence 'At the Supermarket' and work out the correct order of events in 1a. They then tell their neighbour why they have chosen that order in 1b. Write the example from 1c on the board and explain the use of 'has just picked up'.

Provide further examples by asking students to stand up/sit down/pick up a book etc and asking 'What has she just done?'. When students are familiar with the new structure they match the sentences and photographs in 1c while you monitor and check. Provide feedback by asking students questions eg "What has she just done in photograph A?"

Students complete the speaking activity in 1d. Provide feedback by asking pairs to demonstrate their activity. Students then complete the speaking activity in 1e. Check by asking students the questions. In pairs students complete the activity in 1f. Provide feedback by students telling you about their neighbour.

2 Introduce the listening activity by setting the scene in 2a and telling students they will hear the dialogue twice. While they are listening they are to write down who is going to buy what. Ask students to tell you what Jamie and Gillian are going to buy. Students work in pairs and try and answer the questions in 2b about the dialogue. Play the cassette a third time for them to check if necessary.

Students then complete the speaking activity in 2c while you monitor and check.

In pairs students put together a list of 9 items they need to buy from the supermarket.

Demonstrate the speaking activity in 2e with one student before pairs discuss who will buy what. When they are finished demonstrate 2f by telling the class what you are going to buy and what the other student is going to buy.

Students then tell you what they have decided.

3 Students read the questions and find the answers in the advert in 3a. Ask students the questions to provide feedback.

Students then complete the speaking activity in 3b while you monitor and check.

Students then complete the speaking activity in 3c. Provide feedback by students telling you about their neighbour. Set up the roleplay in 3d by explaining the situation and establishing who is the customer and who is the shop assistant. Explain that the customer is going to telephone the shop about the TV and has to ask if the shop still has one; they have to check the price, how they are going to pay and arrange when they will collect it.

Students then act out the roleplay while you monitor and check.

Revise all the structures and vocabulary before moving on to the next lesson.

At home students prepare for the next lesson by looking up the vocabulary in 4a of Unit 25.

Tapescripts

Exercise 2a

Gillian	We'll go to the big supermarket in town because there's always space to park in their car park. I'll go to the supermarket and you can walk into town to get the rest.
Jamie	Okay.
Gillian	First, we need cooking oil, washing up liquid, washing powder, and toilet rolls erm... I'll get the oil, the washing up liquid and the washing powder in the supermarket and you can get the toilet rolls in the chemist's because they're cheaper there. While you're in the chemist's you can get some toothpaste, soap and cat food. Er... We also need bread; you can get that in the baker's - get a large white loaf and a small brown loaf. I'll get the vegetables and fruit in the supermarket. Let's see, we need some ... we need potatoes, onions, peppers, mushrooms, garlic, lettuce and cauliflower. I'll get some apples too. We need some meat as well. I'll get a frozen chicken from the supermarket. Er... Can you go to the butcher's and get some mince, pork chops and sausages. Oh, and a piece of beef for Sunday. I'll get the tinned food in the supermarket. I need tins of tomatoes, mushrooms and peas. And I'll get the milk too. What about eggs?
Jamie	I'll get some eggs from the butcher's - he sells free-range eggs which are good.
Gillian	Okay. Can you think of anything else?
Jamie	Oh, we need some silver foil. Can you get that from the supermarket?
Gillian	Yes okay.
Jamie	And I'll get a bottle of wine from the off-licence oh... and a newspaper from the newsagent's.
Gillian	Fine. Let's just check through again. I'm going to get cooking oil, washing up liquid, washing powder, potatoes, onions, peppers, mushrooms, garlic, lettuce, cauliflower, apples, frozen chicken, tinned tomatoes, tinned mushrooms, tinned peas, milk and silver foil.
Jamie	And I'm going to get the toilet rolls, toothpaste, soap, cat food, a large white loaf and a small brown loaf, mince, pork chops, sausages, beef, eggs, bottle of wine and a newspaper.
Gillian	Right. Let's go.

Answers

Exercise 1a

1 B
2 E
3 F
4 G
5 A
6 D
7 C

Exercise 1c

1 E
2 D
3 G
4 C
5 A
6 B

Exercise 2a

Jamie	Gillian	
toilet rolls	cooking oil	tinned mushrooms
toothpaste	washing up liquid	tinned peas
soap	washing powder	milk
cat food	potatoes	silver foil
large white loaf	onions	
small brown loaf	peppers	
mince	mushrooms	
pork chops	garlic	
sausages	lettuce	
piece of beef	cauliflower	
eggs	apples	
bottle of wine	frozen chicken	
newspaper	tinned tomatoes	

Exercise 2b

1 In the supermarket car park.
2 From the chemist's because they're cheaper.
3 From the butcher because they're free-range eggs.
4 A bottle of wine.
5 A newspaper.

Exercise 3a

1 Walker's Electrical Shop
2 0161 793211
3 Mon - Sat 9am - 5.30pm
4 TV's and video recorders/electrical goods
5 42-44 Sands Way, Oldham, OD21 5TU

1

UNIT 25

Which department is it in?

1 a **Ask your neighbour the following questions.**

1 Is there a department store in your town?
2 What is it called?
3 Where is it?
4 How often do you go there? Why?
5 Is it cheaper or more expensive than other shops?

b **Match the objects and the words.**

h dog food
___ tennis racket
___ sheet and pillow case
___ pens
___ flowers
___ watch
___ glasses
___ perfume
___ loaf of bread
___ earrings
___ china plate
___ woollen cardigan
___ computer
___ cup of coffee
___ bottle of wine

c **Point at the pictures and ask your neighbour.**

eg *What's this? It's a tennis racket. What are these? They're pens.*

d **Here are approximate prices for some items in England. Ask your neighbour and fill in the prices for his/her country.**

eg *In England a cup of coffee costs about £1.35. How much does it cost in your country?*

a cup of coffee	£1.35	______	a set of glasses	£18.99	______
a packet of dog food	£1.22	______	a bottle of perfume	£24.99	______
a tennis racket	£32.49	______	a loaf of bread	72p	______
a sheet and pillow case	£12.79	______	a pair of earrings	£3.99	______
a set of pens	£14.99	______	a china plate	£6.25	______
a bunch of flowers	£3.99	______	a woollen cardigan	£23.49	______
a watch	£29.99	______	a computer	£999.99	______

e **Tell your teacher.**

eg *A cup of coffee is more expensive in England than it is in my country but a loaf of bread is cheaper in my country.*

2

Department Store Guide

Basement	First Floor	Third Floor
coffee shop	ladies' accessories	boutique
telephone	knitwear	restaurant
shoe repairs	men's accessories	furs and leather
glass and chinaware	tobacco	lingerie
jewellery	magazines	WC/ladies
	children's clothes and shoes	ladies' fashions

Ground Floor	Second Floor	Fourth Floor
bakery	ladies' shoes	bed linen
cosmetics	men's fashions and shoes	electrical equipment
florist	customer service department	fabrics
watches	stationery	furniture
health food shop	suitcases	paints and wallpapers
information	WC/men	household equipment
cash machine	hair salon	pet supplies
wine shop	sports wear and equipment	accounts

2 a **Which department would you go to? Look at the Department Store Guide and write the department next to the word.**

dog food ______	watch ______	china plate ______
tennis racket ______	glasses ______	woollen cardigan ______
sheet and pillowcase ______	perfume ______	computer ______
pens ______	bread ______	cup of coffee ______
flowers ______	earrings ______	bottle of wine ______

Check with your neighbour.

b **Fill in the following. Which floor would you go to?**

eg *If I wanted a cup of coffee, I would go to the coffee shop in the basement.*
If I wanted to buy a diary, I would go to the stationery department on the second floor.

1 If I wanted to change my hairstyle, ______
2 If I wanted to exchange a cardigan, ______
3 If I wanted to go to the toilet, ______
4 If I wanted to make a phone call, ______
5 If I couldn't find what I wanted, ______

c **Ask your neighbour.**

eg *Can you name 3 things you would buy in the wine shop?*
A bottle of red wine, a can of beer and a bottle of whisky.

1 Can you name 3 things you would buy in the furniture department?
2 Can you name 3 things you would buy in the stationery department?
3 Can you name 3 things you would buy in the men's fashion department?

d **Ask your neighbour the following questions.**

eg *Which floor is the cash machine on? It's on the ground floor.*
Why would you go there? I would go there to take out some money.

1 Which floor is the restaurant on? Why would you go there?
2 Which floor is the health food shop on? Why would you go there?
3 Which floor are the magazines on? Why would you go there?
4 Which floor is the telephone on? Why would you go there?
5 Which floor is the customer service department on? Why would you go there?

3

3 a **You are going to listen to an announcement in a department store on the cassette. Put a question mark (?) next to the information you think you will hear.**

? ✓		? ✓	
❑ ❑	the time now	❑ ❑	what to do in case of fire
❑ ❑	information about special offers	❑ ❑	information about departments which are closed today
❑ ❑	what each department sells	❑ ❑	where to go if you have any questions
❑ ❑	where the exits are	❑ ❑	where the nearest car park is

b **Listen to the cassette and put a tick (✓) next to the information you hear. Did you hear what you expected?**

c **Here is the layout plan for 2 floors of the department store. Listen again and make notes below.**

GROUND FLOOR LAYOUT PLAN

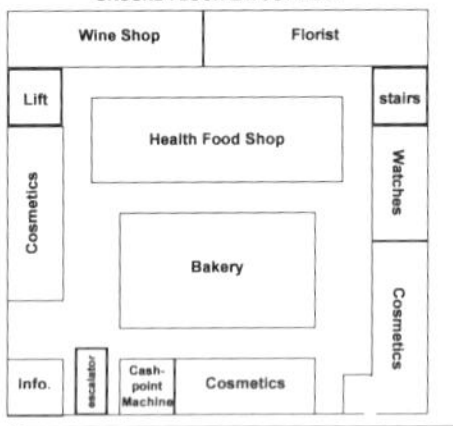

SECOND FLOOR LAYOUT PLAN

Opening Times: Mon - Sat 9am - 6pm / Late Night Shopping: Thu 9am - 8.30pm

✍ **Notes**

d **Ask your neighbour the following questions and then check with your neighbour.**

1 What is £3 cheaper than normal today?
2 What time is the demonstration of fitness equipment?
3 How long is the WC closed?
4 Which special offer is available only while stocks last?
5 Which day of the week is it? Why?

e **Roleplays in the supermarket. Work with your neighbour.**

1 You bought a dress for your daughter last week but it is too small. Go to the customer service department and see if you can exchange it for a larger one.
2 You have heard that there is a special offer in the hair salon. You decide to change your hairstyle. Go to the hair salon and arrange an appointment.
3 You are at the information desk on the ground floor. You want to buy a tennis racket. Find out which department you should go to and how to get there.

4

4 a **Translate the following.**

Vocabulary

a packet of dog food ______	men's accessories ______
a tennis racket ______	tobacco ______
a sheet ______	children's clothes ______
a pillow case ______	second floor ______
a set of pens ______	customer service point ______
a bunch of flowers ______	stationery ______
a set of glasses ______	WC men ______
a bottle of perfume ______	hair salon ______
a loaf of bread ______	sportswear and equipment ______
a pair of earrings ______	third floor ______
a china plate ______	boutique ______
a woollen cardigan ______	restaurant ______
guarantee ______	furs and leather ______
latest technology ______	lingerie ______
ready to go ______	WC ladies ______
department store guide ______	bed linen ______
basement ______	electrical equipment ______
coffee shop ______	fabrics ______
shoe repairs ______	furniture ______
glass and chinaware ______	paints and wallpapers ______
ground floor ______	household equipment ______
bakery ______	pet supplies ______
cosmetics ______	accounts ______
wine shop ______	to exchange ______
first floor ______	to return ______
knitwear ______	

Structures

What's this? It's a tennis racket. ______
What are these? They're pens. ______
In England a cup of coffee costs £1.35. ______
How much does a cup of coffee cost in your country? ______
A cup of coffee is more expensive in England than it is here. ______
A loaf of bread is cheaper in England than it is in my country. ______
If I wanted a cup of coffee, I would go to the coffee shop in the basement. ______
If I wanted to buy a diary, I would go to the stationery department on the second floor. ______
Can you name 3 things you would buy in the wine shop? ______
A bottle of red wine, a can of beer and a bottle of whisky. ______
Which floor is the cash machine on? ______
It's on the ground floor. ______
Why would you go there? ______
I would go there to take out some money. ______

Teaching Notes

Warm-up

Ask students questions from earlier Units eg "What do you use a sewing machine for? Do you live in a block of flats?"

Revision

Revise all the structures and vocabulary from the previous Unit by asking students questions eg "Where do you buy your vegetables from? Why? What did you buy to eat last week? Can you name 5 vegetables?"

Presentation and Practice

1 In pairs students complete the speaking activity in 1a while you monitor and check. They then complete the matching task in 1b. Check their work by asking students questions eg "What is A?"

Students then complete the speaking activity in 1c while you monitor and check.

In pairs students discuss the prices of the items shown in their country and write this next to the price for England. They then compare prices in the speaking activity in 1e.

2 Find out which students have a department store in their town/city and ask them what it sells and how customers find their way around it. Explain to them that the information given is a guide to a department store. Ask them questions about the information eg "How many floors does the store have? Which floor is the hair salon on?" When they are familiar with the information they complete 2a and then compare their work with their neighbour.

They then complete the writing activity in 2b while you monitor and check. Provide feedback by asking students to tell you what they have written.

Students complete the speaking activity in 2c. Provide feedback by eliciting as many items as possible from students.

Students complete the speaking activity in 2d. Provide feedback by pairs asking and answering.

3 Ask students what kind of information they are likely to hear on an announcement in a department store. Students then read through the information and put a question mark next to the information they think they will hear. Before they hear the cassette tell them that all they are to do is to put a tick next to the information which they hear. When you have played it once check which boxes students have ticked. Students then look at the diagram of the store and ask and answer questions in order to familiarise themselves with the layout eg "Where is the WC? What is between the cosmetics and the stairs?" When students are familiar with the plan, play the cassette a second time so that they can complete the activity in 3c. They then compare their work with their neighbour and complete the speaking activity in 3d. Provide feedback by asking pairs to demonstrate their activity. Students then act out the roleplay in 3e.

Revise all the structures and vocabulary before moving on to the next lesson.

At home students prepare for the next lesson by looking up the vocabulary in 4a of Unit 26.

Tapescripts

Exercise 3b & c

Ladies and gentlemen. Today we have 4 special offers in the store. BW Whisky is £14.99; this is £3 off the normal price of £17.99. You can find this in the wine shop on the ground floor on the left when you come out of the lift. While you're on the ground floor we have a special offer on our own brand of day cream for ladies - 2 tubes for the price of one. Available from cosmetics only while stocks last. Everybody who makes a hair appointment today, will get it for ½ price. The appointment must be within the next 2 weeks. There is a sale of summer shirts in the men's fashion department this week. The men's fashion department is in the middle on the second floor. There is a demonstration of fitness equipment in the sports department at 3.30pm. This will last half an hour.

Our new bakery, which is situated on the ground floor, opposite the health food shop, has a range of fresh brown and white bread. If you have any questions please visit our information stand on the ground floor, and if you have any articles you wish to exchange or return please go to our customer services department on the second floor. It's on the left when you come out of the lift. Please note that the WC is closed between 3pm and 3.30pm as the water is turned off.

And don't forget, tonight is late night shopping and the store is open until 8pm.

Answers

Exercise 1b

a tennis racket
b cup of coffee
c computer
d pens
e perfume
f flowers
g earrings
h dog food
i glasses
j bottle of wine
k watch
l woollen cardigan
m loaf of bread
n china plate
o sheet and pillow case

Exercise 2a

dog food	pet supplies
tennis racket	sportswear and equipment
sheet and pillow case	bed linen
pens	stationery
flowers	florist
watch	watches
glasses	glass and chinaware
perfume	cosmetics
bread	bakery
earrings	jewellery
china plate	glass and chinaware
woollen cardigan	knitwear
computer	electrical equipment
cup of coffee	coffee shop
bottle of wine	wine shop

Exercise 2b

1 If I wanted to change my hairstyle, I would go to the hair salon on the second floor.
2 If I wanted to exchange a cardigan, I would go to the customer service department on the second floor.
3 If I wanted to go to the toilet, I would go to WC on the second/third floor. (men/women)
4 If I wanted to make a phone call, I would go to the telephone in the basement.
5 If I couldn't find what I wanted, I would go to the information on the ground floor.

1

UNIT 26

What's the code for Cork?

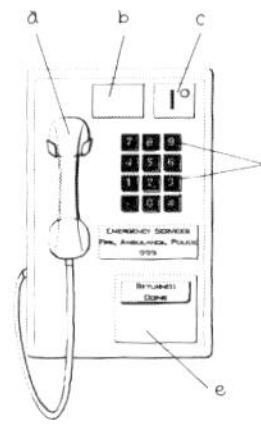

1 a Match the letters and the words.

a receiver
___ coin slot
___ returned coins slot
___ display
___ keys

b Point at the pictures and ask your neighbour.

eg What's this? It's the receiver. What do you do with it? You speak into it.

c Read the instructions below and put them in the correct order.

___ listen for the dialling tone
1 pick up the receiver
___ dial the number
___ take the returned coins
___ replace the receiver
___ insert your money (minimum 10p)
___ speak
___ listen for the ringing tone

d Close your book and tell your neighbour how to make a phone call.

eg First you lift up the receiver. Then...

e Ask your neighbour the following questions.

eg What number do you dial if you want the police? You dial 999.

1 Do the 3 emergency services all have the same number?
2 What are the number(s) for the emergency services in your country?
3 In what situations would you ring for the fire brigade?
4 In what situations would you ring for the police?
5 In what situations would you ring for an ambulance?

f Look at the information on telephone rates and ask your neighbour the following questions.

eg When is cheap rate? It's from 8pm - 8am

1 When is peak rate?
2 How much are long distance calls per minute cheap rate?
3 How much are local calls per minute peak rate?
4 How much are long distance calls per minute peak rate?
5 How much are local calls per minute cheap rate?

Telephone Rates

Peak rate times	8am - 8pm
Cheap rate times	8pm - 8am
Local Calls (up to 15 miles away)	
Cheap rate	8p per minute
Peak rate	16p per minute
Long Distance Calls (over 15 miles away)	
Cheap rate	12p per minute
Peak rate	24p per minute

g Ask your neighbour the following questions.

1 How much is a 5 minute conversation to another country at peak times?
2 How much is a 10 minute conversation to a friend living in the same village at 10.30am?
3 How much is the same conversation at 10.30pm?
4 How much is a 20 minute conversation with a business colleague in another town 50 miles away at 9.45am?
5 How much is a 30 minute conversation with a relative in another town 20 miles away at 8.30pm?

2

2 a You are on holiday in London. Look at the information below and ask your neighbour 5 questions.

eg What's the area code for Cork? It's 21.

Area Dialling Codes

- UK -				- Republic of Ireland -			
Bath	01225	London - central	0171	Athlone	902	Roscommon	903
Birmingham	0121	London - outer	0181	Cork	21	Shannon	61
Blackpool	01253	Manchester	0114	Donegal	73	Sligo	71
Cardiff	01222	Oxford	01865	Dublin	0001	Tipperary	62
Edinburgh	0112	Portsmouth	01705	Galway	91	Waterford	51
Glasgow	0116	Southampton	01703	Kildare	45	Wexford	53
Harrogate	01423	York	01904	Limerick	61	Wicklow	404
Liverpool	0117						

International Codes

To call overseas:

1 Dial the international code 00.
2 Dial the code of the country you require.
3 Dial the area code, remembering to omit the first 0 (or in the case of Spain, 9).
4 Dial the telephone number you wish.

Australia	61	India	91
Belgium	32	Republic of Ireland	353
Denmark	45	Japan	81
France	33	Spain	34
Germany	49	Taiwan	886
Greece	30	Turkey	90
Hong Kong	852	USA	1

b Ask your neighbour.

eg How do I make an international call?

c Fill in the following.

What's your area code? ______________________

What's your telephone number? ______________________

What's your number from the UK? ______________________

Telephone Numbers

Kevin Thompson (Central London)	2298566
Linda Dooley (Cork, Ireland)	32990
José Gonzalez (Spain)	(937) 25614
Pierre Lafayette (France)	(0623) 943211
Bob Thornton (Glasgow)	2913214
Barbara Grundmann (Germany)	(0201) 259432
Susi Kerr (USA)	(0971) 3949527
Hiromi Suzuki (Japan)	(0332) 4933215
Tania Connor (Outer London)	8922599
Daniel O'Neill (Sligo, Ireland)	49156

d Use the page from the address book and write the number you would call from Glasgow.

eg Kevin Thompson (0171) 2298566

1 Bob Thornton ______________________
2 Linda Dooley ______________________
3 Barbara Grundmann ______________________
4 José Gonzalez ______________________
5 Tania Connor ______________________
6 Susi Kerr ______________________
7 Hiromi Suzuki ______________________

e Ask your neighbour.

eg What is Kevin Thompson's number? It's 0171 double 2 985 double 6.

Now ask your neighbour about the other people.

f Ask 5 other people about their telephone numbers.

3

3 a Look at photograph sequence 4 'Making a Phone Call' on the next pages. Describe the lady to your neighbour.

b Ask your neighbour.

eg What's Mrs Jackson doing in picture 1? She's opening the door of the phone box. What's she going to do next? She's going to step inside the phone box.

1 What's she doing in picture 2? What's she going to do next?
2 What's she doing in picture 3? What's she going to do next?
3 What's she doing in picture 4? What's she going to do next?
4 What's she doing in picture 5? What's she going to do next?
5 What's she doing in picture 6? What's she going to do next?

c Tell your neighbour about Mrs Jackson.

eg In picture 1 she's opening the door of the phone box. She's going to step inside it next because she's going to make a phone call.

d Mrs Jackson is telephoning Susi's Hair Salon. Listen to the cassette and make notes.

Notes

Mrs Jackson	Susi's Hair Salon

e Which of these phrases did you hear? Listen again and tick the phrases you hear.

☐ Hello
☐ Can I help you?
☐ I have an appointment for Thursday.
☐ I'd like to change it.
☐ Would 3pm suit you?
☐ That's fine.
☐ Goodbye.

f Practise telephoning with your neighbour. Use the following situations.

1 You ring up a restaurant to make a reservation for yourself and some friends this evening.
2 You ring an estate agent to make an appointment to see a house and arrange a meeting place.
3 You ring a shopping centre to find out what time they close tonight.
4 You ring the railway station to reserve a seat on a train to London tomorrow. You need to be in London by 10.30am at the latest.
5 You have an appointment with Dr Giles at 10.30am next Tuesday. You would like to change it to 11.15am on Friday. Ring the surgery and rearrange the appointment.

4

4 a Translate the following.

Vocabulary

receiver	___	peak rate	___
coin slot	___	cheap rate	___
returned coins slot	___	local call	___
to listen for	___	long distance call	___
dialling tone	___	business colleague	___
to lift up	___	relative	___
to dial	___	20 miles away	___
to replace	___	dialling codes	___
to insert	___	to call	___
to speak	___	overseas	___
ringing tone	___	international code	___
emergency services	___	country code	___
fire brigade	___	area code	___
police	___	to remember	___
ambulance	___	to omit	___
telephone rates	___	wish	___

Structures

What's this? ______________________
It's the receiver. ______________________
What do you do with it? ______________________
You speak into it. ______________________
First you lift up the receiver. ______________________
What number do you dial if you want the police? ______________________
You dial 999. ______________________
When is cheap rate? ______________________
It's from 8pm - 8am. ______________________
What's the area code for Cork? ______________________
It's 21. ______________________
How do I make an international call? ______________________
What is Kevin Thompson's number? ______________________
It's 0-1-7-1-double-2-9-8-5-double-6. ______________________
What's Mrs Jackson doing? ______________________
She's opening the door of the phone box. ______________________
What's she going to do next? ______________________
She's going to step inside the phone box. ______________________

Teaching Notes

Warm-up

Ask students questions from earlier Units eg "Have you ever been sailing? What are you wearing? Are you wearing a tie?"

Revision

Revise all the structures and vocabulary from the previous Unit by asking students questions eg "Is there a department store in your town? Can you name 3 things you would buy in the cosmetics department?"

Presentation and Practice

1 Find out who has got a telephone and ask them to explain how to use it. Provide vocabulary where necessary. Students then complete the matching task in 1a. Check by asking students questions eg "What is A?" before they complete the speaking activity in 1b.

In pairs students read the instructions and try to work out the correct order. Provide feedback by asking one pair to tell you the order they have put the instructions in.

Students complete the speaking activity in 1d while you monitor and check.

In pairs students complete the speaking activity in 1e. Provide feedback by students telling you about themselves.

Introduce the activity in 1f by asking students questions about the 'Telephone Rates' information sheet eg "When are peak rate times? Is peak rate more expensive than cheap rate?" Students then complete the speaking activity in 1f while you monitor and check.

Students then ask their neighbour the questions in 1g. Ask students the questions to check their answers.

2 Ask students what their area code is and then introduce the list of dialling codes in 2a.

Students complete the speaking activity in 2a while you monitor and check.

In pairs students then complete the speaking activity in 2b. Provide feedback by asking students to tell you how to make an international call. In 2c students answer the questions about their own number.

Introduce the page from the telephone numbers book by asking students about the information eg "What is Kevin Thompson's number? Where does Susi Kerr live?" Explain to students that they are in Glasgow and want to telephone some of the people on the list. They then complete the activity in 2d. When they are finished ask them what numbers they would ring for the 7 people, checking how they are saying the numbers and that the numbers they are dialling are correct.

Students then complete the speaking activity in 2e while you monitor and check.

In 2f students ask 5 other students for their numbers. Check by asking students to give you their number.

3 Students look at the photograph sequence 'Making a Phone Call' and describe the lady to their neighbour.

In pairs students then ask and answer the questions from 3b while you monitor and check. Students then tell their neighbour about Mrs Jackson as in the example.

Introduce the listening activity by telling students that they are going to listen to Mrs Jackson's conversation. While they listen they should make notes. Play the cassette twice and then ask students to tell you what the conversation was about. Students then read the phrases in 3e and put a question mark next to the phrases they think they heard on the cassette. Play the cassette again for them to check and then ask students to tell you which phrases they heard. Revise the telephone phrases for answering and finishing a call and then demonstrate the speaking activity in 3f with one student.

In pairs students then complete the speaking activity while you monitor and check.

Revise all the structures and vocabulary before moving on to the next lesson.

At home students prepare for the next lesson by looking up the vocabulary in 4a of Unit 27.

Tapescripts

Exercise 3d

A Susi's hair salon. Can I help you?

B Yes please. I have an appointment for Thursday at 10am and I'd like to change it.

A Yes certainly. What's the name?

B It's Mrs Jackson.

A Okay. And when would you like to change it to?

B Thursday afternoon, if possible.

A Yes of course. How about 3pm?

B That's fine.

A See you on Thursday at 3pm Mrs Jackson.

B Okay. Goodbye.

A Bye.

Answers

Exercis2 1a

a receiver
b display
c coin slot
d keys
e returned coins slot

Exercise 1c

1 lift up receiver
2 insert money (minimum 10p)
3 listen for the dialling tone
4 dial the number
5 listen for the ringing tone
6 speak
7 replace the receiver
8 take the returned coins

Exercise 2d

1	Bob Thornton	2913214
2	Linda Dooley	00 353 21 329 90
3	Barbara Grundmann	00 49 201 259432
4	Jose Gonzalez	00 34 37 25614
5	Tania Connor	0181 8922599
6	Susi Kerr	00 1971 3949527
7	Hiromi Suzuki	00 81 332 4933215

1

UNIT 27

Do you have a driving licence?

1 a Ask your neighbour the following questions.

1 Do you have a driving licence?
2 Do you have a car?
3 What kind of fuel does it take?
4 Where do you normally get petrol?
5 Why do you normally go to this petrol station?

b Look at photograph sequence 5 'Filling up with Petrol' on the next pages and answer the following questions.

1 Which photograph do you think is first in the sequence? ___________
2 Which photograph do you think is second in the sequence? ___________
3 Which photograph do you think is third in the sequence? ___________
4 Which photograph do you think is fourth in the sequence? ___________
5 Which photograph do you think is fifth in the sequence? ___________

c Tell your teacher about the photograph sequence.

eg *I think the first photograph in the sequence is photograph C because the car is coming into the garage. I think the second photograph is...*

d Ask your neighbour.

1 What is happening in photograph A?
2 What is happening in photograph B?
3 What is happening in photograph C?
4 What is happening in photograph D?
5 What is happening in photograph E?

e Ask your neighbour about the pictures.

eg *How much is diesel per litre? It's 52.9 pence per litre.*

1 What is the car registration number?
2 How much is unleaded petrol?
3 What is the man wearing?
4 Can you pay by credit card at this garage?
5 What is the woman wearing?

f Discuss the following questions with 2 neighbours.

1 Is petrol cheaper or more expensive in your country than in Britain?
2 Are most petrol stations self-service in your country?
3 What information does the registration plate in your country give?
4 Can you buy alcohol and/or sweets at petrol stations in your country?
5 Do you pay before or after you fill up in your country?

2

2 a Which services do you think post offices in the UK provide? Put a tick (✓) next to the ones you know they definitely provide, a cross (x) next to the ones you know they definitely don't provide, and a question mark (?) next to the ones you're not sure about.

___ sell stamps
___ issue driving licences
___ deliver letters
___ sell phonecards
___ issue passports
___ have savings accounts
___ sell lottery tickets
___ issue TV licences
___ issue gun licences
___ change foreign currencies
___ pay pensions

Check with your teacher.

b Write 5 sentences.

eg *I didn't know that post offices in Britain sold phonecards.*

1 ___________
2 ___________
3 ___________
4 ___________
5 ___________

c Discuss this with your neighbour.

eg *I didn't know that post offices in Britain sold phonecards, did you? In our country they don't.*

d Fill in the following. Which licences do you need in your country?

gun licence ____ dog licence ____
TV licence ____ radio licence ____
driving licence ____ trading licence ____

e Discuss with your neighbour.

eg *In our country we need a gun licence, don't we? I don't think we need a dog licence...*

Where would you get these licences from?

f Tell your teacher.

3

3 a Read the following situations and tell your neighbour what you would do.

1 You are lying in bed one night. It's 3am and very dark outside. You suddenly hear a scream.
2 You are driving along the road. A car pulls out of a side street and crashes into the side of your car. Nobody is hurt.
3 You return home from a party at 11pm. You get your key out to open your door. The door is unlocked and a light is on inside. You had locked the door before you left.
4 You are walking along a street. You see a small bag lying on the floor. You pick it up and find it is full of money.
5 You finish work one evening. You go outside to the car park and go to where you left your car. It is not there.
6 You are walking home one evening. You notice a man climbing out of a window of a house. The house is in darkness. He is carrying something.

b Look at the following and tick the box (✓) if you would go to the police if it happened to you.

Somebody has broken into your house and has stolen your TV. ❑
Somebody has stolen your passport. ❑
Somebody has broken a window in your car but has not stolen anything. ❑
Somebody is playing loud music at 3am on a Wednesday morning. ❑

c Tell your neighbour why you would go to the police.

d Imagine one of the situations in 3a has happened to you. Tell your neighbour what happened.

eg *I was driving along the road, concentrating and watching the other cars. Suddenly a car pulled out of a side street and crashed into the side of my car. Nobody was hurt. I was getting out of the car when the other car drove off. I grabbed a piece of paper and a pen and while he was driving away, I wrote down the car number. I went to the police and told them about the accident. They looked in their computer and said that the car had been stolen. They told me to write to my insurance company so I wrote to them and explained what had happened.*

e Look at the pictures for 30 seconds and then cover the page. Try to remember where the person was, what he/she was wearing and what he/she was doing.

eg *He was in a library. He was wearing a dark suit and sunglasses, and he was sitting at a table reading a book...*

4

4 a Translate the following.

Vocabulary

fuel ___________
diesel ___________
per litre ___________
car registration number ___________
unleaded ___________
number plate ___________
credit card ___________
4 star petrol ___________
lead ___________
registration plate ___________
alcohol ___________
petrol station ___________
to sell ___________
stamps ___________
to issue ___________
driving licences ___________
to deliver ___________
letters ___________
phone cards ___________
savings accounts ___________
passports ___________
lottery tickets ___________
TV licences ___________
gun licences ___________
to change ___________
foreign currencies ___________
pensions ___________
dog licence ___________
radio licence ___________
trading licence ___________
to hear ___________
scream ___________
side street ___________
to crash into ___________
nobody ___________
hurt ___________
to return home ___________
unlocked ___________
to lock ___________
to notice ___________
to climb out of ___________
darkness ___________
to break into ___________
to steal ___________
to break ___________
to concentrate ___________
to drive off ___________
to grab ___________
accident ___________
insurance company ___________
to explain ___________

Structures

I think the first photograph is C because the car is coming into the garage. ___________
How much is diesel per litre? ___________
It's 52.9p per litre. ___________
I didn't know that post offices in Britain sold phone cards, did you? ___________
In our country, they don't. ___________
In our country we need a gun licence, don't we? ___________
I don't think we need a dog licence. ___________
I was driving along the road. ___________
I was getting out of the car. ___________
While he was driving away I wrote down the car number. ___________
He was in a library. ___________
He was wearing a dark suit and sunglasses. ___________
He was sitting at a table reading a book. ___________

Teaching Notes

Warm-up

Ask students questions from earlier Units eg "Is there a department store in your town? What is a parking meter? Have you ever been to the USA?"

Revision

Revise all the structures and vocabulary from the previous Unit by asking students questions eg "What number do you dial in your country to call the police? Have you ever telephoned the fire brigade? What is your telephone number from the UK?"

Presentation and Practice

1 In pairs students complete the speaking activity in 1a while you monitor and check. Students look at the photograph sequence 'Filling up with Petrol' and answer the questions in 1b. Check that students have the correct order before they complete the speaking activity in 1c. Provide feedback by one student telling you about the sequence.

In pairs students then complete the speaking activity in 1d. Provide feedback by asking students the questions and checking their answers.

Students then look at the photographs in more detail and ask each other the questions in 1e. Check their answers.

Students complete the speaking activity in 1f while you monitor and check. Ask pairs to tell you about their neighbour.

2 In 2a students look at the information and mark it with a tick (✓), cross (x) or question mark (?). Ask students to tell you what they think and then give them the correct answers.

Students complete the writing task in 2b. Provide feedback by asking students to tell you what they have written.

Students then complete the speaking activity in 2c while you monitor and check. Provide feedback by asking pairs to demonstrate their activity. Students work in pairs and complete the task in 2d before going on to the speaking exercise in 2e. Provide feedback by asking students to tell you about their own country.

3 Write the first situation on the board and ask students what they would do. Elicit as many answers as possible.

In pairs students continue the speaking activity with their neighbour.

Provide feedback by asking students what they would do in each of the situations. Ask how many of the class would go to the police for any of the situations in 3a. They then look at the situations in 3b and say if they would go to the police for any of these situations.

Students then complete the speaking activity in 3c. Provide feedback by asking students to tell you in what situations their neighbour would go to the police.

Students then complete the speaking activity in 3d while you monitor and check. Provide feedback by asking students to tell you what happened.

Students look at the pictures of the people in 3e for 30 seconds. They then close their books and try to remember what the person was doing, where he/she was and what he/she was wearing. Provide feedback by asking students to tell you about the people.

Revise all the structures and vocabulary before moving on to the next lesson.

At home students prepare for the next lesson by looking up the vocabulary in 4a of Unit 28.

Answers

Exercise 1b

1 C
2 E
3 D
4 A
5 B

Exercise 2a

✓ sell stamps
x issue driving licences
✓ deliver letters
✓ sell phonecards
x issue passports
✓ have savings accounts
x sell lottery tickets
✓ issue TV licences
x issue gun licences
x change foreign currencies
✓ pay pensions

1

UNIT 28

Who do you bank with?

1 a **Now read the following information.**

"I bank with Lloyd's bank. I've been with them since I left school and got my first job, where I was paid by cheque every Thursday. After work I took my cheque to the bank and paid it in. I only had a deposit account then, so I had no cheques or cash cards. At the same time as I paid my cheque in I took most of my wages out, so I had some money for the weekend. Now I have a current account, so I have a cheque book and cheque card. The cheque card can be used in cash machines, so I can get money wherever and whenever I want. I get a salary every month which is paid into this account. I still have my deposit account and I try to save a little bit each month, so I can go somewhere nice for my summer holidays, but it's too easy to spend it now."

b **Say whether the following statements are true (T) or false (F).**

eg *John banks with Lloyds. T.*

1 He was paid in cash in his first job. ____
2 He was paid weekly in his first job. ____
3 His first account was a current account. ____
4 Now he has two accounts. ____
5 Now he is paid monthly. ____

Check with your neighbour.

c **Fill in the questionnaire about yourself.**

Banking Questionnaire

1 Who do you bank with? ____________________

2 How many accounts do you have? ____________________

3 Which of the following do you have?
current account ☐ deposit account ☐ other ☐

4 Do you have a ...?
cheque book ☐ cash/cheque card ☐ cash card ☐ cheque card ☐

5 Are you paid ...?
hourly ☐ weekly ☐ monthly ☐

6 Are you paid / is your salary paid ...?
in cash ☐ by cheque ☐ into your account ☐

d **Tell your neighbour about yourself.**

eg *I bank with Lloyd's bank.*

2

2

a **Ask your neighbour the following questions.**

1 What is the man in the picture doing?
2 How often do you use these machines?
3 Why do you use them?
4 Do you prefer using them to going into the bank?
5 Do you have to pay for the card?
6 When was the last time you used one?
7 Why did you use that cash machine?
8 What did you do with the money?
9 Did you get a receipt?
10 Do you think cash machines are a good idea? Why (not)?

b **How to use a cash machine. Put the instructions in the correct order.**

___ Key in your Personal Identification Number (PIN).
___ Take your card.
___ Request which service you would like.
_1_ Insert your card.
___ Key in the amount you wish to withdraw.
___ Take your money.
___ Wait while your request is being processed.

Check with your neighbour.

c **Ask your neighbour the following questions.**

eg *What do I do first? Insert your card.*

1 Do I key in the service I want or the amount I want first?
2 When do I key in my PIN number?
3 Why do I have to wait?
4 Do I take my card or my money first?
5 What's the last thing I do?

d **Close your books and ask your neighbour how to use a cash machine.**

eg *What do I do first? First you insert your card.*

3

3 a **Look at photograph sequence 6 'Changing Money' on the next pages. Describe the man and tell your neighbour what the photograph sequence is about.**

b **Ask your neighbour.**

1 Where do you think these photos were taken?
2 Why does the man go to the foreign enquiries counter?
3 Why would you go to this desk?
4 What time of day do you think it is? Why?
5 What do you think he's holding in his hand?

c **A bank clerk is talking to a customer. Listen to the cassette and fill in the missing information. (B = Bank Clerk / C = Customer)**

B Good afternoon. Can I help you?
C Yes please. I want to change some ______________ into ______________.
B Certainly. How much would you like to change?
C ______________ German Marks.
B Can I see your ______________ please?
C Yes of course. Here you are.
B Thank you. Can you ______________ this form here please? Thank you. That's ______________.
C Thank you. Goodbye.

d **Here are some phrases you can use in a bank. Read them through and then practise the dialogue with your neighbour.**

1 I want to change some French Francs.
2 I want to order some traveller's cheques.
3 I want to pay a cheque in.
4 I want to take some money out.
5 I want to order a new cheque book.

e **Now complete the following sentences.**

eg *I want to change some German Marks.*
He said he wanted to change some German Marks.

1 I want to change some French Francs.
He said ______________________________

2 I want to order some traveller's cheques.
He said ______________________________

3 I want to pay a cheque in.
He said ______________________________

4 I want to take some money out.
He said ______________________________

5 I want to order a new cheque book.
He said ______________________________

f **Now ask your neighbour these questions.**

1 Have you ever changed money? Where? Why?
2 Have you ever ordered traveller's cheques. When? Why?
3 When you go on holiday, do you take cheques or cash? Why?

4

4 a **Translate the following.**

Vocabulary

by cheque ______	Personal Identification Number (PIN) ______
to pay in ______	to request ______
deposit account ______	service ______
cash card ______	to withdraw ______
to take out ______	to wait ______
wages ______	to be processed ______
current account ______	counter ______
cheque book ______	to change money ______
cheque card ______	passport ______
salary ______	to sign ______
to spend ______	form ______
in cash ______	signature ______
weekly ______	to order ______
account ______	traveller's cheques ______
hourly ______	

Structures

I bank with Lloyd's bank. ______
I have a current account. ______
I have a cheque book and cheque card. ______
I get a salary every month. ______
My salary is paid into my account. ______
John banks with Lloyd's bank. ______
What do I do first? ______
First you insert your card. ______
Can I help you? ______
I want to change some German Marks into pounds. ______
Can I see your passport please? ______
Can you sign this form please? ______
I want to change some French Francs. ______
I want to order some traveller's cheques. ______
I want to pay a cheque in. ______
I want to take some money out. ______
I want to order a new cheque book. ______
I want to change some German Marks. ______
He said he wanted to change some German Marks. ______

Teaching Notes

Warm-up

Ask students questions from earlier Units eg "How do you make a telephone call? What's your neighbour wearing?"

Revision

Revise all the structures and vocabulary from the previous Unit by asking students questions eg "How much does a litre of petrol cost in your country? What services do post offices provide in your country? What would you do if someone broke into your house?"

Presentation and Practice

1 In pairs students look at the photograph and describe the person and the background. Ask them what they think he does for a living. Students then read the information about John and say whether the statements in 1b are true or false. When they have checked with their neighbour introduce the banking questionnaire in 1c reading the questions and answering about yourself. When students are familiar with the new vocabulary they complete the questionnaire and tell their neighbour about themselves. Provide feedback by asking students to tell you about themselves.

2 In pairs students complete the speaking activity in 2a while you monitor and check.

In 2b students put the instructions in the correct order and compare their work with their neighbour. They then complete the speaking activity in 2c while you monitor and check. Provide feedback by asking pairs to explain how to use a cash machine.

Students then complete the speaking activity in 2d.

3 Find out who has changed money in a bank before and ask them where, when, why and what currency they were changing.

Students look at the photograph sequence 'Changing Money' and complete the speaking activity in 3b. Ask students what they think the people are saying before introducing the listening activity in 3c.

Play the cassette once for students to fill in the missing information and check by asking two students to read the dialogue. If possible find a current list of exchange rates for further practice. Students then use the phrases in 3d and practise asking for different things in a bank.

Introduce 3e by writing the examples on the board and explaining how to change the statements into reported speech.

Students then compete the task in 3e while you monitor and check.

Students then complete the speaking activity in 3f and tell you about their neighbour.

Revise all the structures and vocabulary before moving on to the next lesson.

At home students prepare for the next lesson by looking up the vocabulary in 4a of Unit 29.

Tapescripts

Exercise 3c

B Good afternoon. Can I help you?

C Yes please. I want to change some German marks into pounds.

B Certainly. How much would you like to change?

C 250 German Marks.

B Can I see your passport please?

C Yes of course. Here you are.

B Thank you. Can you sign this form here please?

Thank you. That's £100 (10-20-30-40-50-60-70-80-90-100).

C Thank you. Goodbye.

Answers

Exercise 1b

1 F
2 T
3 F
4 T
5 T

Exercise 2b

1 Insert your card.
2 Key in your Personal Identification Number.
3 Request which service you would like.
4 Key in the amount you wish to withdraw.
5 Wait while your request is being processed.
6 Take your card.
7 Take your money.

Exercise 3c

B Good afternoon. Can I help you?

C Yes please. I want to change some German marks into pounds.

B Certainly. How much would you like to change?

C 250 German Marks.

B Can I see your passport please?

C Yes of course. Here you are.

B Thank you. Can you sign this form here please? Thank you. That's £100

C Thank you. Goodbye.

Exercise 3e

1 He said he wanted to change some French Francs.
2 He said he wanted to order some traveller's cheques.
3 He said he wanted to pay a cheque in.
4 He said he wanted to take some money out.
5 He said he wanted to order a new cheque book.

1

UNIT 29

Where's the nearest car park?

1 a **Answer the questions below.**

1 **Which of these do you have in your town?**
___ a tourist information office ___ public toilets ___ car parks ___ a library
___ a swimming pool ___ recycling banks ___ cinemas ___ a park

2 **Who pays for these services?** ______

3 **Who pays for new roads?** ______
rubbish collection? ______
street cleaning? ______
playgrounds? ______
litter bins? ______

4 **Which of these do you have in your town?**
restaurants ______ a taxi service ______ an old people's home ____

5 **Do you need a licence for these? If so, who do you get it from?**
______

6 **If you want to build a house, do you need permission? Who from?**
______

7 **If you want to build a factory, do you need permission? Who from?**
______

8 **Do you have cheap accommodation for old people?**
______

9 **If you eat in a restaurant and get food poisoning, who can you complain to?**
______

10 **Who maintains parks, grass areas, trees?**
______

b **Tell your teacher.**

c **Read the following information.**

In Britain many of these services are provided by the local council. The public elect councillors who serve for 4 years and a chairman is elected to chair council meetings. Their aims are to provide efficient services to residents and visitors in their district. Most meetings are open to the public.

Tourist information offices, libraries, recycling banks and public toilets are provided by the local council. Some car parks and swimming pools are provided by the council, although many are privately owned. New roads, sewers and playgrounds are planned, paid for, and maintained by the local council, who also provide rubbish collection and street cleaning. If you want to open a cinema, taxi service, pub, restaurant or kennels you need a licence and you apply for this licence to the local council. You cannot build a house or a factory, or alter your house if you do not have permission from the local council. If you are an old aged pensioner (OAP) you can apply for a cheaper flat from the council. There are sometimes waiting lists. And if you have food poisoning you will, of course, complain to the restaurant but you can also complain to the council. They will then check the restaurant. The local council also maintains parks, grass areas and trees.

These are just some of the services the local council provide. This all costs a lot of money and so the residents have to pay a council tax. The amount you pay is different in different areas.

2

2 a Look at the diagram below.

Local Council - Departments and Sections

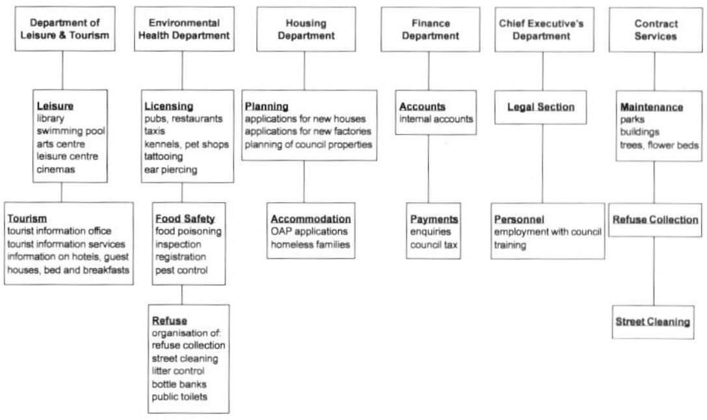

b **Now answer these questions.**

eg *Where should you go if you want to open a restaurant?*
You should go to the licensing section in the Environmental Health Department.

1 Where should you go if you want to find a good hotel? ______
2 Where should you go if you have had food poisoning? ______
3 Where should you go if you want to pay your council tax? ______
4 Where should you go if you want a job? ______
5 Where should you go if you want to build a factory? ______

c **Listen to the cassette and make notes. You will hear a recorded message giving telephone numbers.**

Housing Department Planning Accommodation	**Environmental Health Department** Licensing Food Safety Refuse
Finance Department Accounts Payments	**Chief Executive's Department** Personnel Legal
Department of Leisure and Tourism Tourism Leisure	**Contract Services Department**

d **Ask your neighbour questions.**

eg *What's the number for the Housing Department? It's 251.*

3

Tynedale Council

How to Get in Touch

By Phone

Ring (01434) 604011 and ask for the department you require. If you are not sure who to contact, explain briefly to the switchboard, who will transfer you to the correct department and section.

In Person

The main departments are located in Hexham and are marked on the map.

Office Hours

8am - 5pm

In case of emergency please contact (0831) 580888

Important changes

Please note the following changes:

Main Council - old 604022
Tel No new 652448

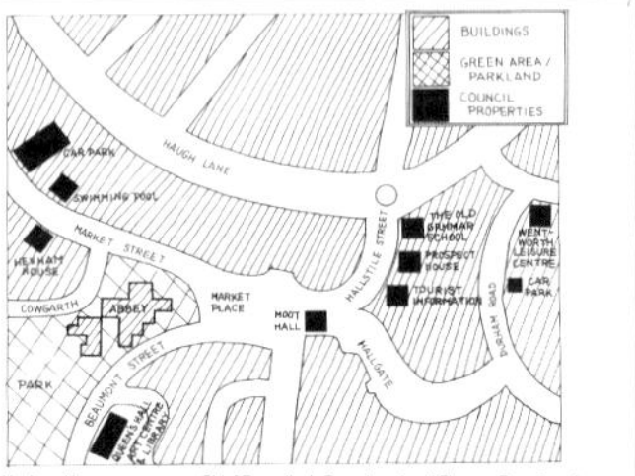

Hexham House - Chief Executive's Department and Finance Department
Prospect House - Housing Department and Department of Leisure and Tourism
The Old Grammar School - Environmental Health Department
Moot Hall - Contract Services Department

3 a **Ask your neighbour the following questions.**

eg *What time do the council offices close? At 5pm.*

1 What time do the council offices open?
2 When would I ring (0831) 580888?
3 Where is the Finance Department?
4 Which departments are in Prospect House?
5 Which is the number for the main council?

b **Answer the following questions.**

eg *Where is Hexham House? It's in Market Street opposite the swimming pool.*

1 Where is the tourist information office? ______
2 Where is the swimming pool? ______
3 Where is the leisure centre? ______
4 Where is Prospect House? ______
5 Where is the Queen's Hall Arts Centre? ______

c **Ask your neighbour for directions to 5 places.**

eg *How do you get from the swimming pool to the library? You come out of the swimming pool and turn left. You go along Market Street and turn right at the Market Place. You go along Beaumont Street past the Abbey on your right and the library is on the left opposite the park.*

d **Ask your neighbour the following questions.**

eg *Where is the Housing Department? It's in Prospect House in Hallstile Street.*

1 Where is the Finance Department?
2 Where is the Contract Services Department?
3 Where is the Department of Leisure and Tourism?
4 Where is the Environmental Health Department?
5 Where is the Chief Executive's Department?

4

4 a Translate the following.

Vocabulary

public toilets ______	to apply for ______
new roads ______	to alter your house ______
rubbish collection ______	old age pensioner (OAP) ______
street cleaning ______	waiting lists ______
playgrounds ______	council tax ______
litter bins ______	department of leisure and tourism ______
taxi service ______	environmental health ______
old people's home ______	housing ______
licence ______	finance ______
permission ______	chief executive ______
factory ______	contract services ______
food poisoning ______	kennels ______
to complain to ______	pet shops ______
to maintain ______	tattooing ______
park ______	ear piercing ______
local council ______	inspection ______
councillors ______	registration ______
to elect ______	pest control ______
chairman ______	refuse ______
to chair ______	litter control ______
council meetings ______	property ______
public ______	homeless ______
aims ______	payments ______
to provide ______	personnel ______
efficient ______	employment ______
residents ______	training ______
district ______	buildings ______
privately owned ______	flower beds ______
planned ______	switchboard ______
maintained ______	

Structures

Where should you go to if you want to open a restaurant? ______
You should go to the licensing section of the Environmental Health Department. ______
What's the number for the Housing Department? ______
It's 251. ______
What time do the council offices close? ______
At 5pm. ______
Where is Hexham House? ______
It's in Market Street opposite the swimming pool. ______
How do you get from the swimming pool to the library? ______
You come out of the swimming pool and turn left. ______
You go along Market Street and turn right at the Market Place. ______
You go along Beaumont Street past the Abbey on your right and the library is on the left opposite the park.
______
Where is the Housing Department? ______
It's in Prospect House in Hallstile Street. ______

Teaching Notes

Warm-up

Ask students questions from earlier Units eg "Can you name 3 electrical items which have switches? What did you do yesterday?"

Revision

Revise all the structures and vocabulary from the previous Unit by asking students questions eg "Who do you bank with? Do you have a current account? How do you use a cash machine?"

Presentation and Practice

1 Students fill in the questionnaire about the town/city where they live while you monitor and check. Students then tell you about their town/city.

Students read the information in 1c and compare it with the answers in their questionnaire.

2 Introduce the diagram in 2a by asking students questions about the information eg "How many departments are there? Which section is ear piercing in?"

Students then answer the questions in 2b. Provide feedback by asking students the questions and checking their answers.

Introduce 2c by explaining that they are going to hear a recorded message which will give them information about the telephone numbers of the various departments and sections. While they are listening they are to note down the numbers. They will hear the cassette twice.

Students then complete the speaking activity in 2d.

3 Students look at the information and complete the speaking activity in 3a while you monitor and check.

Students then answer the questions in 3b. Provide feedback by asking students the questions and checking their answers.

In pairs students revise directions by asking 5 questions as in the example in 3c. Provide feedback by asking pairs to demonstrate their activity.

Students then complete the speaking activity in 3d.

Revise all the structures and vocabulary before moving on to the next lesson.

At home students prepare for the next lesson by revising all the vocabulary and structures from Units 21 -29.

Tapescripts

Exercise 2c

Good morning. This is the local council offices. Unfortunately the switchboard is closed but you may dial direct when you hear the tone. The housing department is 251 for general enquiries. Specific enquiries about planning should dial 252 and enquiries about accommodation should dial 253. The finance department is closed all day today so please try again tomorrow if you wish to speak with them. General enquiries for the department of leisure and tourism should dial 200; the tourism section is 201 and the leisure section is 204. General enquiries for the environmental health department should dial 220; specific enquiries for the licensing section should dial 223, and food safety should dial 229 and for refuse dial 227. The personnel section is 794 and the legal department is 860. The contract services department has moved and has a new number, enquiries should ring 01434 652211. Have a nice day.

Answers

Exercise 2a

1 You should go to the tourism section in the Department of Leisure and Tourism.
2 You should go to the food safety section in the Environmental Health Department.
3 You should go to the payments section in the Finance Department.
4 You should go to the personnel section in the Chief Executive's Department.
5 You should go to the planning section in the Housing Department.

Exercise 2c

Housing Department	251
Planning	252
Accommodation	253
Finance Department	closed all day
Accounts	
Payments	
Department of Leisure and Tourism	200
Tourism	201
Leisure	204
Environmental Health Department	220
Licensing	223
Food Safety	229
Refuse	227
Chief Executive's Department	
Personnel	794
Legal	860
Contract Services Department	01434 652211

Exercise 3b

1 It's in Hallstile Street just before Prospect House.
2 It's in Market Street opposite Hexham House.
3 It's in Durham Road next to the car park.
4 It's in Hallstile Street between the tourist information and the old grammar school.
5 It's in Beaumont Street opposite the park.

1

UNIT 30

Revision

1 a **What do you buy in the following containers? Work with your neighbour and see how many items you can think of.**

eg *packet - cigarettes, dog food, tissues, cereals.*

1 jar 2 bottle 3 box 4 tin 5 aerosol can 6 carton

b **Ask your neighbour these questions.**

1 What do you do with your empty bottles?
2 What do you do with your old newspapers?
3 What do you do with your empty tins?
4 What do you do with your plastic bags?
5 What do you do with your old clothes?

c **Tell your neighbour what you would use these objects for.**

1 a plaster
2 string
3 hairspray
4 fly spray
5 wall paper

d **Discuss these sentences with your neighbour.**

1 I don't buy products if the packaging is not nice.
2 I think supermarkets should charge for plastic bags.
3 I buy brand products because they're better quality.
4 I don't think packaging is important.
5 I always buy refillable containers if I can.

2 a **Can you name 3 things you would buy in these shops?**

1 Jeweller's ______ ______ ______
2 Newsagent's ______ ______ ______
3 Stationer's ______ ______ ______
4 Chemist's ______ ______ ______
5 Electrical Shop ______ ______ ______

b **Which of these would you give to a friend, or relation as a present? Put a tick (✓) next to the ones you would give, and a cross (x) next to the ones you wouldn't give as a present. When you're finished, tell your neighbour who you would give your presents to.**

1 flowers ___	6 a map ___
2 socks ___	7 perfume ___
3 sticky tape ___	8 envelopes ___
4 belt ___	9 chocolate ___
5 petrol ___	10 hairdryer ___

c **Tell your neighbour about the last time you gave somebody a present. What was it? Who did you give it to? Why did you give the person a present?**

2

3 a **Ask your neighbour these questions.**

1 When was the last time you bought something in a sale?
2 What was it?
3 Was it something you needed or did you buy it because it was a special offer?
4 Was it good value for money?
5 "You get what you pay for." Do you agree with this statement?

4 a **Jamie is going shopping this afternoon. Here is his shopping list. Read it through and then complete the sentences.**

1 He's going to buy some eggs.
2 He isn't going to buy any potatoes.
3 ______ mushrooms.
4 ______ toothpaste.
5 ______ oil.
6 ______ garlic.
7 ______ toilet rolls.
8 ______ mince.
9 ______ tomatoes.
10 ______ apples.

b **Ask your neighbour these questions.**

1 Have you got a TV?
2 How did you pay for it?
3 Do you prefer to pay when you buy something, or later? Why?
4 Do you think it is cheaper paying monthly? Why (not)?
5 What monthly instalments do you pay?

5 a **Match up the following and compare with your neighbour.**

1 a packet of	___ flowers
2 a bunch of	___ coffee
3 a loaf	_1_ dog food
4 a pair of	___ pens
5 a cup of	___ earrings
6 a bottle of	___ whisky
7 a set of	___ bread

b **Ask your neighbour these questions.**

1 Is there a department store in your town?
2 What is it called?
3 Where is it?
4 How often do you go there?
5 Is it cheaper or more expensive that other shops?

3

5 c **Name 3 things you would buy in the following departments.**

1 furniture department ______ ______ ______
2 stationery department ______ ______ ______
3 men's fashion department ______ ______ ______
4 electrical department ______ ______ ______
5 ladies' fashion department ______ ______ ______

d **Which department would you go to if...**

1 ... you wanted to change your hair style? ______
2 ... you wanted to exchange a jumper? ______
3 ... you wanted to buy some cat food? ______
4 ... you wanted to pay a bill? ______
5 ... you wanted to buy a pillow? ______

6 a **Explain to your neighbour how to make a phone call from a public phone box. Your neighbour will do the actions as you explain them.**

eg *First you open the door and go into the phone box.*

b **Ask your neighbour these questions.**

1 What are the number(s) for the emergency services in your country?
2 In what situations would you ring for the fire brigade?
3 In what situations would you ring for the police?
4 In what situations would you ring for an ambulance?
5 Have you ever telephoned the emergency services? When? Why?

c **Write down the names and telephone numbers of 5 people you know in 'your telephone book'.**

your telephone book	your neighbour's telephone book
1	1 ......
2	2 ......
3	3 ......
4	4 ......
5	5 ......

Your neighbour will now give you his/her 5 names and numbers. Listen and write down the names and numbers in 'your neighbour's telephone book'. Compare your work with your neighbour.

7 a **Ask your neighbour these questions.**

1 Do you have a car?
2 How old is it?
3 What make is it?
4 What kind of fuel does it take?
5 Where do you normally get petrol?

4

7 b **Can you name 3 services which post offices in Britain provide and 3 services which post offices in your own country provide? Work with your neighbour.**

c **What would you do? Read these situations and then tell your neighbour what you would do.**

1 You lend a friend your car while his is in the garage. He rings you next morning to say he drank too much last night and crashed the car while he was driving home.

2 You are on holiday in Britain and go to a restaurant for lunch. When you want to pay you find that somebody has stolen your purse.

3 You go shopping one Saturday afternoon. When you return to the car park, the window in your car is broken and the radio has been stolen.

4 You are lying in bed one night and hear somebody moving around in your flat.

5 You are walking home one night and you see a baby lying by the side of the road.

8 a **Ask your neighbour these questions.**

1 Who do you bank with? Why?
2 How many accounts do you have?
3 What type of account(s) do you have?
4 Have you got a cheque book?
5 Are you paid weekly or monthly?

b **Your neighbour has just received a cash card from the bank. He/she has never used a cash machine before. Explain how to use it. Remember you have to explain every stage.**

c **Ask your neighbour about their holiday. When you are on holiday in a foreign country how do you pay for:**

1 your hotel?
2 a meal in a restaurant?
3 the hire of a car?
4 shopping?
5 sun cream?

9 a **Ask your neighbour these questions about their country.**

1 How often is the street where you live cleaned? Who by?
2 Who collects your rubbish? Do you have to pay for it?
3 Who provides playgrounds and litter bins?
4 Do you have cheap accommodation for old people?
5 Do you need permission to build a house? Who from?

10 a **You are going to tell your neighbour about yourself. Try and talk for at least 5 minutes. Here are some topics you can talk about.**

- what you recycle and why
- what you think of brand names and packaging
- why you would(n't) buy things from sales
- how you pay for things (eg cars, TV's)
- shopping facilities in your town
- post office services in your country
- local council services in your town
- who you bank with and why

Teaching Notes

Warm-up

Ask students questions from earlier Units eg "Have you ever changed money in a bank? Have you ever travelled by plane?"

Revision

Revise all the structures and vocabulary from the previous Unit by asking students questions eg "Who provides street cleaning in your town? What does OAP stand for?"

1 In pairs students complete the speaking activity in 1a while you monitor and check.

Students then complete the speaking activity in 1b. Provide feedback by asking students to tell you about their neighbour. Students then explain to their neighbour what they would use the objects in 1c for. In 1d students discuss the statements with their neighbour while you monitor and check.

2 Students complete the task in 2a and then compare their work with their neighbour. Students then decide who they would give the items in 2b to as a present and tell their neighbour.

They then complete the speaking activity in 2c while you monitor and check.

3 Students complete the speaking activity in 3a. Provide feedback by asking students to tell you about their neighbour.

4 Students then complete the writing task in 4a. Provide feedback by asking students to read you their sentences.

Students then complete the speaking activity in 4b while you monitor and check.

5 Students complete the matching task in 5a and then complete the speaking activity in 5b while you monitor and check. In 5c students name 3 things in each department and then compare their work with their neighbour.

Students then complete the writing task in 5d. Provide feedback by asking students which department they would go to.

6 In 6a students explain to their neighbour how to make a phone call from a public call box while you monitor and check.

In pairs students then complete the speaking activity in 6b. Students then write down the names and numbers of 5 people they know and sitting back to back they give their neighbour the names and numbers. They then compare their work.

7 Students complete the speaking activity in 7a. Provide feedback by asking students to tell you about their neighbour.

Students then complete the activity in 7b and tell you the services they have named.

In pairs students tell their neighbour what they would do in the situations described in 7c. Provide feedback by asking students to tell you about their neighbour.

8 Students ask their neighbour the questions from 8a and then complete the speaking activity in 8b. Students then ask their neighbour how they would pay for the items in 8c. Provide feedback by students telling you about their neighbour.

9 Students complete the speaking activity in 9a. Provide feedback by asking students to tell you about their neighbour's country.

10 Students are given 5 minutes each to practise talking about themselves. They may make a few notes if they wish, but they should follow the points given and talk about themselves for at least 5 minutes.

At home students prepare for the next lesson by looking up the vocabulary in 4a of Unit 31.

Answers

Exercise 4a

1 He's going to buy some eggs.
2 He isn't going to buy any potatoes.
3 He isn't going to buy any mushrooms.
4 He's going to buy some toothpaste.
5 He isn't going to buy any oil.
6 He's going to buy some garlic.
7 He isn't going to buy any toilet rolls.
8 He's going to buy some mince.
9 He's going to buy some tomatoes.
10 He isn't going to buy any apples.

Exercise 5a

1 a packet of dog food
2 a bunch of flowers
3 a loaf of bread
4 a pair of earrings
5 a cup of coffee
6 a bottle of whisky
7 a set of pens

Exercise 5d

1 hair salon
2 customer service department
3 pet supplies department
4 accounts department
5 bed linen department

1

UNIT 31

I've got a headache.

1 a Match the words and the parts of the body.

h toes	___ knee
___ fingers	___ hand
___ ankle	___ waist
___ leg	___ head
___ thumb	___ elbow
___ foot	___ chest
___ wrist	___ neck
___ arm	___ ear
___ hips	___ eye

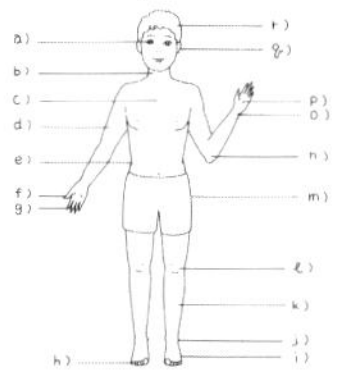

b Tell your neighbour to touch parts of his/her body.

eg Touch your left knee.

c Ask your neighbour these questions.

eg Have you ever had toothache? Yes, I had toothache a lot when I was younger. What did you do? At first I took tablets but they didn't help, so I went to the dentist. He took two teeth out and I've had no problems since then.

1 Have you ever had toothache? What did you do?
2 Have you ever had food poisoning? What did you do?
3 Have you ever had sunburn? What did you do?
4 Have you ever had flu? What did you do?
5 Have you ever had backache? What did you do?

d Now read these dialogues and say whether you agree or disagree with the advice given.

1 Tim: Hello Louise. You look awful. What's the matter?
Louise: I've got terrible toothache.
Tim: Have you taken anything for it?
Louise: Yes, I've taken some tablets but they haven't helped.
Tim: I think you should see a dentist.

2 Christine: What's the matter?
Jane: I've got stomach ache.
Christine: Have you taken anything for it?
Jane: Yes, I've taken a tablet but it still hurts.
Christine: I think you should lie down for a while.

3 Samantha: What's the matter Ian?
Ian: I feel sick.
Samantha: You look terrible. I think you should see a doctor.

e What advice would you give? Read the problems below and give your neighbour some advice.

1 I've got a headache.
2 I've got a sore throat.
3 I've got terrible backache.
4 I think I've got food poisoning.
5 I've got a cold.
6 I've got toothache.
7 I've got flu.
8 I've got stomach ache.
9 I've got sunburn.
10 I feel sick.

f You have a headache and go to the chemist's to get something for it. Read the dialogue and then practise with your neighbour.

Chemist: Hello. Can I help you?
You: Yes. I've got a terrible headache. Can you give me something for it?
Chemist: Of course. Here are some tablets. You should take 2 every 6 hours, but no more than 8 tablets in one day.
You: Thanks. How much are they?
Chemist: The 10-pack is £1.20 and the 20-pack is £1.90. Which would you like?
You: I'll take the 10-pack thanks.

2

2 a Look at the following information.

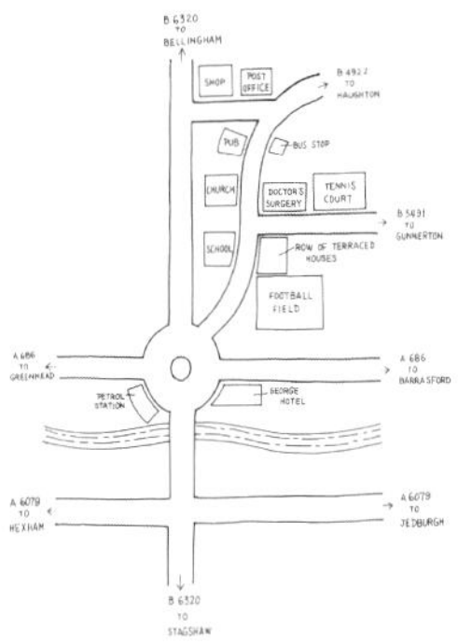

Surgery

Dr G Jones
Dr J Walter
Dr S Revell

Pharmacy Open
Monday to Friday 8.30am - 5.45pm

Doctors' Consulting Hours
Monday to Friday 8.30am - 10am
3.45pm - 5.45pm
Saturday 10am - 10.30am

Telephone (01493) 681281

b Ask your neighbour the following questions.

1 Can I see a doctor on Saturday afternoon?
2 How many doctors work at the surgery?
3 Can I collect a prescription at 2pm on Monday?
4 Can I see a doctor at 4pm on Monday?
5 What is the telephone number?

c Here are the directions to get to the surgery from Hexham.

> Coming from Hexham you go along the A6079 towards Jedburgh. At the crossroads you turn left towards Bellingham on the B6320. You go across the bridge, then round the roundabout and take the third exit. You go past a football field on your right, then a school on your left and some houses on your right. Take the first right turn after the row of terraced houses and the surgery is on your left - you can't miss it. It's opposite the church.

d Now give your neighbour directions to get to the surgery from Bellingham, Barrasford, Haughton, Gunnerton and Jedburgh.

e You think you have food poisoning. Telephone the surgery and make an appointment to see a doctor. You usually see Dr Revell. Say which direction you are coming from and ask for directions.

3

3 a Look at photograph sequence 7 'At the Doctor's' on the next pages and ask your neighbour the following questions.

1 What can you see in photograph 1?
2 What can you see in photograph 2?
3 What can you see in photograph 3?
4 What can you see in photograph 4?
5 What can you see in photograph 5?
6 What can you see in photograph 6?

b Now ask your neighbour these questions.

1 What do you think is the matter with the woman?
2 What do you think she is saying to the receptionist in photograph 2?
3 What do you think the doctor is saying in photograph 3?
4 What do you think the doctor is doing in photograph 4? Why?
5 What do you think the doctor is saying in photograph 5?
6 What do you think he is holding in his right hand in photograph 5?
7 What do you think the doctor is giving the lady in photograph 6?
8 What do you think he has in his pocket in photograph 6?
9 What is the lady wearing?
10 Describe the doctor.

c Give the lady a name and make up a short story, explaining why she is ill, what she tells the doctor, what advice he gives her and what she does after she leaves the surgery.

d The following signs are on the wall in the waiting room of the surgery. Look at them and ask your neighbour the questions below.

> Please report to the receptionist on arrival.

> Please hand any unused tablets back to your pharmacy for safe disposal.

> **Hypothermia Kills**
> Last winter 2,000 people died of hypothermia. Don't be one of them this year.
> Keep warm this winter.

> **Prescription Charges**
> With effect from 1 April 1996, prescription charges have been increased to £5.75 per item.

> **Nurses Treatment Sessions**
> For: blood pressure, weight, dressings, etc.
> Monday: 9.30am - 10.30am
> Wednesday: 9.30am - 10.30am
> 4.00pm - 5.00pm
> Friday: 9.30am - 10.30am

1 What is the first thing you should do when you enter the surgery? ______
2 How many people died of hypothermia last winter? ______
3 If the doctor prescribes 2 items, how much do you have to pay? ______
4 What should you do with any unused tablets you have? ______
5 Can I have my blood pressure taken on Friday afternoon? ______

4

4 a Translate the following.

Vocabulary

toes ______	toothache ______
fingers ______	tablets ______
ankle ______	dentist ______
leg ______	sunburn ______
thumb ______	flu ______
foot ______	backache ______
wrist ______	awful ______
arm ______	terrible ______
hips ______	headache ______
elbow ______	sore throat ______
knee ______	surgery ______
hand ______	pharmacy ______
waist ______	prescription ______
head ______	charge ______
chest ______	nurse ______
neck ______	treatment ______
ear ______	blood pressure ______
eye ______	

Structures

Have you ever had toothache? ______
I had toothache a lot when I was younger. ______
What did you do? ______
I took tablets. ______
They didn't help. ______
So I went to the dentist. ______
He took two teeth out. ______
I've had not problems since then. ______
You look awful. ______
What's the matter? ______
I've got terrible toothache. ______
Have you taken anything for it? ______
Yes, I've taken some tablets. ______
I think you should see a dentist. ______
I've got a terrible headache. ______
Can you give me something for it? ______
You should take 2 every 6 hours. ______

Teaching Notes

Warm-up

Ask students questions from earlier Units eg "Can you name 3 things you would buy in men's accessories in a department store? What did your neighbour did yesterday?"

Presentation and Practice

1 Write 'parts of the body' on the board. Point at your head and write 'head' on the board. Point at your hand and elicit the word 'hand' from your students. Elicit more words by pointing and write them on the board. Ask students if they know any more and then point at the word 'head' and say 'This is my head'. Point at other words and get students to do the same.

Students then complete the task in 1a while you monitor and check.

Students then complete the speaking activity in 1b. Ask students questions using the vocabulary in 1c eg "Have you ever had toothache?" Find out who has had toothache and what they did.

Students then complete the speaking activity in 1c while you monitor and check. Provide feedback by asking students the questions and checking their answers. Write the words eg 'toothache', 'food poisoning', etc on the board and ask students what advice they would give to someone who had these problems.

Students then read through the dialogues in 1d and say whether they agree with the advice given. They then complete the speaking task in 1e. Provide feedback by asking students for their advice.

Students read through the dialogue in 1f and practise with their neighbours while you monitor and check.

2 Find out if students have a regular doctor and if they think it is important to see the same doctor. Ask if they have to make an appointment or whether the doctor has consulting hours.

Students then look at the information in 2a and complete the speaking activity in 2b with their neighbour while you monitor and check.

In pairs students then revise directions in 2c and 2d. Provide feedback by asking students to give you directions from different directions.

In pairs students act out the roleplay in 2e. Provide feedback by pairs demonstrating their roleplay to the rest of the class.

3 Students look at the photograph sequence 'At the Doctor's' and in pairs ask and answer the questions in 3a while you monitor and check. Students then complete the speaking activity in 3b.

In pairs students then make up a story about the lady in the photographs. When students are ready they tell their story to the rest of the class. Provide feedback by asking students the questions.

Ask students what kind of signs they have seen in doctor's waiting rooms. Students then complete the writing task in 3d.

Revise all the structures and vocabulary before moving on to the next lesson.

At home students prepare for the next lesson by looking up the vocabulary in 4a of Unit 32.

Answers

Exercise 1a

a eye
b neck
c chest
d arm
e waist
f thumb
g fingers
h toes
i foot
j ankle
k leg
l knee
m hips
n elbow
o wrist
p hand
q ear

Exercise 3d

1 You should report to the receptionist.
2 2,000
3 £11.50
4 You should hand them back to your pharmacy.
5 No.

1

UNIT 32

Rescue at Sea

1 a Read the text below and put the verbs in the correct place.

walked	saw	drove	sailed	lit	telephoned
packed	heard	put	took	parked	
was	switched	shouted	helped	explained	

1 Claire Haycroft is a bank clerk in Brighton. Her hobby is sailing and on May 6 she had an experience that she will never forget.

2 It was 7.15am on Saturday May 6 when Claire got into her car and __________ to the marina. She __________ on the radio and listened to the weather report. The forecast was ideal for sailing - sunshine and wind. At 7.30am she turned into the marina and __________ her car. She picked up her bag, locked her car and __________ to the boat where she met Nigel and Sarah. They __________ their supplies onto the boat and checked the safety equipment. At 8 o'clock they left the marina and sailed out to sea.

3 It was a lovely day and they __________ a long way out to sea. At 11 o'clock the weather changed. There was a strong wind and it started to rain heavily. They __________ on their waterproof clothes and brought the sails in. Suddenly a wave hit the boat and overturned it. All 3 of them were thrown into the water. Nigel swam to the surface and climbed onto the upturned boat. He saw Sarah and __________ her out of the water but he couldn't see Claire. They __________ her name again and again. She didn't reply and they thought she was dead. Nigel __________ a flare and hoped that someone would come and help.

4 After a few minutes Sarah __________ someone shouting 'help'. They looked around but couldn't see anyone. They listened again. They heard Claire shouting their names and realised that she was trapped inside the upturned boat. They were very happy that she was alive but were worried about her.

5 It was about 12 o'clock when Nigel __________ a lifeboat coming towards them. The rescue team took Sarah and Nigel to the lifeboat. Nigel __________ that Claire was trapped inside the upturned boat. A diver tried to rescue Claire but her feet were caught in the ropes and she couldn't get out. The diver came back and told the rescue team that he couldn't get her out. It was now almost 1 o'clock and Claire had been trapped for nearly 2 hours. The weather was getting worse.

6 The wind was very strong by now and it was not safe to stay there. The diver swam back to Claire with some oxygen and the rescue team started to tow the boat back to the marina. Claire __________ very frightened and was glad that the diver was with her. After an hour they arrived in the marina. It was now 3 hours since the boat had overturned and trapped Claire. One of the rescue team __________ 999 and asked for an ambulance to come to the marina.

7 In the marina the water was calm. The diver untied the ropes and freed Claire's foot. They swam through the ropes and sails and up to the surface. She __________ a deep breath of fresh air. At that moment she was the happiest person alive.

b Compare with your neighbour.

2

1 c Match the paragraph and the summary.

eg 7 The diver rescued Claire.

___ The lifeboat arrived.
___ Claire drove to the marina.
___ The boat overturned.
___ Nigel and Sarah realised Claire was trapped.
___ Claire's job and hobby.
___ The lifeboat towed the boat back to the marina.

d Answer these questions.

eg What time did Claire leave home on Saturday May 6? She left home at 7.15am.

1 What time did she arrive at the marina? ______________________
2 Who did she meet at the marina? ______________________
3 What did they check before they left the marina? ______________________
4 What did they pack on to the boat? ______________________
5 What happened at 11 o'clock? ______________________

e Now make up 5 more questions and ask your neighbour.

eg How long was Claire trapped for? She was trapped for 3 hours.

f Have you ever had an experience you will never forget? Ask your neighbour.

2 a Read the following situations and discuss with your neighbour what you would do.

1 A motorcyclist is driving along a road. A car pulls out of a pub in front of him. The motorcyclist pulls out to overtake the car. The car turns right. The motorcyclist drives into the side of the car. The motorcyclist has a broken leg. The car driver is not hurt.

eg What would you do in this situation? I would ring for an ambulance first, and then warn any traffic.

2 A young mother is cooking the evening meal. She takes the pan with the potatoes in it to the sink and drains the water. Her 8 year old daughter Tania wants to help. Tania reaches for the pan with the carrots in it but it is too heavy. She drops the pan and boiling water covers her legs. The mother tries to help and drops her pan of potatoes. Both are badly scalded.

3 A young couple go out for a meal one night. They ask one of the grandparents to look after their two children. They decide the two children will stay the night at the grandparents. Grandfather, the dog and the two children are playing with a ball in the garden. One of the children runs for the ball. The dog jumps for the ball at the same time. The dog misses the ball but catches the child's arm. The child has to go to hospital for stitches.

4 A couple are invited to friends for dinner. The host asks them what they would like to drink. The man asks for white wine and the lady asks for red wine. The host gives the man the white wine and the man takes it. He does not have hold of the glass properly and drops it. The glass breaks. The host picks up the pieces of glass and cuts his hand badly.

5 An old lady is cleaning her house and puts her electric fire on a chair while she is vacuuming. When she has finished vacuuming she takes out the vacuum cleaner plug and replaces the electric fire plug. She takes her vacuum cleaner to the next room and continues cleaning. The electric fire heats up and sets fire to the chair covers.

b Ask your neighbour these questions about his/her own experience.

1 Have you ever had an accident? What happened?
2 Have you ever been scalded? When? What happened?
3 Have you ever had stitches? Where? How many? What happened?
4 Have you ever been trapped? Where? What happened?
5 Have you ever cut yourself? Where? What happened?

3

3 a Look at the following pictures.

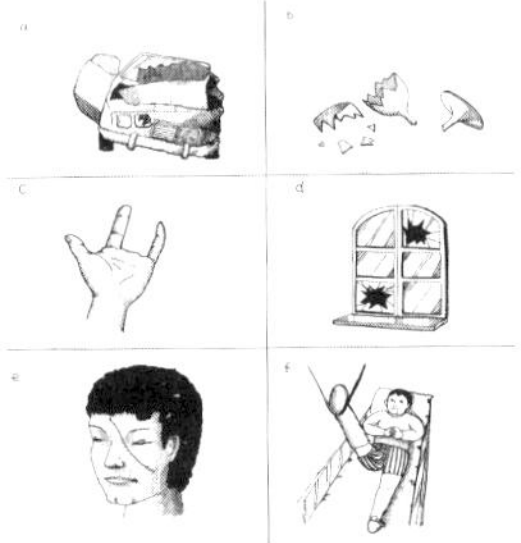

b What do you think happened in each picture? Discuss with your neighbour.

eg I think somebody went to a party, had a lot to drink and while he was driving home he crashed the car.

c Choose one picture and make up a story about it. Tell the other people in your class.

d Listen to the cassette. There are 6 people saying how the situation in the picture happened. Note down which picture they are talking about and how it happened.

person	picture	how it happened
1	___	______________________
2	___	______________________
3	___	______________________
4	___	______________________
5	___	______________________
6	___	______________________

e Read the following sentences and underline the correct verb form.

eg I was driving/drove along the road when the car was skidding/skidded on some ice.

1 I was playing/played tennis when I was slipping/slipped and broke my arm.
2 I was doing/did some shopping when I was falling/fell over.
3 I was dropping/dropped the cup while I was washing/washed up.
4 I was spraining/sprained my ankle while I was jogging/jogged.
5 I was walking/walked by the river when I was tripping/tripped and fell in.

4

4 a Translate the following.

Vocabulary

experience ________	worse ________
to forget ________	oxygen ________
marina ________	to tow ________
to switch on ________	calm ________
weather report ________	to untie ________
supplies ________	to free ________
boat ________	fresh air ________
to check ________	to pull out ________
to sail ________	to overtake ________
safety equipment ________	to drain ________
heavily ________	to drop ________
sails ________	boiling water ________
wave ________	to cover ________
to hit ________	scalded ________
to overturn ________	to jump ________
to throw ________	to miss ________
surface ________	stitches ________
to climb ________	host ________
upturned ________	to cut ________
to help ________	to vacuum ________
to shout ________	ice ________
to reply ________	to skid ________
to think ________	window ________
dead ________	scar ________
to light ________	last minute shopping ________
flare ________	to hurry ________
to hop ________	to slip ________
to realise ________	to fall ________
trapped ________	to sprain ________
alive ________	to trip ________
worried ________	to catch ________
lifeboat ________	ropes ________
rescue team ________	diver ________
to rescue ________	to tell ________

Structures

What time did Claire leave home on Saturday May 6? ______________________
She left home at 7.15am. ______________________
How long was Claire trapped? ______________________
She was trapped for 3 hours. ______________________
What would you do in this situation? ______________________
I would ring for an ambulance. ______________________
While he was driving home he crashed the car. ______________________
I was driving along the road when the car skidded on some ice. ______________________
Have you ever had an accident? ______________________
What happened? ______________________

Teaching Notes

Warm-up

Ask students questions from earlier Units eg "What did you do at work yesterday morning? What are the advantages of travelling by train?"

Revision

Revise all the structures and vocabulary from the previous Unit by asking students questions eg "What should you do if your feet hurt? Why is it dangerous to throw old tablets away?"

Presentation and Practice

1 Find out if any of your students have ever been sailing. Ask those who have questions eg "Where did you go sailing? What sailing experience do you have?"

In pairs students then read the complete text and put the verbs from 1a in the correct place. Students compare their work with their neighbour in 1b and then in 1c match the paragraphs and the one-line summary. Provide feedback by asking one student to read out the summary and the paragraph number. As a final check ask one student to read out the whole story in the correct order.

Students then answer the questions in 1d. Provide feedback by asking students the questions. Students then make up 5 more questions about Claire and ask their neighbour.

Students complete the speaking activity in 1f while you monitor and check.

2 Read out the first situation and ask students what they would do in this situation. Elicit as many suggestions as possible.

In pairs students then complete the speaking activity in 2a while you monitor and check. Provide feedback by asking pairs to tell the rest of the class what they would do.

In 2b students ask their neighbour about his/her own experience while you monitor and help. Provide feedback by asking students the questions.

3 Ask students to describe what they can see in the pictures and ask them to say what they think had happened in the first picture. Elicit various answers from students.

They then complete the speaking activity in 3b while you monitor and check. Provide feedback by asking students to tell the rest of the class what they think happened.

Students then choose one of the pictures and make up a story about it while you monitor and help. Students then tell their story to the rest of the class.

Introduce the listening activity by telling students that they are going to hear 6 people explaining how the situation in the picture happened. They will hear the cassette twice and they are to note down which picture the person is referring to and how it happened. Students then compare their work with their neighbour. Provide feedback by asking students to tell you what happened.

Introduce and explain the past continuous using the example and then students complete the activity in 3e. Provide feedback by asking students to read out their sentences.

Revise all the structures and vocabulary before moving on to the next lesson.

At home students prepare for the next lesson by looking up the vocabulary in 4a of Unit 33.

Tapescripts

Exercise 3d

1 Oh, that glass! I had visitors last night. After they left I cleared up. I picked up the glass and dropped it on the floor and it broke.

2 This is a picture of my mother's car. I was driving home from work one night in January and I drove on to some ice. The car skidded into a wall. My mother was not very happy.

3 The picture shows a broken window. When I was about 12 I was playing tennis in the garden and a ball hit the window and broke it.

4 This is me in hospital. I had an accident on a motorcycle and had to spend 4 months in hospital. I was very pleased to leave.

5 That's my hand. I lost 2 fingers when I was 17 working in a factory which made furniture.

6 I got that scar on Christmas eve 1994. I was doing some last minute shopping. I was hurrying from one shop to the next when I slipped on some ice and fell through a shop window. That wasn't a good Christmas for me.

Answers

Exercise 1a

1	drove	9	shouted
2	switched	10	lit
3	parked	11	heard
4	walked	12	saw
5	packed	13	explained
6	sailed	14	was
7	put	15	telephoned
8	helped	16	took

Exercise 1c

1 Claire's job and hobby.
2 Claire drove to the marina.
3 The boat overturned.
4 Nigel and Sarah realised Claire was trapped.
5 The lifeboat arrived.
6 The lifeboat towed the boat back to the marina.
7 The diver rescued Claire.

Exercise 1d

1 She arrived at 7.30am.
2 She met Nigel and Sarah.
3 They checked their safety equipment.
4 They packed their supplies onto the boat.
5 The weather changed.

Exercise 3d

1 b Dropped it on the floor and it broke.
2 a Skidded into a wall.
3 d Tennis ball broke window.
4 f Motorcycle accident.
5 c Lost fingers in factory.
6 e Fell through shop window.

Exercise 3e

1 I was playing tennis when I slipped and broke my arm.
2 I was doing some shopping when I fell over.
3 I dropped the cup when I was washing up.
4 I sprained my ankle when I was jogging.
5 I was walking by the river when I tripped and fell in.

1

UNIT 33

Do you live a healthy life?

1 a Put the words/phrases in the column you think suitable.

exercising every day
smoking
living in the country
dairy products
alcohol
vegetarian food
dieting
working outside
fried food
meat
body building
fresh fruit
8 hours sleep a night
living in a town
jogging
eating raw fish

healthy	not sure/it depends	unhealthy

b Explain to your neighbour why you put the words and phrases in each column.

eg *I put exercising every day in the healthy column because I think it's very important to keep fit. Where did you put it? I put it in the same column for the same reason.*

c Now discuss with another neighbour.

eg *I think that exercising every day is healthy. What do you think?*
I disagree with you. I think that exercising every day is unhealthy. It's too much. Your body needs to rest. I think exercising four times a week is healthy.
Yes, I suppose you're right.

d Complete the questions using 'a lot' or 'a lot of'.

		you: yes	you: no	your neighbour: yes	your neighbour: no
1	Do you smoke .... ?	....	....	....	....
2	Do you exercise .... ?	....	....	....	....
3	Do you live in the country?	....	....	....	....
4	Do you eat .... dairy products?	....	....	....	....
5	Do you drink .... alcohol?	....	....	....	....
6	Do you eat .... vegetarian food?	....	....	....	....
7	Do you diet .... ?	....	....	....	....
8	Do you work outside .... ?	....	....	....	....
9	Do you eat .... fried food?	....	....	....	....
10	Do you eat .... meat?	....	....	....	....
11	Do you do .... body building?	....	....	....	....
12	Do you eat .... fresh fruit?	....	....	....	....
13	Do you sleep for 8 hours a day?	....	....	....	....
14	Do you live in a town?	....	....	....	....
15	Do you go jogging .... ?	....	....	....	....
16	Do you eat .... raw fish?	....	....	....	....

e Answer the questions about yourself then ask your neighbour the questions. Who do you think is the healthiest - you or your neighbour?

2

2 a Are you fit? Discuss these questions with your neighbour.

1 What is physical fitness?
2 How can you improve your level of physical fitness?
3 How can you measure physical fitness?
4 What factors affect your level of physical fitness?
5 Do you think you are fit? Why (not)?

b Now read the text below.

The American Academy of Physical Education recently described fitness as a person who can carry out daily tasks efficiently and have plenty of energy to take part in leisure time activities. Physical fitness can be measured by 4 criteria: strength, endurance, coordination and flexibility. Fitness can be improved by regular exercise. Swimming, running, jogging, cycling, energetic dancing, and walking are good examples. There are many places which offer the facilities to do these: schools, gymnasiums, clinics, sports centres. It is important that the instructor is fully trained and qualified and can give you an individual programme. People with health problems eg diabetes, high blood pressure should see a doctor before beginning a programme of physical exercise. However, exercise alone will not guarantee physical fitness, healthy eating is also important. A bad diet will cause a drop in fitness levels. People who are underweight, overweight or weak will have a lower than average level of physical fitness.

c Read the following questions and tick the appropriate box in the column marked 'you' ....

		you: yes	you: no	you: sometimes	your neighbour: yes	your neighbour: no	your neighbour: sometimes
1	Do you sleep badly at night?	.....	......	....	......	....	.....
2	Do you find it difficult to relax?	.....	......	....	......	....	.....
3	Do you feel there is not enough time to do everything?	.....	......	....	......	....	.....
4	Do you lose your temper easily?	.....	......	....	......	....	.....
5	Do you often rush things to get everything finished?	.....	......	....	......	....	.....
6	Do you often take work home with you?	.....	......	....	......	....	.....
7	Do you ever have bad dreams?	.....	......	....	......	....	.....
8	Do you find it difficult to concentrate for a long time?	.....	......	....	......	....	.....
9	Do you ever think that everybody else is an idiot?	.....	......	....	......	....	.....
10	Do you make mistakes in your work?	.....	......	....	......	....	.....

d Before you ask your neighbour, fill in the answers you think he/she will give ....

e Ask your neighbour and see if you were correct.

3

3 a Read the following questions and discuss them with your neighbour.

1 Do you know what AIDS stands for?
2 Do you know what the symptoms of AIDS are?
3 Do you know when or where the first case of AIDS was identified?
4 Do you know what the connection between HIV and AIDS is?
5 How many cases of AIDS do you think there were world-wide between 1979 and 1989?

b What do you know about AIDS? Make a few notes in the boxes below.

things I know	things I've heard but am not sure of

c Now read this text about AIDS.

Acquired Immune Deficiency Syndrome, also known as AIDS, is a disease of the body's immune system. Symptoms include weight loss and tiredness. The first known case of AIDS was in New York in 1979. The disease comes from a virus known as HIV (Human Immunodeficiency Virus). This virus was first identified in 1983-84 by scientists at the National Cancer Institute in the United States. AIDS is passed on through blood and sexual contact. Needles used by drug-abusers are a major means of transmitting the disease. The disease was passed on through blood transfusions at first, but now all blood donations are tested for AIDS. Once the body has the virus it may be up to 10 years before the AIDS symptoms appear. In 1990 the World Health Organisation (WHO) reported over 203,599 known cases of AIDS so far world-wide, but say the actual number is nearer 600,000.

d Ask your neighbour these questions about AIDS.

1 Can you name one symptom of AIDS?
2 Where was the virus first identified?
3 What is a major means of transmitting the disease among drug-abusers?
4 Can you have the virus but not have any symptoms of AIDS?
5 What does WHO stand for?

e Here are some notes about influenza. Read them through and then write a short article about influenza.

influenza - also known as flu
disease - of the body's breathing system
symptoms - dry cough, sore throat, blocked or runny nose, burning of eyes, fever, headache, aching muscles and joints
first case - England - 16th Century
cause - These are 3 types of virus: Virus A identified in 1993; Virus B identified in 1940 and Virus C identified in 1950
transmission - by breathing in contaminated air
symptoms appear - 2-3 weeks
number of cases - 20 million known - actual 25 million (WHO 1987)

4

4 a Translate the following.

Vocabulary

unhealthy ____________	to sleep badly ____________
exercising ____________	difficult ____________
vegetarian food ____________	to relax ____________
dieting ____________	to lose your temper ____________
fried food ____________	easily ____________
body building ____________	to rush things ____________
jogging ____________	bad dreams ____________
raw fish ____________	to make mistakes ____________
physical education ____________	AIDS ____________
to carry out ____________	symptoms ____________
daily tasks ____________	case ____________
efficiently ____________	to identify ____________
energy ____________	HIV ____________
to take part in ____________	disease ____________
leisure time ____________	immune system ____________
criteria ____________	weight loss ____________
strength ____________	tiredness ____________
endurance ____________	virus ____________
coordination ____________	scientists ____________
flexibility ____________	to transmit ____________
to improve ____________	blood ____________
level ____________	sexual contact ____________
energetic ____________	needles ____________
facilities ____________	drug-abusers ____________
clinics ____________	blood donations ____________
instructor ____________	blood transfusions ____________
fully trained ____________	actual ____________
qualified ____________	dry cough ____________
health problems ____________	blocked nose ____________
diabetes ____________	runny nose ____________
bad diet ____________	fever ____________
underweight ____________	aching ____________
overweight ____________	muscles ____________
weak ____________	joints ____________

Structures

Do you live a healthy life? ____________
I think that exercising every day is healthy. ____________
What do you think? ____________
I disagree with you. ____________
I think that exercising every day is unhealthy. ____________
Yes, I suppose you're right. ____________
Do you smoke a lot? ____________
Do you exercise a lot? ____________
Do you eat a lot of dairy products? ____________
Do you drink a lot of alcohol? ____________.

Teaching Notes

Warm-up

Ask students questions from earlier Units eg "Do you think that it is important to recycle things? Do you have to pay for prescriptions in your country?"

Revision

Revise all the structures and vocabulary from the previous Unit by asking students questions eg "What can you remember about Claire Haycroft? What were you doing at 8 o'clock last night?"

Presentation and Practice

1 In pairs students ask their neighbour what he/she ate and drank yesterday. Ask students to tell you about their neighbour and then ask the rest of the class if they think what other students ate and drank was healthy. Ask students if they think that jogging is healthy.

In pairs students list 5 activities which they consider healthy and 5 activities which they consider unhealthy. Pairs tell you what they have written and ask the rest of the class to see if they agree.

Students then complete the activity in 1a. When they are finished they explain to their neighbour why they have put the words in the categories as in the example in 1b while you monitor and check. Students then discuss their opinions with another neighbour while you monitor and check.

Students complete the writing task in 1d by completing the questionnaire. Ask one student to read out the questions before students fill in the column marked 'you'. They then ask their neighbour and make notes. Provide feedback by asking students to tell you about their neighbour.

2 Ask students if they think they are fit. Find out why they think they are fit or why they don't think they are fit and try to build up a definition of what fitness is.

In pairs students complete the speaking task in 2a while you monitor and help. Provide feedback by pairs telling the rest of the class their answers to the questions.

Students then read through the text in 2b and discuss the questions from 2a again based on this information.

Read through the questions in 2c explaining where necessary and telling students how you would answer and then students answer the questions about themselves in the column marked 'you'. In the column marked 'your neighbour' students then put a question mark next to the answer they think their neighbour will give. They then ask their neighbour the questions and see if they were correct. Provide feedback by asking students to tell you about their neighbour.

3 Students read the questions in 3a and discuss their answers with their neighbour. They then make notes of 'things they know' and 'things they've heard but are not sure of' about aids. Write the 2 column headings on the board and ask pairs to tell you what they have written. Put all the ideas on the board.

Students then read the text in 3c. Find out if they now know something which they were unsure of before. Students then answer the questions in 3d.

Students write an article about influenza based on the notes in 3e. Check their articles are correct where necessary.

Revise all the structures and vocabulary before moving on to the next lesson.

At home students prepare for the next lesson by looking up the vocabulary in 4a of Unit 34.

Answers

Exercise 1d

1 a lot	3 -	5 a lot of	7 a lot	9 a lot of	11 a lot of	13 -	15 a lot
2 a lot	4 a lot of	6 a lot of	8 a lot	10 a lot of	12 a lot of	14 -	16 a lot of

Exercise 3e

Influenza, also known as flu, is a disease of the body's breathing system. Symptoms include a dry cough, sore throat, blocked or runny nose, burning of eyes, fever, headache, aching muscles and joints. The first known case of flu was in England in the 16th century. The disease comes from 3 types of virus. Virus A was first identified in 1933; virus B in 1940 and virus C in 1950. Influenza is passed on by breathing in contaminated air. Once the body has the virus it may be up to 3 weeks before the flu symptoms appear. In 1987 the World Health Organisation (WHO) reported over 20 million known cases of influenza so far world-wide, but say the actual number is nearer to 25 million.

1

UNIT 34

Do you have medical insurance?

1 a What do you know about medical care in Britain? Read the following statements and put a tick in the appropriate column.

	true	false	don't know
1 Medical care is provided by the government.	.....	....	....
2 Prescriptions are free.	.....	....	....
3 If you choose private medical insurance, you still have to pay for state insurance.	.....	....	....
4 Not many people take out private medical insurance.	.....	....	....
5 One disadvantage of the NHS is that you may have to wait for an operation.	.....	....	....

b Now read the text below and see if you are correct.

The NHS

In Britain there is a National Health Service (NHS). Everybody pays a small amount from their wages to the government and in return the government provides medical care, free of charge, for everybody.

If you have a problem and you see a doctor, there is no charge. If you have an operation, there is no charge. However, if your doctor gives you a prescription, you have to pay for this.

The advantages of the service are that everybody has medical care, whether they are unemployed, homeless or working. The disadvantages are that you may have to wait for a long time to get an appointment with a doctor or for an operation. Or you may be in a ward with 20 other people after an operation. You may decide to take out private medical insurance. If you do this, you still have to pay towards the National Health Service. Many people do it because they say the service is better.

c Explain to your neighbour about the health service in your country. Use the following questions to help.

1 Is medical care private?
2 Is medical care provided by the state?
3 Can you choose your own health insurance?
4 Can you choose which doctor you see?
5 Who pays for prescriptions? Operations?

d Discuss the advantages and disadvantages of private medical care.

eg *I think one of the advantages is that you don't have to wait.*

2

2 a Match the words and the pictures.

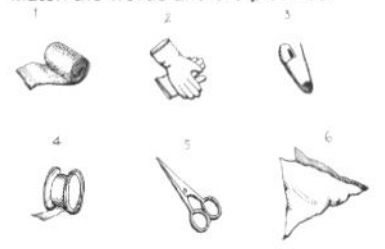

3 safety pin
___ scissors
___ bandage
___ plaster
___ plastic gloves
___ triangular bandage

b Which of these items would you use if you had to treat a cut or a sprained wrist? Tell your neighbour.

c If you were going on holiday to another country (eg India, Japan, Africa), what first aid equipment would you take and why? Would you go to a doctor before you went? Why? Discuss this with your neighbour.

d The following pictures show what to do in different situations. Match the pictures and what you should do.

1 What to do if somebody cuts him/herself. ______
2 What to do if somebody faints. ______
3 What to do if somebody has a nose bleed. ______
4 What to do if somebody stops breathing. ______
5 What to do if somebody has a cardiac arrest. ______

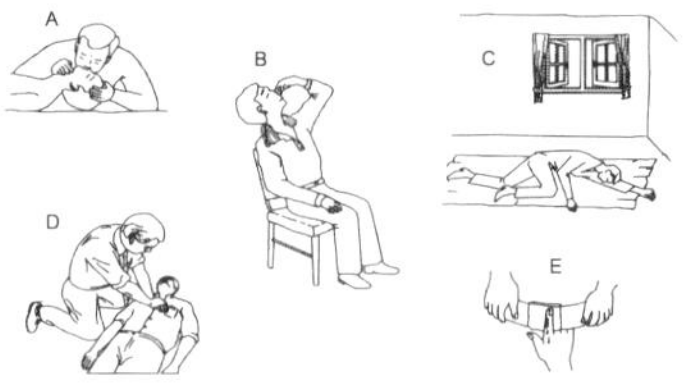

e Now ask your neighbour these questions.

eg *I had first aid training when I was at school. It was only two days but it was useful. I learnt what to do if somebody has a cardiac arrest or if somebody stops breathing. I've never given first aid treatment but I know what to do and it may save a life.*

1 Have you ever had first aid training? When? Where? Why?
2 Do you have a first aid kit in your house? What is in it? Have you ever used it? When? Why?
3 Have you ever needed first aid help?
4 Have you ever given somebody first aid help? When?
5 Do you think it is important to have first aid training? Why (not)?

3

3 a Look at the following plan of a hospital.

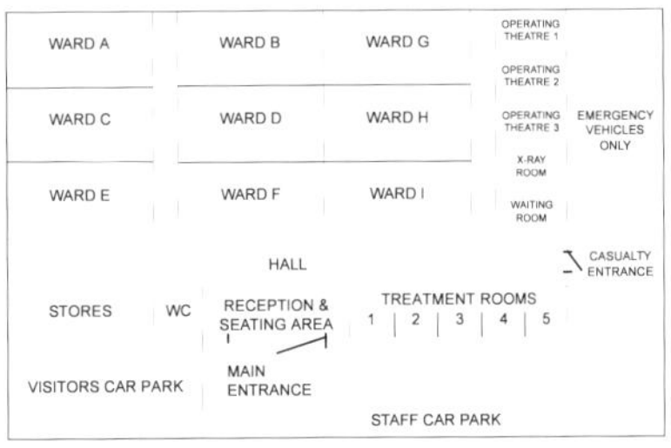

b Answer the following questions.

1 Where is the X-ray room? ______
2 How many treatment rooms are there? ______
3 Which entrance would be used for an emergency? ______
4 Which entrance do visitors use? ______
5 How would you get from the X-ray room to ward B? ______

c Listen to the cassette and make notes. You will hear it twice.

Notes

d Compare your notes with your neighbour. What other information can you remember?

4

4 a Translate the following.

Vocabulary

National Health Service ______
government ______
in return ______
medical care ______
no charge ______
operation ______
advantages ______
ward ______
private medical insurance ______
bandage ______
plastic gloves ______
triangular bandage ______
cut ______
sprained wrist ______
first aid ______
to cut yourself ______
to faint ______
nose bleed ______
to stop breathing ______
cardiac arrest ______
operating theatre ______
X-ray room ______
casualties ______
treatment rooms ______
stores ______
main entrance ______
regulations ______
emergency vehicle ______
staff car park ______

Structures

I think one of the advantages is... ______
I think one of the disadvantages is.... ______
I think the advantages are... ______
I think the disadvantages are... ______
If somebody faints you should... ______
I had first aid training when I was at school. ______
It was only two days but it was useful. ______
I learnt what to di if somebody faints. ______
I've never given first aid treatment. ______
But I know what to do and it may save a life. ______

Teaching Notes

Warm-up

Ask students questions from earlier Units eg "What were you doing at 10 o'clock last night? What are you going to do tomorrow?"

Revision

Revise all the structures and vocabulary from the previous Unit by asking students questions eg "Do you smoke a lot? Do you eat a lot of fresh fruit? Do you lose your temper easily?"

Presentation and Practice

1 Students read through the statements in 1a and mark whether they think they are true/false or if they don't know. Students then read the text in 1b and compare their answers. Provide feedback by asking students to read the statements aloud, say whether they are true or false and quote reasons from the text.

In pairs students then discuss the questions in 1c while you monitor and check. Elicit 3 advantages of private medical care and 3 disadvantages of private medical care before students complete the speaking activity in 1d.

As further practice you can set up a debate where one group of students prepares and presents a case for state medical care and another group prepares and presents a case for private medical care. The rest of the students would listen to both sides and take a vote at the end to see which system is better for them. It is useful to have a chairperson to control the debate. Writing minutes for the debate is also a useful exercise.

2 Students complete the matching activity in 2a. Provide feedback by asking students questions eg "What is A?" Students then work with their neighbour and complete the activity in 2b. Ask students to tell you what they would use.

Find out if any of your students have been to India, Japan or Africa on holiday. Ask them if they took a first aid kit with them and if so what was in it.

In pairs students then complete the speaking activity in 2c. Provide feedback by pairs telling you what they would take and why.

In 2d students match the situations and what you should do in these situations. Check their answers and then students complete the speaking task in 2e while you monitor and check. Provide feedback by students telling you about their neighbours.

3 Introduce the plan in 3a by asking students questions eg "How many car parks are there? How many treatment rooms are there?" When students are familiar with the plan they answer the questions in 3b.

Introduce the listening activity by explaining to students that they are going to hear a conversation between the hospital receptionist and a man wanting to visit his wife. They will hear the cassette twice and are to make notes while they listen.

In pairs they compare their notes with their neighbour and listen for a third time to check any discrepancies.

Revise all the structures and vocabulary before moving on to the next lesson.

At home students prepare for the next lesson by looking up the vocabulary in 4a of Unit 35.

Tapescripts

Exercise 3c

A Is this the reception?
B Yes it is. Can I help you?
A Yes please. I'm looking for my wife. She had a baby yesterday and I don't know which ward she's in. Her name's Elaine Johnson.
B How do you spell that?
A E L A I N E J O H N S O N
B Hold on one moment, I'll just check.
A She's tall with long, dark curly hair and she came in on Friday afternoon.
B Do you know who her Doctor is?
A I think it's Dr Douglas.
B Oh yes. Here she is. Yes, she's in Ward A.
A Thank you. How do I get there?
B Well I'm afraid it's not visiting time yet. Visiting hours are between 1pm and 3pm and it's only ten to one.
A But I've got to see her now, I have to get back to work by 1pm.
B Well, all right. Go through the doors into the hall, then turn left. Take your first right, it's sign-posted Wards A-F. Ward A is the last ward on your left at the end of the corridor. Be careful, because they're washing the floors in that corridor.
A Thank you very much.
B Not at all.

Answers

Exercise 2a

bandage	1
plastic gloves	2
safety pin	3
plaster	4
scissors	5
triangular bandage	6

Exercise 2d

1	What to do if somebody cuts him/herself.	E
2	What to do if somebody faints.	C
3	What to do if somebody has a nose bleed.	B
4	What to do if somebody stops breathing.	A
5	What to do if somebody has a cardiac arrest.	D

Exercise 3b

1 Between operating theatre 3 and the waiting room.
2 5 treatment rooms.
3 The casualty entrance.
4 The main entrance.
5 Turn left and take the corridor on your right. Go past the reception and turn right. Ward B is at the end of the corridor on the right.

1

UNIT 35

What do you do for a living?

1 a Match the pictures and the job titles. *eg f shop assistant.*

___ policeman	___ chef	___ DJ (disc jockey)
___ teacher	___ receptionist	___ company salesman
___ housewife	___ bus driver	___ nurse

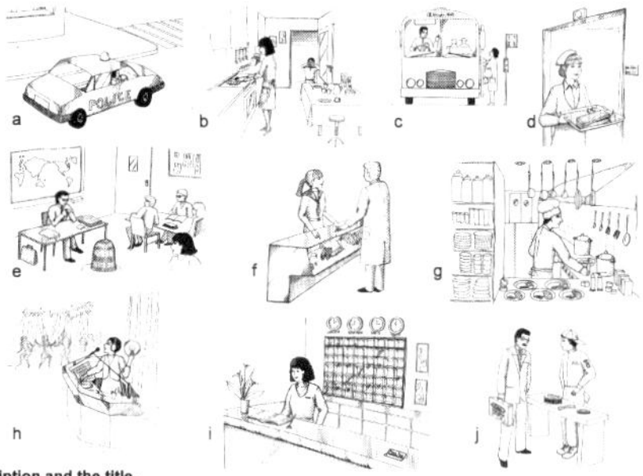

b Match the job description and the title.

1 I wear a uniform to work. I drive around my area to see that everything is all right or I do administration work in the police station. The hours are not regular - Friday and Saturday nights are always busy when the pubs close. ☐

2 I get up first in the morning and wake the children. I help them to get washed and dressed. I wake my husband and then I make breakfast. We eat breakfast together then the kids go off to school and my husband goes to work. I go shopping, clean the house, tidy up and prepare the evening meal. ☐

3 I work in a school. I have to do a lot of preparation for my lessons. I teach geography to 12 and 13 year olds. I like my pupils. It's quite well paid and I get long holidays. ☐

4 I work in the evenings but not every evening. On Friday and Saturday evenings I always work in the same club. I start at 7pm and finish at 1am. It takes an hour to put all my equipment in the van again. I play music so that people can dance all evening. ☐

5 I work regular hours. I drive to work by car and then get into my bus. I drive the same route every day and I see the same people quite a lot. I work 8 hours a day and then I go home. ☐

6 I work for a company which sells steel plate. I have to go to trade fairs and make contact with new customers. We sell a lot to car factories so I have a lot of regular customers, who I have to visit quite often. ☐

7 I work behind a counter all day. I start at 9am and finish at 5pm and I have one hour lunch break from 12pm - 1pm. When customers come in I say "Hello. Can I help you?" When they have everything they need I take the money, put it in the till and give the customer a receipt. *f*

8 I work in the kitchen of a big hotel. You don't normally see me but I'm very important. I prepare food and cook dishes that are good enough for a king. ☐

9 I work in a ward in a hospital. I work very long hours and often it's hard work. I look after the patients in my ward - they all have back problems and there are 27 of them in the ward. It's not very well paid. ☐

10 I work in a hotel. I'm normally the first person the guests speak to. I find rooms for them, ask them to fill out registration cards and take payment from them. ☐

Check with your neighbour.

c Point at the pictures and tell your neighbour about the people.

eg She's a shop assistant. She works behind a counter all day. She starts at 9am and...

2

2 a Fill in the following questionnaire about yourself. Put a tick (✓) in the relevant boxes.

Your Name: ______________________

Your Address: ______________________

1 **Where do you work?**

factory ☐ office ☐ shop ☐ hotel/restaurant ☐
school ☐ hospital ☐ other ☐ ____________

Name of Work: ______________________

Address of Work: ______________________

2 **When do you work?**

	yes	no
Do you start work at the same time every day?	☐	☐
Do you finish work at the same time every day?	☐	☐
Do you work the same number of hours every day?	☐	☐
Do you ever work in the evening?	☐	☐
Do you ever work on Saturdays?	☐	☐
Do you ever work on Sundays?	☐	☐

3 **Which field do you work in?**

production ☐ education ☐ services ☐ research ☐
administration ☐ sales ☐ other ☐ ____________

4 **Which of these activities does your work involve?**

working on a computer	☐	giving presentations	☐
travelling on business	☐	writing letters	☐
speaking on the telephone	☐	using a calculator	☐
working at home	☐	going to meetings	☐
going to trade fairs	☐	wearing a uniform	☐
working behind a counter	☐	taking payment from people	☐
asking people to fill forms out	☐	other	☐

5 **What's your position?**

(in your language) ______________________

(in English) ______________________

b Ask your neighbour the questions.

c Tell your teacher about yourself.

3

3 a Look at photograph sequence 8 'At Work' on the next pages and find the following objects. When you've found them, ask your neighbour where they are.

filing cabinet	folder	mug	drawer	tray	box file

b Match the question and the answers.

eg What has she just done? She has just taken out a folder.

1 What has she just done?	___ She was reading the information in the folder.
2 What is she doing?	*1* She has just taken out a folder.
3 What do you think she'll do next?	___ I think she'll put the folder back in the filing cabinet.
4 What did she do first?	___ She had opened the drawer.
5 What was she doing while she was telephoning?	___ She opened the drawer and took out a folder.
6 What had she done before that?	___ She's telephoning.

c Ask your neighbour the following questions about the woman in the photographs.

1 What is she doing in photograph 1? Why do you think she's doing this? What had she done before this? What is she going to do next?

2 What is she doing in photograph 2? Why do you think she's doing this? What had she done before this? What is she going to do next?

3 What is she doing in photograph 3? Why do you think she's doing this? What had she done before this? What is she going to do next?

4 What is she doing in photograph 4? Why do you think she's doing this? What had she done before this? What is she going to do next?

5 What is she doing in photograph 5? Why do you think she's doing this? What had she done before this? What is she going to do next?

d Now ask your neighbour these questions.

1 What does the woman look like?
2 What is she wearing?
3 What time of day do you think it is? Why?
4 What kind of company do you think she works for? Why?
5 Which department do you think she works in? Why?
6 What do you think her job is? Why?
7 Who do you think she's telephoning? Why?
8 Why does she go to the filing cabinet before she makes the phone call?
9 Why does she put her glasses on?
10 What do you think she does after the phone call?

e Make up a story about the photographs and tell your neighbour.

eg The photographs show a lady at work. I know that she's at work because there's a desk, a filing cabinet and lots of box files. She's wearing smart clothes, too. I think she's a Sales Manager in a large company. She's going to make an important telephone call to one of her customers. Before she makes the phone call she goes to the filing cabinet to get out a folder. She looks at the folder to check that it's the right one and then...

4

4 a Translate the following.

Vocabulary

shop assistant ______	car factories ______
policeman ______	till ______
teacher ______	receipt ______
housewife ______	important ______
chef ______	king ______
bus driver ______	to work long hours ______
disc jockey ______	hard work ______
company salesman ______	back problems ______
uniform ______	guests ______
police station ______	to fill out ______
to wake ______	registration cards ______
to tidy up ______	to take payment ______
evening meal ______	production ______
to teach ______	education ______
lesson ______	services ______
geography ______	administration ______
12 year olds ______	sales ______
pupils ______	research ______
well paid ______	trade fairs ______
equipment ______	presentations ______
van ______	position ______
to work regular hours ______	filing cabinet ______
route ______	folder ______
company ______	mug ______
steel plate ______	drawer ______
to make contacts ______	tray ______
customers ______	box file ______

Structures

What does she do? ______
She's a shop assistant. ______
She works behind a counter all day. ______
What has she just done? ______
What is she doing? ______
What do you think she'll do next? ______
What did she do first? ______
What was she doing while she was telephoning? ______
What had she done before that? ______
She was reading. ______
She has just taken the folder out of the filing cabinet. ______
I think she'll put it back in the filing cabinet. ______
She had opened the drawer. ______
She opened the drawer and took the folder out. ______
She's telephoning. ______
What is she doing in picture 1? ______
What had she done before this? ______
What is she going to do next? ______

Teaching Notes

Before the lesson fill out the questionnaire in 2a for yourself and photocopy it for your students. On the other side photocopy the blank form from 2a.

Warm-up

Ask students questions from earlier Units eg "What should you do if you have a headache? Do you think you are fit?"

Revision

Revise all the structures and vocabulary from the previous Unit by asking students questions eg "Do you have medical insurance? Do you have to pay for prescriptions in your country? How long do you have to wait to get an appointment with a doctor in your country? Do you have a first aid kit at home?"

Presentation and Practice

1 Write 'shop assistant' on the board and explain where a shop assistant works and what he/she does. Write 'policeman' on the board and elicit the same information about a policeman.

Continue with the rest of the words from 1a eliciting information. At the end clean everything off the board apart from the job titles.

Students then complete the matching task in 1a. Check by asking students questions, eg "What does A do for a living?"

Students then complete the matching task in 1b. Provide feedback by asking one student to read the description out and another to say which occupation it refers to.

Students complete the speaking activity in 1c while you monitor and check. Provide feedback by asking students to close their books and then point at the job titles on the board and ask "What does a shop assistant do?" etc.

2 Give students a copy of your completed questionnaire and explain what you have filled in. Students then complete the questionnaire in their books about themselves while you monitor and help. Students then ask their neighbour the questions and note down the answers on the photocopy. Provide feedback by asking students to tell you about themselves.

3 Write the words from 3a on the board and ask students to explain where you would find them and what you would do with them. Students then look at the photograph sequence 'At Work' and complete the speaking activity in 3a. Provide feedback by asking students to tell you which photograph the items are in and also to describe their position, eg "You can see the filing cabinet in photograph 1. It's at the end of the room. On top of it you can see..."

Students then match the questions and answers in 2b. Provide feedback by students reading out the questions and answers.

In pairs students then complete the speaking activity in 3c while you monitor and check. Bring one student to the front to ask the questions and ask different students to answer.

In 3d students complete the speaking activity making up information where necessary. Provide feedback by asking students the questions and eliciting different answers.

In pairs students then complete the story in 3e. They may make notes and when they are ready they read their story to the rest of the class. Students then decide which story they find the most entertaining and why. If students need more practice with the tenses you can ask the questions from 3c about the other photograph sequences.

Revise all the structures and vocabulary before moving on to the next lesson.

At home students prepare for the next lesson by looking up the vocabulary in 4a of Unit 36.

Answers

Exercise 1a

a	policeman	f	shop assistant
b	housewife	g	chef
c	bus driver	h	DJ (disc jockey)
d	nurse	i	receptionist
e	teacher	j	company salesman

Exercise 1b

1	a	6	j
2	b	7	f
3	e	8	g
4	h	9	d
5	c	10	i

Exercise 3b

1	What has she just done?	She has just taken out a folder.
2	What is she doing?	She's telephoning.
3	What do you think she'll do next?	I think she'll put the folder back in the filing cabinet.
4	What did she do first?	She opened the drawer and took out a folder.
5	What was she doing while she was telephoning?	She was reading the information in the folder.
6	What had she done before that?	She had opened the drawer.

1

UNIT 36

Applying for a job.

1 a Look at the following job vacancies.

Secretary	Computer Programmer	Sales Assistant
International Company is looking for a hard working and ambitious person. Must have computer experience. Typewriting and shorthand skills required. Knowledge of French preferred.	Graduate required with 3 years computing experience.	Part time sales assistant required for electrical goods shop. Sales experience required. 3 days a week and every second Saturday.
£13 K p.a.	Contract for 18 months.	£3.50 per hour.
Apply in writing to:	£17 K p.a.	Send CV to:
ILC International 19-23 Port Road Truro	CV's to Intact Computing Ltd 13 Fordway London W3 2BR	The Manager Robsons Electrical Shop 29-33 Pool Street Durham DH3 49P
The Independent 29.04.96	*The Times 29.04.96*	*The Guardian 29.04.96*

b Ask your neighbour these questions.

1 Which advert appeared in the Independent newspaper?
2 Which job was advertised in the Times?
3 How much is the salary for the position as secretary?
4 How much experience do you need for the job as computer programmer?
5 What should you do if you decide to apply for the position as sales assistant?

49 Garden Road
Penzance
PE5 3PH

30 April 1996

ILC International
19-23 Port Road
Truro

Dear Sirs

Position of Secretary

I saw your advertisement for the above position in the Independent newspaper (29.04.96) and would like to apply for this position.

I am 26 years old and am a qualified secretary with over 5 years experience. I speak conversational French and Italian, and have excellent computing, typing and shorthand skills.

At present I am working for a small company in Penzance. I have been employed there as a secretary since I finished my secretarial training in 1990.

I am interested in working with an international company so that I can broaden my experience and use my languages.

I enclose a CV and photograph and am available for interview at any time.

I look forward to hearing from you.

Yours faithfully

Sharon Olsen

Sharon Olsen

c Read the letter which was sent to ILC in reply to their advert, then ask your neighbour the following questions.

1 Where does Sharon Olsen live?
2 Which job is she applying for?
3 Can she speak French?
4 Why is she applying for the job?
5 How old is she?
6 What is her present job?
7 Can she type?
8 When can she come for interview?
9 How many years experience has she got?
10 Has she sent anything else with the letter?

d Which job would you apply for? Write a letter like Sharon's for one of the jobs in 1a.

e When you are finished, work in groups. Look at your letters and decide who would be the best for each job. Tell the rest of the class who you have chosen and why.

2

2 a Look at the plan of ILC International and ask your neighbour questions.

eg *Where's Room 111? It's between the WC and Room 112.*

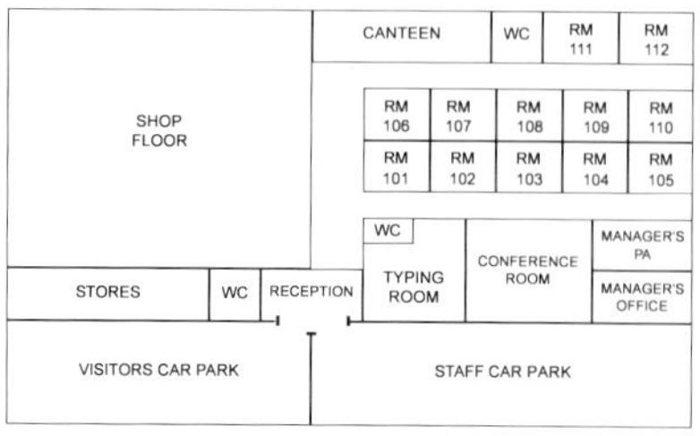

b You are going to hear a telephone conversation between Sharon Olsen and Mike Bell, Personnel Manager at ILC. You will hear the cassette twice. Make notes while you are listening.

Notes

Sharon Olsen	Mike Bell

c Compare your notes with your neighbour.

d Ask your neighbour these questions.

1 Can you remember your first job interview?
2 Before the interview, did you find out information about the company?
3 Before the interview, did you practise what you would say?
4 Before the interview, did you think what kind of questions the interviewer would ask?
5 Did you practise your interviewing techniques with anyone?
6 During the interview, did you say anything you regretted?
7 During the interview, did you ask any questions?
8 Did you learn anything from the interview?
9 Did you get the job?
10 If you got the job, are you still in the same job now?

e Tell your teacher about yourself.

3

3 a You are going to order some items for your office. Look at the price list for Armstrong's Stationery and fill in the details on order form A.

Armstrong's Stationery
Catalogue and Price List
25 George Street, Cheltenham
(tel 01242 262632)

Order No	Description	Colour	Price
SL001	scissors, large	red	£2.50 for set of 3
SS002	scissors, small	black	£2.00 for set of 3
PCL001	pencils	red	£2.00 for 20
PCL002	pencils	black	£2.00 for 20
PN001	pens	red	£3.00 for 20
PN002	pens	black	£3.00 for 20
EB001	elastic bands, large	-	£2.50 per 1000
EB002	elastic bands, small	-	£2.00 per 1000
PCS001	paper clips	-	£1.99 per 1000
FR001	fax roll	-	£8 each
RR001	ruler	clear	20p each

Order Form A

Customer Name ____________________
Customer Address ____________________
____
Date ____________________

Order No	Description	Quantity	Price

Total ....
+ VAT @ 17½% ....
Grand Total ....

Order Form B

Customer Name ____________________
Customer Address ____________________
____
Date ____________________

Order No	Description	Quantity	Price

Total ....
+ VAT @ 17½% ....
Grand Total ....

b Now phone your neighbour who works at Armstrong's to give him/her your order. Sit back to back and your neighbour will note down your order on form B. You start the phone call.

eg *Hello, this is..., I'd like to order the following goods.*

c Compare with your neighbour.

4

4 a Translate the following.

Vocabulary

hard working ____________	Manager's Office ____________
ambitious ____________	PA (Personal Assistant) ____________
computer experience ____________	administration area ____________
skills ____________	catalogue ____________
required ____________	price list ____________
knowledge of ____________	elastic bands ____________
preferred ____________	paper clips ____________
£13 K p.a. ____________	fax roll ____________
to apply ____________	ruler ____________
in writing ____________	clear ____________
Computer Programmer ____________	customer name ____________
graduate ____________	customer address ____________
contract ____________	date ____________
part time ____________	order no ____________
per hour ____________	description ____________
above ____________	quantity ____________
to broaden ____________	total ____________
to enclose ____________	+ VAT @ 17½% ____________
shop floor ____________	grand total ____________

Structures

Dear Sirs ____________
I saw your advertisement for the above position in the ... ____________
I would like to apply for this position. ____________
I am ... years old. ____________
I am a qualified ... with over 5 years experience. ____________
I speak conversational French. ____________
I have excellent ... skills. ____________
At present I am working for ... ____________
I have been employed there as ... since ... ____________
I am interested in working with ... so that I can ... ____________
I enclose a ... ____________
I am available for interview ... ____________
I look forward to hearing from you. ____________
Yours faithfully. ____________

Teaching Notes

Warm-up

Ask students questions from earlier Units eg "What are the advantages and disadvantages of private medical insurance? Have you ever taken a first aid course?"

Revision

Revise all the structures and vocabulary from the previous Unit by asking students questions eg "What do you do? What does a nurse do? Where do you work? What are you going to do after this English lesson? What do you think you'll you do tomorrow?"

Presentation and Practice

1 In pairs students find out how long their neighbour has been working in their present job. Ask students how they got their present job eg through adverts, promotion, contacts etc. Ask students where they would look for job adverts and what information they expect a job advert to contain. Students then look at the adverts for jobs in 1a and complete the speaking activity in 1b. Provide feedback by asking students the questions and checking their answers.

Ask students what information they would include in a letter if they were applying for one of these jobs. They then read the letter in 1c and answer the questions.

In 1d students decide to apply for one of the jobs and write a letter while you monitor and check. Tell them to sign the letter with a made-up name. When they are finished collect all the letters and put the students in 3 groups. One group gets all of the applications for the position of secretary; the second group gets all of the applications for the position of computer programmer; and the third group gets all of the applications for the position of sales assistant. The groups then look at their letters and decide who they think would be best for the position and why. Take all the letters back and return them.

2 Introduce the listening activity in 2a by asking students questions about the diagram eg "What is this a diagram of? Where is Room 102? Where is the conference room? How do you get from Room 101 to the Manager's Office?" When students are familiar with the plan introduce the listening activity by describing the situation in 2b. Play the cassette twice. Students then compare their notes with their neighbour. Provide feedback by eliciting as much information from the conversation as possible and then asking one student to tell you what the conversation was about.

Introduce the speaking activity in 2d by telling your students about your first job interview.

Students then complete the speaking activity in 2d while you monitor and check. Provide feedback by asking students to tell you about their neighbour.

3 Ask students what they have on their desks, when they bought each item and if they can remember how much each item cost.

In pairs students ask and answer questions about the information in 3a eg "How much does a large pair of scissors cost?" When students are familiar with the information on the price list they write 6 items they would like to order on form A. They sit back to back to complete the speaking activity in 3b while you monitor and check. When students are finished they compare their forms and see if they have taken down the order accurately. Provide feedback by asking pairs to demonstrate their activity. The rest of the class can take down the order while they are listening and then check it.

Revise all the structures and vocabulary before moving on to the next lesson.

At home students prepare for the next lesson by looking up the vocabulary in 4a of Unit 37.

Tapescripts

Exercise 2b

A Penzance 582493 Hello.
B Hello, can I speak to Sharon Olsen please?
A Speaking.
B Oh hello, this is Mike Bell from ILC International. We received your letter of application this morning and we would like to invite you for an interview.
A Oh great.
B In your letter you said you were available at any time.
A Yes that's right. Only I can't come tomorrow because I have to work but Thursday's okay.
B That's all right. How about 3pm?
A Yes, I can arrange that.
B Oh good. Do you know Truro at all?
A Yes, I often go shopping there. I know how to find you.
B Good. Well if you're coming by car, park in the visitors car park. It's on the left as you drive in. Come into the building through the main entrance and into reception. There are some toilets on your left. The receptionist won't be there on Thursday - she's ill at the moment, so you'll have to find the room yourself. It's easy though. Go along the corridor and take the first right. Go to the 3rd door on your left - it's marked Room 103. If there's nobody there, go to Room 102 - that's my room. Just come in, you don't have to knock. And if you've got any questions before then, you can call me on 01798 24321, extension 248. Okay?
A Okay, thanks. See you on Thursday at 3pm.
B Okay, goodbye.
A Bye.

1

UNIT 37

Who do you work for?

1 a Look at the names in the box below. Ask your teacher to say any which you can't pronounce, then repeat them. Listen to the cassette and match the names and the people in the photograph.

1 Mary Allinson
2 Colin Reed
3 Nicola Laker
4 Michael Buchanan
5 Mel Roberts
6 George Fraser
7 Scott Hamilton
8 Jo Walker
9 David Young
10 Angus Oliver

Listen again and check.

b Now listen again and write the names of the people under their position. When you've finished, check with your neighbour by asking questions.

eg Who's the Production Manager?
What's Angus Oliver's position?

Managing Director – *Scott Hamilton*

- Production Manager ______
  - Foreman
    - Shop Floor Workers
- Financial Manager ______
  - Customer Accounts Manager ______
    - Accounts Clerks
  - Wages Section Head ______
    - Wages Clerks
- Marketing Manager ______
  - Sales Manager ______
    - Sales Team
  - Advertising Manager ______
    - Advertising Assistants
- Personnel Manager ______
  - Recruitment and Training Officer ______
    - Personnel Department Staff

c Here are some numbers which were on the cassette. Listen again and note down what they refer to.

eg 10 = 10th anniversary last summer. Photo was taken then.

1) 5 2) 90 3) 60 4) 5 5) 28

2

2 a Look at the following five business cards.

Ian McLeary
Sales Assistant
The Computer Superstore
Computer Superstores Ltd
Unit 55 Retail World
Team Valley
Gateshead
NE11 OLP
Tel 0191 491323
Fax 0191 491444

Robson's Electricentre
68 Commercial Street
Dundee
DD1 2AB
Tel 01382 26437
Fax 01382 26451
Tony Robson
Managing Director

Far End Bookshop
99 Harcourt Street
DUBLIN 2
Tel 01-5716554
Fax 01-5715923
Mark Rickwood
Sales Manager

Sheila Kerr
Training Officer
4122 West Avenue 5
Anaheim
CA 92804
USA
Tel 0714 7729201
Fax 0714 7729132
AT
Telephone International

PCL
Software Solutions
6 Davy Way
Llay
Wrexham
Clywd LL12 0PG
Tel 01978 242424 / Fax 01978 255552
Bridget Heale
Financial Manager

b Ask your neighbour these 5 questions.

1 Which company does Sheila Kerr work for?
2 What's the address of the Computer Superstore?
3 Who is the Financial Manager of PCL Software Solutions?
4 What's Ian McLeary's position?
5 If I want to speak to Tony Robson, which number should I ring?

c Now make up another 5 questions about the business cards and ask your neighbour these.

d Fill in your details on business card A.

A
company name ______
your name ______
your position ______
your company address ______
______
your company tel no ______
your company fax no ______

B

C

D

e Ask 3 other neighbours about their work and fill in their details on business cards B - D.

3

3 a You are at the opening of a customer's new premises. You hear the following dialogues. Read them and decide if the people know each other or if they are meeting for the first time.

1 Hi Rob. It's good to see you again.
It's good to see you too, Tom. How are you?
I'm very well. And you?
I'm fine.

2 Hello. I'm Peter Richter. You must be Jeff Shaw.
Yes that's right. Nice to meet you.

3 Hello. I don't think we've met. I'm Janice Ellis.
Nice to meet you. My name's Renate Kennedy, but you can call me Renny.

4 Hello. I'm Patricia Nelson. What's your name?
My name's Alice Barda. Pleased to meet you Patricia.

5 It's Frances Cooper isn't it?
Yes that's right and you're Ben Hutchinson aren't you?
Yes. It's nice to see you again. How are you?

b At the opening Patricia Nelson introduces herself to you. What would you say? What would you say after that? Here are some questions you could use. Match the questions and the answers.

1	Do you work for this company?	*j*	a	Yes, it's because of the rail strike.
2	Have you come far?		b	Machinery for recycling plants.
3	Who do you work for?		c	They're very light and spacious.
4	It's a lovely day, isn't it?		d	Atraverda Ceramics Ltd.
5	What line of business are you in?		e	Yes, dreadful for the time of year.
6	Terrible weather at the moment, isn't it?		f	No, my company is just around the corner.
7	What do you think of the new premises?		g	The Production Department.
8	Which department do you work in?		h	I'm a Production Manager.
9	The traffic is bad today, isn't it?		i	Yes, wonderful.
10	What do you do?		j	No I don't.

c It's now 10.50am and people are starting to leave. You have to be back in your office for 11.15am. Here are some phrases which you can use to say goodbye. Practise the dialogues with your neighbour.

1 A It's been a pleasure talking to you. Goodbye.
B Goodbye.

2 A I'm afraid I have to leave. I have a meeting at 11.15am. Do you have a card?
B Of course. Here you are.
A Thank you. Goodbye.
B Bye.

3 A It was nice meeting you. Here's my card.
B Thank you.
A Goodbye.
B Goodbye.

4 A Why don't you call me next week. Here's my card.
B I certainly will. Thank you.
A Bye.
B Bye.

5 A If you'll excuse me, I must dash. I hope we meet again some time.
B I'm sure we will. Goodbye.
A Bye.

d Now work in groups of 6. You are at the opening of a customer's new premises. Introduce yourself, ask a few of the questions and then say goodbye.

4

4 a Translate the following.

Vocabulary

Managing Director ______	Advertising Assistants ______
Production Manager ______	Recruitment and Training Officer ______
Financial Manager ______	Personnel Department Staff ______
Marketing Manager ______	business card ______
Personnel Manager ______	customer ______
Foreman ______	premises ______
shop floor worker ______	rail strike ______
Customer Accounts Manager ______	machinery ______
Accounts Clerks ______	recycling plants ______
Wages Section Head ______	light ______
Wages Clerks ______	spacious ______
Sales Manager ______	dreadful ______
Sales Team ______	bye ______
Advertising Manager ______	goodbye ______

Structures

It's good to see you again. ______
How are you? ______
I'm very well. And you? ______
You must be Jeff Shaw. ______
Nice to meet you. ______
I don't think we've met. ______
You can call me Renny. ______
Pleased to meet you. ______
Do you work for this company? ______
Have you come far? ______
Who do you work for? ______
It's a lovely day isn't it? ______
What line of business are you in? ______
Terrible weather at the moment, isn't it? ______
What do you think of the new premises? ______
Which department do you work in? ______
The traffic is bad today, isn't it? ______
What do you do? ______
It's been a pleasure talking to you. ______
I'm afraid I have to leave. ______
I have a meeting at 11.15am. ______
Do you have a card? ______
It was nice meeting you. ______
Here's my card. ______
Why don't you call me next week. ______
I certainly will. ______
If you'll excuse me, I must dash. ______
I hope we meet again some time. ______
I'm sure we will. ______

Teaching Notes

Warm-up

Ask students questions from earlier Units eg "What were you doing at 2 o'clock yesterday afternoon?"

Revision

Revise all the structures and vocabulary from the previous Unit by asking students questions eg "What can you remember about your first interview? Where would you look if you wanted a new job?"

Presentation and Practice

1 Five students come to the front and stand in a row. Tell the class where each one is standing eg "Sandra is standing at the end on the left. Alex is second from the left. Silvia is in the middle. Maria is second from the right and Philip is at the end on the right." Ask students questions eg "Where is Maria? Who is second from the left?" When students are familiar with the phrases ask the five students questions eg "Who is on your left? Who is on Sandra's right?"

Students then look at the picture in 1a and describe the people in the picture to their neighbour. Provide feedback by asking students to describe the people to the rest of the class eg "Can you describe the person in the front row second from the left?" Students then describe the people to their neighbour and their neighbour guesses who it is eg "I think it's the man on the left in the second row."

Introduce the listening activity by telling students that they are going to hear somebody explaining who the people in the picture are. They will hear the cassette twice. The first time they are to work out who the people are. Read out the names to the students before you play the cassette. Play the cassette a second time for students to check their work. Provide feedback by asking students to tell you where the people are eg "Where is Mary Allinson?" Look at the organisation chart in 1b and explain to students that they will hear the cassette again and they are to write in the names of the people under the position. Students listen to the cassette and then check their work with their neighbour by asking questions eg "Who is the Production Manager? What is Angus Oliver's position?"

Students then look at the numbers in 1c and see if they can remember what they were for. Play the cassette again for them to check.

2 Students look at the business cards in 2a and then complete the speaking activity in 2b. In 2c they ask their neighbour another 10 questions about the information contained on the business cards.

Students then complete their own information on business card A. Students all stand up and walk around the class asking 3 other people about their work and filling in business cards B, C and D. Provide feedback by asking students to tell you about one other person.

3 Explain the situation in 3a and then students read the dialogues and decide if the speakers are meeting for the first time or if they already know each other. Check this and then students practise the dialogues.

In 3b students match up the questions and answers and then practise the extended dialogues with their neighbour.

Students read through the dialogues in 3c and then practise with their neighbour.

Set up the situation in 3d and then students complete the activity in groups of 6 while you monitor and check.

Revise all the structures and vocabulary before moving on to the next lesson.

At home students prepare for the next lesson by looking up the vocabulary in 4a of Unit 38.

Tapescripts

Exercise 1a & b

This is a photograph of the management of our company. It was taken last summer to celebrate our 10th anniversary. Scott Hamilton is the MD. That's him sitting in the front row, second from the right. Next to him on the right is Mary Allinson - she's our Personnel Manager. On the other side of Scott Hamilton is George Fraser. He joined the company 5 years ago as Financial Manager. 90% of our staff have been with the company right from the start. Next to George is David Young. He's the Recruitment and Training Officer, although most of his work is training as we're only a small company with 60 people working here. That's me in the second row at the left hand end. I'm the Sales Manager and have 5 sales people working under me. On my left is Angus Oliver. He's the Marketing Manager and on his left is Michael Buchanan, he's the Production Manager - there is a foreman and 28 shop floor workers under him. He's also responsible for security. That's Jo Walker in the middle of the back row. She's head of the Wages Section - a very important person (laugh). On her left is Mel Roberts - he's Customer Accounts Manager and on the other side, that's Colin Reed. He's Advertising Manager. So, there you are. That's the happy family.

Answers

Exercise 1a (from left to right)

back row	Colin Reed	Jo Walker	Mel Roberts	
centre row	Me (Nicola Laker)	Angus Oliver	Michael Buchanan	
front row	David Young	George Fraser	Scott Hamilton	Mary Allinson

Exercise 1b

Production Manager	Michael Buchanan
Financial Manager	George Fraser
Marketing Manager	Angus Oliver
Personnel Manager	Mary Allinson
Customer Accounts Manager	Mel Roberts
Wages Section Head	Jo Walker
Sales Manager	Nicola Laker
Advertising Manager	Colin Reed
Recruitment and Training Officer	David Young

Exercise 1c

1 5 years since George Fraser joined the company.
2 90% of staff have been there from the start.
3 60 people work for the company.
4 5 sales people work under Nicola Laker.
5 28 shop floor workers.

Exercise 3c

1	J	6	E
2	F	7	C
3	D	8	G
4	I	9	A
5	B	10	H

1

UNIT 38

What happens to your waste paper?

1 a The sequence of photographs on the next page shows the process of recycling waste paper. Look at the photographs then read the paragraphs below and match the photograph and the description.

☐ 1 Next the waste paper is sorted into bleached (white) paper and coloured paper/cardboard. It is tied together and then stacked in a fenced area. The bleached paper is stacked on the left, and the coloured paper/cardboard on the right.

☐ 2 The sheet of recycled paper is wound onto a roll at the end of the drying machine. When the roll is full, it is taken away and a new roll is started.

☐ 3 The waste paper is collected from the paper banks and delivered to the mill by lorry, where it is emptied into the yard.

☐ 4 The waste paper is mixed with water and left for 24 hours. The mixture is then fed through a machine where the water is squeezed out and the sheet of recycled paper is carried along a conveyor belt. Hot air is blown on it and the recycled paper is dried.

☐ 5 The roll of recycled paper is weighed, then wrapped and loaded onto pallets. It is then ready to be despatched.

b Complete the sentences using the phrases below.

is sorted	is mixed	is left	is started	is emptied
is squeezed	is weighed	is carried	is dried	is loaded

1 The waste paper ________________ into bleached paper and coloured paper.

2 When the roll is full, it is taken away and a new roll ________________.

3 The roll of recycled paper ________________.

4 The waste paper ________________ with water.

5 Hot air is blown on it and the paper ________________.

6 The waste paper ________________ into the yard.

7 The water ________________ out.

8 The recycled paper ________________ along a conveyor belt.

9 The waste paper ________________ for 24 hours.

10 The roll of recycled paper ________________ onto pallets.

c Look at photograph sequence 9 'Recycling Waste Paper' on the next pages and explain what happens to the waste paper when it is delivered to the factory.

2

2 a You have written a letter to your penfriend in Hong Kong. What happens to the letter? Put the sentences in the correct order.

eg _1_ *The letter is weighed.*

___ The letter is put into the post box.
___ The letters are sorted.
___ The letters are sent to Hong Kong.
___ The stamps are stuck on.
___ The post box is emptied.
___ The letters are taken to the sorting room.
___ The letter is delivered to your penfriend.

b Work with someone who has travelled by plane. What happens to your luggage after you check in?

eg *My luggage is put on the scales and weighed.*

c Answer these questions about your place of work.

eg *Is anything emptied regularly in your office? Yes, the bins are emptied every day.*

1 Is anything delivered to your office?
2 Is anything collected from your office?
3 Is anything weighed in your office?
4 Is anything wrapped in your office?
5 Is anything cleaned in your office?

d Can you think of anything else in your place of work...

1 which is sorted?
2 which is tied together?
3 which is taken away?
4 which is filed away?
5 which is checked?

3

3 a You are on a business trip to Britain. You have been invited to visit Fourstones Paper Mill. Look at the information below and answer these questions.

1 When was Fourstones Paper Mill established?
2 Where is the mill located?
3 What is brought from all over the country to the mill?
4 What happens to the waste paper at the mill?
5 What happens to the recycled paper?

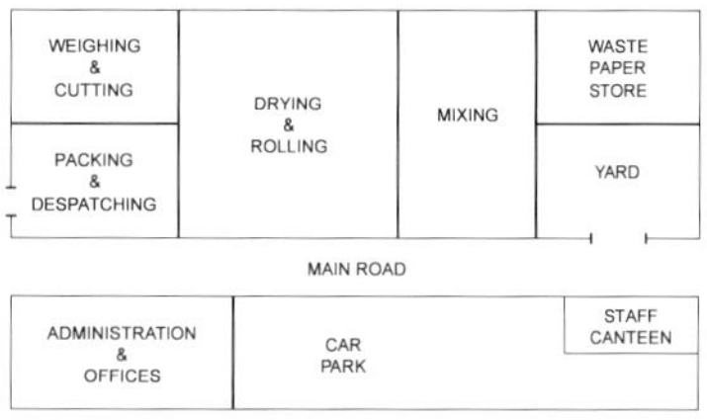

Fourstones Paper Mill was established in 1763 by GT Mandl, a Czech. The mill is located in the heart of Northumbria and has excellent connections by road and rail. Waste paper from all over the country is brought to Fourstones paper mill where it is recycled and the recycled paper is supplied to companies world-wide. Fourstones Paper Mill is committed to the protection of the environment and is working towards a better future.

b While you are at the paper mill you will be given a guided tour of the factory and a presentation of the company's current markets. The guided tour is about to begin and the guide is going to give you some information before you start. What information do you think he will give you? Put a tick (✓) next to the information you think you will hear.

___ the name of the guide
___ where you are now
___ when the company was established
___ where the tour will start
___ what the bleached paper is used for
___ how many people work in the factory
___ where the Marketing Manager will give his presentation
___ the name of the Managing Director
___ the time now
___ how long the tour will take
___ what time you'll be taken back to your hotel

c Now listen to the cassette and see if you were correct. Listen a second time and make some more notes, compare your notes with your neighbour.

4

4 a Translate the following.

Vocabulary

process ________	recycled paper ________
waste paper ________	conveyor belt ________
to sort ________	hot air ________
bleached ________	to blow ________
cardboard ________	to dry ________
to tie ________	to weigh ________
to stack ________	to wrap ________
fenced ________	to load ________
sheet ________	to file away ________
to wind ________	pallet ________
to take away ________	to despatch ________
by lorry ________	to supply ________
to empty ________	worldwide ________
yard ________	to produce ________
to mix ________	wide range ________
mixture ________	products ________
to feed through ________	protection ________
to squeeze out ________	future ________

Structures

The waste paper is sorted. ________
It is tied together. ________
It is stacked. ________
It is wound onto a roll. ________
It is taken away. ________
A new roll is started. ________
Waste paper is delivered. ________
It is emptied into the yard. ________
It is mixed with water. ________
The mixture is fed through a machine. ________
The water is squeezed out. ________
Hot air is blown on it. ________
The paper is dried. ________
The paper is weighed. ________
The paper is wrapped and loaded onto pallets. ________
It is ready to be despatched. ________
The letters are sorted every morning. ________
The waste paper bins are emptied every evening. ________
The rubbish is taken away. ________
It was established in 1763. ________
It was established by ... ________
It is located in... ________

Teaching Notes

Warm-up

Ask students questions from earlier Units eg "Do you find it difficult to relax? Have you ever been skiing? What does a shop assistant do?"

Revision

Revise all the structures and vocabulary from the previous Unit by putting students in groups of 5 to socialise for 3 minutes.

Presentation and Practice

1 Ask students what they do with their waste paper. Ask those who recycle it if they know what happens to it after they have put it in the paper bank. Elicit as much information as possible and help with vocabulary. Ask students if they can name anything which is made of recycled paper.

Students then look at the photograph sequence 'Recycling Waste Paper' and match the photograph to the description before checking with their neighbour. Provide feedback by asking students to read out the paragraphs in the correct order.

Students then complete the sentences in 1b. Check their work and then they complete the speaking activity in 1c.

2 Find out if any students have got penfriends. Ask how often they write and which language they use. Ask students what happens to the letter when they take it to a post office. Help students with vocabulary and then they complete the task in 2a. Check by asking students to tell you what happens to the letter.

In pairs students work out what happens to their luggage after they check in at the airport. Check by asking pairs to tell you.

Students then complete the speaking activity in 2c while you monitor and help. Provide feedback by asking students the questions.

In pairs students then complete 2d and tell you their answers.

3 Students read through the questions in 3a and find the answers in the text below. Check their answers.

Introduce the listening activity by explaining the situation in 3b. Before they listen they put a tick next to the information they think they will hear. They listen to the cassette to see if they were correct. They then listen a second time and note down more detailed information. They tell their neighbour about the company based on their notes while you monitor and check.

Revise all the structures and vocabulary before moving on to the next lesson.

At home students prepare for the next lesson by looking up the vocabulary in 4a of Unit 39.

Tapescripts

Exercise 3c

Welcome to Fourstones Paper Mill. My name's Jonathan and I'm your guide for the tour. As you see, we are now in the car park. We will start our tour in the waste paper store where you will see the waste paper after it has been sorted. We use the bleached paper for better quality paper and the rest for lower quality paper. From there we will go through the factory to show you all the stages involved in recycling the waste paper. We will leave the factory through the side entrance and walk across the road to administration. Please be careful when you're crossing the road as the cars come from the right. We will go through the administration department to the meeting room, Room 11. There the Marketing Manager will give you a presentation of our current sales markets and our future plans and following that we will have lunch in the staff canteen. I hope the Managing Director, Tim Walker, will be present to answer any questions you may have. The time is now 11am. The factory trip and presentation will take about 1½ hours and we've allowed 45 minutes for lunch. I will be explaining things as we go around, but if you have any questions during the guided tour, don't hesitate to ask. Please follow me.

Answers

Exercise 1a

1 A
2 C
3 E
4 D
5 B

Exercise 2a

1 The letter is weighed.
2 The stamps are stuck on.
3 The letter is put into the post box.
4 The post box is emptied.
5 The letters are taken to the sorting room.
6 The letters are sorted.
7 The letters are sent to Hong Kong.
8 The letter is delivered to your penfriend.

Exercise 1b

1 The waste paper is sorted into bleached paper and coloured paper.
2 When the roll is full it is taken away and a new roll is started.
3 The roll of recycled paper is weighed.
4 The waste paper is mixed with water.
5 Hot air is blown on it and the paper is dried.
6 The waste paper is emptied into the yard.
7 The water is squeezed out.
8 The recycled paper is carried along a conveyor belt.
9 The waste paper is left for 24 hours.
10 The roll of recycled paper is loaded onto pallets.

1

UNIT 39

At Work

1 a Read the following questions, then try to find the answers in the text below as quickly as possible.

eg What is the woman's name? Jilly Wright.

1 What is her occupation?
2 How old was she when she left school?
3 What happened when she was 22?
4 When did she start working as a TV presenter?
5 What time does she go 'on air'?
6 What happens at 3.30pm?
7 What time does she go to bed?
8 How much does she earn a year?
9 What is her ambition?
10 How much does she spend on clothes per month?

Name: Jilly Wright
Age: 30
Occupation: Television Presenter

Route to Job

Jilly left school at 16 and worked as a typist for a small company for 3 years. When she was 19 she did a secretarial course which lasted for one year. Her next job was with an international company where she worked as a secretary in the training section of the Personnel Department. When she was 22 she became a trainer and started to train new employees. After another 3 years she left the company to work for a small company who produce training videos. A year ago she started working part time as a TV presenter on one of the cable channels and now she works there full time.

Jilly's Day

I normally get up at 4.30am and go jogging for an hour. I have a quick shower, get dressed for work and have some breakfast - fresh fruit, cereal and orange juice. As I'm a presenter on breakfast television I have to leave home at 5.45am. It takes me about 10 minutes to travel to the television studio, if there are no traffic jams. I arrive there just before 6am. Luckily I have my own parking space so I don't have to worry about that. As soon as I walk in I'm given a cup of strong black coffee and a list of the themes on today's programme. I know all of this because I have to find out information about the themes before the show so I can talk about them or interview people. If there are any last minute questions, for example, how to pronounce someone's name correctly, this is my last chance. At 6.15 am I go 'on air'. I normally start with the news and the weather and then I look at the headlines in all the national newspapers. If something important has happened the producer tries to get experts in to discuss why or what it means, but usually we just have well known faces talking about current affairs. I come 'off air' at 10.30am and grab a sandwich and another coffee. Then I go to the information centre in the TV studio to find out information for tomorrow's programme or practise what I'm going to say tomorrow. I leave the studio about 3.30pm and go to the gym for an hour, then go home and have something to eat. In the evening I watch TV or meet friends, but I'm always in bed by 10pm

Salary: approximately £25,000 p.a.
Monthly Spendings: £500 mortgage / £200 make-up, hair / £50 gym fees / £200 clothes
Ambition: To have my own chat show.

b Now read the text again and make notes about her day. When you have finished, use your notes to tell your neighbour about Jilly. Do you both have the same information?

Notes

2

1 c Ask your neighbour.

1 Would you like to be a TV presenter on breakfast TV? Why (not)?
2 Do you think she earns a lot of money? Why (not)?
3 Do you think her job is easy? Why (not)?
4 Do you think her job is interesting? Why (not)?
5 Do you think she should have been trained to be a presenter? Why (not)?

2 a Other members of the class are going to interview you. They will ask you about your occupation, your work experience and your normal day. Make notes on the form below so you can prepare what you're going to say. Do not use full sentences.

Name ____________ Age ____________ Occupation ____________ Past Jobs:	Notes — A Normal Day Before Work At Work After Work

b You will also be interviewing other members of your class about their occupation, work experience and normal day. Write down 10 questions you can ask them.

1 ____________ ?
2 ____________ ?
3 ____________ ?
4 ____________ ?
5 ____________ ?
6 ____________ ?
7 ____________ ?
8 ____________ ?
9 ____________ ?
10 ____________ ?

c Now ask 3 neighbours your questions. If you need more information, you'll have to think up more questions. Make brief notes of the answers so you can tell your teacher about one of your neighbours.

3

3 a Janice Goulding is receptionist at ABC Office Supplies. Look at the notes she has made in her diary and ask your neighbour questions.

eg Who is at Head Office all morning?

Thursday 10 March

	Mike Smith	Simon Parker	Mandy Wardle	John Banks
9.30		9.30 - 10 Meeting		sick all day
10.00	At Head		10-10.30 Meeting	
10.30	Office all	10.30 - 11.30		
11.00	morning	Meeting		
11.30			11.30-12 Meeting	

b Between 10 and 10.30 Janice has 5 phone calls. What do you think she says to each caller? Match the questions and replies below.

1 Hello. Can I speak to Mike Smith please? ___ Hold the line please. I'll put you through.
2 Hello. Can I speak to Janice Goulding please? ___ She's in a meeting at the moment. Can I ask her to call you back?
3 Hello. Can you put me through to Simon Parker please? ___ I'm afraid he's not here at the moment. Can I take a message?
4 Hello. Can I speak to Mandy Wardle please? ___ I'm afraid he's off sick today. Can I take a message?
5 Hello. Can you put me through to John Banks please? ___ Speaking.

c Janice Goulding is on her coffee break between 11 and 11.15. Your neighbour answers the phone while she is on her break. Telephone your neighbour and ask to speak to different people.

d Later Simon Parker receives a call from Nigel Adinall. Practise the dialogue with your neighbour.

Simon Parker	Nigel Adinall
Simon Parker speaking	Hello Simon. This is Nigel Adinall from ATV. How are you?
Fine thanks. How are you?	Very well. Look Simon I have a small problem with our meeting this afternoon.
Oh, what's that?	Well my car's broken down and I have to take it to the garage. Could we rearrange the meeting for Friday morning?
Yes that's fine. How about 9 o'clock?	9 o'clock's fine by me. Thanks a lot.
No problem. See you then.	Okay. Bye.

e Here are some more useful phrases for telephoning. When would you say them?

1 Could you repeat that please? ___ When the person is speaking too quickly.
2 Could you speak more slowly please? ___ When the person is speaking too quietly.
3 Could you speak a bit louder please? ___ When you want to note something down.
4 Could you hold on while I get a pencil? ___ When you want the person to say something a second time.
5 Could you spell that please? ___ When you want to write something down letter by letter.

f You are going to make some phone calls now. Read the situations and think about what you are going to say and which phrases you are going to use before you begin.

1 You have a meeting at 10.30am tomorrow with Dawn Anderson, Marketing Manager at Aztec Fabrics Ltd. Unfortunately you can't make it as there is a rail strike. Ring her up, explain the situation and rearrange the meeting.

2 You have received a translation of your company brochure to check. You notice that the address is wrong. It reads Normad Exports, 52 Rue de le Victoire, 7509 Paris. It should read Normand Exports, 52 Rue de la Victoire, 75009 Paris. Ring Isabelle Meyer at Intertrans to explain the situation.

3 You have been invited to visit one of your customers, John MacLean at IT Tools. Ring him to let him know the exact time and date you will arrive.

4 You have seen an advert in a magazine which is very interesting. Ring the company (Envirotec) and see if they can send you some general information, a catalogue and a price list.

5 Julian Armitage had an appointment with you at 10 o'clock. He didn't come. Ring him and find out why not.

4

4 a Translate the following.

Vocabulary

television presenter ________	'on air' ________
typist ________	headlines ________
to last ________	producer ________
trainer ________	experts ________
to train ________	well known faces ________
employees ________	current affairs ________
training videos ________	'off air' ________
cable channels ________	gym ________
full time ________	spending ________
breakfast television ________	mortgage ________
television studio ________	make up ________
as soon as ________	gym fees ________
themes ________	ambition ________
programme ________	chat show ________
to interview ________	translation ________
last minute questions ________	brochure ________
to pronounce ________	

Structures

Hello. Can I speak to Mike Smith please? ________
Hold the line please. ________
I'll put you through. ________
She's in a meeting at the moment. ________
Can I ask her to call you back? ________
I'm afraid he's not here at the moment. ________
Can I take a message? ________
I'm afraid he's off sick today. ________
Simon Parker speaking. ________
Hello Simon. This is Nigel Adinall from ATV. ________
Look Simon, I have a small problem with our meeting this afternoon. ________
Could we rearrange the meeting for Friday? ________
Yes that's fine. ________
How about 9 o'clock? ________
No problem. ________
See you then. ________
Could you repeat that please? ________
Could you speak more slowly please? ________
Could you speak a bit louder please? ________
Could you hold on while I get a pencil? ________
Could you spell that please? ________

Teaching Notes

Warm-up

Ask students questions from earlier Units eg "What do you do for a living? What are you doing now? What did you do yesterday? What are you going to do tomorrow?"

Revision

Revise all the structures and vocabulary from the previous Unit by asking students questions eg "What happens to your luggage when you have checked in at the airport?"

Presentation and Practice

1 Introduce the activity in 1a by telling students that they are going to answer some questions about a lady called Jilly Wright. Read the questions through and make sure students understand them. Students then try to answer them as quickly as possible by scanning the text. Provide feedback by asking students the questions. Students then read the text again and make notes about Jilly's day. In pairs they use their notes to tell their neighbour about Jilly while you monitor and check.

Students then answer the questions in 1c. Provide feedback by asking students the questions and checking their answers.

2 Explain that students are going to interview other students and be interviewed in this activity. Before they start they prepare themselves by making notes on the sheet in 2a while you monitor and help. They then make up questions they want to ask when they are interviewing other students. Students then move around the class interviewing other students while you monitor and check. Provide feedback by asking students to tell you about one other student.

3 Introduce the situation in 3a and then students ask and answer questions about the people while you monitor and check.

Explain the situation in 3b and ask students what each person is doing between 10 and 10.30. Students then match the questions and replies. Provide feedback by pairs reading the questions and replies out.

Explain the situation in 3c and ask students what each person is doing between 11 and 11.15. Students then practise telephoning using the phrases from 3b.

In 3d students read through the dialogue and practise it with their neighbour.

Students then match the phrases and when they would use them in 3e. Provide feedback by asking students what they would say if the person is speaking too quickly etc.

In 3f students read through the tasks and make notes about what they will say. They then 'telephone' their neighbour and carry out the tasks while you monitor and check. Provide feedback by students demonstrating their activity to the rest of the class.

Revise all the structures and vocabulary before moving on to the next lesson.

At home students prepare for the next lesson by revising all the vocabulary and structures from Units 31 - 39.

Answers

Exercise 3b

1 Hello. Can I speak to Mike Smith please? I'm afraid he's not here at the moment. Can I take a message?
2 Hello. Can I speak to Janice Goulding please? Speaking.
3 Hello. Can you put me through to Simon Parker please? Hold the line please. I'll put you through.
4 Hello. Can I speak to Mandy Wardle? She's in a meeting at the moment. Can I ask her to call you back?
5 Hello. Can you put me though to John Banks please? I'm afraid he's off sick today. Can I take a message?

Exercise 3e

1	Could you repeat that please?	When you want the person to say something a second time.
2	Could you speak more slowly please?	When the person is speaking too quickly.
3	Could you speak a bit louder please?	When the person is speaking too quietly.
4	Can you hold on while I get a pencil?	When you want to note something down.
5	Can you spell that please?	When you want to write something down letter by letter.

UNIT 40

Revision

1 a Here are the names of some parts of the body. Point at each one and tell your neighbour what it is

eg *This is my ankle. These are my toes.*

elbow	wrist	arm	chest	thumb	leg	waist	head
fingers	hips	hand	neck	ear	foot	eye	knee

b Here are some common problems. What advice would you give?

I've got flu	I've got bachache	I feel sick
I've got toothache	I've got a sore throat	I've got a headache

c What do you do when you want to see a doctor in your country? Discuss these questions with your neighbour. Do you have to make an appointment? Do you have to go to the doctor, or does he come to you? How long do you have to wait for an appointment? How much does it cost?

2 a Work with your neighbour and make up a short story using at least 5 of the words below. Make notes and when you're ready, tell your story to the rest of the class.

started	helped	drove	checked	shouted	saw	sailed
came	thrown	locked	thought	heard	met	explained
freed	arrived	trapped	packed	telephoned	was	tried

b Look at these situations and say what you would do.

1 *Your boss has invited you and your girlfriend/boyfriend out for a meal. The evening is going well and the atmosphere is good. Suddenly your girlfriend/boyfriend coughs and knocks over a glass of red wine. The red wine runs across the table and on to your boss's best suit.*

2 *You are looking after a friend's pet dog while they are on holiday. One morning when you go to feed it, you find that it is lying in its basket. It is very ill.*

3 *You had a job interview last week. This morning you received a letter informing you that you did not get the job. You know that you were the most suitable and best qualified for the job. You also know that you were the oldest.*

4 *Your partner doesn't come home one night.*

5 *You take your boyfriend/girlfriend out to a restaurant. At the end of the meal you ask for the bill and give the waiter your credit card. After a few minutes, he returns and tells you that it has not been accepted.*

c Read these sentences and underline the correct form.

1 The sun was shining/shone when I was arriving/arrived in Hawaii.
2 While I was shopping/shopped, someone was shouting/shouted my name.
3 I was lying/lay in the bath when the telephone was ringing/rang.
4 While I was walking/walked home, someone was screaming/screamed.
5 I was running/ran through the woods when I was tripping/tripped over.

3 a Do you live a healthy life? Ask your neighbour these questions.

1 Do you exercise regularly?
2 Do you eat healthy food?
3 Do you sleep well?
4 Do you find it easy to relax?
5 Do you enjoy life?

b Read these statements and tell your neighbour whether you agree with them or not. Explain why.

1 Eating meat is unhealthy.
2 Too much exercise is bad for you.
3 Fresh fruit is bad for old people.
4 Dairy products are good for children.
5 Vegetarians find it difficult to concentrate for long.

4 a Explain the following words to your neighbour by describing what you use them for: safety pin - scissors - bandage - plastic gloves

b What would you take with you if you were going on holiday to India. You are allowed 10 things in your suitcase. When you've made your list, compare it with your neighbour's. Explain why you need all 10 items on your list.

1	____________	6	____________
2	____________	7	____________
3	____________	8	____________
4	____________	9	____________
5	____________	10	____________

5 a What do you do for a living? Ask your neighbour to explain briefly what the following people do for a living: nurse - teacher - chef - receptionist - policeman

b Now ask your neighbour these questions.

1 What do you do for a living?
2 Which branch do you work in?
3 Do you ever have to work at weekends?
4 Do you work in a factory?
5 What activities does your work involve?

6 a Here are 3 job adverts.

Secretary	**Computer Programmer**	**Sales Assistant**
International Company is looking for a hard working and ambitious person. Must have computer experience. Typewriting and shorthand skills required. Knowledge of French preferred.	Graduate required with 3 years computing experience.	Part time sales assistant required for electrical goods shop. Sales experience required. 3 days a week and every second Saturday.
£13 K p.a.	Contract for 18 months.	£3.50 per hour.
Apply in writing to:	£17 K p.a.	Send CV to:
ILC International 19-23 Port Road Truro	CV's to Intact Computing Ltd 13 Fordway London W3 2BR	The Manager Robsons Electrical Shop 29-33 Pool Street Durham DH3 49P
The Independent 29.04.96	*The Times 29.04.96*	*The Guardian 29.04.96*

Your neighbour has applied to you for one of the jobs and you are going to interview him/her. Before you start, think about the questions you will ask and the information you need to know. Here are a few ideas.

languages - skills - work experience - education - own transport - possible overtime

6 b You need some items for your office. Decide what you need and fill in order form A. (Make up the details). When you are finished, ring your neighbour and place your order. Write down your neighbour's order on form B and then compare your work.

Order Form A

Customer Name ____________
Customer Address ____________
____
Date ____________

Order No	Description	Quantity	Price

Total ....
\+ VAT @ 17½% ....
Grand Total ....

Order Form B

Customer Name ____________
Customer Address ____________
____
Date ____________

Order No	Description	Quantity	Price

Total ....
\+ VAT @ 17½% ....
Grand Total ....

7 a Here are 3 business cards. Ask your neighbour at least 5 questions about them.

Robson's Electricentre
68 Commercial Street
Dundee
DD1 2AB
Tel 01382 26437
Fax 01382 26451
Tony Robson
Managing Director

Far End Bookshop
99 Harcourt Street
DUBLIN 2
Tel 01-5716554
Fax 01-5715923
Mark Rickwood
Sales Manager

PCL
Software Solutions
6 Davy Way
Llay
Wrexham
Clydd LL12 0PG
Tel 01978 242424 / Fax 01978 255552
Bridget Heale
Financial Manager

b You have been invited to the opening of a customer's new premises. Work in groups of 6. You have to socialise with the others. If you have any business cards with you, use them and give them to the people when you are introducing yourself.

8 a Work with your neighbour. You want to send a parcel to your penfriend in England. What happens to the parcel after you take it to the post office?

Here are some words which may help:

delivered	weighed	stacked	sorted
tied together	emptied	loaded	taken away

b Can you think of anything in your place of work...

1 which is emptied?
2 which is collected?
3 which is sorted?
4 which is weighed?
5 which is cleaned?
6 which is checked?
7 which is filed away?
8 which is wrapped?
9 which is tied together?
10 which is delivered?

9 a Read the following situations. You are going to make a telephone call to your neighbour, so sit back to back.

1 *You have received the translation of your company brochure to check, but there are several mistakes. Telephone the company and explain the mistakes. The post code should read NH5 2LP, not NH5 2LB. The telephone area code should have a '1' in front of it, so should be (01978). The address is 19a, not 19, and your surname is also wrongly spelt.*

2 *You are arranging some interviews for next week for a position in your company. Your neighbour has applied for the job. Ring him/her and arrange a time, place and date. You will probably have to give directions.*

3 *You have a meeting with Simon Parker tomorrow but your car has broken down. Telephone him and explain the situation and rearrange the meeting.*

4 *You have just received a delivery from Armstrong's Stationery. There are several mistakes in the order including 500 red pens which you didn't order, fax rolls which are the wrong size, as well as incorrect quantities. Ring your neighbour and complain. Find out when you can expect the missing articles.*

5 *Your boss has just informed you that you will have to work late tonight. You had arranged to go out for a meal with your boyfriend/girlfriend. Ring your boyfriend/girlfriend and explain the situation.*

10 a You are going to tell your neighbour about yourself. See if you can talk for at least 5 minutes. Here are some topics to help you.

- the medical service in your country
- common illnesses, what advice you should give and why
- health and healthy living
- what you do for a living
- your ideal job
- your work experience

Teaching Notes

Warm-up

Ask students questions from earlier Units eg "What do you do? What are you doing? What did you do yesterday?"

Revision

Revise all the structures and vocabulary from the previous Unit by giving students a copy of the situations in 3e of Unit 39 so that students can revise telephoning.

Presentation and Practice

1 In pairs students complete the speaking activity in 1a. Students then give their neighbour advice for the common problems listed in 1b and then complete the speaking activity in 1c while you monitor and check.

2 Students read the words in 2a out, focusing on pronunciation and stress.

In pairs they then make up a story using at least 5 of the words listed. Using their notes they tell the rest of the class their story.

In 2b students read through the situation and say what they would do if they were one of the people involved. Provide feedback by asking students to tell you what they would do. Then ask students what they would do if they were one of the other people involved eg "What would you do in situation 1 if you were the boss? What would you do if you were the girlfriend/boyfriend?"

Students then complete the task in 2c. Provide feedback by asking students to read you their sentences.

3 In pairs students complete the speaking activities in 3a and go on to 3b while you monitor and check.

4 Students try to explain the items in 4a to their neighbour. They then read the situation in 4b and write down 10 things they would take on holiday with them. When they are ready they explain to their neighbour what they would take and why they have chosen those items.

5 In pairs students explain what the people listed in 5a do. In 5b they ask their neighbour about his/ her own job while you monitor and check.

6 Students prepare themselves for the interview in 6a by writing some questions. They then interview their neighbour. Provide feedback by asking students if they would give their neighbour the job based on the interview and explain why/why not.

In 6b students make a list of the items they wish to order on Form A. They then sit back to back to 'telephone' their neighbour, who listens and takes down the details on Form B. Pairs then compare their order forms to make sure that the order has been taken correctly.

7 Students ask and answer questions about the information on the business cards eg "What is the address of Robson's Electricentre."

In 7b students work in groups of 6. They have been invited to the opening of a customer's new premises. Tell students they have to socialise for 5 minutes and time it. See which group managed to keep socialising the longest.

8 In pairs students work out what happens to a parcel after they take it to the post office. Provide feedback by asking students to tell you what happens.

9 Students sit back to back again to 'telephone' their neighbour. They then complete the tasks in 9a while you monitor and check. Provide feedback by asking pairs to demonstrate their activity.

10 Students are given 5 minutes each to practise talking about themselves. They may make a few notes if they wish, but they should follow the points given and talk about themselves for at least 5 minutes.

At home students prepare for the next lesson by looking up the vocabulary in 4a of Unit 41.

Answers

Exercise 2c

1 The sun was shining when I arrived in Hawaii.
2 While I was shopping, someone shouted my name.
3 I was lying in the bath when the telephone rang.
4 While I was walking home, someone screamed.
5 I was running through the woods when I tripped over.

1

UNIT 41

What was your favourite subject at school?

1 a Which subjects did you learn at school? Look at the subjects listed below and put a tick (✓) next to the subjects you learnt at school.

Biology ☐	Geography ☐	English ☐	Business Studies ☐
French ☐	Economics ☐	Maths ☐	Religious Studies ☐
History ☐	Law ☐	Sport ☐	Swimming ☐
Spanish ☐	Typing ☐	Chemistry ☐	Metalwork ☐
Psychology ☐	Computing ☐	Physics ☐	Politics ☐
Music ☐	Art ☐	Cookery ☐	Technical Drawing ☐
Woodwork ☐	Sewing ☐	Shorthand ☐	Astronomy ☐

b Ask your neighbour and then complete the following sentences.

We both learnt ______________________________ at school.

Neither of us learnt ______________________________ at school.

I learnt ______________________________, but my neighbour didn't.

My neighbour learnt ______________________________, but I didn't.

c Answer the following questions in note form, then ask your neighbour.

1 Which was your favourite subject at school? ______________________________.
2 Why was this your favourite subject? ______________________________.
3 Which was your least favourite subject? ______________________________.
4 Why was this your least favourite subject? ______________________________.
5 Who was the best teacher you have ever had? ______________________________.
6 Why was he/she the best teacher you have ever had? ______________________________.
7 Who was the worst teacher you have ever had? ______________________________.
8 Why was he/she the worst teacher you have ever had? ______________________________.
9 Which subjects did you study for your school leaving examinations? ______________________________.
10 What time did school start and finish? ______________________________.

d Jacqueline is 15 and is a schoolgirl. Her mum, Lilian, is 42 and works in a supermarket. Look at the sentences below. Who do you think is speaking, Jacqueline or Lilian?

1 I learnt history and physics at school.
2 I'm going to do french and maths next year.
3 I went to school for 10 years.
4 School started at 9am and finished at 3.30pm.
5 My least favourite subject was chemistry.
6 I'm learning biology.
7 I've been going to school for 10 years.
8 We don't have school on Saturdays.
9 I didn't do economics.
10 My favourite subject at school is maths.

2

2 a Here is the weekly timetable for class 5b. You are going to hear a cassette informing you of some changes. Before you listen to the cassette ask your neighbour these questions and then make up 5 more questions.

eg What do 5b have at 1310 on Friday? English in Room 21.

1 What time is French on Wednesday?
2 What is first two on Friday?
3 Who teaches history?
4 When is Mrs Wheeler teaching?
5 Which room is computing in?

Now listen to the cassette and make the changes.

TIMETABLE CLASS 5b

	MON	TUE	WED	THUR	FRI
09:10 - 09:45	English Room 21 Miss Fisher	Biology Room 35 Mrs Lambard	French Room 17 Mr Normand	Maths Room 10 Mrs Wheeler	Swimming Pool Miss Brown
09:45 - 10:20	English Room 21 Miss Fisher	Biology Room 35 Mrs Lambard	Geography Room 06 Miss Crosfield	Computing Room 09 Mr Graham	Swimming Pool Miss Brown
10:20 - 10:35	B	R	E	A	K
10:35 - 11:10	Computing Room 09 Mr Graham	French Room 17 Mr Normand	Maths Room 10 Mrs Wheeler	History Room 12 Mr Bell	French Room 17 Mr Normand
11:10 - 11:45	Maths Room 10 Mrs Wheeler	Computing Room 09 Mr Graham	English Room 21 Miss Fisher	Geography Room 06 Miss Crosfield	Maths Room 10 Mrs Wheeler
11:45 - 13:10	L	U	N	C	H
13:10 - 13:45	French Room 17 Mr Normand	Physics Room 32 Mr Middleton	Sport Hall Mr Johnson	Chemistry Room 33 Mr Marshall	English Room 21 Miss Fisher
13:45 - 14:20	History Room 12 Mr Bell	Physics Room 32 Mr Middleton	Sport Hall Mr Johnson	Chemistry Room 33 Mr Marshall	Computing Room 09 Mr Graham
14:20 - 14:55	Chemistry Room 33 Mr Marshall	Geography Room 06 Miss Crosfield	Physics Room 32 Mr Middleton	Music Room 29 Miss Reid	History Room 12 Mr Bell
14:55 - 15:30	Chemistry Room 33 Mr Marshall	Geography Room 06 Miss Crosfield	Physics Room 32 Mr Middleton	Music Room 29 Miss Reid	History Room 12 Mr Bell

b Read these words and phrases. Would you say them when you agree(✓), when you're unsure (?), or when you disagree (x)? Compare with your neighbour.

___ I don't think so ___ of course ___ perhaps ___ it depends ___ definitely
___ of course not ___ certainly not ___ I agree ___ I suppose so ___ definitely not
___ I think so ___ certainly ___ I'm not sure ___ I don't agree ___ sometimes

c Work in groups of 3. Look at the statements and ask your neighbour.

eg Do you think that all children should learn English at school?
Yes definitely. I think it's important to be able to speak English.
I agree with you. It's much harder to learn a language when you're working.

1 All children should learn English in school.
2 All children should learn maths in school.
3 Naughty children should be smacked.
4 It's easier to teach 10 year olds than to teach 16 year olds.
5 Bad exam results are because of bad teaching.
6 Children should be able to choose which classes they go to.
7 Teachers should be paid more.
8 Parents should be able to choose which school their children go to.
9 Classes should be no more than 15 pupils.
10 Education should be free.

3

3 a Listen to the cassette and fill in the missing information on the CV.

C V

Surname ______________ **First Name** ______________
Address 27 Park Avenue **Tel No** ______________
Blackpool ______________ **Date of Birth** October 12 ______________

Education

Name and Address of Institute	*From*	*To*	*Qualifications*
Fylde Primary School, Blackpool	1965	____	
Queen Elizabeth Middle School, St Annes	____	1972	
Fylde High School, Blackpool	1972	____	______ 'O' Levels and 3 'A' Levels ______________
Leeds University, Leeds	____	1981	BSc ______________

Work Experience

Name and Address of Employer	*From*	*To*	*Position*
Holdsworth Electronics, Skipton	1981	____	______________
Holdsworth Electronics, Skipton	____	1988	Sales Manager
Strathdale Systems, Halifax	____	now	General Manager

Skills and Languages ______________
Hobbies and Interests Skiing ______________

b Now fill in one of the forms below about yourself. When you've finished ask your neighbour and fill in the details on the other form.

Surname ______________ **First Name** ______________
Address ______________ **Tel No** ______________
______________ **Date of Birth** ______________
____

Education
Name/Address of Institute *From* *To* *Qualifications*

Work Experience
Name/Address of Employer *From* *To* *Position*

Skills and Languages ______________
____
Hobbies and Interests ______________
____

Surname ______________ **First Name** ______________
Address ______________ **Tel No** ______________
______________ **Date of Birth** ______________
____

Education
Name/Address of Institute *From* *To* *Qualifications*

Work Experience
Name/Address of Employer *From* *To* *Position*

Skills and Languages ______________
____
Hobbies and Interests ______________
____

4

4 a Translate the following.

Vocabulary

biology ______________
history ______________
psychology ______________
woodwork ______________
economics ______________
law ______________
typing ______________
computing ______________
art ______________
maths ______________
chemistry ______________
physics ______________
shorthand ______________
business studies ______________
religious studies ______________
swimming ______________
metalwork ______________
politics ______________
technical drawing ______________
astronomy ______________
favourite ______________
least favourite ______________
best ______________
worst ______________
certainly not ______________
I suppose so ______________
I'm not sure ______________
I agree ______________
certainly ______________
I don't agree ______________
of course ______________
perhaps ______________
definitely ______________
definitely not ______________
I don't think so ______________
of course not ______________
I think so ______________
naughty ______________
to be smacked ______________
results ______________
surname ______________
date of birth ______________
institute ______________
qualifications ______________
work experience ______________
manager ______________
languages ______________

Structures

We both learnt biology, chemistry and maths. ______________
Neither of us learnt woodwork. ______________
I learnt economics but my neighbour didn't. ______________
My neighbour learnt technical drawing but I didn't. ______________
What do 5b have at 1310 on Friday? ______________
English in Room 21. ______________
Do you think that all children should learn English at school? ______________
Yes definitely. ______________
It's very important to be able to speak English. ______________
I agree with you. ______________
It's much harder to learn a language when you're working. ______________

Teaching Notes

Warm-up

Ask students questions from earlier Units eg "What are the advantages and disadvantages of state medical care? What do you think you'll do at the weekend?"

Presentation and Practice

1 Introduce 1a by telling students which subjects you had at school. Write the subjects on the board and elicit what you learn in that subject eg in biology you learn how the body works, in history you learn about the past. Ask students about the rest of the subjects in 1a in the same way and then students tick the subjects which they had at school. In pairs they ask their neighbour and then they complete the sentences in 1b. Provide feedback by asking students to tell you what they have written. Write your note answers to the first two questions from 1c on the board, emphasising that students are not to write full sentences. Students then complete the task in 1c while you monitor and check. In 1d students read the introduction and then decide whether the sentences are said by Jacqueline or Lilian. Provide feedback by asking students to tell you who they think said each sentence.

2 Ask your students questions about schools in their country eg "How many terms are there? What age do children start school? What age do children leave school? What time does school start? What time does school finish?"

Introduce the timetable in 2a by asking students questions eg "Where is English on Monday? Who teaches French? What does Mr Bell teach? Which lesson is in Room 29 at 2.20pm on Thursday?"

In pairs students ask and answer questions about the information while you monitor and check. When they are familiar with the information tell them they are going to hear a recording of the Head of School working out some changes to the timetable for next week. While they are listening they are to make the changes to the timetable. Tell them that they will hear the cassette twice. Play the cassette twice and then students compare their work with their neighbour. Provide feedback by asking students to tell you what changes they have made.

In pairs students read the phrases in 2b and then put them in one of the categories. Check by asking students which phrases they have put into which categories.

In pairs students then read through the statements in 2c and say what they think using the phrases from 2c while you monitor and check.

3 Write your own CV based on the layout in 3a and copy it for each of your students. Talk them through it, explaining any new vocabulary. In pairs students then ask and answer questions eg "What is his/her name? Where did he/she go to school? What qualifications has he/she got?" When students are familiar with the information ask them if they have ever written a CV and ask them what they used it for? Introduce the cassette by telling students they are going to hear a short interview which will be played twice. While they are listening they are to fill in the missing information. Students then complete the listening activity in 3a and compare their work with their neighbour. Provide feedback by asking students the information eg "When did Joanne start school? What did she study at university?" Students then fill in their own details on the CV in 3b while you monitor and check. They then ask their neighbour about him/herself and fill in the details on the other form. Provide feedback by asking students to tell you about themselves.

Revise all the structures and vocabulary before moving on to the next lesson.

At home students prepare for the next lesson by looking up the vocabulary in 4a of Unit 42.

Tapescripts

Exercise 2a

The swimming pool is closed on Friday so we'll move the swimming lesson to last two on Monday and chemistry will be first two on Friday in Room 33 with Mr Marshall. physics on Wednesday afternoon will be in Room 31. Room 17 is being painted on Thursday, so all lessons timetabled for Room 17 on Thursday and Friday will now be in Room 18. Mrs Wheeler telephoned to say she is ill and will be off on Monday, Tuesday and Wednesday. Miss Thomson will take her lessons on these days. Mr Bell is on holiday on Thursday and Friday. Students will have extra computing lessons in room 09 with Mr Graham in these periods.

Exercise 3a

A What's your surname?
B Stephens - that's S T E P H E N S
A And your first name?
B Joanne - J O A double N E
A What's your address?
B 27 Park Avenue, Blackpool, FY29 2PH
A When were you born?
B 12 October 1960
A Do you have a telephone number?
B Yes it's 01253 959272
A When and where did you go to school?
B I went to Fylde Primary School in Blackpool from 1965 to 1969 and then to Queen Elizabeth Middle School in St Annes from 1969 to 1972. After that I went to Fylde High School until 1978.
A What qualifications did you get?
B 8 'O' levels and 3 'A' levels in Physics, Biology and Maths.
A Did you go on to University?
B Yes, I went to Leeds University from 1978 to 1981. I got a BSc in Economics.
A What work experience have you got?
B My first job was as Trainee Manager at a small company in Skipton called Holdsworth Electronics. After 2 years I became Sales Manager at Holdsworth's and stayed there for another 5 years. In 1988 I joined Strathdale Systems as General Manager in Halifax.
A Do you have any skills and languages?
B I have a clean driving licence and my own car. I also have a lot of experience with computers, and I can type. I learnt French at school and can get by.
A Hobbies and Interests?
B Yes, I like skiing and photography.

Answers

Exercise 1d

1 Lilian
2 Jacqueline
3 Lilian
4 Lilian
5 Lilian
6 Jacqueline
7 Jacqueline
8 Jacqueline
9 Lilian
10 Jacqueline

Exercise 3a

C V

Surname	***Stephens***	Name	***Joanne***
Address	27 Park Avenue Blackpool ***FY29 2PH***	Tel No Date of Birth	***01253 959272*** October 12 ***1960***

Education

Name/Address of Institute	*From*	*To*	*Qualifications*
Fylde Primary School, Blackpool	1965	***1969***	
Queen Elizabeth Middle School, St Annes	***1969***	1972	
Fylde High School, Blackpool	1972	***1978***	***8*** O' Levels / 3 'A' Levels: ***Physics, Biology, Maths***
Leeds University, Leeds	***1978***	1981	BSc ***Economics***

Work Experience

Name/Address of Employer	*From*	*To*	*Position*
Holdsworth Electronics, Skipton	1981	***1983***	***Trainee Manager***
Holdsworth Electronics, Skipton	***1983***	1988	Sales Manager
Strathdale Systems, Halifax	***1988***	now	General Manager

Skills and Languages: ***Clean driving licence and my own car. Experience with computers and can type. School French.***

Hobbies and Interests: Skiing, ***Photography***

1

UNIT 42

How long have you been learning English?

1 a **Look at the questionnaire below. Fill in your details.**

Language Learning Background

1 **Did you learn English at school?** No ☐ Yes ☐
How many years of English did you have? ______

2 **Since leaving school have you taken part in any English courses?** No ☐ Yes ☐
Name of Institute(s) ______
Number of hours of course ______
Qualification ______

3 **Have you ever been on holiday to an English speaking country?** No ☐ Yes ☐
How often? ______
Which country(ies)? ______
How long did you stay? ______
When was the last time? ______

4 **Do you have any English speaking penfriends?** No ☐ Yes ☐
How many? ______
What nationality are they? ______
How often do you write? ______

5 **Do you have any English speaking friends?** No ☐ Yes ☐
How often do you speak with them? ______

6 **Do you ever listen to music in English?** No ☐ Yes ☐
What is your favourite group? ______

7 **Do you ever listen to English radio?** No ☐ Yes ☐
Which radio station? ______

8 **Do you ever watch TV or films in English?** No ☐ Yes ☐
How often? ______

9 **Are you a member of any English speaking society?** No ☐ Yes ☐
How often do you meet? ______
How long have you been a member? ______

10 **What do you think is the best way of learning English?**
living in an English speaking country ☐ going to language school in your country ☐
other ☐

b **Now ask your neighbour about his/her English background.**

c **Tell your teacher about yourself.**

d **Complete the following sentence about yourself and then ask your neighbour.**

eg *How long have you been learning English?*
I've been learning English for .... years.

2

2 a **You are spending a year abroad at Nottingham University to improve your English. Look at the map of the campus opposite and ask your neighbour these questions.**

1 Which hall is on my right when I come in from the West Entrance?
2 Which is the best entrance if I want to go to the computing centre?
3 How do you get from the sports centre to the arts centre?
4 How many book shops are there and where are they?
5 Which residential hall is nearest to the library?

b **Now ask your neighbour 5 more questions.**

eg *Where is Derby Hall?*
It's on Beeston Lane between Sherwood Hall and Lincoln Hall.

c **Today is your first day at Nottingham University and the foreign student coordinator is about to give you some information. Tick (✓) the information you think you will hear.**

☐ The name of the foreign student coordinator.
☐ The telephone number of the foreign student coordinator.
☐ How to register with the University Administration Department.
☐ How to register with the Students' Union.
☐ Which hall you are staying in.
☐ How to meet people.
☐ Which bus to take into Nottingham city centre.
☐ How to register at the library.
☐ How to register at the health centre.
☐ Opening times of the sports centre.
☐ Opening times of the computing centre.
☐ Days and times of your lectures.
☐ Where and when your next meeting will take place.

d **Listen to the cassette. Did you hear what you expected?**

e **Listen again and make notes and then tell your neighbour.**

eg *I heard the number 251 but I'm not sure what it was for.*

✍ **Notes**

f **Ask your neighbour these questions.**

1 Where is the University Administration Department?
2 What do I need £10 for?
3 When is the library open?
4 What do I need to take with me to the health centre?
5 Where am I ringing if I dial 273?

3

3 a **You are on a full time training course which has a 3 month work experience placement. You would like to do your work experience placement in the UK. Read the questions and find the answers in the information below as quickly as possible.**

eg *What is the name of the company? European Language Skills.*

1 Can I write my letter of application in French? ______
2 Who do European Language Skills bank with? ______
3 How many copies of my CV do I have to send? ______
4 What size do the photographs have to be? ______
5 How much do I have to send with the registration form? ______
6 Do I have to send a letter of application? ______
7 What language do the details of my current training programme have to be in? ______
8 When does the company have to receive all my details? ______
9 What is the bank account number of the company? ______
10 How much do I have to pay 21 days before I start my work placement? ______

Application for Work Experience in the UK

Introduction

European Language Skills is a London based training organisation servicing the European and International business communities in the field of UK Work Experience Placements, Language Learning and Commercial and Cultural Orientation.

In the area of Work Experience Placements, we enjoy official recognition from several key organisations including the London Chamber of Commerce and Industry, of which we are a registered examinations centre, and the Conseil Régional Ile de France.

Over the years we have developed a highly professional service that seeks to satisfy the specific demands of trainees in their search for challenging on the job assignments at an international level. Close attention is paid to individual needs, to the business activity for which trainees are being prepared, and to the sector of industry or commerce in which they would wish to put to good use their newly acquired skills.

For our part, and in order to satisfy all these needs, trainees are encouraged to put their placement dossier together in a very precise and professional manner. Guidelines on how this may be achieved are provided opposite.

Your Dossier

In order to process your application effectively, our Placement Officers need to receive the following items from you **at least 8 weeks** prior to commencement of the placement:

1 **A comprehensive CV** (4 copies). We enclose a *model CV* which will serve as a guide when elaborating your own. This should be as detailed as possible. The more we know about your education, training, English language ability and professional experience, the easier it is to find you a **tailor-made** placement.

2 **A passport size photograph** (x 4). Please look smart and don't forget to say *cheese!*

3 **A letter of application**. This should be in English and should briefly describe (a) the training programme you are currently attending, (b) what you hope to achieve while on placement in a UK company, and (c) your professional aspirations for the future.

4 **Details of your current training programme**. Your training organisation, college or university will provide you with a programme syllabus. UK companies will require a brief summary, **in English**, of this syllabus.

With this four-fold contribution, we can help to ensure that your placement period in the UK is a worthwhile and satisfying experience.

Placement Fees

1 Our placement fee is **£260**. This is paid in two instalments.
  i Placement Administration Fee £60 (non refundable). This sum should be sent with your Placement Registration Form.
  ii **£200** is due **21 days** before the commencement of your work experience placement.

Payment should be made by direct transfer to: **European Language Skills**

Details for direct bank transfer of fees: Account Number 19815573
Sorting Code 60-50-09
National Westminster Bank, 50 Ilford Hill, Ilford, IG1 2AP, ESSEX, England

4

3 b **Now ask your neighbour for his/her details and fill in the application form.**

European Language Skills
Roman House
9/10 College Terrace
LONDON
E3 5AN

PLACEMENT REGISTRATION FORM

Trainee's Name:
Address:

Post Code:
Tel No:

Training Organisation:
Address:

Post Code:
Tel No:

When Would You Like to Train?

From: To:

In Which Field/Sector Would You Like to Train?

Accommodation

	Yes/No
Do you require family accommodation?	
Hotel	
Guest House	

Registration Check List

Before returning this registration form, together with all the documents requested for your placement please complete the following check list by ticking (✓) the appropriate box.

4 copies of CV	
4 photographs (passport size)	
Letter of Application	
Details of your current Training Programme	
Placement Administration Fee: £60 (non-refundable)	
This Registration Form	

c **Look at the following questions and discuss your answers with your neighbour.**

1 Have you ever worked abroad? If so, where, when and why?
2 Would you like to work abroad? Why (not)?
3 In which country would you like to work? Why?
4 In which country wouldn't you like to work? Why?
5 If you worked abroad for 3 months, what do you think you would miss most?

Teaching Notes

Warm-up

Ask students questions from earlier Units eg "What do you do for a living? How often are your waste paper bins emptied at work?

Revision

Revise all the structures and vocabulary from the previous Unit by asking students questions eg "What subjects did you have at school? Which subjects did you like the most? When was the last time you wrote your CV? Why?"

Presentation and Practice

1 Students read through the questionnaire and fill in their answers while you monitor and check. In pairs they then ask their neighbour about his/ her English background. Provide feedback by asking students to tell you about themselves. Students then complete the sentence in 1d and ask other students in the class.

2 Find out if any of your students have lived in an English speaking country and ask what they were doing there (working, studying, etc). Find out who would like to live in an English speaking country and elicit reasons why or why not.

Introduce the listening activity in 2a by telling students that they are going to spend a year at Nottingham University and that 2a shows them a map of the campus.

In pairs students ask and answer the questions in 2b while you monitor and check. Students make up 5 more questions and ask their neighbour. When students are familiar with the diagram they complete the task in 2c. Ask students what information they think they will hear and then students complete the listening tasks in 2d and 2e. Provide feedback by asking students to tell you what they heard. Students then answer the questions in 2f (they may hear the cassette again to check if they wish).

3 Ask if any of your students have had a work placement during their training/ studying. Those who have tell the rest of the class when, where and why.

Introduce 3a by telling students that there are companies which organise international work placements and they are going to look at some information about one of these companies. First students read through the questions in 3a and find the answers in the text as quickly as possible. Give them a time limit of 3 minutes and then provide feedback by eliciting the answers to the questions. Students then read the information and complete the task in 3b while you monitor and check.

In pairs students then complete the speaking activity in 3c. Provide feedback by asking students to tell you about their neighbour.

Revise all the structures and vocabulary before moving on to the next lesson.

At home students prepare for the next lesson by looking up the vocabulary in 4a of Unit 43.

Tapescripts

Exercise 2d & e

Good afternoon ladies and gentlemen, and welcome to the University of Nottingham. My name's Greg Evans. That's G R E G E V A N S and I'm the foreign student coordinator. That means if you have any problems or need someone to talk to, I'm here to help.

If you look at the map I've given you, I'll explain where things are and what's happening.

The most important thing you have to do is register with the University Administration Department which is situated in the Trent Building. Registration for foreign students takes place today between 1pm and 3pm in Room 201 and don't forget to take your passport with you.

The next thing is to go to the Students' Union in the Portland Building and get your Students' Union card. You can do this any day this week between 9am and 5pm. Go to Room 322 on the third floor. It's best to do this as soon as possible. You'll need £10 with you for registration fees. You'll also find cafés and bars in the Portland Building and on the ground floor you can see the notice boards for all the societies and clubs. There are over 70 societies and clubs and this is a good way to meet people or try out something new from surfing, to playing chess, to debating.

Once you have your student card you can go to the library and register there. It's open 7 days a week from 9am to 9pm and there's a café on the ground floor when you need a break.

It's also important to register at the health centre. Take your student card and your passport and proof of any health insurance you have. You can register here on Tuesday, Wednesday or Thursday morning between 12pm and 3pm.

For those of you who like to keep fit, the sports centre is near the residential halls. There are squash courts, badminton courts and fitness rooms as well as 3 large halls where sports clubs meet to train.

Information on which clubs meet when, can be found on the notice board in the reception hall of the sports centre. There is no swimming pool. Always take your students' union card with you when you go, otherwise you won't be allowed in.

Finally, the computing centre, which is not far from the north entrance, is open for all students. You can do courses in word processing or computing, etc, or you can go there to type up your essays. You have to book a computer, so it's best to ring up first and arrange a time. The number is extension 273. There is no charge for using the computers but you pay 5p per sheet for the print out. It's open Monday to Friday 9am - 9pm, and Saturdays from 10am till 5pm.

So, that's all for the moment. I'll see you all again next Monday in Room 32 in the Portland Building for our weekly meeting. If you have any questions before then, you can contact me on extension 251, or you're always welcome for a cup of coffee in Room 53, Sherwood Hall.

Answers

Exercise 3a

1 No.
2 The National Westminster Bank.
3 4 copies.
4 Passport size.
5 £60.
6 Yes.
7 English.
8 8 weeks prior to the placement.
9 19815573.
10 £200.

1

UNIT 43

Why are you learning English?

1 a Fill in the questionnaire below about yourself.

Needs Analysis - You

1 **Why are you learning English?**
☐ for my job ☐ for pleasure ☐ other

2 **Put the following skills in order of importance:**
(1 = I need this the most / 4 = I need this the least)
☐ speaking ☐ listening ☐ reading ☐ writing

3 **Put the following in order of difficulty:**
(1 = I find this the most difficult / 4 = I find this the easiest)
☐ speaking ☐ listening ☐ reading ☐ writing

4 **Speaking Skills. Put a tick in any boxes where you have to speak English.**
☐ face-to-face (with one other person)
☐ face-to-face (with a group of people)
☐ on the telephone

5 **Listening Skills. Put a tick in any boxes where you need to listen to English.**
☐ face-to-face (with one other person) ☐ face-to-face (with a group of people)
☐ on the telephone ☐ cassettes/videos ☐ radio programmes

6 **Reading Skills. Put a tick in any box where you have to read English texts.**
☐ letters/faxes ☐ notices ☐ books/newspapers

7 **Writing Skills. Put a tick in any box where you have to write in English.**
☐ forms ☐ letters/faxes ☐ notes/memos

8 **Which of the following describes you best?**
☐ I speak English slowly but the grammar is correct.
☐ I speak English quickly but I make mistakes in grammar.

9 **Which of the following is true for you?**
☐ I find it easier to speak English to classmates than to other people.
☐ I find it easier to speak English to other people than to classmates.

10 **How will you continue learning English after this course?** __________

b Tell your teacher about yourself.

eg *I'm learning English for my job.*
Speaking is the most important skill for me.
Writing is the least important.

2

2 a Now find out about your neighbour and fill in the needs analysis below.

Needs Analysis - Your Neighbour

1 **Why are you learning English?**
☐ for my job ☐ for pleasure ☐ other

2 **Put the following skills in order of importance:**
(1 = I need this the most / 4 = I need this the least)
☐ speaking ☐ listening ☐ reading ☐ writing

3 **Put the following in order of difficulty:**
(1 = I find this the most difficult / 4 = I find this the easiest)
☐ speaking ☐ listening ☐ reading ☐ writing

4 **Speaking Skills. Put a tick in any boxes where you have to speak English.**
☐ face-to-face (with one other person)
☐ face-to-face (with a group of people)
☐ on the telephone

5 **Listening Skills. Put a tick in any boxes where you need to listen to English.**
☐ face-to-face (with one other person) ☐ face-to-face (with a group of people)
☐ on the telephone ☐ cassettes/videos ☐ radio programmes

6 **Reading Skills. Put a tick in any box where you have to read English texts.**
☐ letters/faxes ☐ notices ☐ books/newspapers

7 **Writing Skills. Put a tick in any box where you have to write in English.**
☐ forms ☐ letters/faxes ☐ notes/memos

8 **Which of the following describes you best?**
☐ I speak English slowly but the grammar is correct.
☐ I speak English quickly but I make mistakes in grammar.

9 **Which of the following is true for you?**
☐ I find it easier to speak English to classmates than to other people.
☐ I find it easier to speak English to other people than to classmates.

10 **How will you continue learning English after this course?** __________

b Tell your teacher about your neighbour.

eg *She's learning English because she's going on holiday to the USA.*
Speaking and listening are the most important so she can ask for things.
She finds listening the most difficult because people speak so quickly.
She may have to speak on the phone and she'll definitely have to speak with people face-to-face.

3

3 a You want to improve your English and have decided to do a language course in your summer holidays. Look at the adverts below and answer these questions.

1 What is the name of the company in Ireland?
2 Where is Perthshire?
3 Where does Mr Lord work?
4 What is the telephone number for the Maraid Language Institute?
5 Who do I stay with in Ireland?
6 Who do I stay with in Scotland?
7 Who offers English for Communication?
8 Who offers English for Special Purposes?
9 What is the address to write to in Ireland?
10 What social activities are offered in Scotland?

Learn English in the Heart of the Highlands

Why not improve your English and enjoy yourself at the same time. We put together a programme of formal study tailored to your needs and offer a programme of activities allowing you to enjoy the natural beauty of the Highlands and practise socialising in English at the same time.

- one-to-one tuition
- English for Special Purposes
- tailored programme
- qualified teacher
- living in the teacher's house
- golf
- visit to whisky distillery
- trip to Highland Games
- evening in a pub
- walking
- traditional food

For more information, contact: *Mr A Lord, Balloch House Language School, Pitlochry, PL24 9ZJ, Perthshire, Scotland*

Come to Ireland

- 2 and 3-week language courses.
- English language
- English for Communication
- English for Special Purposes
- Anglo-Irish literature

Small classes ☆ Practical Courses
Social Programmes ☆ Host Family ☆ All Levels

Maraid Language Institute
25 Donnybrook Road
Donnybrook
Dublin 4
Tel 353 1 6605522
Fax 353 1 6605523

b Which course do you think is better for you? Why? Tell your neighbour.

eg *I think the course in Ireland is better for me because I want to learn in a class.*

c Read the letter below and underline the correct verb form.

Dear Sirs

I saw/have seen your advertisement for 2 and 3-week language courses in the Times yesterday.

I work/worked for a large, international company and I need/needed English in my job. I regularly have to go to meetings where English is speaking/spoken and I find that I do not understood/understand everything. I also feel/felt that I am making/make a lot of mistakes in grammar when I am speaking/I speak.

I am very interested in the 'English for Communication' course advertised and would like to do a 2 week course from 17 August to 28 August.

I learnt/have been learning English in school for 8 years when I was younger and learn/have been learning in an evening class for the last 6 months.

Please could you send me information and prices for the above course.

I look forward to hearing from you.

Yours faithfully

A J Faisel

AJ Faisel (Mr)

d Write a letter in reply to one of the advertisements asking for information about their courses.

4

4 a Translate the following.

Vocabulary

needs analysis ______	tailored ______
for pleasure ______	activities ______
speaking ______	natural ______
listening ______	beauty ______
reading ______	socialising ______
writing ______	one-to-one tuition ______
face-to-face ______	English for Special Purposes ______
faxes ______	qualified teacher ______
notices ______	small classes ______
forms ______	social programme ______
heart ______	host family ______
Highlands ______	all levels ______
to enjoy yourself ______	prices ______
formal study ______	

Structures

Why are you learning English? ______
I'm learning English for my job. ______
Speaking is the most important skill for me. ______
Writing is the least important skill for me. ______
She's learning English because she's going on holiday to the USA. ______
Speaking and listening are the most important. ______
She finds listening the most difficult. ______
People speak too quickly. ______
She may have to speak on the phone. ______
She'll definitely have to speak to people face-to-face. ______
Which do you think is better, and why? ______
I think the course in Ireland is better for me. ______
Dear Sirs ______
Please could you send me information. ______
I look forward to hearing from you. ______
Yours faithfully ______

Teaching Notes

Warm-up

Ask students questions from earlier Units eg "Do you eat a lot of dairy products? What do you do with your waste paper?"

Revision

Revise all the structures and vocabulary from the previous Unit by asking students questions eg "How long have you been learning English? Did you learn English at school? Would you like to live in an English speaking country?"

Presentation and Practice

1 Students complete the 'Needs Analysis' questionnaire in 1a about themselves while you monitor and help.

Ask students some of the questions from the questionnaire and then ask students to close their books and tell you about themselves.

2 Students then ask their neighbour and complete the second 'Needs Analysis' questionnaire. Provide feedback by students telling you about their neighbours.

3 Find out if any of your students have been on a language holiday. Ask them where, when and if they thought it was useful.

In pairs students look at the advertisements in 3a and ask each other the questions in 3a while you monitor and check. Provide feedback by asking students the questions.

They then complete the speaking activity in 3b and tell you about their neighbour.

Students read through the letter in 3c and underline the correct verb form. They then complete the writing activity in 3d while you monitor and check. Find out who chose to go to Ireland and who chose to go to Scotland and ask why. If you have time students can exchange their letters and write a reply to the enquiry.

Revise all the structures and vocabulary before moving on to the next lesson.

At home students prepare for the next lesson by looking up the vocabulary in 4a of Unit 44.

Answers

Exercise 3a

1 The Maraid Language Institute.

2 In Scotland

3 At Balloch House Language School.

4 353-1-6605522.

5 A host family.

6 The teacher.

7 Maraid Language Institute.

8 Balloch House Language School.

9 25 Donnybrook Road, Donnybrook, Dublin 4.

10 Golf, visit to whisky distillery, trip to Highland Games, evening in a pub, walking.

Exercise 3d

Dear Sirs

I saw your advertisement for 2 and 3 week language courses in the Times yesterday.

I work for a large, international company and I need English in my job. I regularly have to go to meetings where English is spoken and I find that I do not understand everything. I also feel that I make a lot of mistakes in grammar when I speak.

I am very interested in the 'English for Communication' course advertised and would like to do a 2 week course from 17 August to 28 August.

I learnt English in school for 8 years when I was younger and have been learning in an evening class for the last 6 months.

Please could you send me information and prices for the above course.
I look forward to hearing from you.

Yours faithfully

AJ Faisel (Mr)

1

UNIT 44

I don't have time to learn vocabulary.

1 a Read the following statements and put a 'T' next to them if you think they are true for you, or an 'F' if you think they are false.

1 I like working with my neighbour and testing each other on new vocabulary. ___
2 I write down new words again and again until I can remember them. ___
3 I say the words aloud when I'm learning them. ___
4 I put the words in a sentence and try to remember full sentences. ___
5 I write down how to say new words (eg through = thru). ___
6 I can remember short words better than long words. ___
7 There are some words which I can never remember (tell your neighbour what they are, if you can). ___
8 I try to categorise new vocabulary with groups of words I already know. ___
9 I record words and sentences on to a cassette and listen to them in the car. ___
10 I don't have time to learn vocabulary. ___

b Compare your answers with 4 or 5 other neighbours. Who put 'T' next to the same statements as you? Do you have other ways of learning vocabulary? Who do most people think learns vocabulary the easiest? How does he/she learn vocabulary?

c Look at the words in box A. You can group the words into furniture (chair, bed, cupboard), languages (Spanish, English, French), and animals (horse, cat, rabbit). You can also group the words into words with one syllable (chair, bed, French, horse, cat) and words with two syllables (cupboard, Spanish, English, rabbit). You can also group the words into words containing the letter 'e' (bed, English, French, horse) and words containing the letter 'a' (chair, cupboard, Spanish, cat, rabbit). Look at the words in boxes B-E and see how many groups of words you can make.

A	chair bed Spanish horse English cat rabbit French cupboard
B	tin Denmark cabbage onions Belgium England apples packet jar
C	apple black advert boat car accident coat bag catch
D	easy boring interesting empty difficult black full tall white short
E	kettle bedroom bathroom ferry saucepan taxi hall bus pot

Compare your categories with your neighbour.

d Look at the words in box A and write down 3 other words which you associate with them. Do the same for the words in boxes B - E.

A	next year
B	work
C	happy
D	doctor
E	English

e Now tell your neighbour why you chose these words.

f Close your book and see how many words you can remember from exercise c. Compare with your neighbour. See if you can remember the words your neighbour always forgets.

2

2 a The following 5 people are all learning English. What do you think motivates them? What do you think they want to learn? Do you think that speaking, listening, reading, or writing is most important for them? What kind of vocabulary and phrases do you think they will need? Discuss your answers with your neighbour.

1 A 15 year old girl going on an exchange visit to Britain.
2 A business man representing his company in meetings abroad.
3 A 65 year old man who wants to visit his English speaking grandchildren.
4 A traffic controller at Mexico City Airport.
5 A doctor who is going to an international conference.

b Do you have a grammar book which explains English grammar in your language? What's it called? Which grammar books do other students have? Which do you find easiest to use?

c Now look at the following sentences and underline the correct form.

1 I telephoned/have telephoned him yesterday.
2 I went not/didn't go to the cinema last night.
3 He work/works every day.
4 She is talking/talks on the phone at the moment.
5 She is going/goes to see the doctor tomorrow.

d This time you have to produce the correct form.

1 I (work) ____________ here since 1967.
2 In 1992 I (get) ____________ a new job.
3 He (get up) ____________ at 6 o'clock every morning.
4 She (not watch) ____________ TV last night.
5 We (speak) ____________ English now.

e Now put the correct preposition in the space (on, in or at).

1 ________ Tuesday
2 ________ 10 August
3 ________ 3 o'clock
4 ________ 24 October
5 ________ September

f Look at the sentences and tell your neighbour the negative form and the question form.

eg I work on Saturdays. I don't work on Saturdays. Do you work on Saturdays?

1 He plays football.
2 I go swimming on Saturdays.
3 We learn English on Wednesday evenings.
4 I drink coffee with milk.
5 She likes pizza.

g Ask your neighbour what he/she normally does on a Saturday. Make notes and then tell your teacher.

h Look at the picture and tell your neighbour about Jack using the notes below.

Jack - works at Smedley's Supermarket, plays football every Sunday morning, goes to the cinema every Sunday evening, girlfriend's name is Karen.

i Look back through this book and discuss the following questions with your neighbour.

1 Which Unit did you find the most interesting? Why?
2 Which activity did you find the most interesting? Why?
3 Which Unit did you find the most boring? Why?
4 Which activity did you find the most boring? Why?
5 Which Units did you find the most difficult? Why?

3

3 a Heidi Fetzer took part in an English course last summer in London. Look at her diary and tell your neighbour about her week in London.

	Sun May 29	Monday	Tuesday	Wednesday	Thursday	Friday	Saturday
Morning	Arrived Heathrow 1030. Bus to hotel "Park View" - nice hotel.	First day of course - 10 people in my class.	Roleplays in the morning.	Everybody gave presentation - very interesting - lots of ideas to learn English better.	Made video in class.	Visited Madame Tussauds.	Went shopping - expensive!
Afternoon	Roast beef, carrots and potatoes for tea.	Practised introductions - watched a video.	Played quiz-game in the afternoon.	Trip into London.	Showed our video to other classes and watched theirs.	Did a test and was given a certificate.	
Evening	Phoned home to say all okay.	After school - coffee with people from course - did homework.	Homework - prepare for presentation "What I do to improve my English".	Theatre - Cats. Enjoyed it very much.	Giovanni's birthday - went to restaurant 'Hollywood Planet' to celebrate - late to bed.	End of course party.	17:30 leave Heathrow - Flight BA 572 home. Mum and Dad collected me.

eg Heidi arrived in Heathrow on Sunday May 29 at 1030. She took the bus from Heathrow to her hotel. The hotel was called 'Park View' and she thought it was a nice hotel.

b Ask your neighbour about Heidi's week.

eg What did she do on Friday morning? She visited Madame Tussaud's with the rest of her class.

c What do you do to improve your English between lessons? Discuss with your neighbour and make a list of 3 things you both do to improve your English. Tell the rest of the class.

d When Heidi was back in Austria she started going to an evening class. At first she didn't think that she was improving so she started to keep records. Here is a card she filled out. Ask your neighbour questions.

eg Was the lesson on Tuesday November 14 a good lesson? Yes. It was a good lesson, probably because she was in a good mood.

DATE *Tuesday November 14*

1 Hello Heidi. How are you feeling today? ☑ I'm in a good mood ☐ I'm in a bad mood
2 How was your English lesson? ☑ good ☐ bad
3 Why was it good/bad? *I prepared the lesson so I understood everything and spoke a lot.*
4 Which skills did you practise? ☑ listening ☑ speaking ☑ reading ☐ writing
5 What can you do better now? *My listening skills are improving.*
6 What can you do now that you couldn't before? *Tell the chemist what's the matter with me.*
7 When are you going to do your homework? *I'll try to do it on Thursday.*
8 What are you going to do before the next lesson?
☑ listen to the cassette again ☑ learn vocabulary from this lesson
☐ learn structures from this lesson ☐ listen to English radio
☐ read English newspapers ☑ meet classmates to practise
9 When are you going to review this? *Sunday afternoon.*
10 When are you going to prepare for the next lesson? *Probably Tuesday afternoon.*

e Ask your neighbour the questions and then make some cards for yourself. Fill them out at the end of each lesson and keep a record of your improvement.

4

4 a Translate the following.

Vocabulary

to test	______	to represent	______
to say aloud	______	abroad	______
to categorise	______	traffic controller	______
exchange visit	______	activity	______
businessman	______	mood	______

Structures

Which Unit did you find the most interesting? ______
I found Unit 32 the most interesting because I like sailing. ______
Which activity did you find the most interesting? ______
I found writing a CV the most interesting because I need a CV in English. ______
Which Unit did you find the most boring? ______
I found Unit 32 the most boring because I don't like sailing. ______
Which activity did you find the most boring? ______
Heidi arrived in Heathrow on Sunday May 29 at 1030. ______
She took the bus from Heathrow to her hotel. ______
The hotel was called 'Park View'. ______
She thought it was a nice hotel. ______
What did she do on Friday morning? ______
She visited Madame Tussauds. ______
How are you feeling today? ______
How was your English lesson? ______
Why was it good/bad? ______
Which skills did you practise? ______
What can you do better now? ______
What can you do that you couldn't do before? ______
When are you going to do your homework? ______
What are you going to do before the next lesson? ______
When are you going to review this Unit? ______
When are you going to look up the vocabulary for the next lesson? ______

Teaching Notes

Warm-up

Ask students questions from earlier Units eg "Is the number 13 unlucky in your country? When was the last time somebody gave you flowers?"

Revision

Revise all the structures and vocabulary from the previous Unit by asking students questions eg "Why are you learning English? Which is the most important skill for you? How do you improve your English outside lesson time?"

Presentation and Practice

1 At the start of the lesson ask students to write down the name of the person in the class who they think learns vocabulary the easiest. Students then read through the statements in 1a and write T (true) or F (false) next to them. In groups they then compare their answers and discuss the questions in 1b while you monitor and check.

Write the words from 1c (box A) on the board. Students look at the words and put them in categories, eg furniture, languages, animals while you monitor and check. Students then do the same for the words in boxes B - E. Students compare their categories with their neighbour. Provide feedback by asking students to tell you their categories.

Students then complete the task in 1d and tell their neighbour which words they have added and why. Provide feedback by students telling you about their neighbour. Students close their books and try to remember the words from 1c. Then ask students to remember any words their neighbour tends to forget. See which pair remembered the most words from 1c.

2 Students read through 2a and complete the speaking activity while you monitor and check. Students then read through 2b and discuss the questions with their neighbour. See if you can get a consensus of opinion about the most popular grammar book which students have.

Students then complete the activity in 2c. Provide feedback by asking students to read the sentences out. Ask them if they found this exercise easy/difficult/interesting/boring and ask them why.

Introduce 2d by telling students that these are different kinds of exercises and this time they have to write the correct form.

Students then complete 2d. Provide feedback by asking students to read the sentences out. Ask them if they found this exercise easy/difficult/interesting/boring or more difficult than the last one and find out why.

Students then complete the task in 2e. Provide feedback in the same way and again ask students if they found the exercise easy/difficult/interesting/boring and why.

Students then complete the task in 2f in the same way and say whether they find this type of exercise easy/difficult/interesting/boring and why.

Students then complete the speaking activity in 2g and report back to you. When students have told you about their neighbours, ask them whether they found this exercise easy/difficult/interesting/boring and why. Complete 2h in the same way and then students work with their neighbour and complete the activity in 2i. Provide feedback by asking students to tell you about themselves.

3 Explain to students that this is Heidi Fetzer's diary which she wrote when she was on a language course in London.

Students then complete the speaking activity in 3a while you monitor and check. Ask students the example question in 3b and then students ask each other about Heidi's week.

Introduce 3c by asking students how they try to improve their language between lessons (eg doing homework, reading newspapers, etc).

In pairs students then complete the activity in 3c.

Introduce the activity in 3d by asking the example question and then students ask and answer questions about Heidi's lesson while you monitor and check.

Students then complete the activity in 3e.

Revise all the structures and vocabulary before moving on to the next lesson.

At home students prepare for the next lesson by looking up the vocabulary in 4a of Unit 45.

Answers

Exercise 2c

1 I telephoned him yesterday.
2 I didn't go to the cinema last night.
3 He works every day.
4 She is talking on the phone at the moment.
5 She is going to see the doctor tomorrow.

Exercise 2d

1 I have worked here since 1967.
2 In 1992 I got a new job.
3 He gets up at 6 o'clock every morning.
4 She didn't watch TV last night.
5 We are speaking English now.

Exercise 2e

1 On Tuesday.
2 On 10 August.
3 At 3 o'clock.
4 On 24 October.
5 In September.

1

UNIT 45

What do you do in your spare time?

1 a Look at the pictures and describe the people to your neighbour. What do you think they like doing in their spare time?

b Read the following sentences. Is the second person agreeing (✓) or disagreeing (x) or uncertain (?). Compare with your neighbour.

1	I think Andy likes sailing.	I don't.	☐
2	I don't think Andy likes cooking.	Neither do I.	☐
3	I think Freda enjoys going shopping.	Hmm, maybe.	☐
4	I think Freda likes knitting.	So do I.	☐
5	I don't think Sandra likes knitting.	Oh, I do.	☐
6	I think Andy enjoys keeping fit.	I don't.	☐
7	I think Sandra enjoys keeping fit.	So do I.	☐
8	I think Sandra enjoys learning English.	Oh, I don't.	☐
9	I don't think Freda enjoys walking.	Neither do I.	☐
10	I don't think Andy enjoys going shopping.	Oh, I do.	☐

c Read these sentences about the people and say whether you agree or disagree using 'I do', 'I don't', 'so do I' or 'neither do I'.

1 I think Sandra likes going to discos. ____________
2 I don't think Freda likes going to discos. ____________
3 I think Andy enjoys going out with friends. ____________
4 I think Freda enjoys reading. ____________
5 I don't think Sandra likes cooking. ____________

d Make up 3 sentences about each person. Your neighbour will tell you his/her sentences. Reply using the phrases above.

2

2 a Look at the hobbies and interests listed below and say whether you like them (✓) or whether you don't like them (x).

☐ skiing	☐ cooking	☐ jogging	☐ knitting
☐ going out with friends	☐ keeping fit	☐ collecting stamps	☐ walking
☐ gliding	☐ playing the guitar	☐ going shopping	☐ going to pop concerts
☐ painting	☐ playing chess	☐ reading	☐ swimming
☐ taking photographs	☐ bird watching	☐ sewing	☐ learning English
☐ walking	☐ gardening	☐ sailing	☐ going to the theatre

b Tell your neighbour.

eg I like jogging. I don't like sewing.

What else do you like doing in your spare time?

c Fill in the following.

1 How many hours are there in a day? ____________
2 How many hours do you work a day? ____________
3 How many hours do you sleep a day? ____________
4 How many hours do you spend travelling every day? ____________
5 How many hours do you spend eating every day? ____________
6 How many hours do you spend watching TV a day? ____________
7 How much spare time do you have left every day? ____________

d You're going to hear Joanne talking about her hobby. Before you hear the cassette, read the statements below. While you're listening, put a (✓) true, or (x) false in the box.

1 ☐ Her hobby is playing the piano.
2 ☐ She bought the piano second-hand.
3 ☐ The piano cost over £400.
4 ☐ She has 3 half-hour lessons a week.
5 ☐ She finds it very relaxing.

Listen again and check, then compare with your neighbour.

e Fill in the following about your favourite hobby.

What is your favourite hobby? ____________
When did you start this hobby? ____________
What equipment do you need? Have you bought all the equipment? ____________
Is it an expensive hobby? ____________
Are you in a club? ____________
How much time a week do you spend on your hobby? ____________
Would you like to spend more time on your hobby? ____________

f Ask your neighbour about his/her hobby.

3

3 a Here are 5 ways of expressing reaction to a statement.

1 I think that's correct.
2 Well, I suppose it could be true.
3 I agree completely with that.
4 I disagree totally with that.
5 I don't think there's much truth in that.

b Now read through these statements. What is your reaction to the statement? Write the number of the phrase in the box.

eg Reading is bad for your eyes. **5**

Going to the theatre is expensive. ☐
Knitting can reduce stress. ☐
Playing the guitar is easy. ☐
Smoking is good for you. ☐
Walking is good for your heart. ☐
Drinking water is good for you. ☐
Skiing is dangerous. ☐
Learning English is fun. ☐
Jogging is bad for your knees. ☐
Eating chocolates is healthy. ☐
Collecting stamps is boring. ☐
Playing the piano is difficult. ☐
Bird watching is interesting. ☐

c Your neighbour will read the statements to you. Tell him/her what you think.

d Now make up 5 more statements. Read them to your neighbour and ask what he/she thinks.

4

4 a Translate the following.

Vocabulary

cooking ____________
shopping ____________
knitting ____________
keeping fit ____________
collecting stamps ____________
sewing ____________
painting ____________
going to pop concerts ____________
taking photographs ____________
bird watching ____________
gardening ____________
gliding ____________

Structures

I think Sandra likes cooking. ____________
So do I. ____________
I don't. ____________
I don't think Sandra likes cooking. ____________
Neither do I. ____________
Oh, I do. ____________
Maybe. ____________
I like jogging. ____________
I don't like sailing. ____________
I think that's correct. ____________
Well, I suppose it could be true. ____________
I agree completely with that. ____________
I disagree totally with that. ____________
I don't think there's much truth in that. ____________
Reading is bad for your eyes. ____________
Do you agree with that? ____________
Walking is good for your heart. ____________

Teaching Notes

Warm-up

Ask students questions from earlier Units eg "Where do you work? How long have you worked there? Where did you work before that?"

Revision

Revise all the structures and vocabulary from the previous Unit by asking students questions eg "Do you think that English is an easy language to learn? Which grammar book do you use? Which dictionary do you use?"

Presentation and Practice

1 Students look at the pictures in 1a and describe the people to their neighbour. Ask students what they think the people like doing and don't like doing in their spare time. Elicit suggestions and write them on the board. Ask other students who agrees and introduce "So do I" and "neither do I".

Students then complete the activity in 1b and compare their work with their neighbour.

Students then read the sentences in 1c and complete the activity. Provide feedback by asking students to read out the sentences and their answers.

Students then write 3 sentences and complete the speaking activity in 1d.

2 Introduce the activity in 2a by telling students what you like doing and what you don't like doing. Students read through the hobbies and interests in 2a and mark whether they like doing them or not.

Students then complete the speaking activity in 2b. Provide feedback by asking students to tell you about their neighbour.

Students then answer the questions in 2c while you monitor and check.

Introduce the listening in 2d and give students a few minutes to read through the statements in 2d. While students are listening they mark whether the sentences are true or false. Play the cassette a second time for students to check and they then compare their work with their neighbour.

Students answer the questions in 2e and then complete the speaking activity in 2f while you monitor and check. Provide feedback by asking students to tell you about their neighbour.

3 Students read through the phrases in 3a and then complete the task in 3b while you monitor and check.

In pairs students then complete the speaking task in 3c. Provide feedback by reading out the statements and asking students what they think. Students then make up 5 more statements and complete the speaking task in 3d while you monitor and check. Provide feedback by asking pairs to demonstrate their activity.

Revise all the structures and vocabulary before moving on to the next lesson.

At home students prepare for the next lesson by looking up the vocabulary in 4a of Unit 46.

Tapescripts

Exercise 2d

My hobby is playing the piano. I only started last year so I'm not very good yet. It was quite expensive at the beginning because I had to buy a piano. I bought it second-hand and it cost about £300 which is quite cheap. I have 2 half-hour lessons a week which cost £10 each and I have to buy music, of course, but I enjoy it very much and I find it very relaxing.

Answers

Exercise 1b

1	x
2	✓
3	?
4	✓
5	x
6	x
7	✓
8	x
9	✓
10	x

Exercise 1c

1	So do I.
2	Neither do I.
3	So do I.
4	So do I.
5	Neither do I.

Exercise 2d

1	T
2	T
3	F
4	F
5	T

1

UNIT 46

Going Swimming

1 a Look at photograph sequence 10 'Going Swimming' on the next pages and match these questions and answers about photograph 1.

1	Where is the girl?	☐	She'll go to the changing rooms and get changed.
2	What is she doing?	☐	She's in a swimming pool foyer.
3	Why is she doing this?	☐	She's buying a ticket.
4	What is she wearing?	☐	Because she wants to go swimming.
5	What will she do next?	☐	She's wearing a T-shirt, leggings, socks and trainers.

b Ask your neighbour these questions about each of the other photographs.

1 Where is the girl?
2 What is she doing?
3 Why is she doing this?
4 What is she wearing?
5 What will she do next?

c Work with your neighbour and answer questions about the photograph sequence and then check with your teacher.

1 What is in her bag in photograph 1?
2 What is she saying to the assistant in photograph 1?
3 What will the assistant give her?
4 What will she do with the ticket?
5 What is she wearing on her left wrist in photograph 2?
6 What has she done with her clothes? Why?
7 Why is she wearing a swimming costume?
8 Do you think the water is warm or cold in photograph 3? Why?
9 What is she holding in her hands in photograph 4?
10 What time of year do you think it is? Why?

d Make up some information about the girl and then tell your neighbour. Here are some questions to help you.

1 What is her name? How old is she?
2 What does she do - schoolgirl? shop assistant?
3 Why is she going swimming on her own?
4 Does she like swimming? How often does she go swimming?
5 What do you think her ambitions are? Why?

e Ask your neighbour these questions.

1 Can you swim?
2 When/where did you learn to swim?
3 Do you like swimming?
4 When/where was the last time you went swimming?
5 Do you think everybody should learn to swim? Why (not)?

2

2 a Ask your neighbour the following questions.

1 Do you play any sports? What? How often?
2 Where do you play?
3 Are you a member of a club?
4 Do you have to pay a registration fee?
5 What do you wear? What do you do with your normal clothes? Why?

b Look at the instructions for a locker in a swimming pool and then explain to your neighbour how the locker works. Use the words: first, then, next, after that, finally.

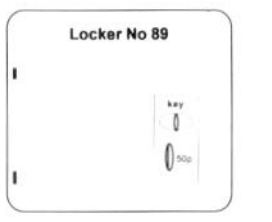

Lockers

Instructions for Use

1 Place your belongings in the locker
2 Insert 50p coin in slot
3 Close door and turn key
4 Fasten the key strap to your wrist
5 Remove your 50p coin when you collect your belongings

c Ask your neighbour these questions.

1 Where else do you find lockers?
2 Have you ever used a locker? Where? Why?

d Look at the information below.

POOL PROGRAMME
6th June - 24th July

	7	8	9	10	11	12 noon	1	2	3	4	5	6	7	8	9 9.45
MON	Early Birds		Schools			Public Swimming							Swimming Club	Over 50's	Lane Swimming
TUE	Early Birds		Schools			Public Swimming						Women's Hour	Swimming Club	Aquarobics 8.00 - 8.40	Lane Swimming
WED	Early Birds		Schools			Public Swimming		Parent & Toddler	Junior Lessons			Aquarobics 6.30 - 7.50	Scouts 7.50 - 8.45	Women 8.45 - 9.30	
THU	Early Birds		Schools			Aqua Babies	Public Swimming					Swimming Club			Lane Swimming
FRI	Early Birds		Schools			Public Swimming						Inflatable Session 6.30 - 8.00			Adult Lessons
SAT		Early Birds	Public Swimming					Fun Session	Canoe Courses			Available for Party Hire			
	7	8	9	10	11	12 noon	1	2	3	4	5	6	7	8	9 9.45

Ask your neighbour these 5 questions then make up some questions of your own.

1 What time does the pool open on Monday?
2 What time does the pool close on Wednesday?
3 When is 'Aqua Babies'?
4 When is the canoe course?
5 Can I book the pool for a party? If so, when?

3

3 a Look at this advertisement for skiing breaks.

Ski Extravaganza Packages

Aviemore Skiing Breaks

Come Skiing

**You know what fun it is.
We've joined forces with the Scottish Norwegian Ski School and the Aviemore Ski School to offer you some super 2, 3 or 5 day skiing packages.**

Package	Adults Low	Adults High	Children Low	Children High
White Lady	£250	£289	£169	£190
Ptarmigan	£73	£79	£47	£53
West Wall	£111	£120	£64	£71

White Lady Package

This holiday includes 5 nights accommodation (Sunday to Thursday) and 5 days skiing (Monday to Friday) in the Cairngorms and is available during January, February, March and April '96 and don't forget this package comes with a "no snow" guarantee.

- welcome drinks reception
- accommodation and breakfast
- 2 table d' hote dinners, to be taken on the days of your choice
- equipment hire (skis, poles and boots)*
- transport to and from ski slopes*
- full area lift pass*
- daily ski tuition*
- best of class races*
- ASSGB international ski school test*
- prize giving ceremony for the ASSGB certificate*

Note Non-skiers who omit items marked * will receive a case of wine on departure. Please indicate on the booking form. (This offer only applies to guests over 18 years of age.)

Ptarmigan Package

- 1 night accommodation and breakfast
- 2 days skiing
- full area lift pass
- either equipment hire (skis, boots and poles) or four hours instruction each day

If you would like both instruction and equipment hire, please add an extra £14.

West Wall Package

- 2 nights accommodation and breakfast
- 3 days skiing
- full area lift pass
- either equipment hire (skis, boots and poles) or four hours instruction each day

If you would like both instruction and equipment hire, please add an extra £21.

Seasons

Low - November, December, January
High - February, March, April

All prices are per person based on two adults sharing a twin/double room. Prices for children under 16 are per child based on sharing a room with 2 adults.

All offers contained herein are subject to availability and all details are correct at the time of printing.

Stakis Hotels Aviemore - Telephone 01479 810661

"No Snow" Guarantee This guarantee is only available on the White Lady Package. If there's not enough snow for skiing on your chosen dates, we will refund £50 per skiing guest. We will also arrange a series of alternative activities which we are sure you will enjoy.

The will include a selection from:
- dry ski slope lessons (every day)
- ice skating
- mountain biking
- ski maintenance clinic
- swimming
- a distillery trip
- curling

4

3 b Now ask your neighbour the following questions.

eg *When is high season? February, March and April.*

1 Which package has 2 nights accommodation and breakfast?
2 Which package has 2 days skiing?
3 Which package has a welcome drinks reception?
4 In the Ptarmigan Package, is equipment hire and four hours instruction each day included in the price?
5 How many days skiing do I get in the West Wall Package?
6 Is an evening meal included in the West Wall Package?
7 Which package has a 'no snow' guarantee?
8 How much is the White Lady Package for one adult in high season?
9 Which package is the cheapest?
10 If I go with my wife and two children on a West Wall Package in January, how much will it cost?

c Ask your neighbour the following questions.

1 Have you ever been skiing?
2 Where and when was the last time?
3 If you have never been skiing would you like to try it? If not, why not?
4 Do you get a lot of snow where you live?
5 What other winter sports can you think of?

4 a Translate the following.

Vocabulary

diagram ________	a selection ________
locker ________	high season ________
to place ________	low season ________
belongings ________	equipment hire ________
to fasten ________	skies ________
strap ________	poles ________
to remove ________	ski slopes ________
coin ________	non-skier ________
skiing package ________	instructions ________
refund ________	

Structures

What is the girl wearing? ________
What is the girl doing? ________
Why do you think she is doing this? ________
What do you think she will do next? ________
What time of year do you think it is? ________
What time of day do you think it is? ________
First you place your belongings in the locker. ________
Then you... ________
Next you... ________
After that you... ________
Finally you... ________

Teaching Notes

Warm-up

Ask students questions from earlier Units eg "How long have you been learning English? Did you learn English at school?"

Revision

Revise all the structures and vocabulary from the previous Unit by asking students questions eg "Do you like gardening? Do you like taking photographs?"

Presentation and Practice

1 Find out which of your students enjoy swimming. Ask them how often they go swimming and then ask them to tell the rest of the class what they do from entering the swimming pool building to leaving it, eg go to the counter, buy a ticket.

Students look at the first photograph and in pairs they complete the matching activity in 1a while you monitor and check. Provide feedback by asking students the questions.

Students then look at the rest of the photographs from this Unit and complete the speaking task in 1b while you monitor and check.

Students then ask and answer the questions in 1c. Provide feedback by eliciting students' answers.

In pairs students make up some information about the girl and then tell their neighbour.

Students then complete the speaking task in 1e. Provide feedback by asking students to tell you about their neighbour.

2 In pairs students complete the speaking activity in 2a while you monitor and check. Provide feedback by asking students to tell you about their neighbour.

Students then complete the speaking activity in 2b. Provide feedback by asking students to explain to you how the locker works.

Students then complete the speaking activity in 2c while you monitor and check. Provide feedback by asking students to tell you about their neighbour.

Students then look at the programme for the swimming pool and answer the questions in 2d. They then make up 5 more questions and ask their neighbour. Provide feedback by asking pairs to demonstrate their activity.

3 In pairs students look at the information in 3a and then ask their neighbour the questions from 3b. Provide feedback by asking students the questions and eliciting the answers. If you have time students can make up more questions and ask their neighbour.

Students then complete the speaking activity in 3c while you monitor and check. Provide feedback by asking students to tell you about their neighbour.

Revise all the structures and vocabulary before moving on to the next lesson.

At home students prepare for the next lesson by looking up the vocabulary in 4a of Unit 47.

Remind students to find a list of 'what's on' for their town/city and bring it to the class next time.

Answers

Exercise 1a

1	Where is the girl?	She's in a swimming pool foyer.
2	What is she doing?	She's buying a ticket.
3	Why is she doing this?	Because she wants to go swimming.
4	What is she wearing?	She's wearing a T-shirt, leggings, socks and trainers.
5	What will she do next?	She'll go to the changing rooms and get changed.

Exercise 2d

1 7am.
2 9.30pm.
3 Thursday 12 noon.
4 Saturday 3pm - 6pm.
5 Saturday 6pm - 9.45pm.

Exercise 3b

1 West Wall Package.
2 Ptarmigan Package.
3 White Lady Package.
4 No - either equipment hire <u>or</u> four hours instruction.
5 3 days.
6 No.
7 White Lady Package.
8 £289.
9 Ptarmigan Package.
10 £350.

1

UNIT 47

What's on?

1 a Look at the list of 'What's On' below and ask your neighbour 5 questions.

eg *What's on at the Central Cinema? Rambo 5 is on from July 21 - 25.*

What's On

Antiques Fair	The Royal Hotel	July 21-23	
Painting Exhibition	Wellington Arts Centre	July 21-25	
Classical Music	High School (Main Hall)	July 22	7pm
Charity Fund Raising Parachute Jump	Catterick Airfield	July 23	
Rambo 5	Central Cinema	July 21-25	
Marathon Run	Start - Wellfield Sports Centre	July 22	11am
Treasure Hunt	Start - The Golden Lion Hotel	July 22	5.30pm
"The Future of the Planet"	High School, Lecture Theatre	July 24	7pm
Hamlet	Beaumont Theatre	July 22-24	7.30pm

b Answer the following questions.

1 Where do you find information about what's on in your local area?

2 Is there a cinema in your town/city? What's on at the moment?

3 Is there a theatre in your town/city? What's on at the moment?

4 Is there a sports centre in your town/city? What's on at the moment?

5 Is there an exhibition centre in your town/city? What's on at the moment?

6 Is there an arts centre in your town/city? What's on at the moment?

7 Where else do events take place?

c Look at your local 'What's On' page. Work with your neighbour and answer the following questions.

eg *Are there any sporting events on this week? Yes there's a football match on Saturday.*

1 Are there any sporting events? When and Where?
2 Are there any charity fund raising events? When and Where?
3 Are there any musical events? When and Where?
4 Are there any events for nature lovers? When and Where?
5 Are there any public lectures? What about? When and Where?
6 Are there any outdoor events? When and Where?
7 Are there any crafts events? When and Where?

d Discuss with your neighbour which events you would like to go to and why.

eg *I would like to go to the Antiques Fair because I'm very interested in antiques. It's on at the Royal Hotel from July 21 - 23. Would you like to come too?*

2

2 a Read the following questions and answer them as quickly as possible using the TV guide opposite.

eg *What's on Grampian at 9.25am? He-Man.*

1 What is on BBC 2 at 4 o'clock? ______

2 How many films are on TV that day? ______

3 Which channel is the Open University on? ______

4 How many news broadcasts are there on BBC 1? ______

5 What time is 'The Bill' on Grampian? ______

6 What is on Channel 4 at 6.30pm? ______

7 What time is the film 'Beyond the Stars' on? ______

8 Which channel closes at 3.15am? ______

9 Which channel is 'True Stories' on? ______

10 How many channels are showing 'Golf - The Open'? ______

Check with your neighbour.

b Now make up 5 more questions and ask your neighbour.

eg *When is 'The Big Breakfast' on? It's on Channel 4 at 7am.*

c Now look more closely at the TV page and answer the following questions. Work with your neighbour.

1 If you were interested in sport, which programmes would you watch?
2 If you were interested in nature, which programmes would you watch?
3 If you were interested in gardening, which programmes would you watch?
4 If you were interested in politics, which programmes would you watch?
5 If you were interested in science fiction, which programmes would you watch?

d Work with 3 neighbours. You are flatmates and only have one TV. Find 3 programmes between 7pm and midnight which you would like to see.

e Now discuss what you would like to watch and decide what all 3 of you will watch.

eg *I'd like to watch 'The Beechgrove Garden' at 8pm. Oh, that's on at the same time as 'The Mind Field'. I wanted to see that! But you watched it last week. Well okay, we'll watch 'The Beechgrove Garden' if I can watch 'Wildlife Showcase' at 8.30pm. Okay.*

f Ask your neighbour these questions.

1 How many hours a day do you spend watching TV?
2 What are the advantages of having a TV?
3 What are the disadvantages of having a TV?
4 What do you watch regularly? Why?
5 When was the last time you watched TV? What did you watch?

3

3 a Look at the 'Calendar of Events, 1995' for Kielder Water, then read the notes below. Make any changes necessary.

Notes

Kielder Board Sailing Marathon on May 15.

Northumberland National Park number is 603942.

Bellingham Show contact is Mrs White on 0191 2324297.

National Bog Day cancelled - no interest.

June 18 should be 'Folk Music' at Falstone.

Hawkhirst Activity Week from August 6 to 13.

English National Fishing Competition August 28 and 29. Contact Ramsay White 01661 823946.

b You are going to hear 15 questions about the Calendar of Events for Kielder Water. Listen to the cassette and write down the answers. Do not write down the questions.

1 ______
2 ______
3 ______
4 ______
5 ______
6 ______
7 ______
8 ______
9 ______
10 ______
11 ______
12 ______
13 ______
14 ______
15 ______

c Listen again and check that you have answered the questions correctly and then compare your answers with your neighbour.

4

4 a Translate the following.

Vocabulary

Antiques Fair ______
painting exhibition ______
classical music ______
parachute jump ______
marathon run ______
treasure hunt ______
lecture theatre ______
exhibition centre ______
charity ______
fund raising ______
nature lovers ______
public lectures ______
outdoor events ______
crafts events ______
channel ______
broadcasts ______
event ______
contact ______
calendar of events ______
festival ______
show ______
nature ______
science fiction ______

Structures

What's on? ______
What's on at the Central Cinema? ______
Are there any sporting events on this week? ______
Yes, there's a football match on Saturday. ______
What's on Channel 4 at 9.25am? ______
He-Man's on Grampian at 9.25am. ______
When is 'The Big Breakfast' on? ______
It's on Channel 4 at 7am. ______
If you were interested in sport, which programmes would you watch? ______
If I was interested in sport, I would watch the golf. ______
I'd like to watch 'The Beechgrove Garden' at 8pm. ______
That's at the same time as 'The Mind Field'. ______
I wanted to see that. ______
But you watched it last week. ______
Well okay we'll watch... ______
We'll watch 'The Beechgrove Garden' if I can watch the 'Wildlife Showcase'. ______
Is there a cinema in your town? ______
What's on at the moment? ______
I would like to go to the Antiques Fair at the Royal Hotel. ______
Would you like to come too? ______
What about you? ______

Teaching Notes

Warm-up

Ask students questions from earlier Units eg "Tell your neighbour about your normal daily routine."

Revision

Revise all the structures and vocabulary from the previous Unit by asking students questions eg "When was the last time you went swimming? Where else would you find lockers?"

Presentation and Practice

1 In pairs students ask their neighbour questions about the information in 1a. Provide feedback by students asking the rest of the class their questions. Students work with their neighbour and answer the questions in 1b while you monitor and check. Provide feedback by students telling you what's on in their local town.

Students look at the 'what's on' page they have brought and answer the questions from 1c while you monitor and check.

In pairs they then complete the speaking activity in 1d. Provide feedback by asking students to tell you what they are planning to visit and when and where it is.

2 In pairs students ask their neighbour what he/she watched on TV last night and then tell you about their neighbour. Ask students how they know what is on TV and how they decide what to watch. Is there any programme that the whole of the class watch?

Students then look at the TV guide and answer the questions in 2a as quickly as possible. When they are finished they compare their answers with their neighbour. Students make up 5 more questions like the example and ask their neighbour. Students work with their neighbour and answer the questions in 2c by looking at the guide in more detail.

Set up the roleplay in 2d by putting students into groups of 4, setting the scene and explaining the task. Students then find three programmes which they would like to watch and mark them. When they have all chosen what they would like to watch they complete the roleplay in 2e while you monitor and check.

Students then ask their neighbours the questions in 2f.

3 Students read through the notes and then complete the task in 3a. Provide feedback by asking students to tell you what is on the 'Calendar of Events'.

Introduce the listening activity by explaining that students are going to hear 15 questions about the Calendar of Events. They are to listen to the questions, find the answer in the Calendar of Events and write down the answer to the questions in their books. (They are not to write down the questions). Play each question separately allowing students time to find and write down the answer. Play the cassette again so that students can check they have answered the question correctly and then students compare their work with their neighbour. If you have time get students to look at the answers and try and remember the questions.

Revise all the structures and vocabulary before moving on to the next lesson.

At home students prepare for the next lesson by looking up the vocabulary in 4a of Unit 48.

Tapescripts

Exercise 3b

1 What is Jack Coates telephone number?
2 When is the Jim Clark Rally?
3 What's happening on 6 - 13 August?
4 Whose telephone number is 01434 250217?
5 Whose telephone number is 603942?
6 Why would I ring Ramsay White?
7 What's happening on 26 August?
8 How many family fun days are there at Leaplish Waterside Park?
9 When is Kielder Festival and Fell Race?
10 Who do I contact for more information on Folk music at Falstone?
11 When is the Forest Life Activity weekend?
12 What number would I ring for Northumbrian Water?
13 Which event was cancelled?
14 If I am interested in birds, which event should I visit?
15 When is Bellingham Show?

Answers

Exercise 2a

1 Golf - The Open
2 5
3 BBC 2
4 7
5 8pm
6 Tour de France
7 11.40pm
8 Channel 4
9 Channel 4
10 2 (BBC1 and BBC2)

Exercise 3b

1 01434 681677
2 July 1st
3 Hawkhirst Activity Week
4 Hawkhirst Adventure Camp
5 Northumberland National Park
6 About the English National Fishing Competition
7 Bellingham Show
8 3
9 August 5th
10 Northumberland National Park
11 June 9th - 11th
12 01434 240398
13 National Bog Day
14 Birds in the Forest
15 August 26th

1

UNIT 48

Where did you go on holiday last year?

1 a Look at the pie chart below which shows you where British people went on holiday in 1995. Using the phrases in the box, complete the sentences below (there may be more than one possibility).

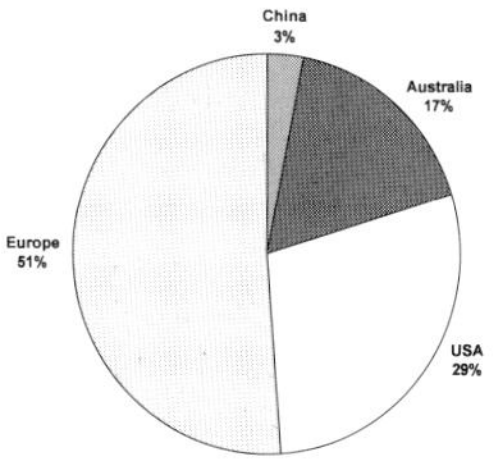

nearly everybody
some people
not many
hardly anybody
just under 30%
just over 15%
more than half
less than half
nobody

1 ______________________ went to China in 1995.
2 Most people went on holiday to ______________________ in 1995.
3 ______________________ went to Australia in 1995.
4 ______________________ went to the USA in 1995.
5 ______________________ went to Europe in 1995.

b Work in groups of 10. Ask each of the other 9 people where they went on holiday last year. Write the name of the countries in column A and the number of people who went there in column B.

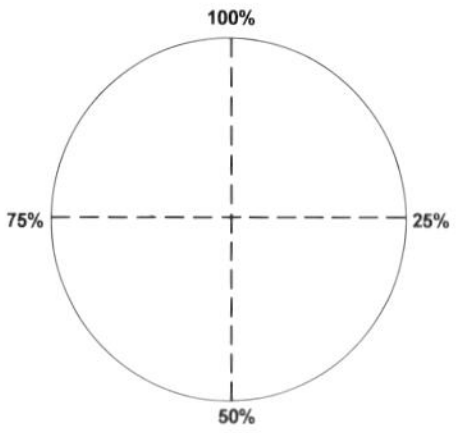

(A) Countries	(B) No of People	%

c Now work out the percentage of your group who visited each country. You can do this by adding a zero to the number in column B. Show this in the pie chart information. When you have finished, make up 5 sentences using the phrases from exercise 1a.

2

2 a You are on holiday in England. You have just arrived in Nottingham with a group of 12 people. The coach driver is about to give you some useful information. Look at the map below and then listen to the cassette. You will hear it twice and may make notes while you listen.

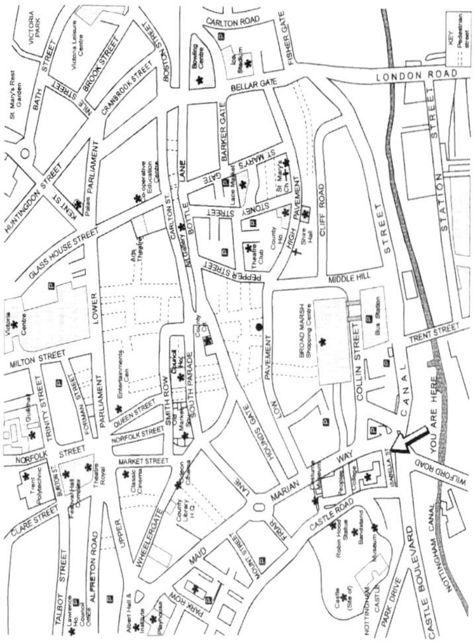

3

2 b Compare your notes with your neighbour.

eg I thought he said the castle was open between 9am and 2pm. No, I'm sure he said between 9am and 1pm.

c Now ask your neighbour the following questions.

1 How much is it to visit the castle?
2 How do you get from the castle to the Victoria Centre?
3 Can I visit the castle at 2pm? Why (not)?
4 Where is the Theatre Royal?
5 How many car parks are there?
6 How do you get from the Victoria Leisure Centre to the Victoria Centre?
7 Can I go to the exhibition in the art gallery if I am 12 years old?
8 What time does the bowling centre open?
9 What is the number of the bus?
10 How do you get from Nottingham Castle to the ice stadium?
11 What is 'the Bell'?
12 What can you find in the Old Market Square?
13 Why would you go to the Ice Stadium?
14 Can I visit St Mary's Church this afternoon?
15 In how many languages do they have information at the Tourist Information Centre?

d Ask your neighbour 5 more questions using the map.

3 a Look at the advert below and answer the questions.

RHINE VALLEY

Dear Reader
Enjoy the delights of the Rhine Valley on this superb value for money tour.

The price includes:
- Return overnight coach travel from Newcastle.
- Return ferry crossings.
- 4 nights accommodation in rooms with hand wash basin at selected family run hotels.
- Breakfast and evening meal each day.
- Services of a tour guide.

Rooms with private bathroom available for a supplement. Single room extra.
Optional excursions to Rudesheim and Rhine Gorge, Bernkastel, Cochem and Koblenz also available.

Deposit £35.00 per person plus insurance of £14.90 per person made payable to Travelscope Promotions.

To request a full colour brochure, complete the coupon below or telephone Reader Holidays

0191 201 6000

Alternatively, call at the Reader Holiday Desk, Front Reception, Thomson House, Groat Market, Newcastle Upon Tyne NE1 1ED

Payment by cheque, credit card or postal order

5 days FROM £99.00 31st July or 23rd October 1996

RHINE VALLEY - Please send me the brochure on the Rhine Valley tour
Mr/Mrs/Ms/Miss Initials Surname
Address
Post Code Tel No

1 What is this an advert for? ______________________
2 Where would you see an advert like this? ______________________
3 Is a mid-day meal included? ______________________
4 If I want a bathroom, do I have to pay more? ______________________
5 Can I pay for the holiday in cash? ______________________
6 Who is organising the holiday? ______________________
7 What costs £14.90? ______________________
8 What number do I call for more information? ______________________
9 What is the difference between 'Mr', 'Mrs', 'Ms' and 'Miss'? ______________________

10 Would you go on a holiday like this? Why (not)? ______________________

4

3 b Now ask your neighbour five more questions about the advert.

c Ask your neighbour the following questions.

1 Where was the best place you have ever been on holiday? Why?
2 Where was the worst place you have ever been on holiday? Why?
3 What is important to you on holiday (weather, food, culture, etc)?
4 Why do you go on holiday?
5 If you could go anywhere on holiday, where would you go? Why?

4 a Translate the following.

Vocabulary

pie chart ______	artist ______
percentage ______	Rhine Valley ______
caves ______	from £99.00 ______
shopping centre ______	return overnight coach ______
ice stadium ______	ferry crossings ______
skates ______	hand wash basin ______
bowling centre ______	family run hotel ______
stained glass window ______	supplement ______
spire ______	optional ______
controversial ______	plus ______

Structures

Most people went to... in 1995. ______________________
Nearly everybody went to... in 1995. ______________________
More than half went to... in 1995. ______________________
Less than half went to... in 1995. ______________________
Some people went to... in 1995. ______________________
Not many went to... in 1995. ______________________
Hardly anybody went to... in 1995. ______________________
Nobody went to... in 1995. ______________________
30% of people went to... last year. ______________________
I thought he said the castle was open between 9am and 2pm. ______________________
I'm sure he said between 9am and 1pm. ______________________
Where was the best place you have ever been on holiday? ______________________
The best place I have ever been on holiday was to... ______________________

Teaching Notes

Warm-up

Ask students questions from earlier Units eg "What do you normally do at the weekend? When was the last time you spoke English on the telephone?"

Revision

Revise all the structures and vocabulary from the previous Unit by asking students questions eg "What did you watch on TV last night? What's on at your local cinema?"

Presentation and Practice

1 Introduce the activity in 1a by asking students where they went on holiday last year. Write the places on the board and how many people went there. Then ask students questions eg "How many people went on holiday to France?" Introduce the phrases from 1a eg "Most people went to France. Hardly anybody went to Italy."

Students then look at the pie chart in 1a and complete the sentences using the phrases in the box. Provide feedback by students reading the completed sentences out.

In 1b students work in groups of 10 and complete the speaking activity. They then work out the percentage of people who went to each country and draw the divisions on the pie chart.

In 1c students make up 5 sentences using phrases from 1a.

2 Introduce the listening activity by setting the scene in 2a. Students listen to the cassette twice and make notes while they are listening. They then compare their notes with their neighbour in 2b while you monitor and check.

Students then complete the speaking activity in 2c. Provide feedback by one student eliciting the answers from other students.

Students make up 5 more questions and complete the speaking activity in 2d while you monitor and check.

3 Introduce this activity by finding out which students have visited Germany, where they went and what they did.

Students then look at the information in 3a and answer the questions. Provide feedback by eliciting the answers to the questions.

Students then complete the speaking activity in 3b while you monitor and check. Provide feedback by students asking the rest of the class their questions.

In pairs students then complete the speaking activity in 3c while you monitor and check. Provide feedback by asking students to tell you about their neighbour.

Revise all the structures and vocabulary before moving on to the next lesson.

At home students prepare for the next lesson by looking up the vocabulary in 4a of Unit 49.

Tapescripts

Exercise 2a

We are in Isabella Street, which as you can see from your maps is near Nottingham Castle and just off Castle Boulevard.

The time now is 9.30am. The coach will leave again at 3.30pm from here. Please remember that it is a yellow coach with the number EXG 235.

Nottingham Castle is open to visitors between 9am and 1pm. Entrance is free. You may also visit the caves underneath the castle between 10am and 12 noon. This costs £3.

There are two large shopping centres in Nottingham, the Broadmarsh Centre which is just behind the bus station, and the Victoria Centre which is on Milton Street.

There are several old pubs in the Old Market Square where you can buy a sandwich and something to drink. One of the oldest is 'The Bell', dating back to 1722.

You will also find restaurants and cafés in this area and I can recommend the Café Royale which overlooks the Theatre Royal in Upper Parliament Street.

The Ice Stadium in Bellar Gate is open all day. Entrance is £3.50 which includes hire of skates. Just opposite this is a bowling centre, which opens at 1pm.

St Mary's Church on High Pavement is open from 12pm to 2.30pm and has one of the largest stained glass windows in England. You can go up the spire for £2.00, and there's a magnificent view from the top.

There is an Art Gallery on Carlton Street which is open all day and this week has an exhibition by the controversial artist, Daniel Forest. Entrance is £4.00 and no under 14 year olds are allowed.

If you need any more information, you can visit the Tourist Information Centre in the Victoria Centre, where they have information in over 30 languages.

I hope you have a nice day and remember we meet again here at 3.30pm.

Answers

Exercise 1a

1 Hardly anybody went to China in 1995.
2 Most people went on holiday to Spain in 1995.
3 Just under 5% went to Australia in 1995.
4 Not many people went to the USA in 1995.
5 Over 20% went to Greece in 1995.

Exercise 3a

1 A holiday in the Rhine Valley.
2 In a newspaper.
3 No.
4 Yes.
5 No.
6 Travelscope Promotions.
7 Insurance.
8 0191 201 6000.
9 -
10 -

1

UNIT 49

What's the best book you've ever read?

1 a **Read the following advert.**

Be a Writer

Earn while you learn and pay your fees.

The Write School, founded in 1952, will show you how to write magazine articles, short stories, novels and TV scripts, which you can sell.

Top professional writers give you expert advice on writing and selling your articles and stories to publishers who are always on the look out for new writers.

Learn At Home

All you need is to spend a few hours each week studying and you can earn an extra income from home.

If you have not recovered the cost of the course by the time you finish, your fees will be refunded.

Please write for our free book: *Learning to Write Successfully*
No stamp needed.
Call: *Freephone 0800 4287912*

The Write School
Freepost LR1
London W4

b **Ask your neighbour the question below.**

1 What is this an advertisement for?
2 What is the name of the advertiser?
3 How old is the school?
4 Who can give you advice on writing?
5 What else can they give you advice on?
6 Where is the school located?
7 Do I have to go there if I want to study?
8 Is it possible to get the course fees back? Why (not)?
9 If I phone, will I have to pay for the call?
10 What is the phone number?

c **What is the best book you have ever read? Fill in the information you can remember about it.**

Title ____________________
Can you remember who it was by? ____________________
How many main characters were there? ____________________
Name(s)? ____________________
Where was it set (your country, another country)? ____________________
When was it set (past, present, future)? ____________________
What was the story about? ____________________

d **Listen to your neighbour and make notes. When he/she is finished, tell him/her about his/her favourite book based on your notes.**

eg *You said the best book you have ever read was called ...*

Here are some phrases to help you.

You said it was by ...
You said there were 3 main characters, ...
Then you said it was set in ...
I think you said it was set in the past. Is that right?
You said the young girl left home when she was 12 and went to live in a city.

2

2 a **The following paragraphs are from 2 articles which appeared in the newspaper. Read the paragraphs and see if you can find the titles for the stories. Then decide whether the paragraphs belong to Story A or Story B.**

Story A	*a b*
Story B	*c*

a It's ten years today since the biggest rock concert ever took place.

b And what help did Liveaid give to Africa in facts and figures? Over £40 million was raised to help the situation.

c The boy was taken to Bristol Childrens' Hospital and is now said to be comfortable.

d When he was breathing again I continued talking to her until the ambulance arrived.

e A short report by Bob Geldof will also show the situation in Ethiopia as it is today 10 years after the famine.

f **Toddler 'serious' in hospital after choking on a grape**

g A two year old boy was seriously ill in hospital yesterday after choking on a grape.

h More than 70,000 people were at Wembley Stadium on July 13, 1985 and the concert was watched by 1.4 billion people in over 170 countries.

i So, if you missed it first time around, make sure you don't miss it tonight.

j Phil Donalds, the telephone operator gave Janice first aid instructions over the phone.

k Between 8.30pm and 9.30pm television presenters will be interviewing musicians, fans and backstage staff who were all at the original concert.

l His mother, Janice, 32 of Bristol rang 999 when he stopped breathing yesterday afternoon.

m "I told her to try and remove the grape by hitting her son on the back" said Mr Donalds.

n 'Liveaid' as the concert was know, was broadcast in 1985 by the BBC and tonight you have a second chance to see it.
The concert will be shown in two parts, from 6pm to 8.30pm and from 9.30pm to 1.35am.

o **The Day the World Rocked**

b **When you have all the parts to the story, work with your neighbour and put the paragraphs in the order you think is correct.**

eg *I think g is the first paragraph of Story B. Do you agree?*

Story A	*o*
Story B	*f*

c **Compare your work with other groups.**

d **Ask your neighbour these questions.**

When was the last time you read a newspaper?
Can you remember what any of the articles were about?

3

3 a **You have travelled to Frankfurt International Book Fair with a group of 15 people. Your tour guide gives you the following map of Frankfurt Exhibition Centre. Look at the information and ask your neighbour 5 questions.**

eg *What is in Hall 1.1?*

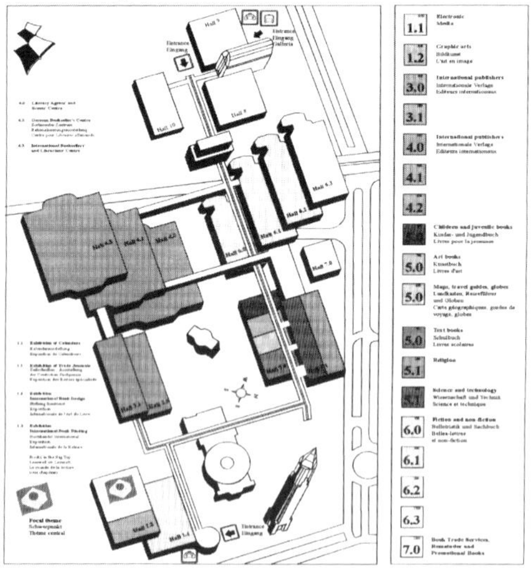

b **Now listen to the cassette and make notes. You will hear it twice.**

c **Ask your neighbour the following questions.**

1 How much does it cost to get into the exhibition?
2 What time will your group leave the fair?
3 What time is the presentation on stand G17 in Hall 5.0?
4 How many people will visit the book fair?
5 Where are the toilets?

d **Now ask your neighbour 5 more questions about the Frankfurt International Book Fair.**

4

4 a **Translate the following.**

Vocabulary

to make money ______	backstage staff ______
to earn ______	billion ______
founded ______	facts and figures ______
novels ______	to raise money ______
TV scripts ______	to stop breathing ______
professional writer ______	toddler ______
expert advice ______	serious ______
publishers ______	to choke ______
on the lookout for ______	grape ______
extra income ______	telephone operator ______
to recover the cost ______	first aid instructions ______
to refund ______	seriously ill ______
freephone ______	exhibitors ______
freepost ______	exhibition ______
to take place ______	multimedia ______
to broadcast ______	discuss ______
BBC ______	pros and cons ______
TV presenter ______	photocopying ______
musicians ______	workshop ______
fans ______	

Structures

What was the best book you have ever read? ______
Can you remember who it was by? ______
You said the best book you have ever read was called ... ______
You said it was by ... ______
You said there were 3 main characters called ... ______
Then you said it was set in ... ______
I think you said it was set in the present. ______
Is that right? ______
You said a young girl left home when she was 12 and ... ______

Teaching Notes

Warm-up

Ask students questions from earlier Units eg "What time did you get up yesterday? What time did you go to bed last night? What happens to your wastepaper after you have thrown it away?"

Revision

Revise all the structures and vocabulary from the previous Unit by asking students questions eg "Where did you go on holiday last year? Would you like to visit the Rhine Valley?"

Presentation and Practice

1 Introduce the activity by asking students who writes in their free time and what they write eg letters, poetry, diary. See how many of the class never write in their free-time.

Students read the advert in 1a and then complete the speaking activity in 1b while you monitor and check.

Introduce 1c by telling students about the best book that you have ever read based on the headings in 1c.

Students then complete the activity in 1c while you monitor and help.

Introduce the activity in 1d by asking students what they can remember about the best book they have ever read, helping them where necessary.

In pairs students then complete the speaking activity in 1d while you monitor and check. Provide feedback by asking students to tell you about their neighbour's favourite book.

2 Students read the paragraphs in 2a and work with their neighbour finding the titles for the two stories. Ask pairs what they think the titles are and ask them to explain why they think it is the title. Students work with their neighbour and decide if the paragraphs belong to Story A or Story B while you monitor and check. Pairs then compare their work with other students. Provide feedback by asking students to tell you the order of the paragraphs.

Students then complete the speaking activity in 2d.

3 Find out who has been to an international fair or exhibition. Ask them where and what it was about. Tell students that they are at the International Book Fair held every year in Frankfurt. Students then look at the plan of the Frankfurt Exhibition Centre and ask each other questions to familiarise themselves with the information eg "What is in Hall 1.1?" Students then listen to the cassette twice and make notes on the plan.

In pairs they ask each other the questions from 3c. Students then make up 5 more questions and ask their neighbour while you monitor and check.

Revise all the structures and vocabulary before moving on to the next lesson.

At home students prepare for the next lesson by revising all the vocabulary and structures from Units 41 - 49.

Tapescripts

Exercise 3b

We are standing in front of the main entrance. The time now is 11am and we will meet again back here at 4pm.

For your information there are toilets at the entrance to all Halls except Hall 6.3 where the toilets are situated next to the emergency exit. There are cafés in Halls 1.2, 3.0, 4.1, 6.1, and 5.0 where you can get a sandwich and a cup of coffee. If you would like something more, there is a restaurant at the entrance to Hall 4.0.

There are over 1,000 exhibitors at this year's exhibition from over 80 countries and it is expected that over 100,000 people will visit it between 4 and 8 October. The entry fee is 25 German Marks which includes a catalogue listing all the exhibitors. As we only have five hours, I suggest you look at this and decide which Halls or exhibitors you would like to see.

Hall 1.1 includes an exhibition on 'Books in multimedia'. You will find this on stands C30 - C45. There is also a display of talking books on stand A15 at 2pm. At 2.30pm in Hall 4.2, there is a discussion on 'The pro's and con's of photocopying'.

In Hall 5.0, stand G17, there is a presentation for teachers called 'How to get the most from your text book'. This starts at 3.30pm and goes on until 4.30pm.

A workshop called 'How to write your first book' is taking place in Seminar Room 2 in Hall 3 at 1pm. Finally, the focal theme is on Brazil and there are lots of interesting stands to visit in Hall 1.2.

Answers

Exercise 2a

Story A a b e h i k n o
Story B c d f g j l m

Exercise 2b

Story A o a n k h i e b
Story B f g l j m d c

1

UNIT 50

Revision

1 a **Ask your neighbour these questions about his/her school days.**

1 Which was your favourite subject at school? Why?
2 Which was your least favourite subject? Why?
3 Who was the best teacher you've ever had? Why?
4 Who was the worst teacher you've ever had? Why?
5 Do you think that school prepares you for working life? Why (not)?

b **Look at these statements and say what you think about them.**

1 Exams should not be marked by teachers.
2 Exams are unfair.
3 Teachers should be paid according to pupils results.

c **Your neighbour is applying for a job with you. Ask him/her for details to fill in the form below.**

Surname ____________ **First Name** ____________
Address ____________ **Date of Birth** ____________
____________ **Telephone Number** ____________

Education
Name/Address of Institute *From* *To* *Qualifications*

Work Experience
Name/Address of Employer *From* *To* *Position*

Skills and Languages ____________

Hobbies and Interests ____________

2

2 a **Tell your neighbour about any courses you have been on since you left school. He/she wants to know where they were, when they were, what they were about, and why you did them.**

b **Ask your neighbour these questions.**

1 Have you ever done a work placement? Where? When?
2 Was it useful? Why (not)?
3 Would you like to work in another country? Why (not)?

3 a **Read these questions and then tell your neighbour about yourself.**

1 Why are you learning English?
2 Which skills do you need the most?
3 How do you practise English between lessons?
4 Do you think you are improving? Why (not)?
5 What do you find most difficult about learning English?

4 a **Read the sentences and underline the correct form.**

1 I wrote/have written the letter last night.
2 He worked/has worked here for 20 years.
3 She went/has gone to America last year.
4 He started/has started University in 1995.
5 I visited/have visited him last week.

b **Read these sentences and put in the correct form.**

1 He (work) ____________ here since 1992.
2 He (live) ____________ in this town for 30 years.
3 She (go) ____________ home early yesterday.
4 She (own) ____________ that car since she was 18.
5 I (live) ____________ here all my life.

c **Read these sentences and say the negative form and the question form to your neighbour.**

1 He is washing his hair.
2 She goes to work at 8 o'clock.
3 I am wearing a jumper.
4 They watched TV last night.
5 She has lived here for 10 years.

3

4 d **Make up 5 sentences using the following words.**

1 yesterday ____________
2 already ____________
3 tomorrow ____________
4 since November ____________
5 now ____________

e **Tell your neighbour 3 things you didn't do yesterday.**

f **Add 3 more words to each of the lists and then compare with your neighbour. Explain why you chose these words.**

1 doctor ______ ______ ______
2 furniture department ______ ______ ______
3 CV ______ ______ ______
4 dog ______ ______ ______
5 Spring Bank Holiday ______ ______ ______

5 a **Can you name 10 spare time activities? When you have 10, ask your neighbour which one(s) he/she likes doing and say whether you agree or not.**

eg *Do you like sailing? Yes, I do. So do I. Do you like sewing? No, I don't. Oh, I do.*

b **Now look at your neighbour's list and say if you think the activities are interesting, boring, expensive, etc.**

eg *I think that bird watching is very interesting. What do you think? Oh, I agree.*

6 a **Ask your neighbour these questions and find out where and when they learnt this skill.**

1 Can you swim?
2 Can you type?
3 Can you speak Italian?
4 Can you cook?
5 Can you drive?

4

7 a **Ask your neighbour these questions.**

1 How much TV do you watch a day?
2 Is the TV in your house switched on every day?
3 How do you decide what to watch on TV?
4 Do you think that there is a lot of rubbish on TV?
5 Do you think that watching TV is relaxing?

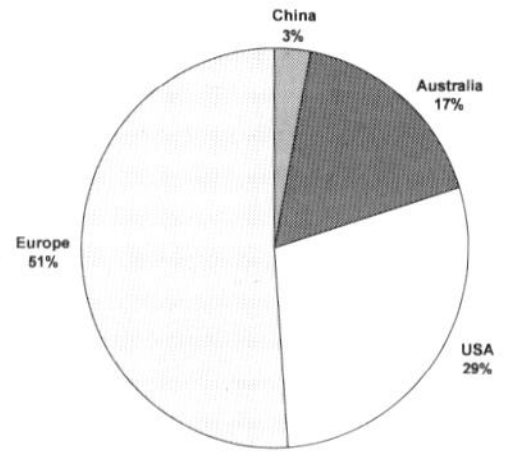

8 a **Make up 5 questions about the information in the pie chart.**

eg *Where did most people go in 1995?*

1 ____________
2 ____________
3 ____________
4 ____________
5 ____________

9 a **Ask your neighbour these questions.**

1 Have you ever been to an exhibition?
2 Where and when was it?
3 Who did you go with?
4 Why did you go?
5 Was it interesting?

10 a **You are going to talk about yourself now. Try and keep going for at least 5 minutes. Here are some guidelines.**

- your school days
- evening courses you've taken
- why you are learning English
- how you practise your English
- skills which you have
- your opinion about TV

Teaching Notes

Warm-up

Ask students questions from earlier Units eg "Have you ever been in a helicopter? Did you enjoy it? Have you ever sailed on a ferry? Where were you going?"

Revision

Revise all the structures and vocabulary from the previous Unit by asking students questions eg "When was the last time you wrote anything in your spare time? Have you ever been to an international exhibition? In what capacity were you there?"

Presentation and Practice

1 In pairs students complete the speaking activity in 1a while you monitor and check. Students then say what they think about the statements in 1b and explain why they think that. In 1c students ask their neighbour questions and fill in the CV about their neighbour while you monitor and check.

2 Students complete the speaking activity in 2a and then continue with the speaking activity in 2b. Provide feedback by asking students to tell you about their neighbour.

3 Students complete the speaking activity in 3a while you monitor and check.

4 Students read the sentences in 4a and underline the correct form. Provide feedback by asking students to read the correct sentence out.

Students complete the task in 4b. Provide feedback by one student reading the completed sentences out.

Students then complete the task in 4c while you monitor and check.

In 4d students make up 5 sentences using the words given. Provide feedback by students reading out their sentences.

They then complete the speaking activity in 4e while you monitor and check. Provide feedback by students telling you 3 things they didn't do yesterday. Students then add 3 more words to the lists and explain to their neighbour why they chose those words. Provide feedback by asking students to tell you about their neighbour.

5 Students list 10 spare-time activities and then complete the speaking activity in 5a while you monitor and check. Provide feedback by asking pairs to demonstrate their activity. Students then complete the speaking activity in 5b. Provide feedback by asking students to tell you about their neighbour.

6 Students complete the speaking activity in 6a while you monitor and check. Provide feedback by asking students to tell you about their neighbour.

7 Students complete the speaking activity in 7a while you monitor and check. Provide feedback by asking students to tell you about their neighbour.

8 Students make up 5 questions based on the pie chart and then ask their neighbour their questions. Provide feedback by students asking the rest of the class their questions.

9 Students then complete the speaking activity in 9a while you monitor and check. Provide feedback by asking students to tell you about their neighbour.

10 Students are given 5 minutes each to practise talking about themselves. In pairs they tell their neighbour about themselves based on the points listed. Tell students when 5 minutes are up so that every student gets a chance to practise talking about themselves. Throughout this activity monitor and encourage students.

At home students prepare for the next lesson by looking up the vocabulary in 4a of Unit 51 and make up 10 questions about their neighbour's family eg "How many brothers and sisters have you got? What are their names? Have you got any children?" etc.

Remind students to bring a newspaper with them next time.

Answers

Exercise 4a

1 I wrote the letter last night.
2 He has worked here for 20 years.
3 She went to America last year.
4 He started University in 1995.
5 I visited him last week.

Exercise 4b

1 He has worked here since 1992.
2 He has lived in this town for 30 years.
3 She went home early yesterday.
4 She has owned that car since she was 18.
5 I have lived here all my life.

1

UNIT 51

Which newspaper do you read and why?

1 a **Here are some comments. Read them and guess who is speaking. Compare with your neighbour.**

1 Elsie Carr, 83, grandmother.
2 Sandra McEwan, 21, student.
3 Ron Barker, 55, banker.
4 George Lawrence, 47, former manager.
5 Mary Adams, 46, teacher.

A "I always buy the Times from the newsagent's in the station. I read it on the train on my way to work. I look at the headlines first to see if there's anything interesting. I'm very interested in politics so I look for anything about that. I played football when I was younger so I usually go to the sports page next and look at the results from last night's games."

B "My daughter lives and works in Rwanda, so I turn to the 'world news' page first. I often buy different newspapers because they report on the situation there from different points of view. She's been out there for 5 years and she's a teacher, like me. I telephone her about once a month and I like to know about the situation there when I speak to her."

C "I was born in this town and I've always lived here. I have 4 children and 9 grandchildren who all live here too. The only newspaper I read is the local paper, the Courier. I'm not interested in what's going on in other places. The paper is delivered every Friday and the first thing I do is look for people I know in the photographs. I read these articles and then go to the births, deaths and marriages column to see if I know anybody there. If there has been something special, like a play in my grandchildren's school, I look for something about that, and then I read the rest of the newspaper."

D "I'm unemployed and I'm looking for a job. The best place to look is in the newspapers. I can't afford to buy newspapers every day so I go to the library in the mornings and look through 2 or 3 different newspapers. I turn to the 'situations vacant' page first and look through the advertisements. If I see a job which I can do I go home and write a letter and a CV. If I can't find anything I read the rest of the newspapers."

E "I always read the Express because I have a friend who is a journalist there. I don't read the headlines or look at the photographs. I look for the name of my friend in the "by" line and if I find her name I read the article. If I don't find her name I don't read any of the articles and throw the newspaper away."

b **Now read the following questions and answer them briefly.**

eg *How often do you read a newspaper? I read a newspaper once a week, usually on Sunday. Which paper do you normally read, and why? I normally read the Sunday Times because I think it reports events well and is not biased.*

1 How often do you read a newspaper? ____
2 Which paper do you normally read? ____
3 When do you read it? ____
4 Do you read all of it? ____
5 Do you look at the photographs or text first? ____
6 Do you turn to a certain page first? ____
7 Do you look at headlines first? ____
8 Do you read the first paragraph of the article and then decide if it's interesting? ____
9 Do you look for certain words in the text? ____
10 Do you look to see who has written the article? ____

c **Discuss your answers with your neighbour and then in small groups. Can you draw any conclusions from your answers?**

2

2 a **Here are one-line summaries of 6 newspaper articles. Read them and then decide if the news is regional news (R), national news (N), or world news (W). When you've finished, compare your answers with your neighbour.**

1 This article is about money raised at a church fete. *R*
2 This article is about current unemployment levels in Britain. ____
3 This article is about the next Grand Prix motor race in Brazil. ____
4 This article is about new tax increases by the government. ____
5 This article is about a famous singer who was born in this town. ____
6 This article is about a meeting of 5 Heads of State to discuss the crisis in Bosnia. ____
7 This article is about a member of the Royal Family. ____
8 This article is about a new supermarket which has just opened. ____
9 This article is about global warming and the greenhouse effect. ____
10 This article is about a man who has won £20 million. ____

b **Now match the one-line summary and the first sentence of the article.**

a Unemployment figures for the last month are down according to new statistics released by the government today. [2]

b 3 points separate world champion Michael Schumacher from Damon Hill before this week's Grand Prix in Brazil. [ ]

c Jed Rover, 29, lead singer of 'Loud and Clear' returned home last night to spend a few days with his parents, Mr and Mrs Harry Rover of 23 Church Avenue, Cirencester. [ ]

d Despite promises that there would be no new tax increases this year, the Chancellor of the Exchequer yesterday announced an increase in income tax of 1%. [ ]

e Heads of States from 5 countries are meeting in Dublin on Saturday to discuss the growing crisis in Bosnia-Herzogovina. [ ]

f At last Saturday's church fete held at St Mungo's church, £4,500 was raised. [ ]

g The health of the Queen is in question after reports that she has been suffering from severe headaches. [ ]

h The new Safeways Superstore was officially opened in St George's Square last Thursday by Ted Aspinall, Director of the Superstore chain. [ ]

i A very happy Mr Nigel Harrison jumped for joy when he received a cheque for £20 million - this week's jackpot in the National Lottery. [ ]

j "The sea level will rise and submerge London by the year 2003 if nothing is done to prevent global warming" was the clear message at this year's Global Care Conference. [ ]

c **Compare your answers with your neighbour.**

d **Now ask your neighbour these questions.**

1 How much money was raised at the church fete?
2 Who won £20 million?
3 How much is the increase in income tax?
4 How old is Jed Rover?
5 Who is Ted Aspinall?

e **Discuss with your neighbour which of these articles you would read. Why?**

eg *I would read the article about the next Grand Prix motor race because I'm very interested in motor racing and I try and watch all of the races.*

3

3 a **You are going to hear the evening news. Before you start ask your neighbour what these words mean:**

injure - planted - stolen - getaway car - exhibitor - decrease - cut

Make notes while you are listening. You will hear the cassette twice.

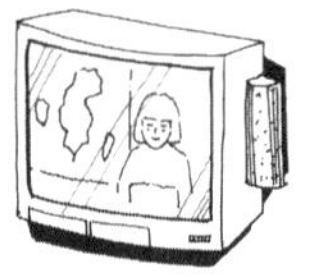

Notes

eg *Bomb attack - London Underground - Kings Cross - 5.30am.*

b **Listen again and then compare with your neighbour.**

c **Now ask your neighbour these questions.**

1 How many stories were there?
2 How many people were injured in the bomb attack?
3 What is the registration number of the getaway car?
4 How many exhibitors were at the International Motor Show?
5 How much was a litre of unleaded petrol before the price cut?

d **You are going to retell one of the stories. Work with your neighbour and use your notes. When you're ready, tell the rest of the class.**

e **Now look at the newspaper you brought with you. Find two articles about local news, 2 articles about national news and 2 articles about international news. Cut them out and then on a separate piece of paper, write a one-line summary of the article. Give your articles and your summaries to your neighbour and see how quickly he/she can match the article and the summary.**

4

4 a **Translate the following.**

Vocabulary

newspaper ____	officially ____
article ____	Chancellor of the Exchequer ____
raised ____	increase ____
church fete ____	to jump for joy ____
current ____	to receive ____
unemployment ____	jackpot ____
levels ____	National Lottery ____
motor race ____	sea level ____
tax increases ____	to rise ____
famous ____	to submerge ____
to discuss ____	to prevent ____
crisis ____	clear message ____
Bosnia ____	Heads of State ____
Royal Family ____	growing ____
global warming ____	bomb attack ____
greenhouse effect ____	to injure ____
won ____	to plant ____
according to ____	getaway car ____
statistics ____	exhibitor ____
released ____	decrease ____
severe ____	to cut prices ____
lead singer ____	

Structures

How often do you read a newspaper? ____
I read a newspaper once a week, usually on Sunday. ____
Which paper do you normally read, and why? ____
I normally read the Sunday Times. ____
I read it because I think it reports events well. ____
This article is about money raised at a church fete. ____
The article is about current unemployment levels. ____

Teaching Notes

Warm-up

In pairs students ask and answer the questions they prepared at home.

Presentation and Practice

1 In 1a students read through the comments and guess who is speaking. They then compare with their neighbour. Provide feedback by asking students who they think is speaking.

Introduce 1b by telling students about yourself. Students then read the questions in 1b and answer them briefly while you monitor and check. Students compare their answers with their neighbour and then with another pair. Provide feedback by asking students to tell you about their neighbour. See if students can draw any conclusions eg everybody in our group looks at the photographs first.

2 Students then read through the sentences in 2a and decide if the articles are regional, national or world news. When they are finished they compare their answers with their neighbour.

In 2b students read through the first sentences of the articles and see if they can match the one-line summary and the first sentence. They then compare their work with their neighbour.

Students then ask their neighbour the questions from 2d and then discuss with their neighbour which article they would read and why. Find out which article most students would read.

3 Introduce the listening activity by asking who listened to the news yesterday. See who can remember any of the news stories and elicit as much information as possible. Tell students they are going to listen to somebody reading the news. They will hear the cassette twice and they are to make notes about the stories.

Play the cassette twice and give them a couple of minutes to compare their work with their neighbour.

They listen again and check and then ask each other the questions from 3c. In pairs students work on one of the stories and prepare themselves to tell it to the rest of the class. Monitor and help and when they are ready students tell their story to the rest of the class.

Students then complete the activity in 3e while you monitor and check.

Revise all the structures and vocabulary before moving on to the next lesson.

At home students prepare for the next lesson by looking up the vocabulary in 4a of Unit 52 and make up 10 questions about their neighbour's home town eg "Where do you live? What facilities are there in your town? Is there any industry? Where do most people work?" etc.

Tapescripts

Exercise 3a & b

Good evening. The main news today is the bomb attack on the London Underground. It happened this morning at 5.30am at King's Cross Station. A train had just left the station when the bomb exploded killing 24 people and injuring 17 others. It is not yet known who planted the bomb.

£15,000 was stolen from the Midland Bank between 2am and 3am this morning. Police believe two men in their thirties were involved. The getaway car was a red Volvo 343 with the registration number H25 XTY. If anybody has seen this car please contact your local police, or call 0181 3249671.

30,000 visitors went to the first day of the International Motor Show at the National Exhibition Centre in Birmingham. The show, which this year has 374 exhibitors from over 50 different countries is on until 27 June.

BP today announced a decrease in the price of petrol. It will cut its prices by 3 pence per litre bringing the price of a litre of unleaded down to 51.9 pence.

Answers

Exercise 2a

1	R	6	W
2	N	7	W/N
3	W	8	R
4	N	9	W
5	R	10	N

Exercise 2b

a	2	f	1
b	3	g	7
c	5	h	8
d	4	i	10
e	6	j	9

1

UNIT 52

What would you do if you won £20 million?

1 a Below is an article about Terry Benson and his wife who won £20 million on the National Lottery. While they were collecting their winnings their house was broken into and lots of things were stolen. Read the questions 1 - 10 through, and then find the answers as quickly as possible in the article.

1 How old is Mr Benson?
2 How did the burglars break in?
3 Where was the family when the house was burgled?
4 What did Terry buy Brenda for their 30th wedding anniversary?
5 How old was Brenda when her mother died?
6 Who is John Benson?
7 How many children do Terry and Brenda have?
8 How much money will their children get?
9 How much does Mr Benson earn a week?
10 Will he continue to work?

£20 million lottery couple's home is burgled.

Lottery multi-millionaire Terry Benson yesterday asked burglars to return jewellery stolen from his home while his family were collecting their £20 million jackpot prize.

Mr Benson (61) said thieves had taken items of sentimental value belonging to his wife Brenda and he would pay a reward to get them back.

The jewellery was stolen between 8pm and midnight from their home in Valentine Street on the Boothferry Estate in Hull while the family was in London at a news conference.

Mr Benson said "I will offer a reward of £1,000 for the pearl necklace I bought Brenda for our 30th wedding anniversary and for the bracelet which Brenda received from her mother for her 21st birthday."

Brenda, whose mother died when she was aged 15, said "This has certainly spoilt our celebrations."

Burglars, who broke in through the back door were disturbed by a relative who was looking after the house. John Benson, Mr Benson's cousin, said "I heard a noise so I got up and put the lights on. By the time I had gone downstairs, they had run away."

When asked about the £20 million win, Terry Benson added, "This is a lot of money, but it won't change our lives." He and his wife Brenda will keep half of the money and the rest will be split between their four children. Mr Benson said he will continue to work at his present £200 a week job.

b Now read the article again and answer the following questions.

1 What kind of things had been stolen from the house? ____________________
2 What will Mr Benson do to try and get the stolen goods back? ____________________
3 When was the jewellery stolen? ____________________
4 Did the burglars leave suddenly? Why? ____________________
5 Are the family upset? ____________________

c Do you feel sorry for the family? Why (not)? Discuss with your neighbour.

eg *I don't feel sorry for the Benson family. Mr Benson has just won £20 million and can afford to buy lots of new things. I think it's unfair that one person can win so much money.*

I don't agree with you. I think he's very lucky to win £20 million, but I don't think that £20 million can replace items of sentimental value. Wouldn't you like to win £20 million? I certainly would.

2

2 a Here is an information sheet from the National Lottery explaining how to play. Look at the information and then answer the questions below.

HOW TO PLAY
INCLUDING "LUCKY DIP"

THE NATIONAL LOTTERY™

PLAYING THE NATIONAL LOTTERY

1 CHOOSE YOUR NUMBERS.

The National Lottery playslip has a number of boxes on it. These boxes are called "boards".

You select your six numbers by marking them on a board.

If you want to pick another six numbers use another board.

Only use a pencil or a blue or black pen. Put a clear, bold, vertical line through each number you've chosen. If you make a mistake, mark the void box and use another board.

2 LUCKY DIP - THE EASY WAY TO PLAY.

With Lucky Dip the terminal randomly selects a set of six random numbers for you. All you have to do is:

- Simply ask your National Lottery retailer for a "Lucky Dip" (You can have as many Lucky Dip selections as you like).

OR

- Mark the Lucky Dip (L. Dip) box on each of those boards on which you wish to play Lucky Dip. (Note: you should not select a set of numbers and mark the Lucky Dip box on the same board.)

3 PAY THE RETAILER.

Next, give your playslip to the sales assistant and pay £1 for every set of six numbers and Lucky Dip selections you have chosen.

4 GET YOUR TICKET.

When you've paid, the retailer will enter your selections into the terminal and give you a National Lottery ticket. It will have your chosen numbers (including any Lucky Dip selections) and the draw date(s) printed on it. **You must check** that the numbers you have selected, the number of selections and the draw date(s) are correct and that the barcoded serial number is clearly readable. Then write your name and address on the back. Keep your ticket safe, you'll need it to check off your numbers in the draw. Don't lose it! You'll need it to claim your prize, as it is the **only proof** that you are a winner.

5 LOOK OUT FOR THE WINNING NUMBERS.

If six numbers on one of your printed selections match the six main numbers that are drawn – in any order – you are a jackpot winner. You also win a prize by matching five, four or even three out of the six.

There will also be a seventh 'bonus number' drawn. If you already have five matching numbers, look out for it. The bonus number gives you the chance to win the second highest prize.

As well as the televised draw, you'll find the winning numbers in national newspapers and clearly displayed in all National Lottery retailers.

b Now ask your neighbour these questions.

1 I am 14 years old. Can I play the National Lottery?
2 How many numbers do I choose?
3 Where can I buy a payslip?
4 What should I use to mark the pay slip?
5 How many numbers can I choose for £2.00?
6 What 3 things do I have to check?
7 Why do I have to keep my ticket safe?
8 When are the numbers drawn?
9 How many numbers do I have to match to win a prize?
10 How many numbers are drawn?

3

2 c Explain to your neighbour how to play the National Lottery.

eg *First you take a payslip. After you have taken a payslip, you choose 6 numbers. After you have chosen 6 numbers, you mark your numbers on the board. After you have marked your numbers on the board, you give your payslip to the sales assistant.*

d If you have a National Lottery in your country and you have played it, explain to your neighbour how to play.

e You work for a regional newspaper and have just heard that somebody in your town has won £5,000 on the National Lottery. You are going to interview them, but before you do, think about what questions you are going to ask. Here are some ideas to start you off.

- Where did they buy their winning ticket? How many times have they played?
- What are they going to do with the money?
- Would they have liked to have won more?
- Are they going to continue buying tickets?
- Will they buy them from the same shop?

When you are ready, start the interview with your neighbour.

3 a Do you think you're lucky? Look at the following sets of numbers and in each set, mark 4 numbers. When you are finished, you will hear the drawn numbers on the cassette. Listen and see if you have the same numbers.

LOTTERY

1.	1	2	3	4	5	6	7	8	9	10
2.	1	2	3	4	5	6	7	8	9	10
3.	1	2	3	4	5	6	7	8	9	10
4.	1	2	3	4	5	6	7	8	9	10
5.	1	2	3	4	5	6	7	8	9	10
6.	1	2	3	4	5	6	7	8	9	10

b How many times did you have...

1 no numbers the same as the draw?
2 one number the same as the draw?
3 two numbers the same as the draw?
4 three numbers the same as the draw?
5 all four numbers the same as the draw?

Did anybody get all the numbers drawn?

c Look at the numbers you chose and then discuss the following questions with your neighbour.

Was there a particular reason why you chose these numbers? Did you choose the same number more than once? How many times did you choose each number? Which number did you choose the most? What do you associate with this number?

d Discuss the following with your neighbour.

1 Do you have a National Lottery in your country?
2 Have you ever played it?
3 Have you ever won anything on the lottery?
4 What would you do if you won £20 million?
5 What wouldn't you do if you won £20 million?

4

4 a Translate the following.

Vocabulary

multi-millionaire ____________	split ____________
burglars ____________	present ____________
stolen ____________	to choose ____________
thieves ____________	to draw numbers ____________
sentimental value ____________	to mark ____________
reward ____________	outlets ____________
news conference ____________	sign ____________
pearl ____________	to claim ____________
wedding anniversary ____________	proof ____________
to spoil ____________	bold ____________
celebrations ____________	vertical ____________
to break in ____________	sales assistant ____________
to disturb ____________	retailer ____________
cousin ____________	randomly ____________
downstairs ____________	winner ____________
added ____________	guaranteed ____________

Structures

I don't feel sorry for the Benson family. ____________
Mr Benson has just won £20 million. ____________
He can afford to buy lots of new things. ____________
I think it's unfair that one person can win so much money. ____________
I don't agree with you. ____________
I think he's very lucky to win £20 million. ____________
I don't think £20 million can replace items of sentimental value. ____________
Wouldn't you like to win £20 million? ____________
I certainly would. ____________
First you take a payslip. ____________
After you have taken a payslip you choose 6 numbers. ____________
After you have chosen six numbers you mark your numbers on the board. ____________
After you have marked your numbers on the board, you give your payslip to the sales assistant. ____________
____
What would you do if you won £20 million? ____________
If I won £20 million, I would buy a house. ____________
If I won £20 million, I wouldn't give any of it away. ____________

Teaching Notes

Warm-up

In pairs students ask and answer the questions they prepared at home.

Revision

Revise all the structures and vocabulary from the previous Unit.

Presentation and Practice

1 Introduce this Unit by asking students if they have a National Lottery in their country. Find out how many people have played it and how many people have won anything in it.

Students then complete the task in 1a as quickly as possible. Provide feedback by eliciting the answers to the questions before students read the article in more detail and answer the questions in 1b. Provide feedback by asking one pair to read out the questions and answers.

Students then complete the speaking activity in 1c while you monitor and check. Provide feedback by asking students whether they feel sorry for the family or not.

2 Students look at the information sheet about the National Lottery and then ask their neighbour the questions in 2b while you monitor and check. Provide feedback by asking students the questions.

Students then complete the speaking task in 2c. Provide feedback by one student explaining what you have to do. The other students listen and help.

In 2d students explain to their neighbour how to play the National Lottery in their country.

Students then complete the speaking activity in 2e. Provide feedback by asking pairs to demonstrate their activity. If you have time students can try writing a simple article based on their interview.

3 In 3a students take part in a small-scale lottery. There are 6 sets of numbers and in each set students mark 4 numbers. Tell them they are going to listen to the 'draw' and while they are listening they are to write down the drawn numbers. They then compare their numbers and the drawn numbers and complete the task in 3b. Provide feedback by asking students the questions from 3b and seeing if they can draw any conclusions.

Students then complete the speaking activity in 3c while you monitor and check. Provide feedback by asking students to tell you about their neighbour.

Students complete the speaking activity in 3d. Provide feedback by asking students to tell you about their neighbour.

Revise all the structures and vocabulary before moving on to the next lesson.

At home students prepare for the next lesson by looking up the vocabulary in 4a of Unit 53 and make up 10 questions about their neighbour's hobbies and interests eg "What are your hobbies? What equipment do you need? How much do you spend on your hobby per month?" etc.

Remember to bring several copies of English newspapers to the lesson next time.

Tapescripts

Exercise 3a

1 And here are the results of this week's draw - 9 - 5 - 1 - 3.

2 And here are the results of this week's draw - 4 - 5 - 8 - 10.

3 And here are the results of this week's draw - 1 - 2 - 3 - 5 .

4 And here are the results of this week's draw - 9 - 7 - 4 - 2.

5 And here are the results of this week's draw - 4 - 5 - 3 - 10.

6 And here are the results of this week's draw - 8 - 2 - 3 - 6.

Answers

Exercise 1a

1 61 years old.
2 Through the back door.
3 In London at a news conference.
4 A pearl necklace.
5 15 years old.
6 Mr Benson's cousin.
7 4 children.
8 £10 million £2.5 million each).
9 £200 per week.
10 Yes.

Exercise 1b

1 Items of sentimental value.
2 He will pay a reward to get them back.
3 It was stolen between 8pm and midnight.
4 Yes. They were disturbed when John Benson came downstairs.
5 Yes. The family are upset.

Exercise 2b

1 No. You must be 16 or over to play.
2 6 numbers.
3 Outlets where you see the National Lottery sign.
4 Pencil/blue or black pen.
5 12 numbers.
6 That your numbers are correct, that the draw date is correct and that the barcoded serial number is clearly readable.
7 It is the only proof that you are a winner.
8 Every Saturday evening.
9 3 out of 6.
10 7 numbers.

Exercise 3a

See tapescript.

1

UNIT 53

What was on the news last night?

1 a Read the following questions and then discuss your answers with your neighbour.

1 How often do you watch the news on TV?
2 What time do you normally watch the news? Why?
3 Which channel do you normally watch it on?
4 Why do you watch the news on this channel?
5 How many TV newsreaders can you name?
6 How often do you listen to the news on the radio?
7 Where do you normally listen to the news on the radio?
8 How many radio newsreaders can you name?
9 Why do you listen to the news on this radio station?
10 Do you prefer listening to news on TV or radio? Why?

b Now work in groups of 5 and answer the following questions.

1 Do most people watch/listen to news at the same time every day?
2 Do most people prefer listening to news on radio or TV?
3 Could people name more newsreaders on TV or on radio?

c When was the last time you heard the news? Think about one of the news items you heard. See what you can remember about it and make notes below. When you're ready, tell your class as much as you can about it. Did anybody else hear the same news item?

eg *I heard an interesting story on the news last night. It happened in Japan the day before yesterday. It was about a bomb attack in Tokyo.*

Notes

When I heard it:

Where it happened:

When it happened:

What it was about:

2

2 a Newspaper headlines have to summarise an article and make you want to read it in a maximum of 7 or 8 words. Look through an English newspaper and see how many words there are in the longest headline. What kind of words are left out? Are the headlines sentences or not? How many words are there in the shortest headline?

b Here are 5 headlines. Try and match the headline and the first sentence of the article. See how many you can match without using a dictionary.

1 Breakthrough on sheep dip-formula.
2 Big cat purrs like a kitten.
3 Graf back at her most graphic.
4 Germans take over UK Car Company.
5 Labour's local choice.

☐ **a** The German Car Company, BMW, yesterday announced its plans to take over the British car manufacturer Rover.
☐ **b** Perth constituency Labour party has chosen its candidate for the next general election.
☐ **c** The most remarkable aspect of the Jaguar XJ6 is how little it has changed over the years.
☐ **d** An Agricultural Supplies company is claiming a breakthrough with a new environmentally friendly formula for its sheep dip.
☐ **e** Steffi Graf fought her way to the Wimbledon singles title and took the plate after winning 4-6, 6-1, 7-5.

c We already know that we can classify news items into regional news, national news and world news, but there are many more ways of classifying news items.

Newspapers divide news into 'sections'. Look at the 5 sections below and decide which section you would find the articles from exercise 2b in.

Sport ☐ Farming ☐
Business ☐ Motoring ☐
Politics ☐

d Look through an English newspaper and see how many sections it is divided into and what these sections are. Make a list of the sections below.

Date ______ Newspaper ______

Section **Page**

e Now find 3 articles which you find interesting. Give them to your neighbour to read and then ask him/her about them.

eg *What do you think of the article on page 45 in the sports section?*
Well I'm not really interested in sport so I didn't really find it very interesting.
And what about the article on fashion?
Oh yes, I thought that was very interesting.

3

3 a Newspapers don't just have news articles in them, they also have a lot of other information. Here are some items you find in newspapers. Can you think of any more?

1 crosswords
2 horoscopes
3 letters to the editor
4 births, marriages and deaths
5 public notices

b Discuss with your neighbour which of these you read and why?

eg *I always read the headlines and then do the crossword while I'm having my morning coffee. I like reading the horoscopes too, but I don't read them until the evening.*

c Now try the crossword below. Some of the letters are already given to help you.

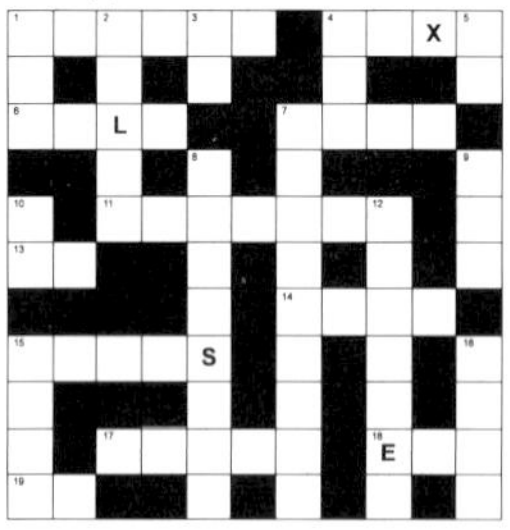

Across

1 You keep your car here at night. (6)
4 This means of transport will take you where you want to go, but it might be expensive. (4)
6 Would you like _ and sugar in your coffee? (4)
7 In the evening, I don't like watching TV. I like reading a good _. (4)
11 When I buy something, I give the cashier some money and she gives me the goods, my change, and a _. (7)
13 Excuse me, can you tell me how to get _ the station please? (2)
14 There are 12 inches (or 30 cm) in a _. (4)
15 My _ are paid into my bank account. (5)
17 They fly in the sky. (5)
18 I come home from work and I ... my evening meal. (3)
19 _ you like the colour blue? (2)

Down

1 You go here to keep fit. (3)
2 You use this to draw a straight line. (5)
3 Every morning I get up and I _ to the bathroom. (2)
4 One plus one. (3)
5 I'm sitting on a chair _ a classroom. (2)
7 You may use one of these to carry your papers to work. (9)
8 You need a pair of these to cut paper. (8)
9 It's a beautiful day. The _ is shining in the sky. (3)
10 I'll meet you _ 7.30pm outside the cinema. (2)
12 When I go shopping in the supermarket, I put my groceries in a _. (7)
15 This is where patients in hospital stay. (4)
16 The opposite of early. (4)

4

4 a Translate the following.

Vocabulary

news ______
newsreader ______
sport ______
business ______
farming ______
motoring ______
crosswords ______
horoscopes ______
editor ______
births ______
marriages ______
deaths ______
public notices ______
market ______

Structures

What was on the news last night? ______
I heard an interesting story on the news last night. ______
It happened in Japan the day before yesterday. ______
It was about a bomb attack in Tokyo. ______
What do you think of the article on page 45 in the sports section? ______
Well I'm not really interested in sport. ______
I didn't really find it very interesting. ______
And what about the article on fashion? ______
Oh yes. I thought that was very interesting. ______
I always read the headlines. ______
I do the crossword while I'm having my morning coffee. ______
I like reading the horoscopes... ______
... but I don't read them until the evening. ______

Teaching Notes

Warm-up

In pairs students ask and answer the questions they prepared at home.

Revision

Revise all the structures and vocabulary from the previous Unit.

Presentation and Practice

1 Students complete the speaking activity in 1a while you monitor and check. Provide feedback by asking students to tell you about their neighbour. In groups of 5 students ask each other the questions from 1a and then answer the questions from 1b. Provide feedback by each group telling you their answers.

Students then make notes about an item they heard recently on the news while you monitor and check. When they are finished they tell the rest of the class about their story and see if anyone else heard it.

2 Introduce 2a by asking students about newspaper headlines eg "Are they usually full sentences?" Give students copies of English newspapers and they then complete the task in 2a.

Students complete the matching task in 2b while you monitor and check.

Students then complete the exercise in 2c. Provide feedback by students telling you which section you would find the articles from 2b in.

Students then complete 2d and compare with their neighbour.

In 2e they find 3 articles which they find interesting and give them to their neighbour. They then ask their neighbour what he/she thinks about them.

3 Ask students what they can find in the newspaper which is not news. In pairs they look through their newspaper and make a list. Students tell you their list of non-news items which they have found. Make a list on the board and then students read through 3a and try to think of anything else. Tell students which of these items you read and why eg "I read the letters to the editor because they are often quite interesting."

In pairs students then complete the speaking activity in 3b while you monitor and check. Provide feedback by asking students to tell you about their neighbour. Ask how many of the class like doing crosswords and then students try and complete the crossword in 3c. Check by reading out the clues and eliciting the correct answer.

Revise all the structures and vocabulary before moving on to the next lesson.

At home students prepare for the next lesson by looking up the vocabulary in 4a of Unit 54 and make up 10 questions about their neighbour's work eg "Where do you work? How long have you worked there? What is your position?" etc.

Answers

Exercise 2b

1 d
2 c
3 e
4 a
5 b

Exercise 2c

Farming	1	d	"Breakthrough on sheep-dip formula."
Motoring	2	c	"Big cat purrs like a kitten."
Sport	3	e	"Graf at her most graphic."
Business	4	a	"Germans take over UK car company."
Politics	5	b	"Labour's local choice."

Exercise 3c

1 G	A	2 R	A	3 G	E	■	4 T	A	X	5 I
Y	■	U	■	O	■	■	W	■	■	N
6 M	I	L	K	■	■	7 B	O	O	K	■
■	■	E	■	8 S	■	R	■	■	■	9 S
10 A	■	11 R	E	C	E	I	P	12 T	■	U
13 T	O	■	■	I	■	E	■	R	■	N
■	■	■	■	S	■	14 F	O	O	T	■
15 W	A	G	E	S	■	C	■	L	■	16 L
A	■	■	■	O	■	A	■	L	■	A
R	■	17 B	I	R	D	S	■	18 E	A	T
19 D	O	■	■	S	■	E	■	Y	■	E

1

UNIT 54

Young French student requires rented accommodation.

1 a Look at these questions and discuss your answers with your neighbour.

eg *If I wanted to buy a second-hand car, I would look in our local newspaper or on the noticeboard of our local supermarket.*

1 If you wanted to buy a second-hand car, where would you look?
2 If you wanted to sell your TV, where would you advertise?
3 If you wanted to rent a flat, where would you look?
4 If you wanted to learn a language, where would you go?
5 If you wanted a part time job, where would you look? Where would you advertise?

b In many countries you can find all kinds of advertisements in the 'classified ads' section of a newspaper. Here are some headings from the classified ads section. See if you can put the advert in the correct column.

CLASSIFIED ADS						
Cars	Pets	Accommodation Wanted	Tuition	Situations Wanted	Situations Vacant	To Let

1 Beautiful kittens, house trained, await loving homes at Willows Cat Shelter. Donations requested. Tel 5366221.
2 House, 3 bedrooms, required for professional family. Medium to long let preferred. Tel 684033. Mobile (0421) 511346.
3 Experienced gardener required two days per week. Tel Mrs Stanton on 843661, after 6pm.
4 English as a foreign language, tuition with experienced EFL teacher, in groups, or one-to-one. Tel 632018.
5 Bedsit, central Haydon Bridge, shared bathroom, kitchen, £32 per week. Tel 684571.
6 GCSE French. Like help? Experienced teacher. Tel 604286.
7 Ford Escort 1.8 Diesel van - G registered. Taxed and tested. Good condition. Long MOT - £900 or nearest offer. Tel 322496.
8 Labrador puppies (3) black, 7 weeks old, 1 dog, 2 bitches, beautiful temperaments, free to a good home. Tel 684256.
9 Young French student, female, requires rented accommodation. Anything considered. Write Box P988.
10 Stone farm house, unfurnished, 3 bedrooms, fitted kitchen, living room, bathroom, central heating, coal fire, double glazing, garage. £350/£400 per calendar month. Tel 229429 business hours.
11 Student, 19, requires gardening/general outdoor work, up to 5 days per week. July to early September. Corbridge area. Tel 673030.
12 Mini 1000, T registered, 4 months MOT, alarm, sun roof, 55,000 miles - £375. Tel 682562.

c Ask your neighbour the following questions.

1 How much is the bedsit in Haydon Bridge?
2 Why would you ring 604286?
3 How much do the Labrador puppies cost?
4 How old is the student looking for gardening work?
5 Why would you ring the mobile phone number?
6 Does the young French student have a telephone?
7 What number would you call if you want to improve your French?
8 Who would you ring after 6pm?
9 When would you ring 229429?
10 What number would you call if you wanted a pet cat?

d Here are some abbreviations which are used in newspaper advertisements. See if you can find what these abbreviations are for. All the answers are contained in the adverts above.

1 pcm 2 pw 3 ch 4 ono 5 wks

2

2 a Your editor has given you the following adverts back because they contain several mistakes. Listen to the cassette and make the necessary corrections. You will hear the cassette twice.

Articles for SALE

TV, black/white, £250, nearly new, Tel (01327) 913249

Bicycle, girl's, 3 gears, blue, with basket, 3 years old, Tel (01375) 29929

Fridge, new, unwanted wedding present, £120, Tel (01325) 912634

3-piece suite, yellow, excellent condition, £325 ono, Tel (01444) 400650

Dining table, solid wood, for 8 people, antique, £350, Tel (01325) 742151

Wardrobe, wood, very good condition, £65, Tel (01375) 422313

Tent, 2-man, lightweight, never used, £80, Tel Mike (01421) 29477

Washing machine, good condition, 10 months old, under guarantee, £245 ono, Tel (01833) 27419

b Read this dialogue and practise with your neighbour.

A 422313. Hello.
B Hello. I saw your advertisement for the wardrobe in the paper last night. Do you still have it?
A Yes.
B What's it like?
A Well, it's solid wood and it's quite big. It's in very good condition, you see, I bought it for my son, but he doesn't like it.
B That sounds all right. How much do you want for it?
A £65, but I'll take £60. At the moment it's in the living room.
B Well I can come and see it at 12 o'clock if that's all right with you?
A Yes that's fine.
B How do I get there?
A Do you know St John's Church?
B Yes.
A Well coming from town you turn left at St John's then take the first right and then second left. I'm at number 14 - it's the second house on your left and there's an orange Ford Escort packed outside.
B Okay, see you then. Bye.
A Bye.

c Now telephone your neighbour and ask about some of the other items which are for sale.

d Ask your neighbour these questions.

1 Have you ever looked through the classified adverts section of a newspaper?
2 Have you ever bought anything through a classified advert?
3 What are the advantages and disadvantages of buying something from a classified advert?
4 What are the advantages and disadvantages of selling something through a classified advert?
5 If you were selling the items in 2a, how would you do it?

e Tell your teacher about your neighbour.

3

3 a Here is a guide to placing an advert in the classified ads section of a newspaper. Look at the information and then answer the questions below.

Your guide to placing an advert in the classifieds.

This guide gives you details of how to get the best results from our classified ads section.

How do I place an advert?
There are a number of ways in which to place an advert and it's so easy.

By Telephone (0114) 2300800.
Our classified line is open from 9am - 5.30pm Mon & Tues and from 9am - 5pm Wed, Thur & Fri.

By Fax (0114) 2300888
Our fax is available at all times during the day and night, 7 days a week.

By Post
Simply post your advert to:

Sheffield Herald
Rotherham Road
Sheffield S31
2LL

In Person
Our front counter will be pleased to receive your advert at our Rotherham Road Office, Sheffield. Office hours are: Mon - Fri, 9am - 5pm.

How do I pay?
£ Our staff will be happy to advise you on payment. You can either pay by cheque - made payable to Sheffield Herald, or you can pay by Mastercard or Visa.

Deadlines
The deadline for advertising is Tuesday evening, for the following Friday's publication.

1 If you want to place an advert, what number would you ring? ____
2 When can I ring on a Wednesday? ____
3 What is the fax number? ____
4 Can I fax this number at 8.30am on a Wednesday? ____
5 What is the address of the Sheffield Herald? ____
6 When can I deliver my advert in person? ____
7 Can I pay for the advert by credit card? ____
8 Who do I make the cheque payable to? ____
9 If I want my advert in next Friday's paper, when does the Herald have to receive it? ____
10 Where is the office of the Sheffield Herald? ____

4

4 a Translate the following.

Vocabulary

bedsit ____	shared bathroom ____
long let ____	taxed and tested ____
second-hand ____	condition ____
to advertise ____	MOT ____
to learn ____	or nearest offer ____
part time job ____	puppy ____
pets ____	dog ____
wanted ____	bitch ____
tuition ____	temperament ____
situations vacant ____	female ____
beautiful ____	unfurnished ____
kittens ____	business hours ____
house trained ____	calendar month ____
cat shelter ____	alarm ____
donations ____	sunroof ____
requested ____	to place an advert ____
professional ____	classified ads section ____
medium let ____	front counter ____
mobile ____	to advise ____
experienced ____	payable to ____
gardener ____	deadline ____
English as a Foreign Language ____	

Structures

If I wanted to buy a second hand car, I would look in the local newspaper. ____
I would look on the noticeboard of our local supermarket. ____
Hello, I saw your advert for the wardrobe in the paper last night. ____
What's it like? ____
Well, it's solid wood and it's quite big. ____
It's in very good condition. ____
You see, I bought it for my son, but he doesn't like it. ____
That sounds all right. ____
How much do you want for it? ____
£65, but I'll take £60. ____
Well I can come and see it at 12 o'clock if that's all right with you? ____
Yes that's fine. ____
How do I get there? ____
Coming from town you turn left at St John's Church. ____
Then take first right and then the second left. ____
I'm at number 14. ____
It's the second house on your left. ____
There's an orange Ford Escort parked outside. ____
Okay, see you then. Bye. ____

Teaching Notes

Warm-up

In pairs students ask and answer the questions they prepared at home.

Revision

Revise all the structures and vocabulary from the previous Unit.

Presentation and Practice

1 In pairs students read through the sentences and discuss their answers with their neighbour while you monitor and check. Provide feedback by asking pairs for their answers. Explain that in many newspapers you can find a section called 'classified ads' where you can find all of the items from 1a. Students then read the selection of adverts in 1b and put them under the correct heading while you monitor and help. When they are finished ask students to count how many they have under each heading and then to tell you what they are.

In pairs students then complete the speaking activity in 1c. Provide feedback by eliciting the answers to the questions.

Students then read through the abbreviations in 1d and try to find the word/phrase among the adverts. Provide feedback by students telling you what the abbreviations stand for.

2 Introduce the listening activity by telling students that they work for a newspaper. The editor has just given them the adverts back because they contain mistakes. They will hear the editor explaining the mistakes on the cassette and while they are listening they are to note down the corrections. Tell them they will hear the cassette twice and then students complete the task in 2a.

Students read through the dialogue in 2b and practise with their neighbour.

In 2c they practise telephoning and enquiring about the other items which are for sale. Provide feedback by pairs demonstrating their roleplays to the rest of the class.

Students then complete the speaking activity in 2d while you monitor and check. Provide feedback by asking students to tell you about their neighbour.

3 Students read through the guide to placing an advert in the classified adverts section and answer the questions in 3a. Provide feedback by students telling you their answers.

Revise all the structures and vocabulary before moving on to the next lesson.

At home students prepare for the next lesson by looking up the vocabulary in 4a of Unit 55 and make up 10 questions about their neighbour's language background eg "How many languages do you speak? How long have you been learning English? Have you ever lived in another country?" etc.

Tapescripts

Exercise 2a

There are far too many mistakes in this. Make sure you correct them all before it's printed. The TV is colour, not black and white, and it's for sale at £230, not £250. The bicycle has 5 gears, not 3 gears and it is 2 years old. The 3-piece suite is yellow and green, and the area code is (01334). The dining table is for 10 people, and the number should be 7421515. The tent is a 3-man tent and is £90, and the number is 29577. The washing machine is in 'fairly good' condition, not 'good' condition. It's also 9 months old and the code is (01332). Make the changes and give the corrections to me by 11 o'clock.

Answers

Exercise 1b

Cars	7, 12
Pets	1, 8
Accommodation Wanted	2,9
Tuition	4,6
Situations Wanted	11
Situations Vacant	3
To Let	5,10

Exercise 2a

TV, colour, £230, nearly new, Tel (01327) 913249

Bicycle, girl's, 5 gears, blue, with basket, 2 year's old, Tel (01375) 29929

3-piece suite, yellow and green, excellent condition, £325 ono, Tel (01334)

Dining table, solid wood, for 10 people, antique, £350, Tel (01325) 7421515

Tent, 3-man, lightweight, never used, £90, Tel Mike (01421) 29478

Washing machine, fairly good condition, 9 month's old, under guarantee, £245 ono, Tel (01332) 27419

Exercise 3a

1 (0114) 2300800
2 From 9am to 5pm
3 (0114) 2300888
4 Yes. The fax lines are open all day and night
5 Rotherham Road, Sheffield, S31 2LL
6 Mon - Fri 9am - 5pm
7 Yes, by Mastercard or Visa
8 Sheffield Herald
9 By 5pm on Tuesday
10 In Rotherham Road

1

UNIT 55

Are you free on Tuesday afternoon?

1 a Listen to the cassette and write the appointments in the diary. Brian Hawthorne is telling you about his appointments during the month of October. You will hear the cassette twice.

October

1 Tue ________	18 Fri ________
2 Wed ________	19 Sat ________
3 Thu ________	20 Sun ________
4 Fri ________	21 Mon ________
5 Sat ________	22 Tue ________
6 Sun ________	23 Wed ________
7 Mon ________	24 Thu ________
8 Tue ________	25 Fri ________
9 Wed ________	26 Sat ________
10 Thu ________	27 Sun ________
11 Fri ________	28 Mon ________
12 Sat ________	29 Tue ________
13 Sun ________	30 Wed ________
14 Mon ________	31 Thu ________
15 Tue ________	
16 Wed ________	
17 Thu ________	

b Compare your work with your neighbour.

c Look at your diary and tell your neighbour about your appointments.

eg *On the first I had a meeting at our Head Office in Lyon. I had a week's holiday from 7 - 11. I had a meeting this morning with David Prescott and next Tuesday I'm meeting Frances Latour at 3 o'clock.*

d Roleplay arranging an appointment. Look at the information below. You work in the purchasing department of Psi Computers. Your neighbour is one of Psi's suppliers - Sigma Supplies. You are selling a lot of computers at the moment and you want to arrange an appointment to discuss a larger discount for your company. Ring Sigma and arrange an appointment. You'll need to sort out when, where, what time and how to get there.

Here are some phrases to help you.

Hello, this is...
Can I speak to...?
I'd like to arrange a meeting to discuss...
Are you free on ...?
Can you make it a bit earlier?
Do you know how to find us?
I look forward to seeing you then.

2

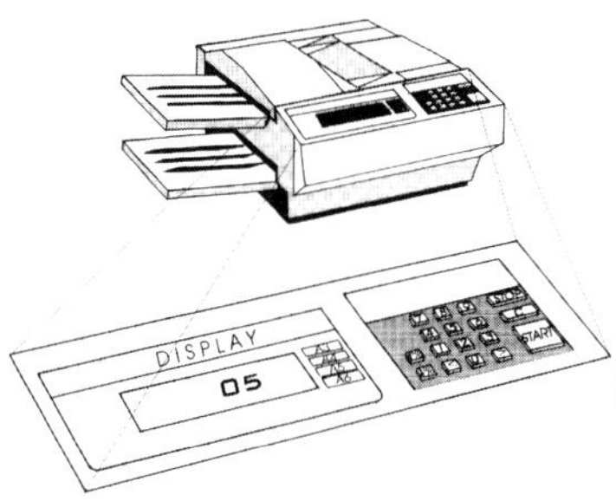

2

Instructions for Use

1. Lift lid and place the text/diagram face down on the glass surface.
2. Close lid.
3. Select paper size (A4 or A3).
4. Select the number of copies required.
5. Press the green start button.
6. If you require double-sided copies, select the double-sided button before selecting the number of copies required. Press the green start button. When the first side is done, open the lid and place the second side face down on the glass surface. Press the green start button.

Note: The photocopier requires a 5 minute warm-up period before operation. If a red light comes on, check that there is enough paper in the copier.

a Look at the information and ask your neighbour these questions, then make up some more.

1. If you want to make a single copy of one side, what do you have to do?
2. Which button do you select first?
3. What colour is the start button?
4. If a red light comes on what should you check?
5. What size paper can you photocopy?

b Now explain to your neighbour how to do the following:

1. You have a single A4 sheet which you need to copy 4 times.
2. You have 2 A4 sheets which you need to copy onto 1 double-sided A4 sheet.
3. You have an A3 sheet which you need to copy 10 times.
4. You have 2 A4 sheets which you need to copy 20 times onto single-sided A3.
5. You have 4 A4 sheets which you need to copy 10 times onto double-sided A3.

c Now ask your neighbour these questions.

eg *Have you ever used a photocopier? Yes I have. I often use a photocopier to copy documents.*

1. Have you ever used a photocopier? Where? When? Why?
2. Do you think photocopiers are useful?
3. Do you think photocopying is a waste of paper?
4. Have you ever had any problems with photocopiers?
5. Can you think of 3 advantages and 3 disadvantages of photocopiers?

d List 5 other pieces of equipment you have in your office and then explain to your neighbour how to use them.

3

3 a Here is a diagram of Sandhouses Trading Estate. There are several companies on this estate and the buildings they rent are called 'units'. This is so that visitors can find the company which they are looking for more easily. Below is a list of who is renting each unit. Ask your neighbour how to get from one unit to another.

eg *Excuse me. Can you tell me how to get to MacMillan's Dog Foods - all it says on the business card is MacMillan's Dog Food, Unit 13, Sandhouses Trading Estate.*

How To Find Us

Unit 1	Storey's Discount Carpet Warehouse	**Unit 8**	R & B T-Shirts
Unit 2	Martin White Car Repairs	**Unit 9**	Z1 Reprographics Ltd
Unit 3	M & S Factory Shop	**Unit 10**	Computer World
Unit 4	Squire's Mountain Bike Centre	**Unit 11**	Discount Jeans Centre
Unit 5	The Fylde DIY Store	**Unit 12**	The Furniture Store
Unit 6	Johnson's Garden Furniture	**Unit 13**	Macmillan's Dog Food
Unit 7	Da Roma's Pizza Delivery	**Unit 14**	Paul Richard's Printers

SANDHOUSE TRADING ESTATE PLAN

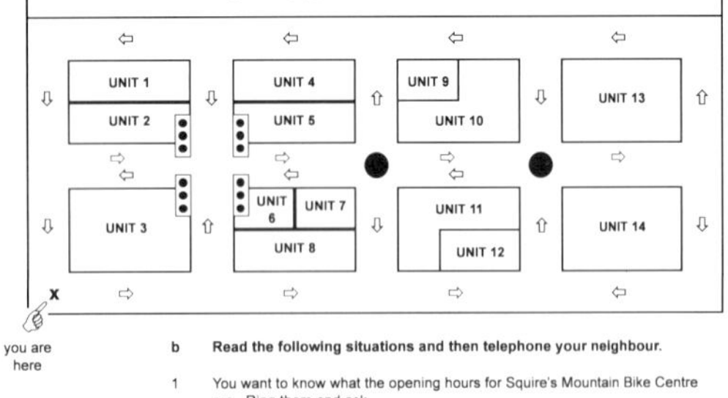

b Read the following situations and then telephone your neighbour.

1. You want to know what the opening hours for Squire's Mountain Bike Centre are. Ring them and ask.
2. You are hungry and decide to order a pizza. Ring Da Roma's Pizza Delivery and tell them what you want and where to deliver it.
3. Somebody crashed into your car yesterday. It is not badly damaged but needs some bodywork. Ring Martin White Car Repairs and arrange a time when you can take your car in.
4. You need some toner for your Hewlett-Packard 4L printer. Ring Computer World and see if they have any. Find out how much it costs and how to get there.
5. You want a bird table. Ring Johnson's Garden Furniture. Find out if they have any in stock, how much they are and if they can deliver.

c Tell your teacher what you have arranged.

4

4 a Translate the following.

Vocabulary

meeting ________
head office ________
project ________
to arrange ________
purchasing department ________
supplier ________
to increase ________
trading estate ________
companies ________
single-sided ________
double-sided ________
to copy ________
10 times ________
sheet of paper ________
units ________
visitors ________
carpet ________
warehouse ________
car repairs ________
factory shop ________
DIY store ________
garden furniture ________
printer ________
photocopier ________
to lift ________
face down ________
to select ________

Structures

On the first I had a meeting at our Head Office in Lyon. ________
I had a week's holiday from 7 - 11 ________
I had a meeting this morning with David Prescott ________
Next Tuesday I'm meeting Frances Latour at 3 o'clock. ________
Hello, this is... ________
Can I speak to...? ________
I'd like to arrange a meeting to discuss... ________
Are you free on...? ________
Can you make it a bit earlier? ________
Do you know how to find us? ________
I look forward to seeing you then. ________
Have you ever used a photocopier? ________
I often use a photocopier to copy documents. ________
Excuse me. Can you tell me how to get to...? ________
All it says on the business card is... ________

Teaching Notes

Warm-up

In pairs students ask and answer the questions they prepared at home.

Revision

Revise all the structures and vocabulary from the previous Unit.

Presentation and Practice

1 Introduce the activity in 1a by telling students that they are going to listen to Brian Hawthorn telling them about his appointments in October. They will hear the cassette twice and are to fill in the appointments in the diary. When you have played the cassette twice students compare their work with their neighbour.

Tell students what appointments you have in the next few days and then in 1c students tell their neighbour what appointments they have in the next few days. Students then tell you about their neighbour.

Introduce the roleplay in 1d by setting the scene and telling pairs which student works for Psi Computers and which student works for Sigma Supplies.

Students then complete the roleplay while you monitor and check. Provide feedback by asking pairs to demonstrate their activity.

2 Ask who has used a photocopier and get students to explain how to use them. Students then look at the 'Instructions for Use' and ask their neighbour the questions in 2a. Provide feedback by eliciting the answers to the questions. Students work in pairs and complete the speaking activity in 2a.

Students then complete the speaking activity in 2c while you monitor and check. Provide feedback by asking students to tell you about their neighbour.

In 2d ask students what other equipment they have (or that you would normally find) in an office. Make a list on the board eg paper shredder, fax machine, coffee - vending machine. They then complete the speaking activity in 2d while you monitor and check. Provide feedback by asking students to explain how to use the pieces of equipment.

3 Find out which students have visited their customer's premises. Ask them how they find their way there.

In pairs students look at the diagram in 3a and ask questions eg "What is Unit 7? Which Unit do Z1 Reprographics have? How do you get to Paul Richard's Printers?" They then complete the speaking task in 3a.

Students read through the situations and complete the telephone calls in 3b while you monitor and check. Provide feedback by students telling you what they have arranged.

Revise all the structures and vocabulary before moving on to the next lesson.

At home students prepare for the next lesson by looking up the vocabulary in 4a of Unit 56 and make up 10 questions about fitness and diet to ask their neighbour eg "Do you think you have a healthy diet? What did you eat and drink yesterday? How often do you exercise?" etc.

Tapescripts

Exercise 1a

October is a quiet month. I'm at an exhibition in France for the first 3 days and then have a review meeting with Jeff Coates and Sandy Rutherford at 10am on Monday. On the 10th I'm giving a presentation at 10am so I want to try and keep the 9th free. At 11am on the 11th there's a Sam Dolan coming from Polar Computers. I'm not sure what he wants, but he knows I have to leave by 12.30pm to get to Head Office in Birmingham by 2pm. I'm meeting Dr Giles who wants to discuss some new projects. On Tuesday the 15th we've got a staff meeting at 3pm. They normally last for about one hour. On the 16th and 17th I'll be in Birmingham again for a training session, which finishes at 1pm so I should be back by mid afternoon. Simon Hall is coming at 4pm so if I'm late, give him some coffee. On the 21st I'm meeting Joanne Sutherland from Lancaster University. She wants to discuss a joint project she's planning - I don't have any details yet, but it sound interesting. I'm back to Birmingham on the 24th for a meeting with Steven Donalds in the Research Department. I've got a day's holiday on the 25th which I'm looking forward to. On the 28th I'm taking my car to the garage for a service, so I'll be in the office all day. On Tuesday morning I have a meeting with Linda Rodgers from the Sheffield branch. She's taking me out to lunch afterwards. I'd like to keep Wednesday the 30th free so that I can prepare my monthly report which I have to give Robbie Ferguson by lunchtime on the 31st.

Answers

Exercise 1a

October

1	Tue	Exhibition in France
2	Wed	Exhibition in France
3	Thur	Exhibition in France
4	Fri	
5	Sat	
6	Sun	
7	Mon	10am Review Meeting
8	Tue	
9	Wed	Free
10	Thu	10am Presentation
11	Fri	11am Sam Dolan (Polar Computers) 2pm Head Office Dr Giles
12	Sat	
13	Sun	
14	Mon	
15	Tue	3pm Staff Meeting (1 hour)
16	Wed	Birmingham (training)
17	Thu	Birmingham (training) 4pm Simon Hall
18	Fri	
19	Sat	
20	Sun	
21	Mon	Joanne Sutherland (Lancaster University)
22	Tue	
23	Wed	
24	Thu	Steven Donalds (Research Department)
25	Fri	Holiday
26	Sat	
27	Sun	
28	Mon	Car service
29	Tue	am and lunch Linda Rodgers (Sheffield Branch)
30	Wed	Free
31	Thu	12.00 - Give report to Robbie Ferguson

1

UNIT 56

She's going to type a letter.

1 a **Look at photograph sequence 11 'Typing a Letter' on the next pages and discuss with your neighbour what the sequence is about.**

b **Describe the woman to your neighbour.**

eg *She's tall and thin with short, dark hair. She's wearing a blouse and...*

c **Ask your neighbour these questions,**

1 What is the lady going to do? What is her job?
2 What is she holding in her left hand?
3 What is she going to do with the paper?
4 What has she done with the paper in the second picture?
5 What has she done with the chair?
6 Why will she need to use the pencil?
7 What has she placed on the desk?
8 What will she do before signing the letter?
9 What has she done before using the pencil?
10 How did she correct her mistake?
11 Before checking the letter, what did she have to do?
12 What did she do after rolling the paper into the typewriter?
13 What was she doing before she sat down to type?
14 How did she check the letter?
15 What will she do after signing the letter?
16 What sort of an office is this?
17 How is the typewriter marked to identify it?
18 How was the office heated?
19 How would you type a letter?
20 Do you think anybody still types in this way? Who?

d **Now ask your neighbour these questions.**

1 Can you type? When/Where/How did you learn?
2 Have you ever used a typewriter like this?
3 Do you think everybody should learn to type?
4 Should children learn to type at school?
5 What are the advantages/disadvantages of typing on a typewriter or on a computer?

2

2 a **Jennifer MacLean works in the Personnel Department of "Urgent Office Supplies". She is working on the holiday plan for July, August and September. Listen to the cassette and mark on the sheet when the employees are taking holiday. You'll hear the cassette twice.**

		HOLIDAY CHART												
		July					August				September			
Name	**Payroll No**	3	10	17	24	31	7	14	21	28	4	11	18	25
Elaine Robertson	95													
David Walker	79													
Michael Craig	17													
Natalie Kerr	32													
Sarah Marshall	34													
Deborah Atkinson	15													
Patricia Oliver	91													
Mark Campbell	12													
Howard Mills	37													
Jennifer MacLean	33													

b **Ask your neighbour about the people.**

eg *When is Elaine Robertson taking her holiday? How long is Michael going on holiday for? Who is taking holiday in the first week of August?*

c **Now ask your neighbour these questions.**

1 How many days holiday do you get per year?
2 Do you get more or less holiday per year as you get older?
3 Who decides when you can take your holiday - you or the company?
4 Have you ever taken unpaid leave? When? Why?
5 Would you prefer to have more days holiday per year? Why (not)?

d **Read these statements and discuss them with your neighbour.**

1 I think the company should let me take holiday when I like, not when the company closes.
2 There is always a lot to do before going on holiday.
3 I think the amount of holiday should increase with age.
4 If I work overtime I should get more holiday.
5 The company is more important than the individual.

e **Now read these statements and discuss them with your neighbour.**

1 If employees are ill, the days should be deducted from their holiday entitlement.
2 Employees should not go on holiday during busy periods.
3 Holiday entitlement should decrease with age.
4 If public holidays fall on Sundays, Mondays should be free.
5 The individuals are more important than the company.

3

The Comptuer Store

- ☆ LHT 7150 Multimedia
- ☆ Intel pentium processor
- ☆ 8Mb RAM
- ☆ 540 Mb hard disk
- ☆ 14" SVGA Monitor
- ☆ Quad speed CD-ROM drive
- ☆ Stereo sound card and speakers
- ☆ Internal fax modem facility
- ☆ Windows 95
- ☆ Many software and CD titles

Specialist Business Centre at every store

- dedicated sales people
- business leasing
- account facilities
- telephone ordering

Where to find us:

Birmingham : Axletree Way, Wednesbury
Tel 0121 505 7950 / Fax 0121 505 7951

Manchester : 750 Chester Road
Tel 0161 877 2120 / Fax 0161 877 2103

Reading : South Park, Rose Kiln Lane
Tel 01325 591265 / Fax 01325 591766

3 a **Ask your neighbour the following questions.**

eg *What is this advertisement for? It's an advertisement for a new computer.*

1 What is the name of the company?
2 How big is the hard disk?
3 How much is the price including VAT?
4 What size is the monitor?
5 Can I send a fax from the computer?
6 How many branches does the company have?
7 What is the fax number of the branch in Manchester?
8 What is the address of the branch in Birmingham?
9 What is the code for Reading?
10 Can my company arrange to lease the computer?

b **Now ask your neighbour these questions.**

eg *Have you ever used a computer? Yes I have. I use one every day at work.*

1 Have you ever used a computer?
2 How often do you use a computer?
3 Do you know what make it is?
4 Do you know what the processor speed is?
5 Which applications do you use most? Why?
6 Which software packages do you use most? Why?
7 Do you ever use CD's? If so, which? Why?
8 When did you first use a computer?
9 What are the advantages of computers?
10 What are the disadvantages of computers?

4

4 a **Translate the following.**

Vocabulary

typewriter ______
Personnel Department ______
to work on ______
holiday plan ______
to take holiday ______
payroll no ______
processor ______
monitor ______
sales people ______
business leasing ______
documents ______
fax ______
modem ______
software ______
application ______
software package ______

Structures

She's going to type a letter. ______
She's tall and thin, with short, dark hair. ______
She's wearing a blouse and... ______
When is Elaine Robertson taking her holiday? ______
How long is Michael going on holiday for? ______
Who is taking holiday in the first week of August? ______
What is this an advertisement for? ______
It's an advertisement for a new computer. ______
Have you ever used a computer? ______
Yes I have. ______
I use one every day at work. ______

Teaching Notes

Warm-up

In pairs students ask and answer the questions they prepared at home.

Revision

Revise all the structures and vocabulary from the previous Unit.

Presentation and Practice

1 Students look at the photographs from this Unit and complete the speaking activity in 1a. Students describe the woman to their neighbour in as much detail as possible in 1b.

Students then complete the speaking activity in 1c while you monitor and check. Provide feedback by eliciting the answers to the questions.

Students ask their neighbour the questions from 1d and then tell you about their neighbour.

2 Introduce the listening activity by explaining the situation in 2a. Students listen to the cassette twice and complete the task. Students compare their work with their neighbour and then complete the speaking task in 2b.

Students ask their neighbour the questions in 2c and then tell you about their neighbour.

Students then read the statements in 2d and discuss what they think about the statements with their neighbour while you monitor and check. Provide feedback by asking students to tell you what they think. Students then do the same with 2e. Provide feedback by asking students to tell you what they think. See if you can get a consensus of opinion.

3 Students look at the advert for the computer and in pairs complete the speaking activity in 3a while you monitor and check. Provide feedback by eliciting the answers to the questions.

Students then complete the speaking activity in 3b while you monitor and check. Provide feedback by asking students to tell you about their neighbour.

Revise all the structures and vocabulary before moving on to the next lesson.

At home students make up 10 questions to ask their neighbour about shopping eg "Where do you normally go shopping? Where would you go if you wanted to buy some new clothes? How do you get there from the main bus station?" etc

Tapescripts

Exercise 2a

Elaine is taking the first two weeks in July. David is taking the last week in July, and the first week in August, as usual. Michael's taking one week from 14 August and then a second week starting 4 September. Natalie has already used up her holiday leave, but has requested a week's unpaid leave for the week beginning 14 August. I've agreed to that. Sarah is taking the last two weeks in July and the first week in August. Deborah has requested four weeks holiday from the 10 July. She wants to go to Hawaii to visit her sister who's just had a baby. I've agreed to this as she's had no holiday so far this year. This means that we'll be a bit short-staffed in the last week of July, but I'm sure we'll manage. Patricia wanted to take the last week in July but has agreed to take the last week in August instead. She's not going away so she said it wasn't a problem. Mark isn't taking any holiday through the summer, he said he'll probably take a week in October. Howard is taking the week beginning 21 August and I'm taking a fortnight from 28 August.

Answers

Exercise 2a

		HOLIDAY CHART												
		July					August				September			
Name	**Payroll No**	**3**	**10**	**17**	**24**	**31**	**7**	**14**	**21**	**28**	**4**	**11**	**18**	**25**
Elaine Robertson	95	X	X											
David Walker	79					X	X							
Michael Craig	17							X			X			
Natalie Kerr	32							X						
Sarah Marshall	34				X	X	X							
Deborah Atkinson	15		X	X	X	X								
Patricia Oliver	91									X				
Mark Campbell	12													
Howard Mills	37								X					
Jennifer MacLean	33									X	X			

1

UNIT 57

Exam Practice 1

1 a Tell your neighbour about yourself. Use the following points as a guide.

- personal details - name, address, tel no; date of birth, place of birth, nationality; marital status
- parents - names, ages, occupations, hobbies
- children - names, ages, birthdays, appearance
- brothers and sisters - names, ages, wives/husbands, relationships

2 a Look at photograph sequence 12 'Buying a Car' on the next pages and discuss with your neighbour what the sequence is about.

b Ask your neighbour these questions. Read the questions carefully.

1. Why have this man and woman parked their car?
2. What is the man doing with his right hand?
3. What have the man and woman done after locking the car door?
4. Why do they lock the car door?
5. What do you think they will do next?
6. What is the salesman trying to do?
7. Why is the salesman sitting at a desk with a pen in his hand?
8. What is the older man going to do?
9. What was the lady doing while her husband was talking to the salesman?
10. What will he do with his old car?

c Now ask your neighbour these questions.

1. Have you ever bought a second-hand car?
2. Have you ever bought a new car?
3. What are the advantages and disadvantages of buying a second-hand car?
4. What are the advantages and disadvantages of buying a new car?
5. Have you ever had any problems with second-hand/new cars?

2

3 a You are going to hear a taped announcement. Before you listen, look at the map of Cambridge. You will hear the cassette twice and you may make notes if you wish.

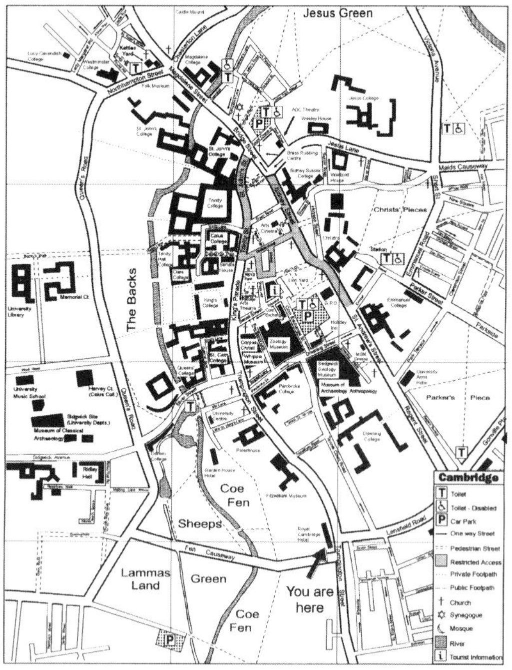

3

3 b Here are 15 questions about the trip to Cambridge. Ask your neighbour and when you've finished, make up 5 more question of your own.

1. Will you go and visit the Fitzwilliam Museum straight away? Why not?
2. Coming out of the hotel on to Trumpington Street, which way would you turn to visit the colleges?
3. From the Fitzwilliam Museum, how would you get to Emmanuel College?
4. From Sidney Sussex College, how would you get to the nearest toilet?
5. How would you get from Clare College to Queen's Road? Would you cross the river?
6. If you wanted to visit two museums in the afternoon after lunch, which would you choose and which direction would you take?
7. If you were at St John's College and needed some tourist information, how would you find it?
8. Supposing it rains, what will happen to the river trip?
9. What are the Backs? Will you see them in the afternoon?
10. Could you walk from Queen's College back to the hotel? How?
11. If you are at Jesus College and want to go to church, where might you go?
12. How long will you have in the Zoology Museum if you arrive at 3.45pm and spend the rest of the visit there?
13. Would you expect to find traffic on King's Parade?
14. If you got a taxi at Magdalen College in a rush back to the hotel at 5.50pm, what route would the taxi take?
15. Supposing you were having a drink at the University Arms Hotel and needed to get back to the coach quickly, how would you go?

4 a Ask your neighbour these 15 questions about the advertisement on the next page. When you've finished, make up 5 more questions.

1. What is this an advertisement for?
2. What is the address of the vineyard?
3. How would you get there?
4. What is the nearest town or village?
5. What roads are nearest to the vineyard?
6. Is the vineyard open every day?
7. Is the visit free?
8. What is the winter season for the vineyard?
9. How long is the vineyard open (a) in summer, (b) in winter?
10. Could you take a group to visit?
11. What are Bank Holidays?
12. How much does a conducted tour cost?
13. Can you eat and drink on such a tour?
14. How could you arrange a conducted group tour?
15. Are children admitted?

5 a Read the following statements and say whether you agree with them or not. Discuss your reasons with your neighbour.

1. Tax on alcohol should be much higher.
2. People who drive the most should pay more car tax.
3. Medical care should be provided by the state.
4. Everyone has the right to work.
5. Unemployment benefit is far too high.

4

Come and drink English Wine at an English Vineyard

How to find us...

St George's English Wines
Waldron Vineyards
Heathfield East Sussex
Telephone: Horam
(014353) 2156

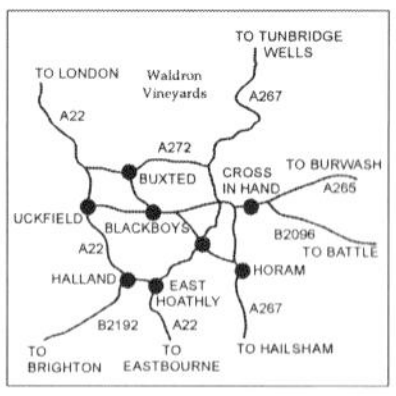

Conducted Tours (by appointment)

Includes talk, colourslide presentation, vineyard tour, tasting and a selection of optional buffets. Ideal for groups and clubs. Daytime, evenings and weekends. £2 - £4.50

Light lunches and cream teas are served on certain days. Ample free parking.

Our Summer season starts on St George's Day, April 23 and from then to September 30 we are open daily 11am to 5pm, including Sundays and Bank Holidays.

During winter, October 1 - April 22, our vineyard shop is open every Thursday, Friday, Saturday and Sunday 1pm - 4pm.

Vineyard Walkabout

Walk at your leisure through the vineyards followed by a tasting of St George's English Wine £1.25
Children Free

Teaching Notes

Warm-up

In pairs students ask and answer the questions they prepared at home.

Explain the Threshold exam to the students, telling then how many parts there are, how long each part lasts and what the tasks are.

Exam practice
(Exam material from 1990)

1 This is practice for part 1 of the exam - general conversation. Write the points from 1a on the board and then bring one student out to the front. Tell students you are going to have a conversation about the student and his/her family. Give another student the job of telling you when 5 minutes are up. Start the conversation by asking the student to tell you something about him/herself, where he/she is from, if he/she is married etc. Encourage the student to talk and steer the conversation to cover the points on the board. Do not correct any mistakes. When time is up ask the student if the time went quickly. Ask other students if they noticed any mistakes.

In pairs students tell their neighbour about themselves while you monitor and check. When 5 minutes are up students change over so that both students have the chance to practise.

2 This is practice for part 2 of the exam - the picture sequence. Students are shown a sequence of pictures and then asked questions about them.

In 2a students look at the photographs and complete the speaking activity in 2a. Students then answer the questions in 2b while you monitor and check. Provide feedback by asking students to tell you what they have written.

Students then ask and answer the questions in 2c about the photographs while you monitor and check. They then ask and answer the questions in 2d about their own experience while you monitor and check.

3 This is practice for part 3 of the exam - pathfinding on the basis of a taped announcement. Students are given a diagram or plan and some paper to make notes on. They listen twice to a cassette recording and are then asked questions about the information.

In 3a students look at the diagram for a few seconds before they listen to the cassette. Play the cassette twice and then students ask their neighbour the questions from 3b while you monitor and check. Provide feedback by eliciting the answers from students.

4 This is practice for part 4 of the exam - reading and reacting. Students are given an advert or other information and asked questions about it.

In 4a students look at the advert and then ask their neighbour the questions. Students then ask their neighbour 5 more questions of their own. Provide feedback by students asking and answering the questions.

5 This is practice for part 5 of the exam - attitudinal conversation. Students express their opinion using statements, headlines or pictures as stimuli.

In 5a students read the statements and tell their neighbour if they agree or not and why. Provide feedback by eliciting opinions from students.

At home students make up 10 questions about when their neighbour needs English eg "Do you use English in your job? Do you have to write faxes? How often do you receive phone calls in English?"

Tapescripts

Exercise 3a

A Day in Cambridge

Now the examiner will test whether you can find your way around on the basis of a map or diagram and a taped announcement. The tape will be played twice. You may look at the map of Cambridge and you may make notes if you wish.

(Pause)

You are a tourist visiting Cambridge. Your guide gives you instructions for the day.

Ladies and gentlemen. Here we are at the Royal Cambridge Hotel where the coach will park and where we shall have lunch at 1 o'clock. Please be back by 12.45pm. It is now 9.45am so you have 3 hours for sightseeing. We return to London at 6pm.

The quickest way to see the colleges is to walk down Trumpington Street and it's continuations, then return by Sidney Street and Downing College.

The Zoology and Geology Museums can be visited this afternoon.

After lunch, weather permitting, we shall be taking a river trip through the meadows behind the colleges, known as the Backs. That's at 3pm.

Don't miss King's College with its famous Chapel or Trinity College with its great courtyard.

The Fitzwilliam Museum does not open until 2.30pm today. Most of the churches will have a morning service on as it's Sunday. You can go into the college chapels, however.

1

UNIT 58

Exam Practice 2

1 a Tell your neighbour about yourself. Use the following points as a guide.

- personal details - name, address, tel no; date of birth, place of birth, nationality; marital status
- family - parents, children, brothers and sisters
- work - work experience (where, when, what, how long); - current occupation (what, where); - ambitions

2 a Look at photograph sequence 13 'A Rep Calls' on the next pages and discuss with your neighbour what the sequence is about.

b Ask your neighbour these questions.

1. Why has the man arrived with 2 small cases?
2. Why do you think the receptionist took the rep's calling card?
3. Where will the rep go after the receptionist's phone call?
4. Who is the lady in the light coloured dress? What is she doing?
5. Describe the room where the three people are. What are they doing?
6. What do you think the Director was doing before the rep arrived?
7. What will the Director say to the rep?
8. Describe the sales techniques of the rep. What do you think of them?
9. What is the lady in the light coloured dress bringing in for the two people? What is on the tray?
10. What is the man writing?
11. Why are they shaking hands?
12. After visiting the company, what will the rep do?
13. In which season is this visit taking place?
14. How is the rep dressed?
15. In your opinion, what sort of company is this?

c Now ask your neighbour these questions.

1. What do you think about Sales Reps?
2. Would you like to work as a Sales Rep? Why (not)?
3. What do you understand by 'sales technique'?
4. What do you think is important for a successful Sales Rep?
5. Do you think languages are important for Sales Reps?

2

3 a You are going to hear a taped announcement. Before you listen, look at the diagram of the Winchester Conference Building. You will hear the cassette twice and you may make notes if you wish.

FIRST FLOOR

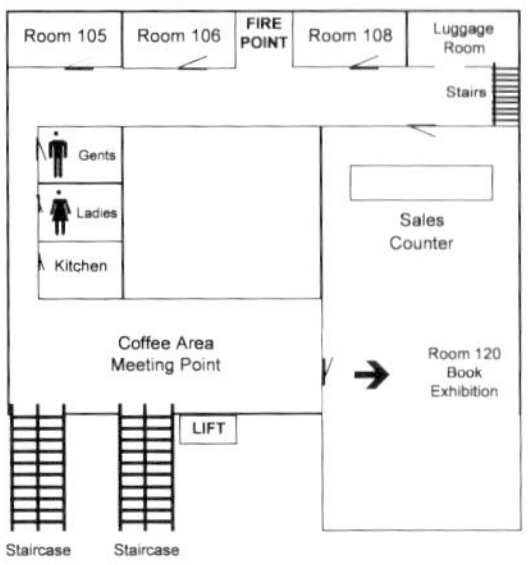

GROUND FLOOR

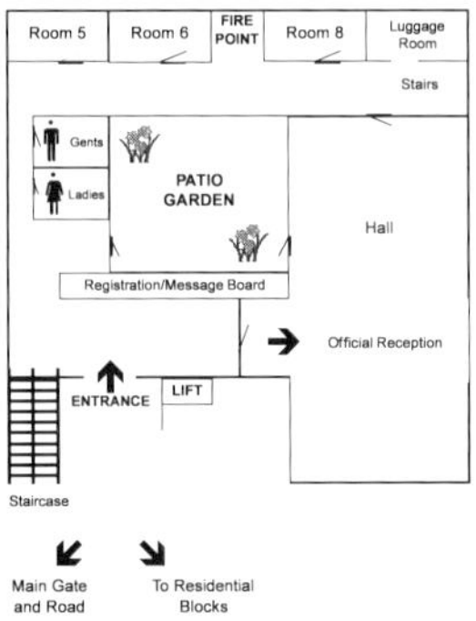

3

3 b Now ask your neighbour these questions.

1. From the kitchen, how would you reach the official reception?
2. After registration you want to store a heavy box of leaflets. Where would you go?
3. Will the weather affect the official reception? How?
4. From the first floor lift, you want to attend the lecture on 'Safety standards'. How would you go?
5. After attending the women's discussion group on Monday afternoon, how would you get coffee?
6. If you want a snack at 4 o'clock in the afternoon, where should you go?
7. After registration you want to buy some books. Where would you go?
8. After hearing a talk in Room 108 you want to go to your residential block. How do you get there.
9. If you were in Room 108 and the fire alarm rang, what would you do?
10. You want to leave a message for a friend who is also at the conference. How would you do it?
11. If you went into the hall at 8pm this evening, what would you find? Why?
12. Could you get tea or Coca Cola at the kitchen? When?
13. Can you buy books at the book exhibition?
14. At the reception you find the Hall very hot and smoky. What could you do?
15. How would get from the patio garden to Room 105?

4 a Ask your neighbour these questions about the advertisement on the next page.

1. If you were an employer, would you be interested in this scheme?
2. Why (not)? Is it simple?
3. How much would you get for each new worker?
4. How much should you pay each new worker?
5. Which people are eligible?
6. Can you benefit if you take on new workers part time?
7. How can you find out more about the scheme?
8. Can you find out information on a Sunday? How?
9. What kinds of businesses can take advantage of this scheme?
10. Why should this attract small businesses?
11. Do you have to pay for telephone calls to find out more?
12. If you were out of a job, could you make use of this scheme? How? Why not?
13. Where has this advertisement come from?
14. Do you think it is a good idea?
15. What other schemes do you know for creating jobs in your country?

5 a Read the following statements and say whether you agree with them or not. Discuss your reasons with your neighbour.

1. School education does not prepare people for the real world.
2. There is no point in training people for jobs which don't exist.
3. Unemployment is increasing because of cheap foreign labour.
4. Working people should pay more tax to support the unemployed.
5. Factories are being closed down and replaced by supermarkets and retail parks.

4

Now you can give young people a job and get paid for it.

There's a new scheme which allows you to take on young workers at realistic wages, and be paid £15 a week for each one.

It's as simple as that. No administrative problems. No complicated red tape.

Jobcentres and Careers Offices will be glad to tell you about eligible young people. You'll be helping out young people, and helping yourself expand, without getting involved in unrealistic labour costs.

It's called the New Workers Scheme. Ideal for small and medium-sized businesses, but still attractive to large businesses.

The jobs must be full time for one year. The wages must be no more than £55 (under 20), or £65 (aged 20).

You can take on as many workers as you like.

The people must be under 21 and in their first year of employment.

For more information dial 100 and ask for FREEFONE NEW WORKERS. (Lines are open from 9.00 am to 9.00 pm, seven days a week). Or send in the coupon below.

ACTION FOR JOBS

To: New Workers Scheme, FREEPOST, Curzon House, 20-24 Lonsdale Road, London NW6 4YP. Please send me details of the New Workers Scheme.
Name: ______ DE2
Company: ______
Position: ______
Address: ______

New Workers Scheme
Department of Employment DE

Teaching Notes

Warm-up

In pairs students ask and answer the questions they prepared at home.

Exam Practice
(Exam material from 1992)

1 Students tell their neighbour about themselves based on the points in 1a. Check the time and after 5 minutes students change over.

2 Students look at the photographs and complete 2a. They then ask and answer the questions in 2b while you monitor and check. Provide feedback by eliciting the answers to the questions. They then complete the speaking activity in 2c while you monitor and check. If students need more practice use the photograph sequences from earlier Units.

3 Students cover the questions in 3b. They look at the diagram and then listen to the cassette twice making notes while they are listening. One student uncovers and asks the questions and the other tries to answer using his/her notes and the diagram. Provide feedback by eliciting the answers from students. If students need more practice use the diagrams and recordings from earlier Units.

4 Students work in pairs. One student looks at the advert. The other student asks the questions. Provide feedback by eliciting the correct answers. If students need more practice use the adverts from earlier Units.

5 Students read the statements and then discuss their opinion with their neighbour while you monitor and check. Provide feedback by eliciting students' opinions. If students need more practice find out what interests them and encourage students to present an idea and support it, while other students try to put forward the other side of the case.

At home students make up 10 questions to ask their neighbour about their home eg "How long have you lived there? Would you like to move? Why (not)? Do you have a mortgage?" etc.

Tapescripts

Exercise 3a

Winchester Conference Building

Now the examiner will test whether you can find your way around on the basis of a map or diagram and a taped announcement. The tape will be played twice. You may look at the plan of the conference centre and you may make notes if you wish. (Pause).

A small-scale conference is being held and an announcement is made from the registration desk.

Could I have your attention please, ladies and gentlemen? There have been last minute changes to the programme and I'd like you to note them.

The lecture on ‘Safety Standards’ to be given on Monday at 3pm in Room 8 will now take place in Room 106 on the first floor. The women’s discussion group to be held at that time will now take place in Room 8.

The official reception will start at 8pm this evening, not 7.30pm as advertised, and if the weather stays fine, it will be held in the patio garden as well as the hall.

The kitchen on the first floor will be open for drinks and snacks from 11am till 5pm.

There are firepoints on the ground floor and first floor. If you hear the alarm you should leave the building by either the main entrance or by emergency doors at the fire points.

If you have heavy cases or equipment, these should be left in the luggage room on the ground floor.

The book exhibition will open at 10am on Monday and close at 3pm on Wednesday. Books may be purchased as well as inspected. That’s all. Thank you.

1

UNIT 59

Exam Practice 3

1 a Tell your neighbour about yourself. Use the following points as a guide.

- personal details - name, address, tel no
  date of birth, place of birth, nationality
  marital status
- family - parents, children, brothers and sisters
- work - work experience (where, when, what, how long)
  - current occupation (what, where)
  - ambitions
- hobbies and interests - what/how often/when/how much travelling/what equipment you need
  - how it started/training
  - ambitions

2 a Look at photograph sequence 14 'Buying a Dress' on the next pages and discuss with your neighbour what the sequence is about.

b Ask your neighbour these questions.

1 What was the lady wearing when she went into the clothes shop?
2 Why do you think she is going into the clothes shop?
3 What did the shop assistant do first?
4 What is she doing in the third photograph?
5 How did she pay for the dress?
6 Why do you think she paid by credit card?
7 What did the shop assistant do with the dress after the customer had paid?
8 Why do you think she bought the dress?
9 Where do you think she will go now?
10 Describe the shop.
11 What did the lady do before trying on the dress?
12 Describe the shop assistant.
13 What kind of clothes shop is this?
14 Would you go to this kind of shop to buy your clothes? Why (not)?
15 When was the last time you bought a new suit or dress?

2

3 a You are going to hear a taped announcement. Before you listen, look at the floor plan. You will hear this cassette twice and you may make notes if you wish.

Plan of 4th Floor (not to scale)

INTERNATIONAL BUSINESS COLLECTION

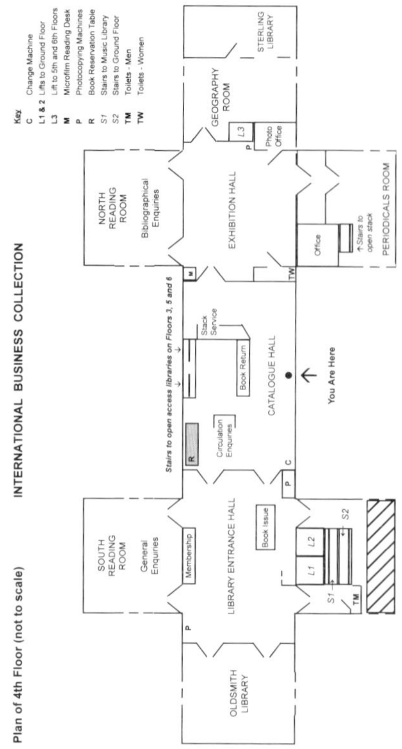

PETERSTONE BUSINESS COLLEGE - THE LIBRARY

3

3 b Now ask your neighbour these questions.

1 When will the group reassemble? And where?
2 Supposing you are in the South Reading Room at 2.55pm, what must you do?
3 Why must you keep your voices down?
4 If you want to make a bibliographical enquiry, that is, about a particular book, what will you do?
5 Supposing you are in the Geography Room and wish to reserve a book, what should you do?
6 Supposing you wanted to photocopy something in Japanese, what would you do?
7 How would you get to the parts of the library on other floors?
8 If you wanted to visit Singapore on a business trip, what might you do?
9 You have been looking at a display of Italian business documents and need to go to the toilet. What would you do?
10 When you take out your Membership Card, where will you get it? Will it be free?
11 You want to look at the latest issue of The Economist and Management Today. Where would you find them and how would you get there from the Sterling Library?
12 After reserving a book you go to the nearest lift. How do you get there?
13 You find something in the South Reading Room which you would like to photocopy but you first need change for the machine. What would you do?
14 After you reassemble, how much longer will the library stay open?
15 Where would you look up details of a book in the catalogue?

4 a Ask your neighbour some of these questions about the advertisement on the next page.

1 What is the object of this advertisement?
2 If you come home and smell gas, what should you do first?
3 If you come home at night and the house is dark, what should you remember?
4 Where would you find the telephone number of the Gas Emergency Service?
5 Where can you write it?
6 What two things should you do after opening doors and windows?
7 If you ring the Gas Emergency Service at midnight will someone be there?
8 What if you are a smoker?
9 If the lights are on, should you switch them off?
10 How do you turn the gas off at the meter?
11 How would you recognize the meter main outlet?
12 What would the most common cause of a gas problem be?
13 Do you use gas in your home? From a bottle or mains supply?
14 What are the dangers and advantages of gas?
15 Who are British Gas?

5 a Read the following statements and say whether you agree with them or not. Discuss your reasons with your neighbour.

1 Testing of nuclear weapons is necessary.
2 Credit cards are dangerous.
3 People should spend their holiday in their own country to support the economy.
4 Thin people are unhappy.
5 Children should be seen and not heard.

4

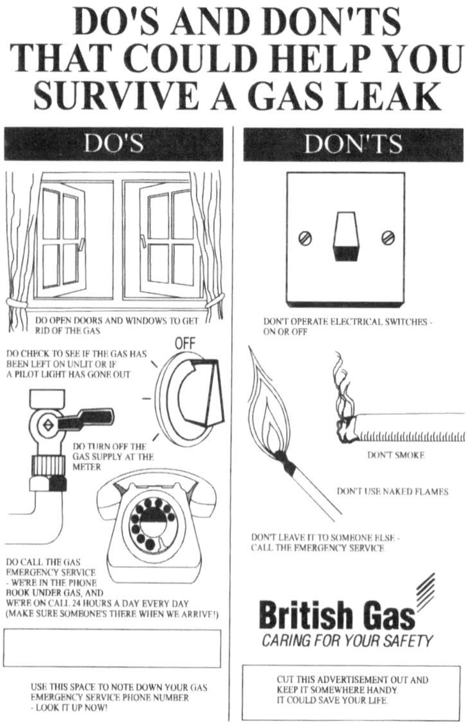

DO'S AND DON'TS THAT COULD HELP YOU SURVIVE A GAS LEAK
DO'S
DON'TS
DO OPEN DOORS AND WINDOWS TO GET RID OF THE GAS
DON'T OPERATE ELECTRICAL SWITCHES - ON OR OFF
DO CHECK TO SEE IF THE GAS HAS BEEN LEFT ON UNLIT OR IF A PILOT LIGHT HAS GONE OUT
OFF
DO TURN OFF THE GAS SUPPLY AT THE METER
DON'T SMOKE
DON'T USE NAKED FLAMES
DON'T LEAVE IT TO SOMEONE ELSE - CALL THE EMERGENCY SERVICE
DO CALL THE GAS EMERGENCY SERVICE - WE'RE IN THE PHONE BOOK UNDER GAS, AND WE'RE ON CALL 24 HOURS A DAY EVERY DAY (MAKE SURE SOMEONE'S THERE WHEN WE ARRIVE!)
British Gas
CARING FOR YOUR SAFETY
USE THIS SPACE TO NOTE DOWN YOUR GAS EMERGENCY SERVICE PHONE NUMBER - LOOK IT UP NOW!
CUT THIS ADVERTISEMENT OUT AND KEEP IT SOMEWHERE HANDY. IT COULD SAVE YOUR LIFE

Teaching Notes

Warm-up

In pairs students ask and answer the questions they prepared at home.

Exam Practice
(Exam material from 1991)

1 Students tell their neighbour about themselves based on the guidelines in 1a. Check the time and after 5 minutes students change over.

2 Students look at the photographs and complete 2a. They then ask and answer the questions in 2b while you monitor and check. Provide feedback by eliciting the answers to the questions. If students need more practice use the photograph sequences from earlier units.

3 Students cover the questions in 3b. They look at the diagram and then listen to the cassette twice making notes while they are listening. One student uncovers and asks the questions and the other tries to answer using his/her notes and the diagram. Provide feedback by eliciting the answers from students. If students need more practice use the diagrams and recordings from earlier units.

4 Students work in pairs. One student looks at the advert. The other student asks the questions. Provide feedback by eliciting the correct answers. If students need more practice use the adverts from earlier units.

5 Students read the statements and then discuss their opinion with their neighbour while you monitor and check. Provide feedback by eliciting students' opinions. If students need more practice find out what interests them and encourage students to present an idea and support it, while other students try to put forward the other side of the case.

At home students make up 10 questions to ask their neighbour.

Tapescripts

Exercise 3a

Introduction to the Library

Now the examiner will test whether you can find your way around on the basis of a map or diagram and a taped announcement. The tape will be played twice. You may look at the plan of the library and you may make notes if you wish.

(Pause)

It's your first day at business school. A senior student shows you and a group of other students round the library facilities.

(Clears throat) Let us just stop here before we go in. I don't want to disturb the readers so I'll tell you what you need before you go in.

This is the special collection of international business books and periodicals. There are over 300,000 titles in 18 different languages. The Japanese and Arabic material is all in the Oldsmith Library at the south end.

You will get your library tickets from the Membership Desk on payment of a £20 deposit.

At present the Exhibition Hall has a display of Italian business documents from the Middle Ages.

The Geography Room at the north end has a unique collection of maps and town plans for planning business ventures. The Periodicals Room holds all the magazine material in languages other than Japanese and Arabic.

The Library is open most of the year between 9am and 9pm. It's closed on Sundays and on Saturday afternoons. At present the North Reading Room is closed for repairs.

Please go in and wander round on your own. We'll reassemble in the Library Entrance Hall at 3pm. There are toilets on this side of the building - women's to the right, men's to the left.

You can't borrow books yet but if you want to reserve some or photocopy anything, you may. The reservation table is almost opposite you on the other side of the Catalogue Hall.

The main photocopying area is through the Exhibition Hall.

Please use your floor plan as a guide and keep your voices down. Thank you.

1

UNIT 60

Exam Practice 4

1 a **Tell your neighbour about yourself. Use the following points as a guideline.**

- personal details
  - name, address, tel no
  - date of birth, place of birth, nationality
  - marital status
- family
  - parents, children, brothers and sisters
- work
  - work experience (where, when, what, how long)
  - current occupation (what, where)
  - ambitions
- hobbies/interests
  - equipment, training, ambitions
- town
  - how big/where
  - tourist attractions
  - industry
  - unemployment levels

2 a **Look at photograph sequence 15 'A Business Trip' on the next pages and discuss with your neighbour what the sequence is about.**

b **Describe the people to your neighbour.**

c **Ask your neighbour some of these questions.**

1 What did the businessman do before leaving on his trip?
2 What is he going to take with him?
3 After packing his suitcase, where did he go and why?
4 What did the secretary have ready for her boss?
5 Describe the woman's office.
6 What does the man have to do first at the airport?
7 How did the businessman get to the airport?
8 Describe the woman at the airport.
9 What will the businessman do when he arrives at his destination?
10 Who do you think he spoke to before going to his meeting?
11 At the hotel, what did he do before making a phone call?
12 What do you imagine the two men said to each other when they met?
13 How many people attend the meeting? Who do you think they are?
14 What do you think the person presenting the businessman says?
15 What will the businessman do after the speech of the man on his right?

2

3 a You are going to hear a taped announcement. Before you listen, look at the diagram. You will hear the cassette twice and you may make notes if you wish.

THE GOLD SHOPPING CENTRE - LOWER MALL

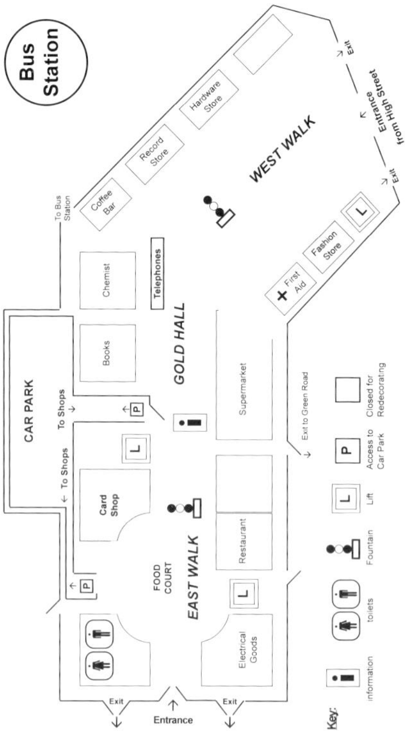

3

3 b **Now ask your neighbour these questions.**

1 At what time of day do you hear this announcement?
2 Why is this called 'late night shopping'?
3 Until when are the shops open? Could you get coffee after they close?
4 Supposing you are Peter's mother, where would you find him? How would you get there from the High Street entrance?
5 Will you be able to have dinner or supper in the Mall? Where?
6 Could you buy some reduced-price records next week? Why not?
7 Suppose you had been buying some cheap records, how would you go to get some Italian food?
8 Which shops are not open? Why?
9 If you are in the restaurant and want to go to the car park, how could you go?
10 You have been buying a video recorder and want to go to the next floor up. How would you get there?
11 You enter the shopping centre from the High Street and want to go directly to the top floor. How would you go?
12 What will you find if you come out of the coffee shop when it closes and go to the toilet?
13 You would like to buy some apples and oranges. Where would be the best place to go?
14 Your friend has an accident and needs urgent medical attention - where would you go?
15 Can you get 30 per cent off music cassettes?

4 a **Ask your neighbour these questions about the advertisement on the next page.**

1 Who lived in this house?
2 How long did he live here?
3 Who was Keats?
4 Can I visit Keats' house on a Sunday morning?
5 Is it open on public holidays?
6 Can I go by car?
7 Where can I park?
8 If I arrive, hot and tired, can I get tea at the house?
9 Can I take a group of visitors to the house?
10 Do I have to make any special arrangements for taking a group of visitors?
11 How much does it cost to go in?
12 Is the house near Hampstead Heath?
13 Where is the nearest underground station?
14 Could I walk from Belsize Park? How far is it?
15 Would you like to visit Keats' house? Why (not)?

5 a **Read the following statements and say whether you agree with them or not. Discuss your reasons with your neighbour.**

1 People who don't exercise should not get medical care.
2 Young people have no respect for their parents.
3 All murderers should be executed.
4 Television is the best source of information.
5 Intelligence is inherited.

4

Information

OPENING HOURS	Monday to Saturday 10 - 1 and 2 - 6, Sunday 2 - 5. Easter, Spring and Late Summer Bank Holidays 2 - 5. Closed Christmas Day, Boxing Day, New Year's Day, Good Friday and May Day.
PARKING	Hampstead Heath 200 yards.
MUSEUM SHOP	Publications, souvenirs
REFRESHMENTS	No catering, nearby tea shops.
PARTIES	Guided parties (limited to 25 persons) by arrangement with the Curator.
DISABLED	Not suitable for wheelchairs
ADMISSION	Free

HOW TO GET THERE

BUSES	268 to Rosslyn Hill; 24, 46 and C11 to Hampstead Heath.
UNDERGROUND	Northern Line (Edgware branch) to Hampstead or Belsize Park
BRITISH RAIL	North London Line to Hampstead Heath.

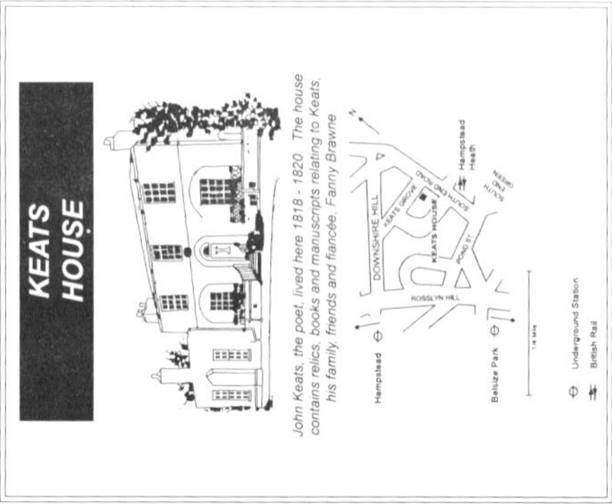

KEATS HOUSE
John Keats, the poet, lived here 1818 - 1820. The house contains relics, books and manuscripts relating to Keats, his family, friends and fiancée, Fanny Brawne.

Teaching Notes

Warm-up

In pairs students ask and answer the questions they prepared at home.

Exam Practice
(Exam material from 1993)

1 Students tell their neighbour about themselves based on the guidelines in 1a. Check the time and after 5 minutes students change over.

2 Students look at the photographs and complete 2a. They then ask and answer the questions in 2b while you monitor and check. Provide feedback by eliciting the answers to the questions. If students need more practice use the photograph sequences from earlier units.

3 Students cover the questions in 3b. They look at the diagram and then listen to the cassette twice, making notes while they are listening. One student uncovers and asks the questions and the other tries to answer using his/her notes and the diagram. Provide feedback by eliciting the answers from students. If students need more practice use the diagrams and recordings from earlier units.

4 Students work in pairs. One student looks at the advert. The other student asks the questions. Provide feedback by eliciting the correct answers. If students need more practice use the adverts from earlier units.

5 Students read the statements and then discuss their opinion with their neighbour while you monitor and check. Provide feedback by eliciting students' opinions. If students need more practice find out what interests them and encourage students to present an idea and support it, while other students try to put forward the other side of the case.

Make sure that students know when and where their exam is and answer any last minute questions students may have.

Tapescripts

Exercise 3a

The Gold Shopping Centre

Now the examiner will test whether you can find your way around on the basis of a map or plan and a taped announcement. The tape will be played twice. You may look at the plan of the shopping centre and you may make notes if you wish.

(Pause)

You go to do some late night shopping in a large shopping centre and you hear the following announcement.

Good evening. Welcome to the Gold Shopping Centre. The time is now 6.30pm. All shops will stay open until 8.30pm. We hope you enjoy your visit.

A very young child has been found near the fountain on West Walk. His name is Peter and he's wearing a green jacket and jeans. Would the person responsible for him please report to the information desk in Gold Hall.

Note that the restaurant and coffee bar will be open until 9.30pm if you wish to take a break after shopping. The restaurant specialises in Italian food.

The record store is offering a 30% reduction on classical records. This offer ends at the close of business tomorrow. The supermarket is now selling all bread and fresh fruit at half price.

There are toilet facilities behind the food court which will stay open until 9.00pm.

First Aid facilities close at 5.00pm daily - contact the information desk in an emergency.

We apologise that some shops are closed for redecorating. They will open in 3 week's time.

Thank you for your attention.

break
breakfast television
bridge
briefcase
broadcasts
brochure
brooch
buildings
bungalow
burglars
bus driver
bus station
bus stop
business
business card
business colleague
business hours
business leasing
business lunch
business studies
businessman
busy
butcher's
butter
button
by cheque
by lorry
bye
cabbage
cabin crew
cable
cable channels
calendar month
calendar of events
Californian
calm
camping
can
cancelled
car factories
car park
car registration number
car repairs
cardboard
cardiac arrest
cargo sales
carpet
carton
case
cash card
cash machine
casserole dish
cassette
castle
casualties
cat
cat food
cat shelter
catalogue
cauliflower
caves
CD
CD player
celebrations
central heating
cereals
certainly
certainly not
chairman
chalets
Chancellor of the Exchequer
channel
charge
charity
chat show
cheap rate
check in
checkouts
cheese and biscuits
chef
chemist's
chemistry
cheque
cheque book
cheque card
cherries
chest
chief executive
children's clothes
Chinese
chopped
Christmas Day
church fete
cigarette packet
cinema
classical music
classified ads section
clean
clear
clear message
climbing
clinics
closed
closed on Sundays
closing down sale
closing time
clothes shop
cloud
clubhouse
clubs
coal fire
coat hanger
coat stand
coconut
coffee machine
coffee shop
coin
coin slot
cold
cold meat
collecting stamps
come downstairs
comfortable
comments
companies
company
company car
company salesman
competition
computer
computer experience
Computer Programmer
computing
condition
congestion
contact
containers
contract
contract services
controversial
convenient
conveyor belt
cooking
cooking oil
cool
coordination
coordinator
cosmetics
council meetings
council tax
councillors
counter
country
country code
courses
cousin
crafts events
cream
credit card
crisis
crisps
criteria
crossroads
crosswords
crowded
crushed
cuisine
current
current account
current affairs
curry sauce
customer
Customer Accounts Manager
customer address
customer name
customer service point
customers

Alphabetical Vocabulary Section

cut
daily
daily tasks
dairy products
darkness
darts
date
date of arrival
date of birth
date of departure
dated
dead
dead end
deadline
deaths
debating
decrease
definitely
definitely not
degrees
delay
delayed
delivery service
dentist
deodorant
department of leisure and tourism
department store
department store guide
departures
deposit account
derailment
description
desk
despite
destination
detached house
developed countries
diabetes
diagram
dial
dialling codes
dialling tone
diary
diesel
dieting
difficult
dining room
disadvantage
disc jockey
discount
discuss
disease
display
district
diver
diversion signs
DIY store
documents
dog
dog food
dog licence
donations
dossier
double
double-sided
downstairs
drawer
dreadful
dress
dried
drink
drinking up time
drive-ins
drivers
driving licences
drug-abusers
dry
dry cough
due to
duty free goods
ear
ear piercing
earrings
easily
Easter Monday
eat
economics
editor
education
efficient
efficiently
eggs
elastic bands
elbow
electric kettle
electric shaver
electrical equipment
electrical shop
emergency exit
emergency services
emergency vehicle
employees
employment
empty
enclose
end of season sale
endurance
energetic
energy
English as a Foreign Language
English for Special Purposes
English speaking
enjoyable
enquiries
entrance
entrance hall
envelope
environmental health
environmentally friendly
equipment
equipment hire
essay
estate agent
estimated arrival time
evening meal
event
exchange visit
exciting
exercising
exhaust fumes
exhibition
exhibition centre
exhibitor
exhibitors
exit
exotic
expensive
experience
experienced
expert advice
experts
expiry date
express
extra care
extra income
eye
fabrics
face down
face-to-face
facilities
factory
factory shop
facts and figures
family run hotel
famous
fans
far too close
farming
favourite
fax
fax roll
faxes
female
fence
fenced
ferry
ferry crossings
festival
fever
fewer
field
file
filing cabinet
final call
finally
finance
Financial Manager

fine
fingers
fire brigade
first
first aid
first aid centre
first aid instructions
first floor
fishing
fitness rooms
flare
flexibility
flies
flight information
flight number
florist's
flour
flower beds
flowers
flu
fluid ounce
fluids
fly spray
foggy
folder
food poisoning
foot
for pleasure
for sale
foreign currencies
foreign newspapers
foreign student
Foreman
forest
form
formal study
forms
founded
free of charge
free-range
freephone
freepost
freeze
French
frequency
fresh air
fresh meat
fried food
from £99.00
front counter
front door
frozen chicken
fruit
fruit trees
frying pan
fuel
full payment
full time
fully trained
fund raising
furniture
furniture polish
furs and leather
future
game
garage
garden
garden furniture
gardener
gardening
garlic
garment bag
gate
geography
German
get dressed
getaway car
give way
glass and chinaware
glasses
gliding
global warming
go off
going to pop concerts
golf
golf club
Good Friday
good news
goodbye
government
graduate
gram
grand total
grape
grapes
green fees
greengrocer's
greenhouse effect
ground floor
group
growing
guarantee
guaranteed
guests
gun
gun licences
gym
gym fees
hail
hair salon
hairdryer
hairspray
half-day closing
hall
hand
hand wash basin
handbag
handle
happy hour
hard work
hard working
hat box
have meetings
hay bale
head
head office
headache
headache tablets
headlines
Heads of State
health centre
health insurance
health problems
healthy
heart
heavily
hectic
hedges
helicopter
helmet
high season
Highlands
hips
history
HIV
hold
holdall
holiday apartment
holiday plan
homeless
horoscopes
hospital
host
host family
hot
hot air
hot-air balloon
hotel
hourly
house keys
house trained
household equipment
household rubbish
housewife
housing
hovercraft
hurt
husband
I agree
I don't agree
I don't think so
I suppose so
I think so
I'm not sure
ice
ice cream
ice stadium

Alphabetical Vocabulary Section

immune system
important
in cash
in return
in the afternoon
in the evening
in the morning
in writing
increase
Indian
individual
injured
insert
inside lane
inspection
institute
instructions
instructor
insurance company
international code
iron
it depends
item
jacket
jackpot
jams
jar
jeweller's
jewellery
jogging
joints
journey
jumbo jet
junction
junior return
junior single
juniors
karaoke
keeping fit
kennels
key
keyboard
killed
king
kitchen
kittens
knee
knitting
knitwear
knowledge of
lake
landed
landed time
landlord
lane
languages
large white loaf
last minute questions
last minute shopping
last night
last orders
latest technology
law
lead
lead singer
lean over
least favourite
lecture theatre
leeks
left luggage locker
leg
legal
leisure centre
leisure time
length
lesson
letters
lettuce
level
levels
library
licence
licensed bar
lid
lie
lifeboat
lifejacket
lifestyle
light
lightning
lingerie
listening
litter bin
litter bins
litter control
living room
local call
local council
locker
long distance call
long let
lottery tickets
low season
lucky
luggage
lump sum
machinery
magazine
main entrance
maintained
make phone calls
make up
manager
Manager's Office
Managing Director
maniacs
maps
marathon run
marina
market
Marketing Manager
marmalades
marriages
master bedroom
mastercard
maths
max. fill level
May Day Holiday
mayonnaise
meanwhile
measurements
meat
medical care
Mediterranean
medium
medium let
meeting
meeting point
member
men's accessories
mend
metalwork
mild
milk
milk bottles
millilitre
min. fill level
mince
mini bus
mints
mirror
mixer
mixers
mixture
mobile
modem
modernised
monitor
monthly instalments
mood
mortgage
mosquito repellent
MOT
motels
mother
motor race
motorbike and sidecar
motorcycling
motoring
motoring holiday
mountain biking
mountains
mug
multi-millionaire
multimedia
muscles
museum

mushrooms
music shop
musicians
narrow
National Health Service
National Lottery
natural
nature
nature lovers
naughty
neck
necklace
needles
needs analysis
never
new roads
New Year's Day
news
news conference
newsagent's
newspaper
newsreader
next
next to
no change is given
no charge
no entry
no extra charge
nobody
noisy
non-recyclable items
non-skier
normal price
normally
northbound
nose bleed
noticeboards
notices
novels
number plate
nurse
occasionally
of course
of course not
off-licence
offer
officially
often
old age pensioner (OAP)
old people's home
olive oil
on the dot
on the left
on the lookout for
on time
on/off switch
one-to-one tuition
one-way street
onion
open
opening hours
opening time
opening times
operate
operating theatre
operation
opposite
optional
or nearest offer
order no
ordinary
outdoor events
outlets
outside
oven
overseas
overturned
overweight
owner
oxygen
PA (Personal Assistant)
packaging
packet
painting
painting exhibition
paints and wallpapers
pair of scissors
pallet
paper bank
paper clips
parachute jump
parcels
park
parking meter
part time
part time job
party bookings
passport
passports
paté
patio
pavement
pay your fare
payable to
payments
payroll no
peak hours
peak rate
pearl
peas
pedestrian crossing
pedestrians
penfriend
pensions
pepper
peppers
per hour
per litre
per person
percentage
perfume
perhaps
permission
Personal Identification Number (PIN)
personnel
Personnel Department
Personnel Department Staff
Personnel Manager
pest control
pet food
pet shops
pet supplies
petrol
petrol station
pets
pharmacy
phone cards
photocopier
photocopying
physical education
physics
pick-up truck
picnic lunch
pie chart
piece of beef
pile-up
place
placement
placement fee
planned
plants
plasters
plastic bag
plastic gloves
playgrounds
playing chess
pleasantly situated
plug
plus
poles
police
police station
policeman
politics
pollution
pony trekking
pork chops
position
post office
pot
potato
pound
prawn cocktail
preferred
premises
prescription

present
presentations
press
price
price list
prices
print-out
printer
private facilities
private medical insurance
privately owned
privatised
process
processor
produce
producer
production
Production Manager
products
professional
professional writer
programme
project
proof
property
pros and cons
protection
psychology
public
public lectures
public notices
public toilets
public transport
publishers
pullover
punctual
pupils
puppy
purchasing department
put on
qualifications
qualified
qualified teacher
quantity
questionnaire
queue
quiet
quiz night
radio licence
radio station
rail strike
railway station
rain
raining
raised
randomly
rarely
raw fish
read the post
reading
ready to go
rebuilding
receipt
receiver
reception
receptionist
recipe
Recruitment and Training Officer
rectangular
recycled paper
recycling plants
redecoration
reduced
refillable
refund
refuse
registration
registration cards
registration fees
registration plate
regular
regulations
relative
released
religious studies
remote control
repair work
repairs
requested
required
rescue team
research
reservation
reservations
residents
responsibility
restaurant
results
retailer
return overnight coach
returned coins slot
reward
Rhine Valley
rice
ring
ringing tone
road repairs
roadworks
roast beef
roast lamb with mint sauce
roast pork with apple sauce
roast turkey with cranberry jelly
roasting tray
rod
roll
rope
ropes
round
roundabout
route
Royal Family
rubbish bin
rubbish collection
rucksack
ruler
runny nose
safe
safety
safety equipment
safety pin
sailing
sailing boat
sails
salad dressing
salary
sale price
sales
sales assistant
Sales Manager
sales people
Sales Team
salmon
salt
sandals
satellite TV
saucepan
sauces
sausages
save-a-can bank
savings accounts
scalded
scar
scarf
scheduled arrival time
science fiction
scientists
scream
sea level
seaside
second floor
second-hand
see people
select
semi-detached house
sentimental value
serious
seriously ill
seriously injured
service
services
set of scales
severe
sewing
sewing machine
sexual contact
shampoo
shared bathroom

Alphabetical Vocabulary Section

sheep
sheet
sheet of paper
shirt
shoe box
shoe repairs
shoe shop
shoes
shooting
shop assistant
shop floor
shop floor worker
shopping
shopping basket
shopping centre
shopping facilities
shopping list
shops
shorthand
shorts
show
shower
shower gel
showers
side roads
side street
sign
signature
signed
silver foil
single
single-sided
situations vacant
skates
ski slopes
skies
skiing
skiing package
skills
skirt
slice of bread
slot
slow
slowly
small brown loaf
small classes
smelly
smoke
smooth
snow
snowing
soap
social programme
socialising
societies
society
socket
socks
software
software package
solution
sometimes
sore throat
soup of the day
south facing
spacious
speaking
special offer
specialist
specialities
speed
spending
spice
spire
spirits
split
spokeswoman
sport
sports bag
sportswear and equipment
spout
sprained wrist
Spring Bank Holiday
square
square metre
squash courts
staff car park
stained glass window
stamps
stand
stationer's
stationery
statistics
steel plate
sticky tape
stitches
stock
stolen
stop
stores
strap
strawberry
stream
street cleaning
strength
string
strong winds
student card
students
Students' Union
study
suddenly
suit
suitcase
Summer Bank Holiday
sunburn
sunny
sunroof
supermarket
supplement
supplier
supplies
surface
surfing
surgery
surname
swimming
swimming pool
switch
switch off
switch on/off
switchboard
symptoms
T-shirt
tablespoon
tablets
tailbacks
tailored
take
takeaway
taking photographs
talk
tattooing
tax increases
taxed and tested
taxi
taxi service
teacher
teaspoon
technical drawing
teddy bear
telephone
telephone operator
telephone rates
television presenter
television studio
temperament
temperature
temperatures
tennis court
terraced house
terrible
textile bank
the day after tomorrow
the day before yesterday
the weather turned bad
themes
then
thieves
third floor
this afternoon
this morning
thoroughly
thumb
thunder
tie
till

time please
tin
tinned food
tinned fruit
tinned peas
tinned vegetables
tiredness
tissues
to fall
to add
to advertise
to advise
to alter your house
to apply
to apply for
to arrange
to avoid
to be processed
to be smacked
to blow
to brake hard
to break
to break in
to break into
to breathe in
to broadcast
to broaden
to build
to buy
to call
to carry
to carry out
to catch
to categorise
to chair
to change
to change money
to check
to choke
to choose
to claim
to climb
to climb out of
to collect
to complain to
to concentrate
to contain
to continue
to copy
to cover
to crash into
to cut
to cut yourself
to cut prices
to decorate
to deliver
to despatch
to dial
to discuss
to disturb
to drain
to draw numbers
to drive away
to drive off
to drop
to dry
to earn
to elect
to empty
to enclose
to enjoy yourself
to exchange
to explain
to faint
to fasten
to feed through
to file away
to fill out
to find
to forget
to free
to fry
to grab
to head west
to hear
to heat
to help
to hit
to hop
to hurry
to identify
to improve
to include
to increase
to injure
to insert
to interview
to invite
to issue
to jump
to jump for joy
to key in
to last
to learn
to leave
to lift
to lift up
to light
to listen for
to load
to lock
to look after
to lose your temper
to maintain
to make contacts
to make mistakes
to make money
to mark
to miss
to mix
to notice
to omit
to order
to overtake
to overturn
to pack
to pay for
to pay in
to pick up
to place
to place an advert
to plant
to prefer
to prevent
to produce
to pronounce
to provide
to pull out
to put
to put out
to raise money
to realise
to receive
to recommend
to recover the cost
to recycle
to refund
to register
to relax
to remember
to remind
to remove
to replace
to reply
to represent
to request
to rescue
to retrieve
to return
to return home
to rise
to roast
to rush things
to sail
to save
to say aloud
to see the sights
to select
to sell
to serve
to shout
to sign
to simmer
to skid
to sleep badly
to slip
to soften

to sort
to speak
to spend
to spoil
to sprain
to squeeze out
to stack
to steal
to stir
to stop breathing
to submerge
to suffer from
to supply
to switch on
to take
to take away
to take holiday
to take out
to take part in
to take payment
to take place
to taste
to teach
to tell
to test
to think
to throw
to throw away
to tidy up
to tie
to tie up
to tow
to train
to transmit
to trip
to untie
to vacuum
to wait
to wake
to wash
to weigh
to wind
to withdraw
to work long hours
to work on
to work regular hours
to wrap
toast
toaster
tobacco
toddler
toes
toilet paper
toiletries
tomato sauce
tomatoes
tomorrow afternoon
tomorrow morning
tomorrow night
tonight
toothache
toothpaste
total
tourist information centre
town
tractor
trade fairs
trading estate
trading licence
traditional
traffic controller
traffic jams
traffic lights
traffic news
trainer
trainers
training
training course
training videos
translation
trapped
travel
traveller's cheques
tray
treasure hunt
treatment
treatment rooms
triangular bandage
trolley
trolleys
trousers
TRUE
try
tube
tuition
turn
TV
TV licences
TV presenter
TV scripts
twin
type
typewriter
typing
typist
underground
underweight
unemployment
unfortunately
unfurnished
unhealthy
uniform
units
unleaded
unless
unlock
unlocked
upturned
vacuum cleaner
van
vanilla
vanity case
VAT (Value Added Tax)
vegetables
vegetarian food
vertical
via
video recorder
village
virus
visa
visibility
visitors
wages
Wages Clerks
Wages Section Head
waist
waistcoat
waiting lists
walking
wallpaper
wanted
ward
warehouse
warm
wash basin
wash his face
washing machine
washing powder
washing up liquid
waste of money
waste paper
watch TV
waterproof trousers
wave
wc ladies
wc men
weak
wear
weather report
wedding anniversary
weekdays
weekends
weekly
weight
weight loss
well known faces
well paid
whether
whiplash
wide range
wider
wife
window
windy
wine
wine cellar

wine list
wine shop
winner
wish
won
wonderful views
woodwork
work experience
workshop
worldwide
worried
worse
worst
wrapping paper
wrist
write
write letters
writing
X-ray room
yard
yesterday afternoon
yesterday morning
yet
yoghurt
yorkshire pudding